Gender on the Borderlands

GENDER ON THE BORDERLANDS

The *Frontiers* Reader

Edited by Antonia Castañeda with
Susan H. Armitage, Patricia Hart,
and Karen Weathermon

UNIVERSITY OF NEBRASKA PRESS · LINCOLN AND LONDON

Gender on the Borderlands was originally published as a double issue of *Frontiers: A Journal of Women Studies* 24, nos. 2–3 (2003).

Library of Congress Cataloging-in-
Publication Data
Gender on the borderlands: the Frontiers
reader / edited by Antonia Castañeda with
Susan H. Armitage, Patricia Hart, and Karen
Weathermon.
p. cm.
"Originally published as a double issue of
Frontiers: a journal of women studies 24,
nos. 2–3 (2003)."
Includes bibliographical references and
index.
ISBN-13: 978-0-8032-5986-7 (pbk.: alk.
paper)
ISBN-10: 0-8032-5986-7 (pbk.: alk. paper)
1. Mexican American women—Mexican-
American Border Region—Social conditions.
2. Women immigrants—Mexican-American
Border Region—Social conditions. 3. Mexi-
can American women—Mexican-American
Border Region—Intellectual life. 4. Sex
role—Mexican-American Border Region 5.
Mexican-American Border Region—Social
conditions. 6. Mexican-American Border
Region—Ethnic relations. 7. Mexican-
American Border Region—Intellectual life.
8. Mexican American arts—Mexican-
American Border Region 9. Mexican
American women—Texas—San Antonio. 10.
San Antonio (Tex.)—social conditions.
I. Castañeda, Antonia. II. Frontiers (Boulder,
Colo.)
F790.M5G46 2007
305.48'868720721—dc22   2007012899

Gracias

Acknowledgments

Gracias to all whose labor of mind, body, and spirit made possible the Gender on the Borderlands Seminar and Conference at St. Mary's University, San Antonio, Tejas, July 12–14, 2001. An institutional grant from the National Endowment for the Humanities provided the funds to sponsor the seminar for St. Mary's faculty and professional staff, as well as to meet conference expenses. St. Mary's University provided outstanding institutional support. *Gracias* to visual artist Alma López for her powerful art, and to Claudia Rodríguez for bodily representing gender on the borderlands in López's work—part of her *1848* series—which graced the cover of the conference brochure and program. *Gracias* to Jen Simmons for the design of the call for proposals brochure. *Gracias* to the Esperanza Peace and Justice Center and to Hispanas Unidas for the photographic exhibit *Mujeres de San Antonio,* and to the Guadalupe Cultural Arts Center and Dr. Gwendolyn Díaz of St. Mary's University for sharing the Latina Letters Conference space. *Gracias,* most especially, to the Conference Committee: Mercedes Elías, Mariulu AbiRached-Reyna, Sylvia Y. Acosta, Cristina Domínguez, and Patricia Mejía. Cory Elías, a middle school student in 2001, and Mercedes Olivia Elías and Stacy Rader, then in high school, immeasurably added to the Committee's labor power before and during the conference. We dedicate this volume to their generation.

CONTENTS

Introduction

Gender on the Borderlands

ANTONIA CASTAÑEDA *Yananawa/San Antonio*

Gender on the Borderlands is based on *testimonios*, papers, *ponéncias*, and *pláticas* from the conference by the same name held at St. Mary's University, July 12–14, 2001. As this volume goes to press, we are compelled to address the persistent absence of gender from public discourse, although gender ideologies are pivotal in the geopolitics shaping new imperial borderlands. The 2001 Conference was held in Yananawa/San Antonio; center of the Payaya-Coahuilteco homeland, core of Atzlán, Chicano homeland/place of first migration, and home of the Alamo, a "Shrine of Texas freedom," according to hegemonic national history. The gender politics of the present war on Iraq mirror those of the wars that fashioned and refashion the U.S-Mexico borderlands. From this historical space of both intimate recognition and opposition, the authors in this volume expose, inscribe, oppose, and write/right the gendered politics of domination on borderlands, old and new. Let us be clear.

Terrorism, militarism, and war masculinize the world, irrespective of how many women serve in the military or conduct suicide missions.[1] Using gender to justify war in the twentieth century—bombing Afghanistan to "liberate" Afghan women from Afghan men, for example—recodes gendered hierarchies and relations of power that have, since the sixteenth century, sexualized conquest and justified European imperialism. The gender and sexual politics of religious fundamentalism, whether in the name of contemporary Christianity, Islam, or Judaism, continue to reify patriarchal, misogynist, and heterosexist structures of domination worldwide. "Global capitalism," our postmodern restructured economy, exploits the labor of men, women, and children within gendered and sexed structures of power framed centuries ago. In the "global market place" women and girls of color remain the target of brutal sexual violence and murder, only now in "free trade zones"; are prey to rape by human smugglers and "law enforcement" agents, including border patrols; and are kept captive in homes where they are maids, housekeepers, and nannies in the "domestic economy of service." The expanding market in "sexual tourism" is a hugely profitable, global phenomenon.

The rapacity of capitalism is well documented, as is the brutality of war, even as both are occluded from public discussion and/or sanitized in public media owned by a few conglomerates. What is not well documented, and what the articles in this volume elucidate, is the inseparability of gendered politics and other politics that produce/reproduce the U.S.-Mexico borderlands to create the issues we live with today: terrorism, war, and imperial hegemony.

On the U.S.-Mexico borderlands, the edge of barbed wire that is home to most of the authors in this collection, the gendered discourses, contestations, and transformations *Tejana* lesbian theorist Gloria Anzaldúa first mapped in *Borderlands/La Frontera* in 1987 are the substance of daily life. In academic papers, *testimonios*, oral histories, songs, prayer, poetry, art, and other narrative and performative forms presented at the Gender on the Borderlands conference, contributors recover and tell multilayered, complex borderlands "*historia,*" (counter-history) that "official histories" have marginalized, distorted, or erased. Threaded within, between, underneath, around, inside, and outside of sanctioned colonial, national, and transnational histories, *historia*/story re-members and recodes the borderlands, bearing witness to the living past, the present, and the future, belying officialdom's visible and invisible technologies of power to silence, deny, and obliterate. Re-membering draws on the metaphor of the body to signify *historia* beyond memory—recalling, telling, writing, and performing to re-piece the body that the violence of history has dismembered and discarded (literally and figuratively). *Historia* re-members the physical body (gendered, racial, and sexual), and the social, political, cultural, and historical body in order to explain what happened and why. From those in-between spaces—the decolonial imaginary that historian Emma Pérez delineates as the third space, that Chicana poets and artists call Nepantla, where Chela Sandoval locates the wellspring of oppositional consciousness—the authors in this volume gather the threads and reweave the fabric of individual, family, and collective history. In so doing they reconstitute regional, state, national, and global histories of the U.S.-Mexico borderlands.[2]

Gender, mapped on the mind, body, and spirit, "is itself a borderland," as Alma López's art powerfully renders in the image that represented the conference, the historical and contemporary borderlands etched on a butch woman's (Claudia Rodríguez's) back.[3] The articles elaborate the complex histories, knowledge systems, genders, sexualities, spiritualities, politics, economies, cultures, conflicts, and identities that López's visual representation signals.

The readings in this collection articulate the processes of recovery in its myriad meanings: The readings thematically traverse, intersect, and connect across the six sections. Section titles denote the agency and action of living gender on the borderlands and denote scholarship about that process. The essays, which focus largely on the twentieth and twenty-first centuries, articulate themes and issues set in motion centuries ago, as previously noted.

In Part 1, Claiming, contributors re-member and reconstitute the land embodied in personal, family, and community stories at specific locations on the U.S.-Mexico borderlands as well as in the Americas more generally. The borderlands, watered with the blood of generations, is home. Bearing witness and telling stories/*historia* of home, from Indigenous America's "precise and studied intimacy with the land . . . its languages . . . rhythms, and epistemologies of place"[4] to coming home to Juárez/El Paso to recover the stories buried beneath *fronteras* of nation-states and to heal from the trauma of history is the act of claiming, writes Yolanda Chávez Leyva. Contemporary notions of gender and sexuality, of masculine and feminine, of compulsory heterosexuality, are not of this land, Gabriel S. Estrada reminds us. They are constructions imposed and sustained in the violence of colonialism, in its structures and relations of power. Duality, not opposition, is at the center of Nahuatl cosmology in Indigenous America. Dualities resound in multiple sexualities evident in the movement of the sun that "begins with masculine rising energy in the east becomes descending feminine energy as it crosses to the west, only to become masculine in the east again in a never-ending cycle of night and day," writes Estrada.

In Part 2, Contextualizing, contributors place the recurrent themes we read in *testimonios* and *historias* within the most recent frameworks and scholarship in Chicana/o, labor, cultural, feminist, lesbian, and borderlands history. Deena J. González teaches "truth to power" in her synthesis of the last thirty years of researching and writing Chicana/o history in the academy, including in Chicana/o studies, wherein gender and sexuality have only recently joined other categories of analysis. Katherine Benton-Cohen delves into the pluralities that González points to in order to examine how racial, class, gender, and political hierarchies are deployed in social constructions of masculinity, manhood, manliness, and the "American worker" during a period of war, revolution, and the Bisbee deportation of 1917. As Clara Lomas confirms in her article, for *Mejicana/Tejana* writers, newspaper publishers, editors, and political activists during the Mexican Revolution (1910–1930), home is the transnational borderlands. No less than today, Latinas then articulated, fought against, and linked gender, racial, class, and political oppression on both sides of the U.S.-Mexico border.

In Part 3, Revisioning, Performing, Liberating, pieces enact politics of art, culture, and representation. Rooted in traditions of art as social critique and culture as a human right, Graciela I. Sánchez's essay explains the origins of the

Esperanza Peace and Justice Center. Esperanza and its community sued the City of San Antonio when the homophobic city council tried to silence cultural expressions that challenged sociopolitical domination and cultural imperialism. Visual and performance artists at the Esperanza, who have included the artists, individual performers, and performance collectives that contributors Yolanda Broyles-González and Judith L. Huacuja's readings present, make visible the politics of cultural distortion. They draw upon and reconfigure multiple aesthetic traditions from *raquachi* to *high-ton* in order to re-envision, perform, and liberate the borderlands in advocacy of community and social justice, which Huajuca affirms, "constitutes the thesis of their art."

In Part 4, Excavating, selections unearth that which is still invisible and unheard in borderlands life and cultures. Here decolonial imaginaries are focused by Emma Pérez's queer gaze and historical novel, which centers lesbian desire and agency. Her critique of colonialist, heteronormative historical scholarship offers new methodologies and theories to disidentify, disrupt, and decolonize borderlands history. Histories of racial pluralities, like those of sexuality, while still largely invisible are nevertheless critical recovery projects that provide archaeologies of multiracial memory. Tracking silences in family stories, Virginia Grise traces her Chinese-Mexican ancestry from Canton, China, to Monterey and Tampico, Mexico, to San Antonio. The fault lines of gender, race, and class surface in Priscilla Falcon's oral history of Chicana/*Mejicana* workers' agency in the historic strike women floral workers organized in Brighton, Colorado, in 1969.

Living San Antonio, Part 5 of the collection, vivifies in one location the history of domination and the decolonial imaginary that testifies to, performs, and writes/rights history. María Antonietta Berriozábal's eloquent *testimonio* of growing up in the deep Westside of San Antonio challenges entrenched structures of power from that location and embodies the meanings of working-class *Tejana* agency. Faith, work, family, and community are the wellsprings of Berriozábal's agency.

Deborah Vargas documents the challenges of cultural production in her oral history interviews with the celebrated Rosita Fernández, "La Rosa de San Antonio." In the late 1990s those same political challenges exposed the city's homophobic heterosexist ideology, culminating in the court case *Esperanza Peace and Justice Center v. the City of San Antonio.* Amy Kastely reflects on community, social justice, and the unprecedented lawsuit that the women-founded, *lesbiana*-led Esperanza brought—and won—against the city. Then, Gabriela González locates us in Depression-era San Antonio to probe class differences in the distinctive approaches taken by community activists and organizers Carolina Mungía and Emma Tenayuca, which González analyzes as "the politics of benevolence and radical reform." Both women organized in *Mejicano* diasporic communities, comprised largely of refugees and exiles from the Mexican Revolution. Mungía organized the Círculo Cultural "'Isabel, la Católica' to improve the women of *la raza* through domesticity, motherhood, and self-education." Tenayuca identified with her Indigenous ancestry, committed herself to social and economic justice for the poor and working classes of San Antonio, joined the Communist Party, and led (with Manuela Sager and others), the pecan shellers strike in 1938. The majority of the pecan shellers were women, *Mejicanas y Tejanas*.

Visual artist Terry Ybáñez memorializes Tenayuca, Fernández, and Berriozábal in the only Chicana-centered public arts mural project in San Antonio. True to her own and her subjects' working-class origins, Ybáñez emblazoned the exterior walls of two Southside public spaces, a local *lavendería* (laundromat) and a restaurant. Ybáñez's choice of colors for her public art (reproduced here in black and white) powerfully symbolizes the brilliant, multihued agency of San Antonio's *Mejicana/Tejana/*Chicana activists, leaders in the struggle for civil, labor, political, educational, and cultural rights.

Tenayuca, whom the religious powers in San Antonio condemned for her radical politics and Communist Party affiliation, was a deeply spiritual woman. At her death in 1999 the family invited María Antonietta Berriozábal to lead the community in reciting the rosary, traditionally proclaimed the night before the burial. At the funeral mass the following day, San Antonio poet Carmen Tafolla eulogized Tenayuca in the poem she wrote for the occasion. We include "María *y* Emma," Berriozábal's recomposition of the liturgy of the Five Glorious Mysteries of the rosary, and Tafolla's "*La Pasionaria.*" Berriozábal's prayer and Tafolla's poem honor and document Tenayuca's spirituality, intellect, and life of struggle for social justice worldwide.

Finally, Part 6, Globalizing, exposes and critiques the virulent injustices of postmodern global capitalism. Economic restructuring removes national regulatory barriers to world trade on the one hand, and on the other constructs draconian barriers to control the transnational flow of labor. Capital knows no national borders, while immigration policies and militarized borders heavily regulate and restrict labor, criminalizing those who cross national borders to seek work. Evelyn Hu-DeHart exposes the hierarchical structures of power and exploitations of globalization. In particular, Hu-DeHart analyzes the gendered, raced, and sexed nature of the international division of labor and the subcontracting system of production, the global processing factories and assembly lines that rest on the transnational exploitation of women in sweatshops worldwide. In the global economy, Latina and Asian women workers' bodies are reduced to "nimble fingers," the ideological construct that rationalizes the nonlivable wages transnational corporations pay women workers, including in the 11,500 *malquiladoras*/assembly plants that line the U.S.-Mexico border.

Mexicanas speak the unspeakable in the narratives of border crossing they tell to María de la Luz Ibarra. Their diverse voices bring the bloodied terrain of the borderlands "that lie somewhere between leaving and arriving" into stark focus. Grounded in lived experience and the agency of the individual women migrants whose stories she records, Ibarra critiques U.S. scholars' tendency to portray transnationalism and border crossing principally in positive terms as a transformative or liberatory process in alternative identity formation.

We heed Ibarra's critique. One of the purposes of this volume is to document and connect the history of the "violence that explodes the imaginary," as well as the agency of those who have lived that violence. By naming the violence that women, families, and communities have experienced, as Chávez Leyva and others tell us, one asserts one's own agency, adding to the collective tide of oppositional voices that becomes a critical base of recovery.

Here we note, if only briefly, the growing strength of organized transnational opposition to the ravages of globalization, particularly among women workers on the line. Beginning in the early 1990s, women of color pioneered new forms of community-based labor organizations with their peers in low-wage industries who were left jobless by garment, electronics, and other companies that restructured and moved factories to Mexico, Costa Rica, Taiwan, Indonesia, or other third world countries. These organizations are best described as "projects rooted in the community, involving women's collective self-leadership and a lived understanding of the necessarily international nature of their struggle" and include, among others, Fuerza Unida (San Antonio), Asian Immigrant Women Advocates (Oakland), Mujer Obrera (El Paso), Chinese Progressive Association (Boston), and Mujer a Mujer in Canada.[5] They work closely with related community-based organizations, including the tri-national Coalition for Justice in the Maquiladoras, Women on the Border, and Mujeres Para el Diálogo to organize feminist and other global oppositional movements, and to draw on the agency of women of all ages, experience, and identities.

We close with the oppositional voice and agency of the future. In her *testimonio* with Anita Tijerina Revilla, delia, a young Mexicana Chicana student, re-members her own and her family's history and makes her own connections between the past, present, and future. In recounting her life, from the terrors of border crossing when she was eight to her present advocacy with public school students she tutors/mentors in South Central Los Angeles, delia marks, makes, and re-makes gender on the borderlands with her generation of Raza Woymn de UCLA, their peers, families, and communities.

Gender on the Borderlands—the seminar, conference, and volume—contributes to the body of work that makes visible the ways in which gender has historically been, and is, the site of violence and oppression, of struggle and liberation. To best organize against the mind-numbing torture, rape, murder, and dismemberment that are the currency of our contemporary world, we place the past in the present to re-member ancestor India/Africana/mestiza women upon whose bodies the global "postmodern" borderlands rest. Their voices, like those the women of Afghanistan, Iraq, Iran, and other Islamic countries, whose history is inseparable from ours, call us to action.[6]

NOTES

1. See Cynthia H. Enloe, *Maneuvers: The International Politics of Militarizing Women's Lives* (University of California Press, 2000); and Cynthia H. Enloe, *The Morning After: Sexual Politics at the End of the Cold War* (University of California Press, 1993). In the U.S. war against Iraq, the first three women killed, captured, and/or wounded were two women of color and one working-class white woman, all belonging to the 507 Maintenance Unit. Lori Piestewa, a member of the Hopi tribe from Tuba City, Arizona, died in the same convoy in which Shoshana Johnson and Jessica Lynch were captured on March 24, 2003. Piestewa's father is Hopi, her mother is Hispanic. Johnson, born in Panama and raised in the United States, is black; her father learned of her capture while watching Spanish language television. Military film footage of the Special Forces rescue of Lynch converted this working-class white woman from West Virginia into the "poster girl for American resilience and camaraderie" (as quoted in Gary Younge, "What about Private Lori?" *Guardian Unlimited*, April 10, 2003). Younge further states that Piestewa is "the other American face of this war, fought by a military whose ranks have been swelled by poor, non-white women." See also Natasha Walter, "Women at War," *Guardian Unlimited*, April 17, 2003, who notes, "The media were a lot less interested in the black and Native American colleagues of Lynch who were captured with her. The media prefer women who fit into a particular frame, and although the British didn't have a Lynch, they still had their own brave, beautiful and white girl soldiers." On Johnson, see Nadra Kareem, "Family Calls POW 'Strong Individual,' Kind, Popular," *El Paso Times*, April 12, 2003; and Ndara Kareem, "'You're All Right,' Mother Tells Released POW Daughter," *El Paso Times*, April 13, 2003. Melissa Valles, who died from a gunshot wound in the abdomen in a noncombat situation on July 9, was from El Paso. She is identified as the "first Hispanic servicewoman" to die in Iraq. See Mariano Castillo, "Eagle Pass Soldier 'Did a Great Act,'" *The San Antonio Express-News*, July 20, 2003. For women's participation in suicide missions, see "First Palestinian Suicide Bomber," BBC NEWS, January, 30, 2002 (*http://news.bbc.co.uk/t/hi/world/middle_east/1787510.stm*); and "Woman Suicide Bomber Rattles Israel," *The Hindu*, online edition of India's *National Newspaper*, January 29, 2002. (*www*

.hinduonnet.com/thehindu/2002/01/29/stories/2002012900641200.htm). For discussion of women in the Mujahedeen Khalq, see Elizabeth Rubin, "The Cult of Rajavi," *The New York Times Magazine*, July 13, 2003, 26–31.

2. Gloria Anzaldúa, *Borderlands/La Frontera: The New Mestiza* (San Francisco: Spinster/Aunt Lute Books, 1987). Yolanda Broyles-González develops the concept of "*historia*," and Emma Pérez develops the concept of "the decolonial imaginary." See Yolanda Broyles-González, *Lydia Mendoza's Life in Music: Norteño Tejano Legacies/La Historia de Lydia Mendoz* (New York: Oxford University Press, 2001), and *El Teatro Campesino: Theater in the Chicano Movement* (Austin: University of Texas Press, 1994); and Emma Pérez, *The Decolonial Imaginary: Writing Chicanas into History* (Bloomington: Indiana University Press, 1999). Pat Mora, *Nepantla: Essays from the Land in the Middle* (Albuquerque: University of New Mexico Press, 1993); and Chela Sandoval, *Methodology of the Oppressed* (Minneapolis: University of Minnesota Press, 2000).

3. See Deena J. González, "Gender on the Borderlands: Re-textualizing the Classics," this volume.

4. Inés Hernández-Avila, as quoted from her plenary presentation at the Gender on the Borderlands Conference, San Antonio, Texas, July 12, 2003.

5. "Mujer a Mujer: Firsthand Account of Levi's," (*www.hartford-hwp.com/archives/26/147.html*), January, 4, 1998, a reprint of an older article about Fuerza Unida.

6. In homage to young women murdered in Juárez, the MujerArtes ceramics cooperative of the Esperanza Peace and Justice Center, under the direction of internationally acclaimed ceramicist Verónica Castillo, created a community altar/installation featuring a "tree of death," with twenty-five accompanying ceramics pieces. Unveiled at a community gathering on July 26, 2003, "*Lamento por las Mujeres de Juárez*" was commissioned by the University of California, Los Angeles (UCLA) Chicano Studies Research Center, which with Amnesty International is the cosponsor of a three-day international conference on the murder of women in Juárez that will be held on October 31–November 2, 2003, at UCLA. Alicia Gaspar de Alba, Associate Professor of Chicana/o Studies, conceptualized and is organizing the conference to mark the tenth year since the murders began in 1993. The conference, "The Maquiladora Murders, or Who is Killing the Women of Juárez," brings together scholars, activists, artists, journalists, students, and policy specialists, as well as the families of young women who have disappeared or have been murdered in Juárez. The intent is to inform the international community and to engage widespread, transnational action. Human Rights Watch is documenting the abduction, rape, and sexual violence against women in Iraq since the war. See Neela Banerjee, "Rape (and Silence About It) Haunts Baghdad," *The New York Times*, Wednesday, July 16, 2003, A1, A9.

"There is great good in returning"

A Testimonio from the Borderlands

YOLANDA CHÁVEZ LEYVA

There is a great good in returning to a landscape that has had extraordinary meaning in one's life. It happens that we return to such places in our minds irresistibly. There are certain villages and towns, mountains and plains that, having seen them walked in them lived in them even for a day, we keep forever in the mind's eye. They become indispensable to our well-being; they define us, and we say, I am who I am because I have been there, or there.

N. Scott Momaday, "Revisiting Sacred Ground," in *The Man Made of Words*

I moved back home to *la frontera* between Texas and Chihuahua in the summer of 2001, back into the little *casita de piedra* where I had grown up. It had been vacant since the deaths of my parents years ago. I knew living back on the border, where the divisions are so great and painful and the people so resilient and persistent, would be exciting and challenging. Returning to the place where I could say, in the most profound way, "I am who I am because I have been there," meant that I would be confronting an often painful history—my own and, in a myriad of ways, that of my people—on a daily basis. It meant that, for my own survival, I had to continue my efforts to make sense of the painful stories and to find ways to create a healing history.

I had been imagining a healing history for several years, inspired in part by historian, poet, and activist Aurora Levins Morales's essay, "The Historian as Curandera." Her advice to "make absences visible," to "identify strategic pieces of misinformation and contradict them," and to "tell untold or undertold stories" spoke to my own sensibilities as a historian who consciously cultivated ties to my communities of origin.[1]

On my first night back in my childhood home, I stood on the porch and looked south toward the greenish-hued lights of Ciudad Juárez, and I felt my sister Elisa near me. Identical twins, we were born to Guadalupe in the spring of 1956 in a small *clínica* near downtown Ciudad Juárez. Unmarried, impoverished, and just nineteen years old, our mother, Lupe, was frightened to keep us. My great aunt and uncle, Esther and Gerónimo Leyva, took me across the border to El Paso where they adopted me and raised me as their daughter in a lower-middle-class/upper-working-class neighborhood in central El Paso.

My sister Elisa stayed in Juárez with Lupe and died several weeks later of an intestinal disease, still the predominant killer of babies in Juárez. She was buried in the *panteón municipal* in an unmarked grave that I have never seen. Yet, because her bones lie in this earth just south of the Rio Grande/Rio Bravo, I know that I belong here on the border, too. Because generations of my people's bones lie buried in this earth, I am grounded to this place, the border, as a *fronteriza*, and I grew up to be a Chicana lesbian historian.

I left home at nineteen to attend the University of Texas at Austin. My journey was a winding road that led me to a degree in business administration, a decade spent as a social worker in the Chicano and African American neighborhoods of East Austin, and finally back to graduate school in my thirties. In my forties, I earned a Ph.D. in history and began teaching in San Antonio.

From elementary school through high school, history bored me. Yet, at home the *historias* of my family riveted me. Historian Vicki Ruiz has written, "When I was a child, I learned two types of history—the one at home and the one at school. . . . Bridging the memories told at the table with printed historical narratives fueled my decision to become a historian."[2] This is my story as well. At school I learned about the Puritans, George Washington, and what was presented as the inevitable westward movement of Manifest Destiny and "progress." I also noted the invisibility of anything that felt familiar to me.

Around the kitchen table at home, listening to my mother as she cooked *albóndigas* or spaghetti while we waited for my father to come home from his civil service job, I learned another history. Here I learned of what it was like to be a girl child during the Mexican Revolution, taken from a comfortable home in Chihuahua and relocated to a place where nothing seemed recognizable. She cried remembering that her mother had died within six years of immigrating—the result of an increasingly hard life. She sighed as she explained that her baby brother had died shortly thereafter—of a broken heart, missing his mother. Watching her cook, I learned of her work as a nanny to the babies of upper-class families who complimented her for her cleanliness. Here I listened to stories of how she fought to protect her sisters from abusive husbands and insincere suitors. She laughed as she told me about her arrest in the early 1940s. She hit a border patrolman with her purse because he was being disrespectful to my father who was in military uniform at the time. I learned from her what it is to be a strong woman.

Sitting outside in the yard with my father as he carefully tended his beloved lawn, I learned another history. Here I listened to what it was like to be born on a hacienda just as the Mexican Revolution tore the nation apart. I paid close attention as he spoke of his love for his grandmother who was *pura indita*. From his stories I learned to think of *puro indio* as an endearment rather than the shame that the phrase often evokes.[3] I learned to be proud of hard work and to believe that we belonged here, for this was our land. These were my childhood *historias* of common people, faced with small and momentous challenges, struggling to make a good life. I had not yet made the connection between *historias*/stories and histories.

In the mid-1970s I began taking Chicano studies courses. I finally began to see my/our reflection in the mirrors of history. Chicana and Chicano professors taught us about the U.S.-Mexican War, the Mexican Revolution of 1910, and shifting immigration policies, which allowed *Mexicanos* to cross over easily when we were needed as cheap labor, but that pushed us back to Mexico during times of economic crisis. Finally, the *historias* of my family and our neighbors made sense in the larger socioeconomic-cultural context. I remember the anger that burned inside of me when I learned that history is so full of injustices and pain.

There was another anger, another pain, that I carried inside. I had come out at eighteen, and my university years were marked with political activity as a Chicana and as a lesbian. I was often the only Chicana in lesbian spaces and the only out lesbian in Chicana spaces. Those were difficult years. On campus, much of the leadership in Chicana/o organizations was queer, yet that queerness was largely invisible. When several of us challenged that invisibility in the Mexican American Youth Organization (MAYO), the group splintered under the weight of the controversy.

In 1977, Chicano movement activists organized the First National Chicano/ Latino Conference on Immigration and Public Policy. The conference, held in San Antonio, drew over two thousand participants with political views ranging from radical to moderate.[4] In the weeks preceding the conference, a group of gay and lesbian Chicanos and Chicanas—mostly students—had drafted a statement to take before the gathering. We asked that one of the resolutions call for an end to homophobic immigration policies that denied entry to homosexual immigrants. I remember standing at the back of the great hall as the conference proceeded, wondering who would take our proposal forward. We believed that it would have more credibility if it was taken forward by a professor and looked to our allies at the university for help. After several professors declined, one agreed to carry the proposal to the front of the room. As our resolution was read, there were snickers in the audience. When the person reading the proposal did an on-the-spot translation, he used the word *joto* rather than homosexual, and the audience burst into laughter. My memories of this great event in *Movimiento* history are collapsed into that one humiliating and painful moment when my own people dismissed the treatment of gay and lesbian Mexican immigrants with laughter and scorn. For years I tried to forget that day in San Antonio.[5]

Twenty years later, I accepted a job on the faculty at the University of Texas at San Antonio. It was during my time in San Antonio that I began the healing process that eventually led me back home to the border. Soon after I arrived in San Antonio in 1997, I began working with the Esperanza Peace and Justice Center, a cultural arts organization with a national reputation for their multi-issue organizing and progressive politics. For a year I met with a small group of women—Chicana, African American, Anglo, heterosexual and queer—to think about ways to create what would become the Esperanza's Community School *Puentes de Poder/* Bridges of Power Program.

Weekly for two months each one of us would tell "our story." We brought photographs and looked into the faces of each other's ancestors; we made time lines showing how our family histories fit into the context of larger local, regional, national, and international histories; we wrote about our experiences and read them out loud. We remembered the painful stories we often kept hidden deep inside our beings. We cried and laughed. And most importantly, we listened, attentively and respectfully, to each other's words.

In *The Decolonial Imaginary: Writing Chicanas into History*, Emma Pérez writes:

> Voices of women from the past, voices of Chicanas, Mexicanas, and Indias, are utterances which are still minimized, spurned, even scorned. And time, in all its dialectical invention and promise, its so-called inherent progress, has not granted Chicanas, Mexicanas or Indias much of a voice at all. We are spoken about, spoken for, and ultimately encoded as whining, hysterical, irrational, or passive women who cannot know what is good for us, who cannot know how to impress or authorize our own narratives.[6]

Over the course of that year we healed by speaking ourselves into being as women who had survived the traumas inflicted upon us as women and people of color.

One particularly powerful interaction occurred when our facilitator asked the white women in the group to actively listen to what we women of color wanted them to know. The white women would listen, but they could not speak. It was a compelling and emotional moment for all of us. It was our chance to be heard as women of color. For a moment in time we said things we had never said aloud before. That year of listening to and telling stories began my healing from the trauma of history that I had carried inside of me, as had my parents, and their parents, and their parents before them.

Healing from the trauma of history is a process that is ongoing, complex, and felt physically, intellectually, and spiritually. In recent years, for example, when someone makes a racist comment about Mexicans being lazy or about sending "Mexicans back where they came from on a burro," I experience the comment as an overwhelming, almost suffocating, pain in my chest. While working with traditional Chicana and Native American healers, I learned that I carry my own traumas in my heart area. I have begun to understand why the ancient Nahuas attributed not just life, but also emotion, memory, and knowledge to the heart.[7] My heart is responding not just to the comment as it is being said but to the memory of similar slurs against my people over the course of the past one hundred and fifty years. The insults and affronts against Chicanos that I read regularly on right-wing electronic discussion lists are the same ones hurled at us during the Texas Revolution of the 1830s, the U.S.-Mexican War of the 1840s, and the immigration debates of the 1920s onward.

The effects of historical trauma are insidious. Native American scholars Bonnie Duran, Eduardo Duran, and Maria Yellow Horse Brave Heart have explored the effects of historical trauma on contemporary Native peoples. They assert:

> Historical trauma and its effects are complex, multigenerational, and cumulative. A constellation of features that occur in reaction to multi-generational, collective, historical, and cumulative psychic wounding over time—over the lifespan and across generations—historical trauma is characterized as incomplete mourning and the resulting depression absorbed by children from birth onward.[8]

Historical trauma, or soul wound, is a result of colonization. It is a wound we experience in our spirits, our minds, and our bodies.

The forms of colonialism that Duran, Duran, and Brave Heart identify, including the loss of physical territory through military means, ongoing attacks on identity and culture, overwhelming changes in economic and social systems, coerced efforts at assimilation, and sterilization of women, resonate deeply for Chicana and Chicano history.[9] These acts of colonization have deeply affected us, and I see it every day in my family, in my students, and in my community.

My generation and the generation before me have personal memories of the forced sterilizations of poor women of color, of educational policies that mandated corporal punishment for the speaking of Spanish on school grounds, of segregated schools, of forced repatriations, and police brutality. As I teach, I see the effects of these traumas working in the lives of the younger generation even when they cannot yet name the trauma. My Chicana-Kikapu friend and teacher Patrisia Gonzáles writes, "Trauma takes away language. If we can't put language to our experience, either through journaling, therapy, or talking circles, it burrows further inside our beings." [10] Putting language to that pain is one of my responsibilities as a historian.

For example, while speaking to a class recently as a guest lecturer, I casually mentioned that many parents who were born in the 1930s, 1940s, and 1950s had not taught Spanish to their children, and that those children should not be ashamed. In passing, without thinking consciously about it, I had touched upon a historically based trauma that immediately affected two young women in the class. Both were ashamed and angry that they did not speak Spanish. Other Chicanos and Mexicanos criticized them for it. On the border there are tremendous pressures to be an "authentic" Mexican, and these young women felt inadequate as individuals. Their comments opened a space in the class to talk about how Spanish had been taken forcibly from us. I encouraged them not to blame their parents. Their parents, too, had been made to feel ashamed and inadequate by an educational system intent on erasing our Mexican-ness. I related how Americanization programs from the early part of the twentieth century had instilled English as a form of social control. Even in the 1960s, schools in the El Paso area paddled students who spoke Spanish on campus. The pattern was repeated throughout the Southwest to the detriment of children's psychological and physical health. The young women spoke of their desire to learn Spanish and showed relief when I told them I knew other people who had learned Spanish as adults.

The discussion touched me as well in ways I did not expect. As I listened to the pain expressed by the women in class, I thought back to my own childhood pain when, entering catechism, my parents told me to pray only in English. My cousins, a few years older than I was, had entered school knowing only Spanish. As a result they were constantly punished and ridiculed by their teachers. My parents did not want me to suffer what my cousins had suffered and started by taking away my *rezos*, my nightly prayers. I forgot how to pray in Spanish for many years. As part of my own healing and reclaiming, I now pray in Spanish, and I learn prayers in Indigenous languages that tie me spiritually to our ancient roots on this continent. Historical trauma wounds our spirits as well as our minds and bodies.

In the last year of my mother's life, when time was no longer linear and the past and present existed simultaneously, historical trauma came unexpectedly to the surface of her day-to-day existence. Fragile, emotionally and physically vulnerable, she returned to the landscape that had made her who she was. She relived crossing the border as a child almost eighty years earlier. Looking at me and seeing her sister instead, she worried about the move. What would it be like "over there"? Would there be problems for her parents? For days she experienced anxiety. Frequently she asked me if we were still in Juárez, wanting some assurance that we were still on familiar ground. Having learned from the geriatric nurses not to contradict her, I reassured her that we were still in México.

Suddenly one day my mother's mood changed dramatically. The worry was replaced with relief and even self-assurance. *"Ellos saben que somos gente buena,"* she announced. I asked why. "They didn't make us take a bath when we crossed." The words shocked me. As a border historian I knew of the various quarantines, health inspections, and baths that had been imposed on Mexicans crossing into the United States during the time period my family had crossed. In a 1974 interview, longtime El Paso resident José Cruz Burciaga remembered the kerosene baths and the shaving of heads forced on many working-class immigrants in the early part of the century.[11] I had read of the disinfection plant built literally under the bridge connecting El Paso and Ciudad Juarez in 1910 and of the continuing and degrading inspections and disinfections that continued into the 1920s.[12] What I had never considered was that my mother, her mother, and her brothers and sisters had experienced an inspection themselves. That evening, sitting by her bed as she slept, I wondered what other fears and anxieties about crossing the border her child self held inside. Her joy and relief at not having to be disinfected only revealed how fearful the prospect had been to her nine-year-old self. I wondered how much fear and trauma had been instilled in the thousands of women, children, and men who crossed daily.[13]

In *Native American Postcolonial Psychology*, Eduardo Duran and Bonnie Duran argue that the practice of psychology must be historicized. They urge their colleagues to understand the history behind the pain. Only by understanding history will psychologists be able to effectively work with Native Americans and other colonized peoples.[14] As a historian, I would urge my colleagues to acknowledge the pain behind the history.

I am not advocating a history of victimization. Much of the historiography in Chicano studies over the past two decades has consciously steered away from such a model. Historically, people of color have demonstrated their agency and their resistance to oppression in multiple and ingenious ways. I look forward to a growing body of literature documenting this fact. However, I support our commitment to look at the ways in which we carry the traumas of history inside our spirits, our bodies, and our minds. Historians can be healers, as Levins Morales asserts. Living on the border, where the landscape itself holds so much pain, I will continue to look for ways to create a history that heals.

NOTES

1. Aurora Levins Morales, "The Historian as Curandera," in *Medicine Stories: History, Culture and the Politics of Integrity* (Cambridge, Mass.: South End Press, 1998), 23–38.

2. Vicki L. Ruiz, *From Out of the Shadows: Mexican Women in Twentieth-Century America* (New York: Oxford University Press, 1998), xiii.

3. Inés Hernández-Ávila, "An Open Letter to Chicanas: On the Power and Politics of Origin," in *Reinventing the Enemy's Language: Contemporary Native Women's Writings of North America*, ed. Joy Harjo and Gloria Bird (New York: W.W. Norton and Company, 1997), 240.

4. David G. Gutiérrez cites this conference as a landmark in Mexican American politics in his book, *Walls and Mirrors: Mexican Americans, Mexican Immigrants, and the Politics of Ethnicity* (Berkeley: University of California Press, 1995), 201–2.

5. Gutiérrez, *Walls and Mirrors*, 202. Ironically, Gutiérrez quotes one participant as saying that unity had been possible at the conference because, "When they come to deport us, we're all in the same boat." For lesbian and gay Chicanas and Chicanos, we were left to drown when the boat came.

6. Emma Pérez, *The Decolonial Imaginary: Writing Chicanas into History* (Bloomington: Indiana University Press, 1999), xv.

7. Alfredo Lopez Austin, *The Human Body and Ideology: Concepts of the Ancient Nahuas*, vol. 2, trans. Thelma Ortiz de Montellano and Bernard Ortiz de Montellano (Salt Lake City: University of Utah Press, 1988), 244–49.

8. Bonnie Duran, Eduardo Duran, and Maria Yellow Horse Brave Heart, "Native Americans and the Trauma of History," in *Studying Native America: Problems and Prospects*, ed. Russell Thornton (Madison: University of Wisconsin Press, 1998), 64.

9. Duran, Duran, and Brave Heart, *Studying Native America*, 62–63.

10. Patrisia Gonzáles, "Grieving and Transforming Rape," *Column of the Americas* (March 9, 2001), *http://www.uexpress.com/columnoftheamericas*.

11. Quoted in Raul R. Reyes, "'Gringos' and 'Greasers' and the Rio Grande Border: Race Resentment in the Mexican Revolutionary Era in El Paso, 1914–1916" (master's thesis, University of Texas at El Paso, 1997), 80.

12. Alexandra Minna Stern, "Buildings, Boundaries, and Blood: Medicalization and Nation-Building on the U.S.-Mexico Border, 1910–1930," *Hispanic American Historical Review* 79:1 (1999): 41–81.

13. Stern, "Buildings, Boundaries," 44–45. Stern provides a dismal description of the inspection and disinfection process. Individuals were forced to strip naked and their clothes were taken from them for laundering. The heads of the men and boys were shaved while women's hair was washed with a mixture of water, soap, and kerosene. They were then bathed with the same mixture. An attendant watched the entire process.

14. Eduardo Duran and Bonnie Duran, *Native American Postcolonial Psychology* (Albany: State University of New York Press, 1995).

An Aztec Two-Spirit Cosmology

Re-sounding Nahuatl Masculinities, Elders, Femininities, and Youth

GABRIEL S. ESTRADA

•

Quetzalcoatl sparkles on the dark morning horizon as my mother pushes me out of her bleeding body.[1] Quetzalcoatl, the morning star Venus, is a cool and dazzling twin to me, a steaming newborn birthed in the fiery *menudo* of the uterus. My mother's words to my waiting father slowly pop like small pink bubbles on a red pool of adrenaline, "Well, you've got your boy." He doesn't hear her speak. In his dark reflective eyes, I am but a wavering mirage, a small sun waiting to envelop the whole world in my brightness, power, and laughter. Yet around this small mirage, the pale hospital lies like a silver sliver of moon in winter solstice, the longest night of 1970. Quetzalcoatl is but one of the last in a constellation of stars to flash a fading dance across an endless indigo sky. "Gabriel," the name my mother dreams for me, will slowly bleed its indigo form onto the ivory of certificates, journals, or love notes scented in both rose and musk. From nine pulsating months of darkness, I am born into a sequined skywomb of greater darkness. Quetzalcoatl is a brilliant period in the spinning message sung by crystalline star white voices:

> *the farther you go*
> *the more you return*
> *to the Winter Solstice night*
> *of your birth.*

••

In western and colonized mestizo cultures, the darkness of femininity is feared even as it supports and creates all life.[2] This fear of the dark is unnatural. Mammal eggs mature in the protective shade of skin and bones. A plant's first growth is away from the sun and into the wet shadows of earth, and dreams of what is to be flower best at night. Yet, as people mature into the light, they forget their very roots and the darkness that formed them in their youth. As a gay Indigenous person, or two-spirit, I do not forget so easily. After my birth, when the 1970s Chicana/o movements of Orange County, California, were flourishing, my family vanished into the protective darkness of the north. Far from the sunny smog of L.A., I grew up in the blue winter snows of Pullman, Washington, and Moscow, Idaho. I rooted myself at the feet of the soaring Rocky Mountains. There, my parents helped to organize *campesinos* and Chicana/o students to overcome a history of segregation. They also worked to help African Americans, Saudi Arabians, local Nez Perce and Coeur d'Alene Indians, women, and drug addicts around Washington State University. In the white snows and white communities there, I was a dark one. A white girl was so shocked to see my brown Indian skin at school that she asked if I was painted, never knowing the history of Native Americans or the genocide that her own people hid behind the blinding rhetoric of Manifest Destiny and Progress. A white boy asked if I was a boy or a girl; I never bothered to answer the strange and puzzling question until I was older.[3]

•••

Before every winter solstice in these early years, my mom, dad, sister, and I would drive south past waterfalls and even through a huge redwood to my grandmother's house in Orange County. Christmas Eve tamales, cousins, aunts, and uncles waited for us there. People who didn't know me used to ask, "Doesn't having a birthday near Christmas ruin everything?" And I'd tell them, "No, I get two presents from all of my family."

My parents' separation in the mid-1970s paralleled the increasing separation of Chicana and Chicano politics as *mujeres* stood up for their rights when *los hombres* could not accept female power within their colonized brand of machismo. Although those long family trips to California stopped, winter solstice never stopped being my time of year. Far to the south, *Huitzilopochtli*, the small hummingbird sun, is always born as I celebrate another year of life. The winter solstice sun is small, like a child born at night. One year, I had the privilege to go to a Nahuatl village for winter solstice. As part of the celebration, I went with Don Jose, a Nahuatl elder, to gather the heart juices of the maguey. The journey began just as the sun set and the moon began to show its sliver. In growing darkness, I talked to the maguey and then drank from the sweet nectar. Night is the traditional time to gather *aguamiel* from the maguey with long gourds like hummingbird beaks. *Aguamiel*, waterhoney, is a good name for the liquid produced by the maguey. While I've never cared so much for the fermented tequila that comes from the same substance, fresh *aguamiel* is uniquely refreshing, a cross between peanut butter, honey, and water flavors. As we walked back through the maguey fields, Don Jose explained that I should tell of my experiences or they would do little good. His message reverberated in the dark caves of my bat-like ears as we found our way home in the moonlight that poured over the tall spiky leaves of the maguey, pointing every which way.

••••

Night is a valued part of who I am. I could not live actively in the day without resting at night. Night balances day. The Aztec calendar is another way we witness this cosmic harmony. For example, the ideal relationship of the Aztec calendar is the circle, which reflects both the roundness of our Father Sun, Tonatiuh, and our Mother Earth, Tonantzin. The sun that begins with rising masculine energy in the east becomes descending feminine energy as it crosses to the west, only to become masculine in the east again in a never-ending cycle of night and day. A similar movement occurs as the earth tilts north and south toward the sun throughout the solar year. The south is the youth of summer and the north is the age of winter. In both cases, energy only exists in relation to other energies, and one kind can transform into another, just as matter can transform into energy and back if given the right time and place.

Night holds the bigger picture, the cosmic dimensions and dreams of who we are and how we can live during the day. Feminine night is integral to who I am. In a male body, I rely upon the flexibility and strength that my feminine and darker side allows in terms of the inner activities that some mistakenly call "passivity." Inner strength is not weakness. Outer masculine strength cannot succeed until the inner emotional strengths guide outer interests. I feel so strongly about this feminine side that it is an honor to identify as a gay Indian, or two-spirited person.[4] Two-spirit means someone who is androgynous, bisexual, or homosexual, but it also means more than that. Two-spirited people are sexually mixed beings who enjoy a living relation with their Indigenous ways and spirituality. Because of Catholic influence, Hispanicized people often reject what is not heterosexual and male, although the majority of Indigenous people are traditionally respectful of two-spirit people as a group.[5] In fact, because we, as two-spirits, find misunderstanding in most colonized philosophies, we are often the first ones to defend and embody the ways of our ancestors who accept us for the way we carry all our energies at once—both male and female, day and night.[6] I strongly feel that my birth in the epicenter of annual darkness reinforces my respect for a Nahuatl sense of feminine darkness, an obscure internal landscape where emotional needs and desires find space for evolution.

———

Even today, some Nahuatl look up at the Milky Way to see a gigantic snake in the night sky. I close with a poem that I wrote in the Sonoran desert, which extends across the U.S.-Mexico border on what is traditional Tohono O'odham land. I write it in memory of the snakes I used to pick up in the wheat fields of Pullman, Washington. Sometimes, I'd just stare back at those snakes. The prettiest were the rattlers all coiled up. As I move into changing times and places, their rattles echo in the caves of my ears eternally. Shkshkshksshkshs-khskhkssh . . .

Cihuacoatl

I saw her snake
into my redwood bathroom mirror again.
Her slit still eyes fill mine.
I feel the moon polish
my obsidian shields of scales
hear the house rattle in wind
as we slither
through small holes in time.

A coiled mass,
she is slowing molting
beneath the rippling black pools of my eyes,
emerging
with the glittering voice
of hard white
diamond
stars.

Her song circles
with the rhythm
of her rattle:
*"the farther you go
the more you return
to the Winter night
of your birth."*

1. *Quetzalcoatl* is a Nahuatl (Aztec) word that means "feathered serpent" and refers both to the Morning Star and to a series of priests and leaders in Toltec and Aztec history. Over one million Mexican Indians speak Nahuatl today. Nahuatl University was gracious enough to improve my Nahuatl and better my understanding of the codices and Nahuatl cosmologies that includes balanced gender roles (Nahuatl University, *Ilhuikayomachiyotl: Reencuentros en el Cosmos, Agenda 2002*, [Ocotepec, Morelos, Mexico: Asociacion Cultural Mascarones, A.C., 2001], 4).

2. See Inés Hernández-Avila, "An Open Letter to Chicanas: On the Power and Politics of Origin," *Reinventing the Enemy's Language: Contemporary Native Women's Writings of North America*, ed. Joy Harjo and Gloria Bird (New York: W.W. Norton and Company, 1997), 244–45.

3. Indigenous rights, oral traditions, post-AIDS sexual politics, and new media are all bound up in my essay on Indigenous (homo)sexuality. See Gabriel S. Estrada, "The 'Macho' Body as Social Malinche," in *Velvet Barrios: Popular Culture & Chicana/o Sexualities*, ed. Alicia Gaspar de Alba (New York: Palgrave Macmillan, 2003), 41–60.

4. For a detailed and contextualized explanation of two-spirited peoples, see Carolyn Epple, "A Navajo Worldview and Nadleehi: Implications for Western Categories," in *Two-Spirit People: Native American Gender Identity, Sexuality, and Spirituality*, ed. Sue-Ellen Jacobs, Wesley Thomas, and Sabine Lang (Chicago: University of Chicago Press, 1997), 174–91.

5. For a good refutation of the theory that all homosexuality was completely outlawed by the Aztec, see Clark L. Taylor's "Legends, Syncretism, and Continuing Echoes of Homosexuality from Pre-Columbian and Colonial Mexico," *Latin American Homosexualities*, ed. Stephen O. Murray (Albuquerque: New Mexico University Press, 1995), 82.

6. One of the more influential Chicana *lesbiana* works is Gloria Anzaldúa's *Borderlands/La Frontera : The New Mestiza* (San Francisco: Spinsters/Aunt Lute, 1987).

Gender on the Borderlands

Re-textualizing the Classics

DEENA J. GONZÁLEZ

It has not been terribly popular to read against the racial grain, even in western/frontier U.S. history circles. Many texts and other efforts move toward multicultural inclusion or diversity training. To incorporate race or to address racism, however, is not the same as reading against the grain. Including race, or culture, or ethnicity simply means that an effort has been expended in the direction of a contribution, but the effort is not a fundamental reassessment of the old order of things. Reading in a contrary way, or pulling out of texts contradictions and foolish logic on the basis of race or ethnicity, can be a lonely scholarly undertaking, depending on the author's position in the academy. Sometimes it even results in poor teaching evaluations because the modern classroom is still grounded on affirmation and confirmation, on supporting a canon and not its revision. To envision bold and fierce re-readings of the historical record can also result in a divided classroom, a besieged professorate, or a university in crisis. Within ethnic studies endeavors of recent decades, however, a great deal of thought has gone into how one "teaches truth to power." The simple phrase captures eloquently a fundamental university mission (search for truth) as it lays bare the most basic reality: Those speaking truth are sometimes not in control of institutions of higher learning.

Within this context of revision, revising, and reversing, Chicano/a studies has been born. The texts produced by Chicano and Chicana writers and historians in the 1980s laid a foundation for revisionist insights and created a discourse community that continues to serve our study of the twentieth-century experiences of Mexican-origin people in the far West as in the Midwest, and increasingly in the South and Northeast United States.[1]

This historiographic productivity mirrors the problems of last century because many of the books published in the 1980s shied away from the seemingly distant colonial period; the nineteenth century in these history books usually warranted a passing glance, but rarely sustained attention. Some gave the earlier, critical centuries a perfunctory nod, but most stuck closely to English-based sources and documentary evidence written in English in the eighteenth and nineteenth centuries. Until recently, for example, most Chicano/a historians began their history courses in earlier centuries, lingering there only a week or two. This essay will work toward examining the significance of both trends—contributory history as a style or method versus analytical or interpretive work—and a Chicana history still lodged firmly in the most recent century. The trends have much to offer our discussions of gender on the borderlands, the title of the conference in 2001 that brought our work together.

Several aspects of the Chicano/a history written in the 1980s—its distinctly inclusionary tone and its effort and passion for inserting people of Mexican origin into the written historical record—paved the way for a type of history that has yet to achieve much status in the historical profession. Whether considered ethnohistory, Spanish borderlands studies, Southwestern history, ethnic studies, or American studies, the new work challenged older paradigms and made enormous headway in the use of original archival excavation. A few books were even hailed as "firsts." Vicki Ruiz's *Cannery Women: Cannery Lives*, published in 1987, was the first Chicana historical monograph written.[2] A few others have won mainstream professional praise. John Chávez's *The Lost Land*, a survey text, was published in 1984 and was reviewed favorably in the major journals.[3] Arnoldo de León's *The Tejano Community, 1836–1900*, was hailed as a "major contribution to Texas historiography."[4] Most, however, fell under a category akin in history to Siberian exile: They were thought to contribute to the base of knowledge about Chicano/as, but only in a descriptive way. If acknowledged by the mainstream journals or the profession of history at all, the work was usually said to add to the already acceptable field of "borderlands" history. Nevertheless, the books by these 1980s historians were decisively engaged in the process of documentation that Rodolfo Acuña had first originated in the textbook classic, *Occupied America*.[5] Whether marxist, socialist, or feminist, all of the historians like Acuña writing in the period up to 1990 were following a small but growing cohort of Chicano/a academics into research university environments. Each believed passionately in the historian's refrain: Follow the sources.

Follow them they did. Many entered archives to locate primary documents that led them down other paths. Mario García's *Desert Immigrants*, for example, revealed the story of both residents and settlers along the U.S.-Mexican border.[6] De León's *The Tejano Community* investigated politics, labor patterns, and religious life to portray hardships, survival, and resistance among *tejanos*. Embellishing the history of Texas from a Chicano/a and Mexican American perspective, David Montejano offered a comprehensive view of how Texan and

Anglo were conflated or, conversely, how Mexican *Tejas* has been eroded and rendered invisible in the official history of the region.[7] From just these select but important works, the history of one state or locale was clearly being reinvigorated. In other words, the work of Chicano historians on Texas benefitted everyone, including Chicano/as elsewhere. These historians especially put a different spin on the political issues of the period, from supporting bilingualism to documenting the violence and vigilantism of the Texas Rangers. If any single political lesson was to be derived from this region and historiographic period, it was that access to archives—from training to funding—yielded better stories and thicker texts, and made for more interesting social history.

In other regions, another layer was also slowly being peeled away: Chicana graduate students in the 1980s were completing master's theses and dissertations. The previous decade had witnessed a tiny cohort of Chicana scholars who, from a variety of areas, including sociology, anthropology, and history, had explored the Chicana experience. Louise Año Nuevo de Kerr, Shirlene Soto, Marta Cotera, and Adelaida del Castillo each tackled significant areas, contributing a foundation to newer Chicana scholarship.[8] Activist scholars, including Anna Nieto Gómez, Enriqueta Vásquez, and Elizabeth Martínez, bridged formal educational institutions and community organizations, and began adding to the pursuit of facts about Chicanas. They were followed by a group of new and formally trained scholars who were not distinguished—as the men were—by the field of history alone. Ruiz's *Cannery Women: Cannery Lives*, based on her 1982 Stanford dissertation in history on the food processing industry, described labor and societal conditions, but also the broader political context in which labor, union organizing, and women leaders were thwarted. Women were central to the themes she explored in food-processing factories in California, and she used feminist analysis to address the topic.

The same year that Ruiz produced one of the first historical monographs on Chicanas, Gloria Anzaldúa published *Borderlands/La Frontera*.[9] Although rarely considered together or in the same category of academic work because Ruiz had a Ph.D. and Anzaldúa (then) did not, each author offered more than a contributory view of Chicanas. Both wrote Chicanas into the field of history. The earlier classic books or essays by Marta Cotera, Irene Blea, and Adelaida del Castillo in the 1970s, followed by Alma García, Inés Hernández, Norma Alarcón, and Emma Pérez in the 1980s, were evidence of a field beginning to show diverse perspectives.[10]

Although the essays by Pérez and others by Alarcón did not appear in print until 1990, their work carried weight among the listening communities of Chicana scholars, graduate students, assistant professors, and undergraduate audiences. A feminist and lesbian feminist set of debates raged in the Chicana discourse community whose critical junctures can be measured by particular panels, panelists, and conference themes throughout the 1980s. In 1983 at Tempe, Arizona, during the National Association of Chicano Studies' (NACS) annual meeting—still without Chicana in its official title—a panel was put together by a group of graduate students and the only Chicana/Mexicana assistant professor we knew in the entire University of California system, Sylvia Lyzárraga. Our group, *Mujeres en Marcha*, as we identified ourselves, was greeted by an attentive audience of undergraduates, male professors, graduate students, and some parents. They listened with remarkable equanimity as we made the case for equality and feminist perspective through personal memoir, poetry, and story.[11]

The momentum was sustained mostly in article format, with some impressive gains in our work elsewhere, as Chicana assistant professors were beginning to be hired. Steady, tenure-track positions also meant access to publishing. Although published in the same year (1987), Ruiz's and Anzaldúa's books could not have been more focused on a similar goal and yet have been more dissimilar in style and tone. Both sought to write Chicanas into history—consciously so. Anzaldúa was also clearly engaged in her extended essay/autobiography/memoir, placing not only Chicanas and not simply gender, but lesbian feminist sexuality at history's door. As a *tejana* transplanted to California, Anzaldúa's statements and her shattering of silences proved decisive.

Comprised of merely ninety-eight pages of narrative, Anzaldúa's book on the borderlands also contains poetry. As its title suggests, native Spanish-speakers refer to the region as *la frontera*, feminized in Spanish, homeland for many generations as well as more recent immigrants. In Anzaldúa's homeland, some Mexicans became residents of the United States when a war and treaties drew new boundaries. The sociology embedded in her book suggests that the boundaries or borders are still viewed as fiction and not fact. Anzaldúa's negotiation of the muddy waters of history—linking experience, memory, and treaties or wars—signified a new direction in Chicano/a studies but also in Chicana history. From the publication of her book forward, we have recommended that traditional borderlands histories weave archival material with personal memoir, reflection, or family stories wherever appropriate.

Related to personal history as Chicana history, the popularity, reach, and audience of Anzaldúa's work begs the question, What is it about the *tejana* experience that makes the book accessible despite its content and generally taboo subject? In particular, what appeals to undergraduates and literary critics, two groups not often considered in the same breath? Perhaps the political lessons embedded in it are simply important. To the mainstream, for example, English language dominance and English-only initiatives are familiar and overwhelmingly endorsed by voters. Anzaldúa investigates the significance of "linguistic terrorism" and monolingual inflictions in Texas, but its lessons could well extend outward to California and other states interested in pursuing that rather odd American sport—defense of English. *Borderlands/La Frontera* is a bilingual, multilingual text, using standard English, Spanglish, and *caló* throughout. To the mainstream, sexuality is viewed as inappropriate or is dismissed through homophobic stances. Anzaldúa rightfully insists on writing through her lesbian perspective, despite critics who usually disregard this aspect of the work. The book's language and metaphors alone require a grounding, minimally, in feminist analysis, and maximally, in women-of-color, lesbian feminism. Tongue, serpent, wounds, and blood, for example, emerge across her essay, born out of an understanding of war, terror, and colonization, but especially out of their impact on Chicana bodies and identity.

Few know how to begin reviewing the work of a Chicana lesbian, multilingual feminist. Many probably hope to avoid the charge of homophobia. But historians might also be reminded of the utter absence and invisibility in mainstream history texts of Indigenous women, mixed-race women, and Mexicana/Chicanas. All of the inclusions are important in creating a critical dialogue about *Borderlands/La Frontera*, but especially in light of a recent survey of U.S. voters who said that the two most hated "issues" in American life were bilingualism and homosexuality!

Along with *Bless me, Ultima* and *The House on Mango Street*, Anzaldúa's book today occupies the highest rank in its sales category.[12] Few other books about the Chicana/o experience have been so widely sold or translated into so many languages. One success of *Borderlands* lies in its reception. It was read by students and non-Chicano/as long before it became a standard text in the field of Chicano/a studies. Most university curricula are slow to pick up on "fads" or "bestsellers." Chicano/a lag in reading Anzaldúa could also be explained by homophobia, but equally important is the lack of familiarity in the late 1980s with any method that encouraged discussion of sex, gender, and sexuality, much less lesbian feminism. All of these topics remained woefully unexplored by reviewers of Anzaldúa's book, by graduate seminars that began assigning the text and by academic panels whenever her work was examined. Still, Anzaldúa continued to publish scholarly as well as creative work, just as she had done in *Borderlands*, by mixing personal narrative, historical recounting, poetry, and verse. Slowly, audiences have come to appreciate the other aspects of her work.

An entire central section of Anzaldúa's book worked with the concept of mestiza (mixed-race) consciousness that signaled another important turn in the road for Chicana history, and, as the book's subtitle, *The New Mestiza*, reflected, racial and ethnic theory. No longer could Chicanas be termed merely "Mexican American females," as the sociological shorthand would have it. Now, Chicanas were complex characters who spoke several languages, were biracial, bicultural, and were more than heterosexual.[13]

Ruiz, on the other hand, sought to document and investigate the linkages between a worker's consciousness in union organizing and the resistance of female immigrants and citizens within the burgeoning California agricultural structure. Less interested in cultural identity, sexuality, or ethnicity per se, Ruiz argued for the necessity of understanding how women viewed themselves when earning wages. It was a critical contribution to the developing field of Chicana studies, and it occurred roughly at the same time as the research and earliest historiographic writings of Antonia Castañeda were circulating. Working on California's colonial and independence period, Castañeda's work signaled a new direction in Chicana history. Both Castañeda and Ruiz were Stanford-trained historians, and they anchored Chicana history at each end—the contemporary twentieth century and the colonial past.[14]

Meanwhile, Chicanos were busy examining cities and towns, from Los Angeles to the Midwest, uncovering economic and political information or reporting statistical findings to spell out why people of Mexican origin were central to the policy issues of the time: poverty, drugs, crime, and educational "push-out," as well as immigration, globalization, and brain-drain. Most of these scholars valiantly combated the historical stereotyping of Chicano/as. Ricardo Romo's work on Los Angeles focused on the segregation that created East Los Angeles, making it a Mexican enclave and situating it firmly in the context of U.S.-Mexico relations. Women were so little a part of the book's narrative that their mention was restricted to about six pages. Romo's was not the only Chicano history book to neglect women. Most of the historians of his era—as he and others would later admit—would view this neglect as a deficiency. De León's book included chapters with some sections devoted entirely to women's lives, as did García's *Desert Immigrants*. Acuña's second edition of *Occupied America*, in 1988, similarly lagged behind the trend that Ruiz and Anzaldúa had initiated, although it would offer a corrective in the fourth edition twelve years later.[15]

In most Chicano histories of that period and up to the present, women are not central to the analysis or narrative, and are not presented equally. The reasons then and now are not always ideological or political: The evidence on and about women requires a far greater expenditure of time because it must be collected in its original state and then analyzed and reported—the census, for example, did not always count female-headed households or report the number of female-run ranches or farms; church and county records similarly might compile accessible information about public spaces, streets, and services, but these contained minimal information about women. This absence of historical documentation was reflected in Chicano history by a lack of interest and attention to women's presence. It is simply not true that women are absent in the archival record. Rather, we need the historians able and eager to find them.[16]

Symbolically, what can we say about this compressed foray through the secondary literature of the 1980s and its implications for Chicana history, for gender, and for the borderlands? First, two of García's books bracket the decade like a pair of bookends, *Desert Immigrants* (1981), and *Mexican Americans* (1989); each is an effort to understand how Chicano/as are the same, but different, from other ethnic immigrants. Figuratively speaking, however, Anzaldúa is the logical companion to this mixed marriage between men's ways of knowing or doing history and women's or Chicanas' methods: García sustains an abiding hope in the ability of a democratic society to acknowledge some of its mistakes and accord persons of Mexican origin (mostly males) their rightful place in history. Anzaldúa, on the opposite side, refuses this effort. In her essay, there is little endorsement or expectation of any form of democracy. Rather, racial violence, sexual abuse, and linguistic terrorism—each historicized—convinces readers that hers is an alternative vision, but one cognizant of doubtful success in the immediate future. Yet, strangely, we are also left with a sort of familial model, even a femininized one, embedded in García because he works mightily toward a generational understanding of history. As in *Desert Immigrants*, García searches for a way to tell the story of his homeland—the El Paso/Júarez border. The return to the womb in many Chicano historians' work mimes the journey Chicano nationalists themselves undertook in the 1970s when a search for roots required visitations to what many termed the cradle of all *chicanismo*, the Valley of México, land of the mighty and glorious Aztecs, or Mexica, peoples.

García's second book was promising but fell prey to some of the same difficulties as previously mentioned. The organization of the book, *Mexican Americans*, follows the lines of traditional ethnic history or recovery: The book spans 1930–60 and surveys political leadership while it questions the role of organized labor policies in Mexican American daily life. The successive chapters are written innovatively and refreshingly as semibiographical sketches that become the vehicle for unraveling the critical political and policy issues of the period, but again, few women are detailed. The exceptions lie in the more prominent political figures like Josefina Fierro de Bright and the Central American/Mexicana, and the enormously influential organizer, Luisa Moreno.[17]

These works are focused on the twentieth-century Chicano and Chicana experience and are based primarily on English-language sources, documents, interviews, and newspaper accounts. We might speculate about the lack of attention to the nineteenth century and to the older colonial past. Calls for new, more inclusive chronologies date back to 1977 with Judith Sweeney's article, "Chicana History: A Review of the Literature," in the important anthology edited by Rosa Martínez Cruz and Rosaura Sánchez, *Essays on La Mujer*, and extend to 1980 with James Diego Vigil's *From Indians to Chicanos*.[18] Both of these publications argued for an expansive historical time line. Vigil, a social scientist, was interested in how Chicano/a life and culture was grounded in an Indigenous past. This coupling, between traditional historians' concerns for chronology and social science developments that also concerned themselves with topics traditionally significant mainly to historians, such as family structures and economic patterns traced over time, meant that the categories of analysis in Chicana studies were also expanding.

The best way to demonstrate this practice is to look outside the box: When Ruiz published her book on the food-packing industry, anthropologist Patricia Zavella published a book on the impact of women's work on Chicano families.[19] When Acuña's second edition of *Occupied America* appeared in 1981, Vigil's work on mestizo culture had just emerged.[20] Although it might seem that the different disciplines did not speak to one another, they were, in fact, developing companion currents or tracks: Each influenced the next set of books across the field. Meanwhile, literary analysis and literature generally were exploding with themes about sexuality, life, and resistance. By the end of the 1980s, history had to account for the role of women, if only in a very scripted fashion—under a separate section, as a thing apart. The intense interests in femininity, womanhood, and femaleness redefined sexuality, sex, art, and activism, and called for an incorporation of women. These interests also forced many scholars living in solitary confinement to begin attending to the matter of including women or to consciously exclude them.

Still, the problem remained for historians of how to do research and work in periods hundreds of years in the past. Some historians writing about Chicano/as could not read the Spanish language, including medieval Spanish. Others chose to focus on histories that seemed to have more immediate implications—those that would allow faculty or administrators to make the case for Chicano/a studies, for example. A few historians were plagued by issues of economic reality, including part-time employment, the costs of traveling to archives in México, the cost of locating sources that lay in the recesses of many collections, and, overall, of justifying anything but more contemporary topics to publishers, colleagues, and students. In sum, it was not—and probably still is not—popular or easy to write about anything predating 1900. In one article, a Chicano historian argued that the best Chicano historians could do in the

1960s and 1970s was to reach back to the period 1846 to 1848, the period of the U.S.-Mexican War.[21] Considered historically, that paradigmatic scheme or time line allowed for the ongoing attention to racial conflict and class subordination. Anything said about either of those topics in earlier periods would complicate race or gender with the need to explain *mestizaje*, Indigenous history, and Spanish-Mexican struggles with Native peoples. Better, it seemed, to avoid the messiness or complexities embedded in intensifying social relations and stick to the known formula: Mexicans struggled valiantly against the U.S. giant; next, Mexican immigrants fled a war-torn country and were encouraged by an overdeveloped economy to the north. In both centuries, the unifying theme is Mexican displacement. The standard chronology is also unified, albeit artificially, by one other characteristic: Its lack of attention to women lends it the appearance of coherence, a feature quite absent in the primary records of just about every village, town, or community in the borderlands.

The juxtaposition of García's books, which helped to open and close a critical period in Chicano/a historiography, with the work by Ruiz and Anzaldúa in between, provides much fodder for a gendered and sexed interpretation of this historiography. It speaks volumes about the necessity of an improved understanding of gender categories in, and on, the borderlands. Other scholars have provided, as mentioned before with examples from the social sciences, methods for grouping or disaggregating the scholarship of the contemporary period. In 1989, for example, the sociologist Alma García published an essay in *Gender and Society* discussing Chicana feminist discourse in the 1970s. It failed to mention any Chicana lesbian feminism, perhaps because much of that writing remained outside the tight, mainly heterosexual discourse community she was examining. By the time Teresa Córdova published her synthetic treatment of Chicana feminist writings in 1994, it was impossible to omit Chicana lesbian feminism, whether one considered one decade more driven by social science methodologies (as Córdova does the 1980s) than the cultural studies approaches of the 1990s, into which she groups Chicana lesbian writing. Both scholars, in these cited works and in other work, have offered enriched bibliographic and historiographic time lines for evaluating where the study of Chicana feminism resides today. Traversing the sources, both original and secondary, is an experience in differences, each marked by approach, methodology, and orientation. The field is now flourishing, as a result of such engagement.[22]

The thriving 1980s could have predicted the chaos and energy of the 1990s, when so many more scholarly books directly included and sustained an historical analysis of Chicanas. In Euroamerican feminist movements, first-, second-, and third-wave feminisms dominated the debates and creative output, and similar divisions could be seen within the Chicano/a scholarly community. As usual, another moment of epiphany in the borderlands occurred, this time in Albuquerque. At the 1990 meeting of NACCS (by then the Association had added Chicana to Chicano), Emma Pérez delivered an address on sexuality and re-read Chicano nationalism using sexuality as a guide. An audience of nearly one thousand people listened to a Chicana lesbian scholar declare a state of emergency, and the fallout proved heady. Men threatened to crash a woman-only workshop, and others called for the creation of separate caucuses for any and all manner of ridiculous causes. Known harrassers sat in the crowded public spaces, ogling young women who were somewhat oblivious to how the public dynamic mirrored the exact thing Pérez had detailed in her remarks.[23]

Scholarly productivity, and Chicana history in particular, was shaped by these events and outcries. The discussion was embedded in every institutionalized setting, including discussions at tables where fellowships and jobs were offered. Feminists of every persuasion made their cases, and the result—as evidenced in the books and articles of the 1990s, especially in Chicana cultural studies—indicated awarenesses about sexuality and radical feminism lacking in the work of the 1980s. It might well be that some decades from now, scholars will reflect on the number of books in history alone that foregrounded sex and sexuality. Ramón A. Gutiérrez, Vicki Ruiz, Emma Pérez, and I all produced books published in the past decade addressing how and why sex and sexuality matter in the Chicano/a experience. Gutiérrez wrote about the Pueblo and Spanish-Mexican worlds in the colonial past (a book the Pueblo peoples dispute), I wrote on the nineteenth century, and Ruiz and Pérez wrote on the twentieth century.[24] Other works, as in previous decades, embellished the historical monographs: Genaro Padilla described primary literary and autobiographical documents, Rosaura Sánchez also turned to literary criticism to excavate original California narratives, and in cultural studies, Alicia Gaspar de Alba and Yolanda Broyles-González, to name two, looked critically at established cultural institutions, art, and theatre to assist and engage the historiography.[25]

Many more works could be cited, but the majority written in the 1990s brought together some intersecting interests: each focused on women, gender, and sex generally, and even those outside the discipline of history engaged history as a means of understanding particular social issues. Gaspar de Alba wrote the first book in Chicano/a art history and refused to relegate gender, sex, and sexuality to just one chapter in the discussion of mainstream museum reception of Chicano/a art. Broyles-González sustained a rigorous gendered analysis of the most renowned of Chicano theater companies, El Teatro Campesino. The literary critics cited before, Padilla and Sánchez, insisted on assessing women's writings, as well as men's. The results are books more textured and layered with meaning for those interested in the social history of nineteenth-century New Mexico and California. Their lessons are also clear and forceful: Few writing after these scholars can neglect the majority population of nearly every Chicano/a community—women.

Chicana feminism dissuades one from capturing any feminism at all under the rubric of "Gender on the Borderlands," because gender can and does mean male as well as female, men as well as women. The original proposal for the St. Mary's University conference by the same title contained as well an implicit understanding that one other purpose was at play—in addition to surveying Chicana history, art, literature, and culture, an opportunity existed to present new directions in the field. The notion that the entire concept of gender was a borderland itself guided the conference planners and Antonia Castañeda, the conference organizer. The double-sided, three-fold conference announcement depicts a butch woman's back (Claudia Rodríguez, photo by Alma López), which includes the cityscape of downtown Los Angeles and is also reproduced on the cover of this special volume. A public demonstration of women marching with banners was embedded in the art piece.

Today, more than ever before, few would conflate gender and women in the same breath in the way that sexuality was once a code word used for lesbian, gay, bisexual, or transgendered. In fact, Chicana history argued strenuously in the work surveyed earlier in this essay that collapsing categories was insufficient. Gender could thus only mean a plurality: male, female, and many in between and beyond. Sex could mean heterosexual, bisexual, gay/lesbian, and transgendered. Sexuality could mean feminine, masculine, two-spirited, and many other expressions of being between and beyond. Just as social scientists amplified the concept of class to include social location as well as caste and other categories, and just as race now includes color, ethnicity, and mixed-cultural ancestry, few of the original, organizing concepts in Chicano/a studies have remained singular. Pluralism in interpretation reigns.

Earlier in this essay, I suggested that although contributory history played an important role in Chicano/a studies, its place was eroding as analytical and interpretive texts and essays began reorienting the field in the direction of different evidence and trends. Just as at one point in literary studies, race and attitudinal surveys (attitudes toward others, for example), went hand in hand, in Chicana history, descriptive and evidentiary exposés once dominated the field. Increasingly, as literary theory and cultural studies begin to influence discussions of the past, the field of Chicana/o history is similarly enriched. Literary theory might not always look at the whole in favor of the specific, or at context in favor of text, but increasingly, it is turning to history to help make sense of text. In the case of Chicana/o letters, this was difficult because only in the last three decades have we had Chicana/o history books helping to establish a context for a literary work. Similarly, Chicana/o history necessarily relies on cultural critics and theorists—not always the same thing—to interpret events, people, language, or conditions in the past. In the crossover, context becomes to text what story is to history. History holds to truth and not to fiction, but much history is in fact exposed as fiction. Literature holds to words and imaginary worlds, but much literature is in fact historically sound.

The enrichment and possibilities created by a borderlands imaginary cognizant of the past and present, of traditional disciplines as well as of inter-, cross-, and post-disciplinary borders or barriers, is precisely what we seek to accomplish next. Younger scholars no longer have to open dissertations, theses, or papers with the old lament: No one has used these sources or published the first sources on this topic. Instead, they must now manipulate a vast array of contrary perspectives and address a topic coherently using both present and past voices. They must master the traditional historiography of the borderlands and the alternative literatures of those regions as well. Description is a prelude to interpretation, and theory without fact or for theory's sake alone is increasingly suspect. Both new and experienced scholars, however, are bound today as rarely before by a growing respect and emphasis on gender, sex, and sexuality.

NOTES

1. Historians are trained in research institutions, usually large universities; although the number of Chicano/a historians has risen, only twenty-one are women. Their place of origin, birthplace, ethnicity, and class continue to correspond closely, for the most part, with the subjects of their research.

2. Vicki L. Ruiz, *Cannery Women/Cannery Lives: Mexican Women, Unionization, and the California Food Processing Industry, 1930–1950* (Albuquerque: University of New Mexico Press, 1987).

3. John Chávez, *The Lost Land: The Chicano Image of the Southwest* (Albuquerque: Univiversity of New Mexico Press, 1984).

4. Arnoldo de León, *The Tejano Community, 1836–1900* (Albuquerque: University of New Mexico Press, 1982), book jacket.

5. Rodolfo Acuña, *Occupied America: A History of Chicanos*, 2nd ed. (New York: Harper and Row, 1981).

6. Mario Garcia, *Desert Immigrants: The Mexicans of El Paso, 1880–1920* (New Haven: Yale University Press, 1981).

7. David Montejano, *Anglos and Mexicans in the Making of Texas, 1836–1986* (Austin: University of Texas Press, 1987).

8. See Louise Año Nuevo de Kerr, "The Chicano Experience in Chicago: 1920–1970," (Ph.D. diss., University of Illinois, Chicago Circle, 1976); Shirlene Soto, *Emergence of the Modern Mexican Woman: Her Participation in Revolution and Struggle for Equality* (Denver: Arden Press, 1990); Marta Cotera, *Diosa y Hembra: The Chicana Feminist* (Austin: Information Systems Development, 1977); and Adelaida del Castillo, "La Vision Chicana," in *La Gente de Aztlan* (Los Angeles: University of California Press, 1974), 8–10. See also Adelaida del Castillo, "Malintzin Tenépal: A Preliminary Look into a New Perspective," in *Essays on La Mujer*, ed. Rosa Martínez Cruz and Rosaura Sánchez (Los Angeles: UCLA Chicano Studies Center Publications, 1977), 129–49.

9. Gloria Anzaldúa, *Borderlands/La Frontera: The New Mestiza* (San Francisco: Spinsters/Aunt Lute, 1987).

10. The work of these scholars appeared most frequently in the 1980s as articles, and most Chicano historians do not cite them generally, although they were enormously influential in laying the groundwork for Chicana studies. See Alma García, "The Development of Chicana Feminist Discourse, 1970–1980," in *Gender and Society* 3:2 (1989): 217–38. See also Inés Hernández Tovar, "The Feminist Aesthetic in Chicano Literature," in *The Third Woman: Minority Women Writers in the U.S.*, ed. Dexter Fisher (Boston: Houghton Mifflin, 1980); Norma Alarcón, "Chicana's Feminist Literature: A Re-vision Through Malintzin/or Malintzin: Putting Flesh Back on the Object," in *This Bridge Called My Back: Writings by Radical Women of Color*, ed. Cherríe Moraga and Gloria Anzaldúa, (Watertown, Mass.: Perspehone Press, 1981), 182–90; and Emma M. Pérez, "A La Mujer: A Critique of the Partido Liberal Mexicano's Gender Ideology on Women," in *Between Borders: Essays on Mexicana/Chicana History*, ed. Adelaida del Castillo (Los Angeles: Floricanto Press, 1990), 459–82.

11. For details of the panel's remarks and audience reception, see *Chicanas in the 80s: Unsettled Issues* (Berkeley: Chicano Studies Library Publication Unit, 1983). The pamphlet is reprinted in *Chicana Feminist Thought: The Basic Historical Writings*, ed. Alma Garcia (New York and London: Routledge, 1997), 253–60.

12. Rudolfo Anaya, *Bless Me, Ultima* (New York: Warner Books, 1994); and Sandra Cisneros, *The House on Mango Street* (New York: Vintage, 1991).

13. Anzaldúa's book was not the first to name mestiza consciousness or to suggest that Chicanas were biracial and bicultural as well as bilingual and, sometimes, bisexual. Rather, all of these categories and terms underscored—beginning in the 1970s at the height of Chicano nationalistic fervor—the importance of multiple categories of analysis. Although few literary critics and historiographers on the Chicano/a experience existed then, the primary documents point to a complex understanding of the period's significant issues, from identity to national policies. Chicana poets deployed the concepts and terms as gathered handily in the important review of the literature by Teresa

Córdova, "Roots and Resistance: The Emergent Writings of Twenty Years of Chicana Feminist Struggle," in *Handbook of Hispanic Cultures in the United States: Sociology*, ed. Félix Padilla, Nicolas Kanellos, and Claudio Esteva-Fabregat (Houston: Arte Público Press, 1994), 175–202.

14. Before her graduate training in history began, Castañeda had already worked in the field. With Joseph Sommers and Tomás Ybarra-Frausto as coeditors, she published *Literatura Chicana: Texto y Contexto* (New Jersey: Prentice-Hall, 1972). See her "Gender, Race, and Culture: Spanish-Mexican Women in the Historiography of Frontier California," *Frontiers* 11:1 (1990): 8–20, and "Women of Color and the Rewriting of Western Women's History: The Discourse, Politics, and Decolonization of History," *Pacific Historical Review* 61 (1992): 501–33, which won an award for best article published that year. I would situate my own work between that of Vicki Ruiz and Emma Pérez (because they each work on the twentieth century) and Castañeda, who focuses on the colonial and early independence periods. My book, *Refusing the Favor: The Spanish-Mexican Women of Santa Fe, 1820–1880* (New York: Oxford University Press, 1999) is one of the only nineteenth-century secondary monographs available thus far that strictly focuses on the Chicana experience. See literary critic Rosaura Sánchez's *Telling Identities: The Californio Testimonios* (Minneapolis: University of Minnesota Press, 1995) for another nineteenth-century work, not all of it on women. We anticipate important new historical studies on the nineteenth century by Linda Heidenreich (on northern California) and Miroslava Chávez (on late colonial and nineteenth century California).

15. See Acuña's fourth edition of *Occupied America: A History of Chicanos* (New York: Longman, 2000). For articles about the men's books, see the important reviews of the literature by David G. Gutiérrez, "The Third Generation: Reflections on Recent Chicano Historiography," in *Mexican Studies/Estudios Mexicanos* 5:2 (1989): 281–96; and Alex M. Saragoza, "Recent Chicano Historiography: An Interpretive Essay," in *Aztlan* 19:1 (1988/1990): 1–77. An important corrective that begins to integrate the role of Chicana literature in relationship to Chicano/a Studies is found in Ramón A. Gutiérrez, "Community, Patriarchy, and Individualism: The Politics of Chicano History and the Dream of Equality," *American Quarterly* 45:1 (1993): 44–72.

16. See my review of some of these features or patterns in "Chicana Identity Matters," reprinted in revised form in *The Chicano Studies Reader: An Anthology of Aztlan, 1970–2000*, ed. Chon A. Noriega, Eric R. Avila, Karen Mary Davalos, Chela Sandoval, and Rafael Pérez-Torres (Los Angeles: Chicano Studies Research Center Publications, 2001), 411–26.

17. Mario T. García, *Mexican Americans: Leadership, Ideology, and Identity, 1930–1960* (New Haven: Yale University Press, 1989).

18. Judith Sweeney, "Chicana History: A Review of the Literature," in Cruz and Sánchez, *Essays on La Mujer*, 99–123; and James Diego Vigil, *From Indians to Chicanos: The Dynamics of Mexican American Culture* (Prospect Heights, Illinois: Waveland Press, 1980).

19. Patricia Zavella, *Women's Work and Chicano Families: Cannery Workers of the Santa Clara Valley* (Ithaca, N.Y.: Cornell University Press, 1987).

20. Vigil, *From Indians to Chicanos*.

21. See Saragoza, "Recent Chicano Historiography," 21–24; and mention by Gutiérrez in "Community, Patriarchy and Individualism," 66.

22. García, "The Development of Chicana Feminist Discourse, 1970–1980," 217–38; and Córdova, "Roots and Resistance," 175–202. For a contemporary historical treatment finally pulling together these trends, see Emma M. Pérez's critical *The Decolonial Imaginary: Writing Chicanas into History* (Bloomington: Indiana University Press, 1999).

23. For an essay based on her plenary address, see Emma M. Pérez, "Sexuality and Discourse: Notes From a Chicana Survivor," in *Chicana Lesbians: The Girls Our Mothers Warned Us About*, ed. Carla Trujillo (Berkeley: Third Woman Press, 1991), 159–84.

24. See Ramón A. Gutiérrez, *When Jesus Came, the Corn Mothers Went Away: Marriage, Sexuality, and Power in New Mexico, 1500–1846* (Stanford: Stanford University Press, 1991); González, *Refusing the Favor*; Pérez, *The Decolonial Imaginary*; and Vicki L. Ruiz, *From Out of the Shadows: Mexican Women in Twentieth Century America* (New York: Oxford University Press, 1998). For the critiques of Gutiérrez's work by Pueblo scholars, see UNM American Indian Studies, *American Indian Culture and Research Journal* 17:3 (1993): 141–77.

25. See Genaro M. Padilla, *My History, Not Yours: The Formation of Mexican American Autobiography* (Madison: The University of Wisconsin Press, 1993); Rosaura Sanchez, *Telling Identities*; Alicia Gaspar de Alba, *Chicano Art Inside/Outside the Master's House: Cultural Politics and the CARA Exhibition* (Austin: University of Texas Press, 1998); and Yolanda Broyles-González, *El Teatro Campesino: Theater in the Chicano Movement* (Austin: University of Texas Press, 1994).

Docile Children and Dangerous Revolutionaries

The Racial Hierarchy of Manliness and the Bisbee Deportation of 1917

KATHERINE BENTON-COHEN

On July 12, 1917, three months after the United States entered World War I, a dramatic event in a remote copper-mining town near the U.S.-Mexico border grabbed national headlines. On June 26, in Bisbee, Arizona, the Industrial Workers of the World (the IWW, or "Wobblies") had called a strike on several local copper mines, including the Phelps-Dodge (PD) Corporation's famous Copper Queen Mine. By almost all accounts, the strike had remained relatively uneventful until the wee hours of July 12, when county sheriff Harry Wheeler quietly deputized twelve hundred men, who were normally miners, engineers, doctors, and shopkeepers. Mining company officials silenced all out-going phone calls and telegrams. On the front page of the morning newspaper, Wheeler warned women and children to stay off the streets. By four a.m., the gun-toting deputies "appeared as if by magic," as the front page of the *New York Times* reported the following day. The posse of deputies, led by the charismatic sheriff and armed to the teeth, swarmed the narrow, steep streets of the mountain town.[1]

Throughout the mining district, deputies broke down doors and gathered up men from their homes, rooming houses, or places of business, including not just miners, but also restaurant owners, carpenters, and a lawyer. Amado Villalovas was in a neighborhood store when, as he later explained to the Arizona attorney general, "about ten gunmen all armed came in and told me to get out. I asked them to let me take my groceries home to my family. They dragged me out of the store, hit me and knocked me down."[2] Under the hot July sun, the deputies forced Villalovas into a line of over a thousand other captives in a forced march through town, past the mines, to a baseball field two miles away. There, local residents gathered to watch as the deputies loaded their charges into twenty-three boxcars and sent them off nearly two hundred miles into the New Mexico desert. Hours later, an army camp in nearby Columbus, New Mexico, rescued the deported men and set up housing for them. Because vigilantes continued to police Bisbee's borders, the deportees were not allowed to go home for more than two months, and many never returned. The event became known across the country as the Bisbee Deportation, although it was not a "true" deportation across international borders.

The deportation captured national headlines, but it was only the most dramatic of a series of encounters during the summer of 1917 between Wobblies and their opponents. The mining West had been the Wobblies' stronghold since disgruntled leaders of the Western Federation of Miners (WFM) had founded the IWW in 1905. Led by colorful characters like "Big Bill" Haywood and Mother Jones, the IWW organized across class, race, and gender lines. Unlike the American Federation of Labor (AFL), which organized along craft lines, the Wobblies' goal was to create an industrial union—"one big union"— that included all workers, from the washerwoman to the foreman.

There were over forty-five hundred work stoppages in the United States that year, but in the patriotic fervor of World War I, the IWW's radical politics and antiwar stance elicited especially deep antipathy. Two weeks after the Bisbee deportation, IWW organizer Frank Little was lynched in Butte, Montana, another copper-mining center. Other towns tarred and feathered Wobblies or deported a few dozen striking workers, as occurred in Jerome, Arizona, just two days before the Bisbee Deportation.[3] But nowhere did anti-Wobbly responses reach the precision and scale of the Bisbee Deportation, a distinction that has generated many attempts at explanation. The event prompted President Woodrow Wilson to appoint a federal commission to investigate the IWW and vigilante activities in war industries in the West.

Today, the event remains a mainstay of the scholarly literatures on the domestic front in World War I, western labor history, and the history of nativism. Interpretations have varied. One view portrays the deportation as a simple example of wartime nativism intended to purge the country of foreign radicals during the Red Scare. The second major interpretation, developed in the only book-length study of the event, portrays the deportation as cynical opportunism by the mining companies that used the war effort as an excuse to rid Arizona mining camps of an increasingly powerful union movement. One scholar has sharpened the antinativist thesis by examining nascent interracial collaboration among strikers as a motivation for antilabor opposition. A women's historian has explored the gendered implications of the deportation and its effects on racial division, specifically the deployment of the concept of "domesticity" by both strikers and deputies.[4] While each of these approaches is valuable, no single theory has the power to explain an event that involved thousands of people. What is missing is an interpretation that captures the variety of perspectives among the deportation's participants.

In this article, I focus on masculinity—or "manhood" and "manliness," as contemporaries would have put it—to show the links between Bisbee's class, race, and gender anxieties and divisions. As Kristin Hoganson has linked diverse interpretations of turn-of-the-century imperialism to "fighting for manhood," I argue that an understanding of the racial hierarchy of manliness can help explain the multiple motives held by Bisbee residents and also help bridge the multiple interpretations the deportation has generated.[5] The deportation was not about labor relations *or* race *or* gender; it was about all of them. Manliness is a useful lens because it colored all of them. Manliness is not a magic interpretive bullet, and I am not arguing that there is only one definition of manliness, even among white men; neither do I argue that manliness is or was inherently violent or militant or pro- or anti-labor. Manliness is a social construct linking male anatomy, cultural identity, and power. What the theme of manliness will do is reveal how several different perspectives on the strike converged in a mass vigilante action.[6] Understanding manliness can help make sense of the links between social categories that we too often isolate for the sake of analytical clarity at the cost of accurate depiction of their deep interconnections. To explore the relationships between manhood and race in Bisbee more closely, I examine their evolution at three stages in Bisbee's history: first in the social world that had developed in Bisbee before 1917; then during the strike, when Mexican workers challenged the terms of Bisbee's social compact; and, finally, in the stunning vigilante response in the form of deportation and its aftermath.

RACIAL HIERARCHIES OF MANLINESS

Bisbee's most vivid and public expression of the racial hierarchy of manliness was its reputation as a "white man's camp," which dates to the 1880s. The term's meanings changed over time. At first the term indicated the exclusion of Chinese, who were barred from the town altogether.[7] Mexicans, unlike the Chinese, were allowed to live and work in Bisbee, but the town's status as a white man's camp also referred to its exclusion of Mexican workers from the most lucrative jobs underground. In "Mexican camps" like Clifton-Morenci in Arizona, Mexican workers performed most kinds of work, other than supervisory roles, but in Bisbee they were restricted to only the most menial mining jobs. "Mexican" was a racial label, not a national one, and native-born, lifelong residents of the American Southwest were consigned to the "Mexican" category alongside recent Mexican immigrants.

The place of other ethnic groups in the white man's camp was less clear, however. "Bisbee has always been a 'White Man's Camp,'" insisted one local editorial in 1903, but the new "foreign labor" from Serbia and Italy was threatening that status quo. Eastern and southern Europeans occupied an "in-between" racial category, to use a phrase used by several historians. In Bisbee, workers argued among themselves and with employers over where these "in-betweens" should go in a place self-defined as a white man's camp. Other white man's camps, like Cripple Creek, Colorado, had successfully excluded southern and eastern Europeans in the years before the World War I boom, but not so Bisbee. By 1917, hundreds of Slavs and Italians lived in Bisbee, enough to have their own boardinghouses and distinctive neighborhoods. In part, the Bisbee deportation, occurring in the context of World War I and increasing support for immigration restriction, did reflect fears about foreigners, as many historians have noted. Eighty percent of the men deported from Bisbee in 1917 were immigrants. One third of those counted as foreign-born were of Mexican descent, and another 40 percent were Slavic.[8]

The place of Mexicans and these new "in-between" races in the white man's camp differed, however, and the biggest difference flowed from the dual-wage system of Bisbee's mines. People of Mexican descent doing the same work as other mine employees earned one-half to two-thirds of what their non-Mexican counterparts did. Although northern European workers complained that Slavs and Italians would work for less pay, eastern and southern European workers did not actually occupy a separate racial job category; Mexican workers did. Printed pay scales listed Mexican and white (or "American") wages separately, with Serbs and Italians clustered in mid-level "white" jobs. In a context where race so explicitly equaled class, this distinction was critical because an "American" wage was as racially defined as a Mexican wage. In Arizona, the opposite of a white man's camp was a Mexican camp, *not* a Slavic camp or even a foreigners' camp.[9] This linguistic distinction suggested some room for racial maneuvering for eastern and southern Europeans in contrast to opportunities for Mexicans.

The dual-wage system existed throughout the Southwest's mining industry, but white man's camps buttressed racial divisions of labor by excluding Mexican workers from the better-paid jobs underground—the work of Bisbee's famed "he-men." As the *Bisbee Daily Review* explained in 1903, Bisbee "is strictly a 'white man's camp'. . . . Mexicans are employed only in the common or rough labor" above ground. Sometimes, as at Bisbee's Calumet & Arizona Mining Company (C&A), "Mexican" was a job category as well as a racial label. A detailed "nationality report" compiled by C&A for federal investigators listed categories for "Native Born Citizens," "Naturalized Citizens," and "Foreigners." These were totaled and then, below this total and separated by a line, was a column labeled "Mexicans (not included above)." Wage scales never listed a "foreigner" wage; "Mexican" was the only category that appeared in both nationality reports and wage scales. As a result of this combination of wage and job discrimination, almost all non-Mexican mining employees had better jobs than Mexican workers did. During the 1910s, the average Mexican wage was half the average white wage because of combined wage and job discrimination, and the gap was growing.[10]

The wage system was also highly gendered. Mexican wages were defined as a percentage of white wages, which in turn were defined in terms of "family wage ideology." This principle held that a man working full-time should be not just the primary, but *the* breadwinner, in his family. As Marsha May and Linda Gordon have observed, family wage ideology enjoyed wide consensus among workers, employers, and reformers. Historian Alice Kessler-Harris has shown that women's low wages suffered from the assumption that women were not breadwinners.[11]

As in other industrial communities, in Bisbee the family wage ideology was useful to employers and workers alike: Bisbee had a reputation as one of the best-paid mining camps in the West precisely because the mining companies wanted to entice family men in order to reduce turnover. As one C&A official explained in 1907, "the robust American with a growing family and home ties is a better man for us than a man without these things." To entice these robust specimens, companies supplemented wages with family-friendly philanthropy like home-owning schemes, school-building, park maintenance, and a preference for keeping on married men during lay-offs. These were offers benefited mainly those who were earning white wages. Just as David Roediger has summarized W. E. B. DuBois to argue that the "wages of whiteness" include the "psychological wage" of being white, so too did Bisbee's family wage package include forms of compensation not found in a pay envelope. The "wages of whiteness" were family wages.[12]

In theory, white workers and managers agreed on the family wage, but in practice they parted company when it came to defining it in dollars and cents. They had competing visions of the family wage's meaning: Employers saw the family wage as an incentive, but those who earned white wages saw the family wage as a right. The mining companies had established a sliding pay scale according to the price of copper; even if these wages were higher than the industry average, this market-determined pay scale conflicted with workers' conviction that wages should be calculated based on a certain standard of living. One of the strikers' demands in 1917 was to replace the sliding scale with fixed wages. In 1917, as wartime inflation deflated salaries, defenders of the strikers invoked the importance of supporting one's family. When the PD company store raised the price of flour, sympathetic newspaper editor John

Dunbar argued that the price increase was intended to "starve the miners into subjection," but that all the increases would do was to "starv[e] men out who have families."[13] Dunbar was implicitly admitting that some men *would* work for the current wages, but not the most desirable workers—the family men.

Bisbee's debates about the family wage usually invoked the "American standard of living," a concept that national trade unionists had been developing since the Jacksonian period. Although the term was clearly subjective and rarely explicitly defined, it generally referred to providing the sole support for a wife and several school-age children, and usually to home ownership ("a comfortable house of at least six rooms," wrote one labor leader in 1898). By 1917, these claims were well established. At Bisbee, the strikers were simply "asking the American right to maintain their wives and children," argued editor Dunbar in 1917.[14]

Home ownership was the most potent symbol of the American standard of living in Bisbee. Bisbee had long been known as a "city of homes," where a high percentage of miners were also homeowners, and promotional pamphlets bragged about Bisbee's "domesticated miners." Beginning in 1906, C&A created a subsidiary, the Warren Company, to build an entire suburb to entice "American" miners to purchase homes for their families. PD bought the real estate company in 1917. This corporate commitment to home ownership for workers gave miners some leverage. If it was company policy to offer home ownership, workers argued, it ought to be company policy to pay men wages that covered the mortgage as well as the grocery bill. Defenders of strikers in 1917 repeatedly pointed out that the majority of the men deported were homeowners.[15]

The case of housing shows that the family wage and the American standard of living were racialized as well as gendered. Both white workers and managers used housing to show Mexican workers' unfitness for an American standard of living. Mexican families' "domestic equipment" consisted merely of "an adobe hut with an earth floor." This "lower" standard of living became naturalized in white minds, so that white workers continually opposed the inclusion of Mexican laborers into "white" labor categories by arguing that their lower standard of living allowed them to undercut white wages. Managers did the same. Less than a year after the deportation, PD president Walter Douglas thought it "desirable that American employees should own their own homes," but rejected a home-owning plan for Mexican workers, because "where the Mexican is concerned, it will be difficult to induce him to obligate himself to pay for the house in which he is living." Better to "build tenements or cheaply constructed houses" for rental that "might appeal to the Mexican."[16]

White workers and mining officials believed that the gap between American and Mexican standards of living—indeed, the dual-wage system itself—was a natural product of racial difference. As Linda Gordon has pointed out, most Anglos honestly believed that Mexicans did not need a family wage. A well-circulated government report used Mexicans' "lower standard of living" to justify their low wages: "The wants of the Mexican peon are hardly more complex than those of the Indian from whom he is descended." Mexican wages quite explicitly could not support an "American standard of living," nor were they intended to. In this sense, the dual-wage system, and with it the racial hierarchy of manhood, appeared natural.

Specifically, white critics believed that Mexican workers were not "real" men. If anything, this is an understatement. As Yvette Huginnie has shown, Anglo workers and managers infantilized and feminized Mexican workers to reinforce their exclusion from the family wage and the American standard of living. "The Mexican worker intellectually is a child. He is governed by emotion rather than by reason," explained one technical journal. Another article warned, "The Mexican workman will misunderstand an attitude of social equality toward him. . . . He cannot be your equal; he must either be your superior or your inferior." The superiority of Anglo men over Mexican men meshed quite neatly with the superiority of foreman over laborer in a twinned hierarchy of class and race. Mexican workers needed white bosses they could "look up to," according to such articles.[17] That white workers and managers often expressed these stereotypes in terms of benevolent paternalism only accentuates the ways that their rhetoric aimed to emasculate Mexican workers.

MEXICAN WORKERS STRIKE THE RACIAL HIERARCHY OF MANLINESS

These racialized, emasculating characterizations assumed by white bosses and coworkers had little to do with how Mexican workers viewed themselves, however, and the strike was a vivid assertion of their own manly identities. Their strike participation and demands rejected nearly everything about the racial hierarchy of manliness, which, by then, shaped nearly everything about life in Bisbee, from gender to wages, family structure, and housing. No one understood the hierarchy's ideological and material power better than Mexican workers themselves. In the strike of 1917, Anglo Wobbly leaders were calling for an end to the practice of blacklisting, a solidarity strike for copper miners striking in Butte, Montana, and—lastly—a slight wage increase. However, Mexican workers called for dismantling the dual-wage system by demanding the family wage and the right to an American standard of living. Above all, they were rejecting the social compact of the white man's camp, one that denied them full male economic and social citizenship.

Scholars have not adequately explored the challenge Mexican workers raised against the ideology of the white man's camp. Most histories of the Bisbee strike have ignored the prevalence of Mexican workers in the strike or have depicted them as passive, unknowing dupes of Wobbly leaders. One reason, no doubt, is that Wilson's Mediation Commission failed to interview any Mexicans in Bisbee. Few sources exist about Mexicans in Bisbee except quantitative ones (which are difficult to use in the noncensus year of 1917). Others mention groups of Mexicans in only the most vague, stereotypical terms—generally as faceless peons or revolutionaries. The lack of sources on Mexicans in Bisbee is, in fact, prima facie evidence of the power of the white man's camp ideology, because sources on Mexicans elsewhere in Arizona, while not abundant, far outnumber those for Bisbee. I have borrowed from these other sources where necessary. Because of this scarcity of sources, general histories of Arizona's Mexican mine workers have focused on Mexican strikes in Mexican camps—an important story. But that focus has underplayed the ideological significance of their participation in strikes on the white men's camps of Bisbee and Globe-Miami, Arizona. The challenges mounted by Mexican workers in 1917 against the very tenets of the white man's camp were unprecedented. Bisbee had faced union conflict before, in an abortive Western Federation of Miners strike in 1907. But in that incident, strikers had called not for equality for Mexican workers, but for an end to Mexican labor altogether! The 1907 strikers intended to preserve Bisbee's reputation as a white man's camp, not to destroy it. Not so in 1917.[18]

By 1917 Mexicans made up a significant portion of Bisbee's population and workforce. When the strike broke out in late July, the Copper Queen had about three hundred Mexican workers, which added up to nearly 15 percent of the official workforce, second only to "Americans." In addition to the Mexicans employed at the mines, hundreds of new immigrants from Mexico had come to Bisbee looking for work in the month before the strike. The story of Amado Villalovas, the deportee rounded up at the grocery store, is typical in several ways. Countless others suffered injuries and indignities as Villalovas had; two men—a deputy and a deportee—were killed in the confusion of the morning. In addition, at least two hundred twenty-six deportees had wives and families to support, and many of them were Mexican workers like Villalovas, belying the fiction that only white workers needed a family wage.[19] Finally, Mexican workers like Villalovas were disproportionately represented among the deportees. Several witnesses testified that "foreigners," especially Mexicans, were rounded up indiscriminately. It is not even clear that Villalovas was a miner, much less on strike, and in this, too, he was typical, because many of the deportees did not work for the mining companies. A perusal of the deportees' testimonies reveal that they represented many different occupations.

What is clear is that Mexican workers participated in the strike in disproportionate numbers. Several witnesses claimed that at least half of the men on strike were Mexican. Bisbee's mining labor force was about 13 percent Mexican, but at least 27 percent of all deportees were Mexican—and probably more. One mining manager echoed several others when he observed that, alone among the working men, the Mexican workers quit "practically in a body at the first announcement of the strike." At one mine, three hundred of three hundred and fifty Mexican workers appeared on the picket line the first day of the strike.[20] They were the most loyal of the strikers in a workforce of thousands. The question is, why?

Mexican workers had concrete goals and ideological reasons for joining the strike. Above all, Mexican workers were on strike against the dual-wage system. Their chief demand threatened to yank the linchpin from the racial hierarchy of manliness. This demand proposed to raise the wages of *all* surface laborers, regardless of race, from $2.50 to $5.50 per day, while raising wages of underground (white) miners from $5.75 to $6.00—an increase of less than 5 percent. Had both these demands been met, the wages of surface laborers would be within $.50 of what white underground workers earned. If surface workers earned $5.50 per day and underground workers earned $6.00, the dual-wage labor system would have effectively ceased to exist.[21]

Anglo Wobbly organizers had concocted this extraordinary wage demand to entice Mexican workers to their cause, not because of a genuine commitment to it. Strike leaders intended for the Bisbee strike to show support for Wobbly strikes elsewhere, especially in Butte, Montana. As a Wobbly spokesperson explained, "This is a solidarity strike and we must concentrate on that phase of it. The demands made are wholly secondary."[22] Anglo strike leaders were pursuing a national political agenda, while Mexican miners were striking for local demands with broad consequences.

Despite these differences with Anglo leaders, Mexican workers flocked to the Wobblies for sound ideological and practical reasons. The IWW was the first union to take a friendly interest in Bisbee's Mexican workers. The union hired two Mexican organizers, Benito García and Joseph Robles—a first for organized labor in Bisbee. Moreover, while some strikers were surely ignorant of the finer points of Wobbly doctrine, many others would have known about the connections between the IWW and the Partido Liberal Mexicano (PLM), the anarcho-syndicalist organization headed by the Flores Magón brothers. Many Bisbee miners had come from the Mexican copper town of Cananea, where the IWW had participated in the PLM's first important strike in 1906.

There, too, PLM members had been striking against the dual-wage system, where "American" workers imported to Cananea earned twice what the Mexican miners earned. In Bisbee, the sheriff's department used the terms "Magonistas" and "Mexican IWW" synonymously, and a year before the strike, the leader of the Mexican IWW was also a representative for the PLM's newspaper.[23] The PLM had close ties with the Wobblies and the Bisbee area. In other words, Mexican workers, far from being the Wobblies' dupes, knew exactly what they were doing.

Mexican workers also challenged the racial hierarchy of manliness by appropriating the language of manhood long denied to them. Federal and state investigators ignored Mexican workers while they were collecting testimony in Bisbee, but statements gleaned from the Mexican camp of Clifton, where Mexican workers represented such an overwhelming majority that investigators had to question them, speak clearly. When New York reporter Robert Bruére asked Mexican miners in Clifton why they were on strike, they said it was "for an American standard of living," and more say in the improvement of working conditions. Federal investigator Felix Frankfurter, then a young Harvard Law School professor and assistant secretary of labor, was even more concise, specifically invoking the role of manhood. After visiting Bisbee as a member of the Mediation Commission three months after the deportation, Frankfurter observed that the strike had been "a fight for the status of free manhood." The Mexicans and Slavs, he concluded, "feel they were not treated as men." One Mexican striker in Clifton touched on this multiracial alliance, casting the racial hierarchy of manhood in the stark terms of slavery. Critics "were sure that the Mexican element and the Spaniards and Italians would not hold together. [But] the times in which the master class were imposing on us are past and gone. . . . The times of slavery are gone forever." Given the racial division of labor, this was a powerful metaphor, even more so because it appropriated a language many white union workers had long used to embrace free labor ideology.[24]

As this Clifton striker recognized, perhaps the most revolutionary aspect of the Bisbee strike was its ability to subvert and reevaluate established "racial" truths. Surviving on a "Mexican standard of living" had been outstanding training for a war between capital and labor. One white carpenter admitted that "the much vaunted superiority of the so-called Anglo-Saxon fades into a myth" in the face of the dedicated resolve of Mexican strikers, who "lived on less than half of what the average [white] striker would consent to remain loyal on."[25] Did it occur to the carpenter that Mexican workers had been enduring similar conditions for decades?

By claiming their manhood and demanding the American standard of living, Mexican strikers pulled up the stakes that secured the white man's camp.

Outsiders like Bruére and Frankfurter recognized this, but local Anglos could not. To admit the manhood of Mexican workers would be to topple the teetering racial hierarchy of the white man's camp. This is why the sheriff responded to the strike so forcefully.

SHERIFF HARRY WHEELER AND THE MANLINESS
OF PATRIOTIC CHIVALRY

When asked by federal investigators about the strike, Sheriff Wheeler announced, "This is no labor disturbance. We are sure of that."[26] That Wheeler could make the extraordinary statement that a strike was not about labor indicated how deeply racialized the class system was. Race and nation were commingled in a borderlands town populated largely by immigrants, where questions of patriotism and national loyalty were always questions of race. For Wheeler, opposing the strike was a matter of national defense, racialized fears, and—by his own assertion—being a man. Wheeler's commitment to the tenets of American manliness was extraordinary, but it demonstrates the way that divergent views of white manliness could still converge in the decision to participate in the deportation.

For good reason the *New York Times* called Wheeler a "vigorous personage." With his slight stature and modest height, it was not Wheeler's physical stature that made him stand out, but rather his reputation as "a man of splended judgement [sic], cool—skillful, daring, and the right man in the right place at all times." Wheeler had authentic and well-known western manly credentials. The son of a West Point graduate, Wheeler was born and raised on western army forts. After apparently serving in the Spanish-American war, Wheeler worked his way up the ranks until he was captain of the Arizona Rangers, a state militia that patrolled the border, pursued cattle rustlers, and "kept the peace" in labor disputes.[27]

Critics and defenders alike described him as moral and honest. Married with several children, Wheeler was an upright military man and a teetotaler— stern, moralistic, and uncompromising. The Arizona Rangers had sometimes found their captain inflexible and condescending (twenty-six resigned under his watch), but he could also be deeply caring and contemplative. He "grieved" after dismissing an officer whom he had found drunk, praising the fallen man's "exceedingly good character and most lovable traits." Wheeler believed that men were made, not born; he admitted that he had once "fought down some personal habits, but it took me a long time . . . before *I gained the mastery over myself.*"[28]

Wheeler's role in the deportation deserves special mention because, unlike company officials who were eastern aristocrats, the sheriff had a good reputation among union members. As captain of the Arizona Rangers, Wheeler had intervened in several strikes in Arizona, most notably the 1903 strike of mostly Mexican workers in Clifton-Morenci. Yet he had gained a reputation as a fair-minded third party who insisted on equal treatment and nonviolence for both sides of labor conflicts. Mother Jones herself had vouched for Wheeler's good character, calling him "a pretty fine fellow," despite her distrust of law enforcement. She admitted that Wheeler "was an exception to that rule." Because of Wheeler's reputation for fairness, he had not been the mining companies' chosen candidate for sheriff. Wheeler once explained to a friend that he had not run for office until 1911 because "The Copper Queen [management] does not want me and that settles it in this County."[29] In spite of his concern, Wheeler was elected twice, and was immensely popular in the mining towns and the large ranching areas that surrounded Bisbee.

Wheeler's moral probity made a strong impression on federal investigators. After meeting with Wheeler for hours, the commission—although they disapproved of Wheeler's actions—dismissed allegations that Wheeler had been paid off by the mining companies. One commission member, an AFL leader from Illinois, echoed the sentiments of several others when he averred, "I believe [Wheeler] is absolutely honest and clean and courageous." The federal secretary of labor called Wheeler "a man of the type" immune "to any corrupt influence of any kind of character whatever."[30]

Wheeler was neither a company man nor crooked. So why the deportation? Why cooperate with the mining officials? Although his plan of action may have converged with theirs, and he may have even worked at their behest, Wheeler fully believed that he did so for his own reasons and on his own terms, and so did the commission. He did not defend the rights of industrialists, but he did believe that maintaining wartime industry was a patriotic responsibility. In Wheeler's mind, he was preserving national interests, not material ones. It was not antilabor attitudes that led Wheeler to organize the deportation, but rather what he called "pure Americanism," and by that he meant patriotism and loyalty. Wheeler believed that anyone striking against a war industry was potentially treasonous. For him, choosing sides became a question of "Are you an American, or are you not?" He defined his Americanism against the actions of "foreigners," and for him, wartime labor activism, foreignness, and disloyalty were inseparable. He insisted, "We intend to make this an American camp where American working men may enjoy life, liberty and the pursuit of happiness unmolested by any alien enemies of whatever breed."[31]

The Mexican Revolution, which had begun in 1910, had a galvanizing influence on Wheeler. For people on the U.S.-Mexico border, the war-related tensions had begun long before America's entry into World War I. The Zimmermann telegraph, in which the Germans promised to return Arizona, New Mexico, and Texas to Mexico, if Mexico would attack the United States, suggested to Wheeler, and to many others, that the strike was the work of pro-Germany provocateurs who had allied with the Mexicans. The telegram—sent just five months before the Bisbee strike—only confirmed Harry Wheeler's worst suspicions. He believed rumors that Mexican workers kept a cache of rifles just over the line, though he had no evidence. After the deportation, he admonished federal investigators that any one of them would have done the same thing, had he "been a sheriff on this border for six or seven years, and a captain of the Rangers years before it[,] and had seen the things which occurred on the border as I have seen them." Living on the border, he explained, "put a new complexion on" the strike.[32] His choice of the term "complexion" unconsciously captured the racial subtext of the fear over labor troubles.

Wheeler and the deputies targeted Mexicans as a group, whether or not they were on strike. As one deputy explained, "It is hard for an American to tell the faces among the Mexicans." As a result, according to one source, "Innocent suffered alike with guilty." Labor Secretary William B. Wilson asked the sheriff how he had ascertained which residents of Mexican descent were revolutionaries or at least "alien." Wheeler responded, "They were practically all aliens, Mr. Wilson." The labor secretary pressed on, "What steps were taken to take charge of those Mexicans" who were explicit supporters of Mexican revolutionary Pancho Villa? To this, Wheeler responded, "How could you separate one Mexican from another?" When Wilson asked whether the deputies had even tried to distinguish among the men, Wheeler concluded the exchange by announcing that, "I honestly believe today that 80 or 85 per cent of these men were foreigners, some of them Austrians and Germans and Mexicans, and none of them loved the country I love." He rounded up many men whose only crime was their foreign appearance—and Mexican men were the most obvious targets. When Secretary Wilson continued to needle Wheeler about his dragnet techniques, Wheeler replied, "I would repeat the operation any time I find *my own people* endangered by a mob composed of 80 per cent aliens and enemies of my Government."[33]

To Wheeler and others, foreigners—especially Mexicans—were a faceless crowd of mindless, dangerous followers. By 1917, the docile children of years past had been transformed into dangerous revolutionaries in the testimonies of deputies and their defenders. No one articulated this metamorphosis of Anglo perceptions better than did Wheeler, with his references to dangerous "mobs," and his repeated mention of rifle-caches. This was a new tune for Wheeler. Just one year before the deportation, Wheeler had received reports from deputies that "there does not seem to be any plotting and organizing going on" among Bisbee's Mexican population. On the contrary, Mexicans in the area were "somewhat timid for fear that they might be molested by the Americans." At the time of the deportation, however, Wheeler claimed that "all Mexicans hate Americans," and his every action flowed from this premise. Wheeler had little patience with federal investigators who questioned his conclusions. "You eastern people haven't had much experience with Mexicans, but . . . we figured they might do anything."[34]

The Mexican Revolution had surprised many people who had assumed Mexicans were simply childish nuisances incapable of insurrection. Close to home, the border towns of Agua Prieta and Naco, both just miles from Bisbee, had been the sites of significant battles to which U.S. residents had flocked to participate as spectators. Sheriff Wheeler repeatedly referenced "border troubles" in general and the Battle of Naco in particular as he defended his role in the deportation. Then, too, the Mexican camp of Clifton-Morenci had been the site in 1903 and 1915 of large-scale strikes led by Mexican workers, as well as wildcat strikes so common that a new Spanglish term arose to describe them—*strikitos*.[35] Both the revolution and this new labor activism forced many Anglos to revise their stereotypes.

The new stereotype of the Mexican as dangerous revolutionary was not as distant from the older one of the docile child as it might appear, however, because neither was manly. Both failed to resemble the ideal resident of the white man's camp: the independent, loyal, family-supporting "American" worker. Even sympathizers reified this ultimately passive vision of Mexican workers. Mining officials warned Bruére, the New York reporter, that the Mexican camps surrounding Clifton-Morenci were "unsafe" because of the "terrible Mexicans," although the muckraking adventurer reported somewhat disappointedly that he found them to be "the most docile people imaginable."[36] For Wheeler, revolution had not made Mexicans manly and independent, because in his view, they had simply switched their allegiances from American foremen to foreign provocateurs. The Zimmermann telegram indicated to the sheriff that Mexican strikers were dangerous because they had fallen under the sway of "Prussians."

If ideas about manliness shaped Wheeler's understanding of Mexicans' place in the deportation, his own gender identity was inseparable from his decision to take a leadership role in the event. Typical was his statement to investigators that, "I don't shirk anything. If I have done wrong, I am willing to suffer for it. I am not the kind of man who will whimper, and I am not running away from it."[37] Wheeler felt the deportation was necessary to protect Bisbee's most precious social boundaries—those that separated working-class Mexican men from "white women." He worried for weeks, he said, about "foreigners" bothering "women." For Wheeler, the two categories were separate, because "women" were implicitly American, even though thousands of foreign-born women lived in Bisbee.

When Mexican Wobblies approached a group of white female laundry workers to join the union, this was the last straw. In Wheeler's words, "They were so terrorized by visitations of a committee of Mexicans . . . that the women one day left in a body in abject terror. Think of white women in an American town so terrorized by foreigners that they were compelled to quit work in terror of their lives." [38] Like race, gender seemed natural to Wheeler and, thus, the perfect arsenal with which to defend his position. In Wheeler's mind, protecting white womanhood was just as natural as self-defense, and both were at the heart of his understanding of manhood.

Although it was relatively minor, the incident at the laundry came up again and again when vigilantes defended their actions. It was bad enough in their minds when Mexican workers demanded nearly the same wages as Anglo men in Anglo jobs. But when Mexican strikers approached *white women* to join their union—to make common cause with them—the strikers were also challenging *gender* hierarchies that built upon racialized fears. In a world where class differences rested on race and racial boundaries rested on gendered rules, single white women joining a mixed-race miners' union was literally unthinkable. Wheeler could not conceive of it as anything except a potentially violent threat to white womanhood, indeed to "pure Americanism itself."

The deportation was a messy affair, and so were its causes. Unitary theories are tidy, because they insist on parceling race, labor, nation, and gender into separate categories. These interpretations also suppose that one justification trumped another. Yet what is far more striking is the confluence of these ideas. Although the meanings of these categories seemed self-evident, in fact all of them were fluid. The conflation of race and labor was so deeply entrenched in the social system that it was manifested in the most visceral, unself-conscious justifications and behaviors—manliness among them. An emphasis on the role of masculinity—something seemingly natural but never stable—highlights the connections between gender, race, family, labor, and national identity. A threat to one meant a threat to all.

The racial hierarchy of manliness subsumed race, gender, nation, and class into a conception of manliness that did not cause the deportation, but did filter multiple motives into a worldview of white male supremacy that provided a frame for participants to understand their decisions and roles in the strike and the vigilante response to it. For Wheeler, this was the crux of the dual-wage system: to naturalize racial difference to such an extent that any challenge to it was a threat to gender relations and to the integrity of "America" itself.

Ultimately, the strike was a failure by any measure. Many of the deported men never returned. Even worse, Bisbee embraced its status as a white man's camp and "American town" with renewed vigor. As late as 1929, Bisbee advertised as "the last stand of the American miner."[39] Conditions for Mexicans worsened, and with the same circular reasoning they had used before 1917, white workers scapegoated Mexican workers for low wages and labor conflict. Given the odds that were stacked against the workers, it is hardly surprising that the strike was unsuccessful. Still, to attempt it at all meant that the goal of the white man's camp—to make Mexican workers less than men, to deny them agency—had failed.

NOTES

I would like to thank Thomas Andrews, Antonia I. Castañeda, Hal Cohen, Flannery Burke, Linda Gordon, Alexander Shashko, and Marienka Sokol Vanlandingham for their readings and assistance.

1. The President's Mediation Commission appointed by President Woodrow Wilson concluded that the strike had been peaceful (U.S. Department of Labor, *Report on the Bisbee Deportation Made by the President's Mediation Commission to the President of the United Sates, November 6, 1917* [Washington D.C.: Government Printing Office (GPO), 1918, hereafter cited as PMC], 4; George E. Kellogg testimony, PMC, 13; "Women and Children Keep Off Streets Today," *Bisbee Daily Review*, July 12, 1917, 1; and "Arizona Sheriff Ships 1,100 IWW's Out in Cattle Cars," *New York Times*, July 13, 1917, 1).

2. Testimony cited in reports to Gov. George W. P. Hunt, July, 1917, probably from sworn statements to Arizona Attorney General Wiley Jones, RG 1 Governor's Office, Hunt Papers, box 8, Arizona State Legislative and Public Records, hereafter cited as Hunt Papers and ASLAPR.

3. The classic account of the IWW is Melvyn Dubofsky, *We Shall Be All: A History of the IWW* (Chicago: Quadrangle Books, 1969). Thomas E. Sheridan, *Arizona: A History* (Tucson: University of Arizona Press, 1995), 183. Vernon H. Jensen, *Heritage of Conflict: Labor Relations in the Nonferrous Metals Industry up to 1930* (Ithaca, N.Y.: Cornell University Press, 1950), 400.

4. Major interpretations of the deportation include John H. Lindquist and James Fraser, "A Sociological Interpretation of the Bisbee Deportation," *Pacific Historical Review* 37:4 (1968): 401–22; Philip Taft, "The Bisbee Deportation," *Labor History* 13:1 (1972), 3–40; James Byrkit, *Forging the Copper Collar: Arizona's Labor-Management War of 1901–1921* (Tucson: University of Arizona Press, 1982); Philip J. Mellinger, *Race and Labor in Western Copper: The Fight for Equality, 1896–1918* (Tucson: University of

Arizona Press, 1995); Colleen O'Neill, "Domesticity Deployed: Gender, Race, and the Construction of Class Struggle in the Bisbee Deportation," *Labor History* 34:2/3 (1993): 256–73; and Colleen O'Neill, "A Community Divided: A Social History of the Bisbee Deportation" (master's thesis, New Mexico State University, 1989). The most recent study is Christopher Capozzola, "The Only Badge Needed is Your Patriotic Fervor: Vigilance, Coercion, and the Law in World War I America," *Journal of American History* 88:4 (2002): 1354–82.

5. Kristin L. Hoganson, *Fighting For Manhood: How Gender Politics Provoked the Spanish-American and Philippine-American Wars* (New Haven: Yale University Press, 1998). Other works that have influenced my focus on manliness and masculinity include Susan Lee Johnson, "'A Memory Sweet to Soldiers': The Significance of Gender," in *A New Significance: Re-envisioning the History of the American West*, ed. Clyde A. Milner II (New York: Oxford University Press, 1996), 255–78; Gail Bederman, *Manliness and Civilization: A Cultural History of Gender and Race in the United States, 1880–1917* (Chicago: The University of Chicago Press, 1995); and Matthew Basso, Laura McCall, and Dee Garceau, eds., *Across the Great Divide: Cultures of Manhood in the American West* (New York: Routledge, 2001).

6. I focus here mainly on men. On women in Bisbee, see O'Neill, "Domesticity Deployed," and "A Community Divided"; and Katherine A. Benton, "What about Women in the 'White Man's Camp?': Gender, Nation, and the Redefinition of Race in Cochise County, Arizona, 1853–1941" (Ph.D diss., University of Wisconsin–Madison, 2002).

7. Bisbee's exclusion of the Chinese was in explicit contrast to Tombstone, its nearby silver-camp neighbor, which included a sizable Chinese population. See Odie B. Faulk, *Tombstone: Myth and Reality* (New York: Oxford University Press, 1972), 199; William B. Shillingberg, *Tombstone, A.T.: A History of Early Mining, Milling, and Mayhem* (Spokane, Wash.: Authur H. Clark, 1999), 130–32; and U.S. Bureau of the Census, *Eleventh Census of the United States, 1890, Population*, Part 1, Statistics of Population (Washington, D.C.: GPO, 1892), 610.

8. "No Foreign Labor Wanted," *Bisbee Daily Review*, May 27, 1903. Robert Orsi, "The Religious Boundaries of an Inbetween People: Street *Feste* and the Problem of the Dark-skinned Other in Italian Harlem, 1920–1990," *American Quarterly* 44:3 (1992): 313–47. According to Orsi, John Higham coined the term "'in-between' races." James R. Barrett and David Roediger, "In-Between Peoples: Race, Nationality and the 'New Immigrant' Working Class," *Journal of American Ethnic History* 16:3 (1997): 3–44. Elizabeth Jameson, *All That Glitters: Class, Conflict, and Community in Cripple Creek* (Urbana: University of Illinois Press, 1998), 140–60. "Census of the Columbus I.W.W. Refugee Camp," comp. by Ben H. Dorcy, Cavalry Major, Intelligence Officer, Columbus, New Mexico, Hunt Papers, ASLAPR.

9. Mexicans working at the Copper Queen smelter in nearby Douglas earned two-thirds what other men in the same jobs did. I have not found wage scales for Mexicans

in Bisbee on the eve of the strike; but the proportional difference between white and Mexican wages would be similar. Copper Queen Smelter Rate Scales, May 16, 1917, Henry McCluskey Collection, MSS 54, box 2, Arizona Collection, Arizona State University. See Phelps-Dodge Corporation Payroll Records, 1885, Arizona Historical Society, hereafter cited as AHS, and "March 13, 1923 Report Re: Wage Scale for Reduction Works Employees in Douglas," Copper Queen Mining Company Wage Scales, Samuel Truett private collection, Albuquerque, New Mexico. The author wishes to thank Truett for access to these materials. See Michael Parrish, *Mexican Workers, Progressives, and Copper: The Failure of Industrial Democracy in Arizona During the Wilson Years* (San Diego: Chicano Research Publications, University of California, San Diego, 1979), 12–13. Linda Gordon describes the ways that Phelps-Dodge manipulated the dual-wage system in her book, *The Great Arizona Orphan Abduction* (Cambridge, Mass.: Harvard University Press, 1999), 181. The racial underpinnings of American identity were best articulated by Theodore Roosevelt, who believed that, as Gail Bederman has summarized, "the manly American race was forged of various immigrant races, [and] all of those contributing races were European" (Bederman, *Manliness and Civilization*, 179).

10. Ralph Rollins, "Labor Situation in Arizona Points to Mexicanization," *Arizona Mining Journal* 4:4 (1920): 13–14. *Bisbee Daily Review*, World's Fair Edition (1904). "Nationality Report of Men Employed on June 26th, and of Men Deported to Columbus on July 12th, Who Were in the Employ of the Calumet & Arizona Mining Company When Strike Was Called on June 26th," PMC reports, 288–89. The Mexican workers were also the only ones whose marital status was not recorded. Roediger and Barrett found that managers drew up elaborate lists of which races should do which work ("In-Between Peoples," 17). On the average Mexican and white wages, see Joseph F. Park, "The History of Mexican Labor in the Territorial Period" (master's thesis, University of Arizona, 1961), 245. Park found the average wage for Anglo workers to be about $4.00, and the average Mexican wage to be about $2.05 during the early 1910s. Phylis Cancilla Martinelli, unpublished manuscript.

11. Linda Gordon defines the family wage usefully as "the sex/gender/family system that prescribes earning as the sole responsibility of husbands and unpaid domestic labor as the only proper long-term occupation for women," in *Pitied but not Entitled: Single Mothers and the History of Welfare, 1890–1935* (New York: Free Press, 1994), 53. For more on the family wage, see Martha May and Ron Rothbart, "'Homes Are What Any Strike Is About': Immigrant Labor and the Family Wage," *Journal of Social History* 23:2 (1989): 267–84. See Martha May, "The Historical Problem of the Family Wage: The Ford Motor Company and the Five Dollar Day," *Feminist Studies* 8:2 (1982): 404, 419. Alice Kessler-Harris, *A Woman's Wage: Historical Meanings and Social Consequences* (Lexington: University of Kentucky Press, 1990), 1.

12. Cleveland Van Dyke report to Kendric C. Babcock, president of the University of Arizona, December 16, 1907, Warren Company Papers, Private Collection of Charles

Parrott, Lowell, Massachusetts, 8–9. My thanks to Parrott for sharing these valuable materials with me. On the family wage ideology and its relationship to the homeowning plans in the Bisbee suburb of Warren, see Benton, "'What about Women,'" 192–253. David Roediger, *The Wages of Whiteness: Race and the Making of the American Working Class* (1991; reprint, New York: Verso Books, 1999).

13. Byrkit, *Forging the Copper Collar*, 158. John O. Dunbar, "Editorial Comment," *Dunbar's Weekly*, July 7, 1917, 8.

14. Lawrence Glickman, "Inventing the 'American Standard of Living': Gender, Race and Working-Class Identity, 1880–1925," *Labor History* 23: 2/3 (1993): 221–35. On its relationship to the family wage, see May and Rothbart, "Homes," passim, and, in the Jacksonian period, Jeanne Boydston, *Home and Work: Housework, Wages, and the Ideology of Labor in the Early Republic* (New York: Oxford University Press, 1990). Glickman, "Inventing the 'American Standard,'" 221; quotation from 226. Dunbar, "Editorial Comment: Kill The Strikers," *Dunbar's Weekly*, July 14, 1917, 6.

15. World's Fair Edition, *Bisbee Daily Review*. The census of deportees in Columbus found 773 out of 1003 to be "men owning property," including Mexican and those of Mexican descent (Dorcy, "Census," Hunt Papers). For a published example of such defense, see Edward T. Divine, "The Bisbee Deportations," *Survey*, July 21, 1917, 353.

16. Victor Clark, "Mexican Labor in the United States," *Bureau of Labor Bulletin*, 78 (1908): 477–92, as cited in Dru McGinnis, "The Influence of Organized Labor on the Making of the Arizona Constitution" (master's thesis, University of Arizona, 1930), 18. See Glickman, "Inventing the 'American Standard,'" 228. Walter Douglas, president of Phelps Dodge Corporation, to A.T. Thompson, assistant to the president, Douglas, Arizona, March 7, 1918, Truett collection.

17. Gordon, *Great Arizona Orphan Abduction*, 180. Clark, as cited in McGinnis, "The Influence of Organized Labor," 18. My discussion of Mexican workers is indebted to A. Yvette Huginnie's "A New Hero Comes to Town: The Anglo Mining Engineer and 'Mexican Labor' as Contested Terrain in Southeastern Arizona, 1880–1920," *New Mexico Historical Review* 69:4 (1994): 323–44. Alonzo Crittenden, "Management of Mexican Labor," *Mining and Scientific Press* 123 (1921), 267, as cited in Huginnie, "A New Hero," 330.

18. O'Neill, "Domesticity Deployed," 258. Other scholars have made a similar choice. When Michael Parrish tried to offer evidence of Mexican workers' attitudes in Bisbee, he was forced to cite the testimony of Antonio Rodriguez, an immigrant from Spain who lived on Chihuahua Hill. Rodriguez was the only Spanish-surnamed or Spanish-speaking witness at the Presidential Mediation Commission hearings in Bisbee (Parrish, *Mexican Workers*, 16–7; and PMC, 546–57). On the 1907 strike, see Mellinger, *Race and Labor in Western Copper*, 73–79; and Benton, "'What about Women,'" 216–20.

19. Of the two thousand two hundred one surface and underground workers as of June 26, 1917, three hundred fourteenwere Mexican (PMC, 217). These numbers

are generally consistent with the testimony of Copper Queen General Manager G. H. Dowell in the PMC reports. Secretary Wilson had eased immigration restrictions from Mexico in June (Parrish, *Mexican Workers*, 18). Mellinger, *Race and Labor in Western Copper*, 188. This figure comes from Dorcy, "Census."

20. Figures cited by witnesses ranged from 50 percent to 85 percent (Strickland testimony, PMC, 502; and Wheeler testimony, PMC, 166, 256). Workforce numbers compiled from statistics at two major companies on June 26, 1917, the last day before the strike. Percentage of strikers (which no doubt included people born in Mexico as well as Mexican Americans) compiled from Army census of deportees conducted in August, the most reliable figures available. Company officials and IWW leaders concurred on this (G. H. Dowell testimony, PMC, 353; and Grover H. Perry, secretary-treasurer of Metal Mine Workers' Industrial Union No. 800 to William [Big Bill] Haywood, July 6, 1917, Exhibits in *State of Arizona v. Henry Waters*, and *Michael Simmons v. El Paso and Southwestern Railroad* [1919], hereafter cited as *Simmons v. EPSW Railroad*, box 1, University of Arizona Special Collections,).

21. O'Neill briefly suggests these same points in "Domesticity Deployed," 258.

22. Jack Norman, Columbus, New Mexico, to Perry, July 25, 1917, *Simmons v. EPSW Railroad*, box 1.

23. O'Neill, "Domesticity Deployed," 82, 83. J. L. P., Report on "Mexican Matters," to Harry Wheeler, June 5, 1916, in *Simmons v. EPSW*, box 8. The best source on the strike is Michael Gonzales, "United States Copper Companies, the State, and Labour Conflict in Mexico, 1900–1910," *Journal of Latin American Studies* 26:3 (1994): 651–81. For a typical example of the claim that the Cananea strike was the opening shot in the revolutionary battle, see Ramón E. Ruiz, *Labor and the Ambivalent Revolutionaries: Mexico, 1911–1923* (Baltimore: Johns Hopkins Press, 1993), 3; and the classic, though now outdated, Rodney D. Anderson, "Mexican Workers and the Politics of Revolution, 1906–1911," *Hispanic American Historical Review* 54:1 (1974): 94–113. Other sources include Jonathan C. Brown, "Foreign and Native-Born Workers in Porfirian Mexico," *American Historical Review* 98:2 (1993): 786–818; and Marvin D. Bernstein, *The Mexican Mining Industry, 1890-1950* (Albany: State University of New York Press, 1965), 65. See also C. L. Sonnichsen, *Colonel Greene and the Copper Skyrocket* (Tucson: University of Arizona Press), 1994.

24. Robert Bruére, *Following the Trail of the IWW: A First-Hand Investigation into Labor Troubles in the West—A Trip into the Copper Camps and the Lumber Camps of the Inland Empire with the Views of the Men on the Job* (New York: New York Evening Post, 1918), 3. Frankfurter, as cited in Parrish, *Mexican Workers*, 30, 29. Critics as cited in Parrish, *Mexican Workers*, 14. See Glickman, 222–23. On immigrant workers and free labor's meanings, see Gunther Peck, *Reinventing Free Labor: Padrones and Immigrant Workers in the North American West, 1880-1930* (New York: Cambridge University Press, 2000).

25. Worker as cited in Parrish, *Mexican Workers*, 11.

26. Wheeler testimony, PMC, 138.

27. "Arizona Sheriff Ships 1,100 IWW's Out in Cattle Cars," 1. Sheriff John White to Gov. Joseph Kibbey, August 15, 1907, Arizona Ranger Papers, ADLAPR, as cited by Bill O'Neill, "Captain Harry Wheeler, Arizona Lawman," *Journal of Arizona History* 27:3 (1986): 303. There is inconsistency regarding documentation of Wheeler's participation in the Spanish-American War. The soundest overview of Harry Wheeler is Bill O'Neill, "Captain Harry Wheeler."

28. Bill O'Neill, "Captain Harry Wheeler," 304. Capt. Harry Wheeler, Naco, Arizona, to Gov. Kibbey, Phoenix, Arizona, October 30, 1908, Arizona Ranger Papers, RG 42, ASLAPR, emphasis added.

29. See John Greenway's correspondence during these years, passim, John C. Greenway Collection, MS 311, AHS, and discussion of Douglas in Byrkit, *Forging the Copper Collar*, 32, 87, 99, 139, 178, 299, 301. Mellinger, *Race and Labor in Western Copper*, 24. Philip Foner, ed., *Mother Jones Speaks: Collected Writings and Speeches* (New York: Monad Press, 1983), 372. Capt. Harry Wheeler to Mr. Sims Ely, secretary to governor, Phoenix, Arizona, February 23, 1908, Arizona Ranger Papers.

30. Walker testimony, PMC, 589, William B. Wilson testimony, 492.

31. "Sheriff Wheeler's Statement on Strike," *Courtland Arizonan*, July 21, 1917, 2.

32. On the impact of the Zimmermann telegram, see Friedrich Katz, *The Life and Times of Pancho Villa* (Stanford: Stanford University Press, 1998), 612, 660, 663–64. Wheeler testimony, PMC, 161.

33. This pro-company miner thought that around 50 percent of the strikers were Mexican (I. H. Strickland testimony, PMC, 502). See testimony cited in reports to Gov. George W.P. Hunt, July, 1917, probably from sworn statements to Arizona Attorney General Wiley Jones, 20–21, box 8, Hunt Papers. Wheeler testimony, PMC, 166, 256, emphasis added.

34. [J.L.P.], police informant, to Sheriff Wheeler, "Re: Mexican Matters," June 5, 1916, in *Simmons v. El Paso*, box 8. Wheeler testimony, PMC, 224.

35. Linda Hall, "The Mexican Revolution and the Crisis in Naco: 1914–15," *Journal of the West* 16 (July 1977): 27–35. Wheeler testimony, PMC, 161–62. See also Bruére, *Following the I.W.W. Trail*, 13–14. A[ndrea] Yvette Huginnie appropriately named her dissertation for these ongoing challenges to management. "'Strikitos': Race, Class, and Work in the Arizona Copper Industry, 1870–1920" (Ph.D. diss., Yale University, 1991).

36. Bruére, "Following the I.W.W. Trail," 1.

37. Wheeler testimony, PMC, 165.

38. Wheeler testimony, PMC, 253.

39. "Bisbee, the Most Southern Mile-High City in North America," *Arizona Labor Journal*, May 31, 1929, 27.

Transborder Discourse

The Articulation of Gender in the Borderlands
in the Early Twentieth Century

CLARA LOMAS

The U.S.-Mexico border area, especially the urban centers of Laredo, San Antonio, El Paso, and Los Angeles, served as center stage for a vital part of the precursory work for the Mexican Revolution of 1910. At the boundaries of these two nation-states issues of liberalism, anticlericalism, anarchism, nationalism, class, race, and identity were addressed with revolutionary fervor and articulated through periodical publications, autobiographical narratives, and memoirs by women who became involved not only in Mexico's nationalist strife for a more democratic country but also in calling attention to gender issues. Within the counterdiscourses articulated by the divergent factions of the Mexican revolutionary movement, a small but significant number of Spanish-language periodicals published in the United States expounded concern for women's emancipation and subverted patriarchal authority by including women as part of the struggle for justice, at times by manipulating gender for their own particular nationalist ends. Through unsigned articles and editorials, the periodicals *La Voz de la Mujer* (*Women's Voice*) and *El Obrero* (*The Worker*) proclaimed themselves as political tools of the precursor revolutionary movement, and *Pluma Roja* (*Red Pen*) did the same for the internationalist anarchist movement. The writings of specific women, such as Jovita Idar's writing in her family's periodical *La Crónica* (*The Chronicle*) and Leonor Villegas de Magnón's autobiography/memoirs, further problematized the articulation of gender by their "erasure of the geopolitical border," focusing on political/cultural practices across the border and consciously developing a transborder discourse.

Despite the twentieth-century political imposition of a physical national boundary to mark a clear division between two sovereign nation-states, each seeking to develop its distinct national culture, the social position of Mexican women in the borderlands was still dictated by traditional nineteenth-century Mexican social mores. As the revolutionary movement developed, it provided a fertile field for the resurgence of nationalist sentiment among the U.S. Mexican population and created the space to recode the role of women in society.[1] The liberalism of this movement reinforced the secular perspective that openly defied the master narrative of the Catholic Church. Although few women in the borderlands had the cultural capital required to express themselves in writing, the women who did were able to create alternative means to do so. Until now, these women's work as activists and their intellectual, written contributions have remained virtually unrecognized. Either due to their political affiliations or to gender discrimination, their work has not been recognized in Mexico. In the United States, these factors, as well as racial and linguistic biases, have relegated their work to oblivion. Nevertheless, these women's stories and their publishing efforts capture the realities of a people, the significance of whose daily existence transcends the limitations imposed by national, political, gender, and class boundaries. This study begins to trace various instances of their gendered transborder discourse.

THE ALTERNATIVE PRESS IN THE BORDERLANDS

In 1910 the U.S. Consul in Mexico, Luther E. Ellsworth, wrote:

> I have the honor to report increasing activity of the very intelligent class of Mexican exiles in the Cities and Towns along the Mexican-American Border line, between the Gulf and the Pacific Ocean.... [They] are busily engaged [in] writing and publishing inflammatory articles intended to educate up to date, in new revolutionary ideas, the thousands of Mexicans now on the American side of the Border line, and as many as possible of those on the Mexican side.[2]

Indeed, the intellectual political refugees who were forced to migrate north of the border, some with members of their respective families, immediately became engaged in U.S. local community political activism to rally support for their own nationalist cause, to support transborder labor organizing, or both. From 1900 to 1910, the movement to unseat the three-decade-old Porfirio Díaz dictatorship in Mexico was initiated by San Luis Potosí's Club Liberal "Ponciano Arriaga," which advanced traditional liberal ideals of democracy, anticlericalism, and free enterprise. The movement rapidly grew to include workers and peasants, and became involved with the 1905–11 antireelection campaigns of the Partido Liberal Mexicano (PLM), headed by Ricardo Flores Magón, and the Partido Nacional Anti-reeleccionista, led by Francisco I. Madero.

One of the most powerful tools working against the dictatorship was the alternative press, which was constantly subjected to government suppression.

The offices of newspapers, such as *Regeneración* (*Regeneration*), *Renacimiento* (*Renaissance*), *El Porvenir* (*The Future*), *El Hijo del Ahuizote* (*The Emperor's Son*), *El Paladín* (*The Champion*), and *El Demófilo* (*The Demophile*), were raided and closed down. Their journalists were beaten, jailed, and often murdered. In 1903, threats of imprisonment and death prompted several leaders of the San Luis Potosí Club Liberal "Ponciano Arriaga"—Camilo Arriaga, Antonio Díaz Soto y Gama, and Juan Sarabia—to seek refuge in the United States. As liberal newspapers were shut down, a member of the Ponciano Arriaga Liberal Club in Hidalgo, schoolteacher Elisa Acuña y Rosetti, joined journalist Juana B. Gutiérrez de Mendoza in the publication of *Vésper* (*Eve*), which had been established in 1901 in Guanajuato.[3]

Ricardo Flores Magón and other opposition journalists were jailed for several months in 1903. After their release in early 1904, they also went into exile in Texas and from there tried to reestablish their opposition newspaper *Regeneración*, to create liberal clubs (PLM groups), and to launch a revolutionary movement in Mexico. Persistent harassment by President Díaz's foreign agents forced these radicals to flee to St. Louis, Missouri.[4] PLM activity nonetheless persisted and spread throughout the southwestern United States to Texas, Arizona, New Mexico, and California. Headquarters for the PLM leadership were established in San Antonio in 1904 and in El Paso in 1906, where more oppositional newspapers were published: *Humanidad* (*Humanity*), *La Reforma Social* (*Social Reform*), *La Democracia* (*Democracy*), *La Bandera Roja* (*The Red Flag*), *Punto Rojo* (*Red Point*), *La Voz de la Mujer*, and *El Obrero*. The principal propaganda organs of the PLM in Los Angeles were *Revolución* (*Revolution*) in 1907 and *Libertad y Trabajo* (*Freedom and Work*) and *Regeneración* (*Regeneration*) from 1910 through 1918. Out of approximately two hundred newspapers that were published in the Southwest during the period between 1900 and 1920—the majority of which supported the dictatorship of Mexico's President Porfirio Díaz—more than thirty were founded by PLM members or sympathizers.[5] *La Voz de la Mujer*, founded in El Paso in 1907 under the directorship of Isidra T. de Cárdenas, published, as U.S. Consul Ellsworth contended, "inflammatory articles intended to educate" the public about the oppressive and exploitative regime of Porfirio Díaz. *La Voz de la Mujer* also attempted to show through its publication that women were intellectually and morally engaged in the revolutionary effort against the Díaz dictatorship.

The years between 1907 and 1910 were ones of intense activity for the PLM. While their leaders were being arrested in California and Arizona, the forty to sixty-four PLM groups organized on both sides of the border were attempting to foment rebellion in Mexico and escape arrest by U.S. and Mexican authorities.[6] Established in San Antonio, Texas, in 1910 by Teresa Villarreal and aimed at the proletariat, *El Obrero* called for the involvement of all men and women in the new social order. By the time most of the PLM leaders were released from prison in 1910, the political situation in Mexico had dramatically changed. After two unsuccessful armed efforts to establish "local political revolutionary hegemony" in Baja California and Texas in 1911 and 1913, respectively, and a very successful campaign launched by Mexican consular agents to discredit them as traitors, the PLM lost their influence in the border communities.[7] By the time Blanca de Moncaleano published *Pluma Roja* in Los Angeles from 1913 to 1915, the PLM faction in Los Angeles shared the periodical's anarchist ideals. *Pluma Roja* placed the emancipation of women at the center of its anarchist agenda, adding a new dimension to the politics of the revolutionary struggle. *El Obrero, La Voz de la Mujer*, and *Pluma Roja* imploded the nationalist and anarchist discourses of the times by articulating gender issues.

EL OBRERO:
WOMEN SHOULD PARTICIPATE WITH A RIFLE OR WITH A PEN

On December 15, 1910, Teresa Villarreal, director of *El Obrero: Periódico Independiente* (*The Worker: Liberal Newspaper*), published the eighth issue of the periodical intended to educate the proletariat along the U.S.-Mexico border.[8] In her article "*El Partido Anti-reeleccionista*" ("The Anti-reelection Party"), Villarreal cites an incident of female bravery as an illustration of the heroism found within the Anti-reelection Party, and urges PLM members and sympathizers to demand guarantees of democracy and justice from the next president. Her narrative of an incident in Puebla, Mexico, on November 18, 1910, subverts the official account of the event. Additionally, her concern for Mexico's destitute population reveals the importance she gave to issues of human dignity over those of patriotism.

Villarreal recounts the heroic deeds of the Serdán family who, on November 18, 1910, defended their house in Puebla with gunfire as the police chief attempted to arrest them for sedition. According to official history, Aquiles Serdán, along with some eighteen people, including three women and two children, were in a house fully equipped with arms and ammunition, prepared for the first day of the revolution, November 20, 1910. In their attempt to arrest the revolutionaries, Police Chief Miguel Cabrera and his men were surprised when Serdán received them pointing a rifle at Cabrera. Cabrera shot at Aquiles, who shot back, mortally wounding Cabrera and initiating the revolution two days early.

What is particularly interesting about Villarreal's narrative of this event is that contrary to the official record, which attributes the first shots to Serdán,

Villarreal credits a woman with the killing of the despised chief of police. She writes:

> *Recordamos con verdadero entusiasmo la escena que tuvo lugar en Puebla en la casa de Cerdán [sic], donde contestaron con balas a los polisontes, los serviles que por asegurar un salario trabajan en pro del despotismo, y nos regocijamos de que en México aún existan heroínas que sepan levantar su mano para desafiar a los tiranuelos mercenarios. Una mujer, sin tener las policía, a Miguel Cabrera, el hombre degenerado que cometía crímenes para obedecer las órdenes de un gobierno despótico.*[9]

The narration continues, citing the heroic behavior of the unidentified woman as the example for all to follow:

> *Hombres degenerados e indiferentes que soportáis los ataques de la Dictadura y vosotras mujeres mexicanas, hijas de México, de esa bella patria donde han nacido héroes valientes y heroínas sin tacha; imitad el ejemplo de esa mujer que ha muerto pero como mueren los valientes: desafiando á los verdugos. Unamos todos los mexicanos nuestras fuerzas.*[10]

It is noteworthy that Villarreal should attribute the action that initiated the overthrow of the dictator to a woman. Her praise of that action undermines, to some extent, rigid patriarchal notions that relegated women to the domestic sphere and demanded considerably more modesty of them. The vast majority of historical accounts still credit Aquiles Serdán as having taken the first shots that started the Mexican Revolution. According to historian Angeles Mendieta Alatorre, however, there is an undecipherable mystery with regard to the events of November 18, 1910, at the Serdán house. Alatorre suspects that Carmen Serdán, Aquiles' sister, shot Cabrera when he was about to attack Aquiles:

> *Históricamente, la presencia de Carmen Serdán en la vida pública dura escasamente cuatro horas. . . . Quizá fue ella misma la que dio muerte a Cabrera cuando iba a atacar a Aquiles—las primeras versiones dijeron que fue una mujer—ya que éste era zurdo y torpe en el manejo de las armas que ella fue tan certera como acaece con los que disparan por primera vez. . . . Empero, de esas mismas horas, poco también hay que decir, hubo un misterio que la Familia Serdán se encargó de guardar con esa fidelidad leal con la que se guardaban los secretos de familia.*[11]

Mendieta Alatorre was convinced that *"Algo extraño, profundamente conmovedor fue sacado a la conciencia pública."* ("Something strange and deeply moving/emotive was made public.")[12] Perhaps Carmen Serdán herself chose to ascribe the act to her own dead brother. We can speculate that either Villarreal was mistaken, or that, given the choice, she decided to educate her readers by crediting the revolutionary act to a woman.

In the second part of the article, Villarreal urges the members of the PLM to support the reelection campaign in order to construct an effective force against the dictatorship. She also cautions her readers that the reelection must yield a new president capable of providing economic, educational, and cultural improvement for the masses:

> Debemos aspirar al mejoramiento económico de las masas y queremos que México figure como un pueblo culto entre las naciones del mundo civilizado. Esa debe ser la aspiración que nos aliente a todos en la lucha contra la Dictadura actual. Luchemos en pro de la civilización y el adelanto moral y material del proletariado mexicano.[13]

Evidently both Villarreal and the principal character in her narrative shared the conviction that their participation in the revolutionary effort was essential, either with the rifle or with the pen. Clearly, Villarreal's narrative of a woman's heroism inscribed itself in the social text of the borderlands quite differently than did the official account in central Mexico.

LA VOZ DE LA MUJER: "WE MUST BE REBELS!"

Founded in El Paso, Texas, to function as a propaganda tool for the PLM, *La Voz de la Mujer* struggled against threats and harassment from President Díaz's secret agents, as did many other PLM periodicals. On its front page, *La Voz de la Mujer* identifies a staff consisting primarily of women: "Isidra T. de Cárdenas, *Directora* (Director); María Sánchez, *Redactora en Jefe* (Chief Editor); María P. García, *Administradora* (Manager); and León Cárdenas, Secretario de Redacción (Secretary of Edition)."[14]

The publication explicitly states its purpose: "*Semanario Liberal de Combate, Defensor de los Derechos del Pueblo y Enemigo de las Tiranías*" ("Combat Liberal Weekly, Guardian of the People's Rights and Enemy of Tyrannies"). The newspaper's logo summons women's participation in the revolutionary struggle by exhorting their duties and rights: "*La mujer forma parte integrante de la gran familia humana; luego tiene el deber y el derecho de exigir y luchar por la Dignificación de su Patria*" ("Women are an integral part of the great human race; and so it is their duty and right to demand and struggle for the Dignity of their Country"). Purporting to be the voice of women, the majority of the articles and commentaries in *La Voz de la Mujer* are written in the first person plural—*nosotras, las madres* (we, mothers), *las esposas* (wives), *las hermanas* (sisters), *las hijas* (daughters)—and none are individually signed.

From the outset, the newspaper established a communal identity and assumed a collective female voice. Most of the writings are political essays that strongly attack Mexico's autocracy. Its tone is militant, fearless, combative, and similar to the tone of Ricardo Flores Magón's writings. Its style is that of revolutionary romanticism. The newspaper vehemently attacks the harshness and brutality of the regime, passionately denounces the exploitation of the proletariat, and calls for reform within the confines of the nation, as did the PLM during the early phase of their work in exile.

The article "*Unifiquémonos: trabajemos en favor de la Junta de San Louis, Mo.*" ("Let us unite: let us work in favor of the Junta de San Louis, Mo.") asserts:

> *"La voz de la mujer" surgió al estadío de la prensa liberal, defendiendo el principio de libertad; coadyuva con nuestros hermanos de ideales en defensa del pueblo oprimido; sus trabajos son limpios por eso hablamos claro; no somos serviles, por eso fustigamos a los protervos; no tememos despertar su encono, por eso denunciamos sus maldades.*[15]

La Voz de la Mujer follows in the tradition established by journalist, poet, and political radical Juana Belen Gutiérrez de Mendoza with her newspaper *Vésper*, founded in 1901 in Guanajuato.[16] Its language had been characterized as "*viril*" ("manly") and "*estilo en pantalonesi*" ("virile style").[17] Through the use of extremely metaphoric language and a sarcastic tone, *La Voz de la Mujer* attempts to expose the criminal face of the so-called "Mexican peace" and to unveil the bestiality of the Diaz government. In an article entitled "*Apocalipcis* [sic] *de la tiranía*" ("Apocalypse of the tyranny"), which comments on the dictator's iron hand of repression against the PLM, the bourgeoisie are identified as the "*sanguijuelas del erario*" (public funds parasites), the mercenaries as "*los peletas alquilados*" (hired canines), and the consulates as "*las emponsoñadas víboras*" (poisonous snakes). An article which exposes the exploitation of the farmworker warns of the coming upheaval: "[*La labor*] *ha tenido una cosecha de exasperación que ya se manifiesta con el descontento general que ha venido madurándose, y solo bastará con un beso del viento para que desprenda su fruto*" ("Labor has had a harvest of exasperation. This already manifests itself with the general discontent which has been maturing. A kiss of wind will be sufficient to let go of its fruit.")[18]

Some of the most intriguing pieces in the newspaper sum up and comment on the current political events, in the tradition of the Mexican ballad. "*¡Loor a los mártires traicionados!*" ("Hail Betrayed Martyrs!"), a heroic romance, celebrates the betrayed Mexican Liberal Party heroes' feats when captured by the dictator's secret police, who are assisted by Pinkerton detectives and United

States immigration officers. The final stanza addresses the oppressed people directly:

¡Pueblo! tu deber es rebelarte
Contra ese mito que de sangre vive:
Si mártires te sirven de baluarte,
¿Por qué consientes que tu pena avive?
Convierte abyección en rebeldías
Y alcanzarás el medio de salvarte.

[We shall rebel against
the myth that feeds from blood:
if martyrs serve us as bastions
Why do we revive our pain?
Let us turn despicable acts into rebelliousness
And we will/shall find a way to salvation.] [19]

The readers of *La Voz de la Mujer* are challenged to raise their level of social consciousness through the poetic piece, and not remain apathetic to the realities of their circumstances.

The extant issues of *La Voz de la Mujer* do not address the specific condition of women. Their situation is alluded to within the context of the proletariat conditions. There are passages in the articles, however, which pay special attention to how women are affected differently by the new upheaval. The article *"Conviene prevenirse: iniciativa"* ("We should be cautious: Initiative") reports that due to their oppositional discourse, the rebels are being imprisoned. Among them, women run a greater risk as they are always in jeopardy of also being raped:

Como respuesta a sus demandas, son arrancados de sus hogares y por la fuerza se les deporta a los cuarteles, lugar de tormento para los espíritus que no abdican sus derechos y persisten en reivindicar su dignidad, máxime y con mayor abundancia cuando algún miembro femenino de esos REBEL-DES despierta la lujuria de algún cacique vulgar. [20]

Although the newspaper does not analyze women's condition, it does address itself to women, encouraging them to rouse their men to fight for liberty and against peonage:

Hoy el dilema es otro: tomar lo que se necesita, ¡libertad! Y ésta sólo se conquista con rebeldías. ¡Hay que ser rebeldes! Primero morir, antes que consen-

*tir que nuestros hijos lleven el estigma de la esclavitud. A nosotras, madres y
esposas, hermanas o hijas, toca encausar este dilema.*[21]

La Voz de la Mujer counsels women to assume new duties within the public
sphere: to form mutualist societies to raise funds for families of soldiers, as
well as to accept posts men are not willing to assume. Within the domestic
sphere, it urges women to send their sons off to war with blessings and words
of valor, and to expect nothing but heroism from their husbands. It is important to note, however, that women's incorporation into the public sphere was
ultimately intended for the benefit of the state and, therefore, limited within
the constraints of nationalism.

Two aspects of the newspaper had the potential of consciously, or subcon-
sciously, affecting the gender politics of their readers. The first of these was the
newspaper's gendering of political positions. In the article, "*La prensa honrada?
Redactado por pseudo-independientes*" ("Is the press honest? edited by pseudo-
independents"), which promotes the alternative press's position against the
state, the ambiguity of the so-called "independent presses" is attacked through
gender rhetoric:

> *Sirviendo de estribillo que provoca néuceas* [sic], *a diario vemos en cierta
> prensa, que por sí y ante sí se hace los honores de llamarse honrada, inde-
> pendiente, instructiva, un cúmulo de ataques infamatorios contra la prensa
> de oposición al gobierno mexicano; ataque que nunca ha justificado, porque
> si bien es cierto que emplea frases ofensivas contra sus adversarios, es más
> verdad que jamás justifica tales calificativos aunque haga derroche de el-
> ocuencia hasta hipnotizar a los lectores con vastos conocimientos en retórica,
> con un lleno completo en gramática, para expresar conceptos sublimes que
> conmuevan a todo continente.*[22]

La Voz de la Mujer does not tolerate the ambiguity of those who purport to be
between the political Right and Left. "*Estos parásitos,*" it points out, "*son edi-
tores que pertenecen al género neutro.*" ("These parasites are editors who belong
to the neuter genre.") Evidently, it is the women (the voices of women) who, in
opposition to the state, speak out for the oppressed through this publication.
Those who take an ambivalent attitude are neutered. *La Voz de la Mujer,* then,
claims to be the voice of the oppressed. All who are exploited are imagined as
the oppressed sex. They are impoverished, their basic needs and rights denied,
and their existence dehumanized.

The other aspect of the newspaper that draws attention to women's social
position is manifested through the title of the newspaper, *La Voz de la Mujer.*
The collective voices of women is not only vigorous, decisive, and vital, but

calls for the restructuring of society. Readers, the vast majority men, were likely to be prompted to react to women's appropriation of the written word and to their intellectual and revolutionary activity.

Further research on this periodical has revealed a letter regarding the gender of the production staff, which problematizes the issue of authority and raises the question of manipulation of gender by the author of the letter.[23] Dated August 11, 1907, addressed to Antonio I. Villarreal and signed by the secretary, Leonor, the letter claims that this weekly was not produced by women at all:

> *Efectivamente que puede suceder una acusación como Ud. lo prevee al aparecer yo como secretario de La Voz de la Mujer, a ello me he visto obligado porque nuestro amigo Don Lauro [Aguirre] está temeroso de que se crea que él escribe el semanario aludido y esto lo hacía estar inquieto, y además que las damas que en él figuran, sólo tienen un corazón muy grande para trabajar por la causa, pero nada pueden expresar ellas porque no son capaces de escribir y en este caso sólo tomo el nombre de ellas como un impulso para la causa porque supongo que muchos hombres al aparecer señoras en el periódico, deben sonrojarse al encontrarlas en puestos que ellos deberían desempeñar; así, repito, lo que La Voz dice, no lo escriben ellas pero con su abnegación expresan más de lo que se asienta en imprenta.*[24]

One can surmise that this letter, which deprives women of authority, was written by the Secretary of Edition, León Cárdenas. If we take his claim at face value, we would have to address the issue of manipulation of gender by the proponents of the social revolution. Instead of women's appropriation of the written word, we may have here the appropriation of women's "voices" by men. This may account for the fact that the narrative voices in *La Voz de la Mujer* are not at all different from those of the male precursors of the revolution. Why does the newspaper lack an analysis of women's condition, and why are attempts made therein to develop women's sense of state nationalism? This manipulation of gender buttresses Emma Pérez's critique of the PLM's ideology on women. As Pérez has pointed out, "*Regeneración* helped to politicize Mexican women in the Southwest, but women were politicized to serve a nationalist cause—the Mexican revolution."[25]

Cárdenas rationalizes that his manipulation of gender in the newspaper's pages is a way to both humiliate and to motivate men. He suggests that the periodical's call for women's participation in the revolution was a very specific one: to arouse their men's civic pride by overthrowing the dictator. If Cárdenas was correct, it is important to note that his manipulation of gender in the pages of the newspaper also allowed him to have access to the women's private sphere—the home—as did the priests from the pulpit.

Nonetheless, we should remember that Cárdenas was responding to an accusation. We cannot therefore rule out the possibility that he very well could have been responding defensively, inaccurately, and perhaps cleverly, in order to protect his masculine pride.

PLUMA ROJA: "BEFORE ME, THE STAR OF THE IDEAL. BEHIND ME, MEN. I DO NOT LOOK BACK."

Whereas in the 1900s Teresa Villarreal defied established Catholic ideology, and *La Voz de la Mujer* called for liberal democracy through a revolution, in the following decade, *Pluma Roja* proposed anarchism as the solution to oppression.[26] Founded in Los Angeles during the second phase of the revolution, *Pluma Roja* was edited and directed by Blanca de Moncaleano from 1913 to 1915. Although there are no indications that this publication was founded as a political organ of the PLM, it was established to network with the international anarchist movement in which Ricardo Flores Magón participated. Although little is known about Blanca de Moncaleano, John Hart writes, "In early June 1912, Juan Francisco Moncaleano, a Colombian anarchist and political fugitive sought by the Colombian military [and 'his dynamic wife'], arrived in Mexico after a brief stay in Havana ['inspired by the news of the Madero led revolution']." A university professor in Colombia, Moncaleano founded the newspaper *Luz* in Mexico City, which, according to Hart "was a remarkable newspaper. Moncaleano used it to publicize the hopeless cause of Flores Magón and the Partido Liberal Mexicano, the anarchist program, which he enthusiastically endorsed and whose leader he deeply admired."[27] As Moncaleano prepared the opening of the *La Casa del Obrero* in September of 1912, the Madero regime succeeded in arresting him and expelled him from the country. The few issues of *Pluma Roja* located and consulted for this study indicate that the Moncaleanos continued their anarchist work by crossing still another border.

Unlike the nationalist ideology of *La Voz de la Mujer*, *Pluma Roja* did not believe in national borders. It adopted instead José Martí's concept of one united America. "[*Hay que demostrar*] *que las fronteras son un mito.*" ("[We should] demonstrate] that borders are a myth.") appeared in its pages. For *Pluma Roja*, the need to recode the position of women in society was at the center of the struggle for social, political, and economic freedom, and was an integral part of the ideal of anarchism, as it had been for Emma Goldman during that same historical moment. For *Pluma Roja*, unquestioned patriarchal authority upheld by religion and the state was the target of its red pen.

Many of the articles that appeared in the newspaper were directed specifically at women, who were encouraged to break their chains through the acquisition of knowledge. The anarchist program, as defined by *Pluma Roja*, searched for an egalitarian society in which women would be fully emancipated. It proposed women's freedom from their three oppressors: the state, religion, and capital.

As editor and director, Blanca de Moncaleano not only addressed women but men as well, urging them to convert their obedient enslaved women into thinking *compañeras* (partners). For example, although the title, *"Hombre, educad a la mujer"* ("Men, educate women"), appears to be a call for men to educate women, in essence the article addresses the issue of the importance of allowing women to educate themselves: *"Dejen los hombres que la mujer se instruya, que piense y reflexione por sí sola."* ("Men, allow women to educate themselves and to think on her own.")[28]

The articles signed by Blanca de Moncaleano are perhaps the most vehemently critical of those men involved in the struggle for liberation and who were least conscious of their own suppression and enslavement of women. She wrote: *"Engolfados los hombres en su supuesta superioridad, fatuos por su ignorancia, han creído que sin la ayuda de la mujer, pueden llegar a la meta de la emancipación humana."* ("Consumed by their supposed superiority, conceited in their ignorance, men believe they can achieve the goal of human emancipation without the help of women.") Confronting apathy from her male counterparts, she denounces the source of their power, *"El hombre no ha sido otra cosa que el verdadero ladrón de los derechos naturales de la mujer."* ("Men are the real thieves of women's natural rights.") Moncaleano expounded her firm, militant stance through the newspaper's motto: *"Ante mí la estrella del ideal. Tras de mí los hombres. No miro atrás."* ("Before me, the star of my ideal. Behind me, men. I do not look back.")[29]

El Obrero, La Voz de la Mujer, and *Pluma Roja* all had an impact on their audiences as they articulated gender issues. It is highly probable that their audiences consisted of PLM activists and partisans, described by Gómez-Quiñones:

> 1) The large audience was composed of Chicano-Mexicano general sympathizers and intermittently active, for the most part, lower middle class, artisans and laborers; 2) the local cores of leadership, in the majority Chicano, district organizers, chapter officers, local journalists who were transmitters and interpreters of PLM policy usually active for prolonged periods; [and] 3) the bi-national leadership, well educated, self taught or as a result of professional training, they were the policy makers and were mostly Mexicano but with some Chicanos.[30]

Whether that public read privately or listened to someone reading in groups at gatherings, the articulation of gender issues within an environment of revolutionary change must have encouraged rethinking of women's role in society. While we now know that the Mexican Revolution was a catalyst for the women's movement in Mexico, we know little of its repercussions for women's. lives in the U.S. Southwest.[31] Recovery of periodicals such as *Pluma Roja* and research of their impact on various communities and of women's social history should reveal the development of feminist consciousness in the borderlands.

LA CRÓNICA:
"WORKING CLASS WOMEN ARE MEN'S EQUALS, THEIR COMPANIONS"

The extant issues of *La Crónica*—merely one year's publication, that of 1911—reveal the Idar family's position on the contemporary debates on both sides of the U.S.-Mexico border that examined racial politics, challenged legal and social injustices, promoted bilingual education, condemned officially tolerated lynchings of Texas-Mexican residents, and offered a scathing critique of the Catholic Church's oppression of women.[32] In 1911 *La Crónica* responded with a journalistic campaign of resistance, leading to the organization of El Congreso Mexicanista (The Mexican Congress). As José Limón has noted in his germinal essay on this conference, "*El Primer Congreso Mexicanista* (The First Mexican Congress): Precursor to Contemporary Chicanismo," the periodical projects an imagined community based on ethnic solidarity.[33] As principal writers of the family weekly, Jovita, Clemente, and Eduardo Idar regularly reported and commented on these events despite severe political repercussions from Texas authorities. Although her father and brothers occasionally assumed authorship of the articles they had written, Jovita did not. However, through interviews with family members I have identified pseudonyms she used: "A.V. Negra," which phonetically reads "*Ave Negra*" ("Black Bird"), connoting the bearer of tragic news, and "*Astrea*" (Greek goddess of justice). My reading of articles discussed below show Jovita Idar as author and as disseminator of culturally-specific and working-class-based feminist ideas.

Two articles identified by Idar family members as part of Jovita Idar's writings capture the political climate that led to the conference, Primer Congreso Mexicanista. These articles reveal the strong sentiment of nationalist/racial indignation on the part of border area Tejano-Mexicanos for over half a century after the massive invasion by industrial capitalism and "foreigners," as well as the devastating impact of these changes on the younger generation. The article "*Por la raza: la niñez mexicana en Texas*" ("For the Race: Mexican Children in Texas") claims:

> *La niñez mexicana en Texas necesita instruirse. Ni nuestro gobierno ni el de EEUU pueden hacer nada por ella, y no queda otro recurso que el de hacerlo*

por nuestro propio impulso á trueque de no seguir despreciados y vejados por
los extranjeros que nos rodean.[34]

Caught between the overlapping boundaries of two sovereign nation-states, neither of which protects their interests, the author urges the people to organize collectively and specifically proposes community-funded schools for Mexican children. Their own cultural survival depends on concerted community efforts, the author maintains. And, in the follow-up article, *"Por la raza: la conservación del nacionalismo"* ("For the Race: Protection of Nationalism"), the writer advocates bilingual and bicultural education:

> *No debe desatenderse el idioma nacional, porque es el sello característico*
> *de las razas y de los pueblos. Las naciones desaparecen y las castas se hun-*
> *den cuando se olvida la lengua nacional; . . . No decimos que no se enseñe*
> *el inglés a la niñez mexico-texana, sea en hora buena, decimos que no se*
> *olviden de enseñarles el castellano, pues así como les es útil la arimética y*
> *la gramática así les es útil el inglés á los que viven entre los que hablan ese*
> *idioma.*[35]

Cognizant of the difference between official nationalism of the nation-states and the need for cultural community, *nacionalismo* (nationalism) is defined by them as cultural/linguistic preservation for the purpose of community survival. If a child only learns the history and culture of the United States, disregarding the Mexican heritage of his/her parents, that child, warns the essayist, will be caught in a cultural vacuum. Language, the article purports, is a social and psychological bond between generations. Strategies against cultural/linguistic annihilation were the focus of the publication Jovita Idar founded after the Primer Congreso Mexicanista, *El Estudiante* (*The Student*).[36]

Directly linked to her written word was Jovita Idar's community organizing centered on empowering women. As part of the larger conference, she founded the Liga Femenil Mexicanista (Mexican Feminine League) to challenge women to work beyond the confines of their domestic sphere. *La Crónica* reports:

> *[Este] grupo de damas que forman sociedad . . . es de alta trascendencia y*
> *de mucha significación. Muchos huérfanos tendrán pan y muchas mujeres*
> *que aisladas y dispersas era partes* [sic] *tan solo* [sic] *del sexo débil, aliadas*
> *serán fuertes y respetadas.*[37]

Originally comprised predominantly by teachers (*"en su personal está lo más selecto y granado Sembradores Ricardos Flores Magón y el Partido Liberal Mexicano de la intelectualidad femenina,"* in essence, a very selective feminine intelligentsia), the league prioritized the organization of local women of both Laredo, Texas, and Nuevo Laredo, Tamaulipas. The league's agenda was to institute regular study sessions for women; to found some of the first bilingual schools for Tejano children; and to establish benefit fundraisers to finance its cultural project and assist newly-arrived immigrants and their families. Class conscious, the organization identified itself not only by gender and ethnic group, but also as an integral part of the working class:

> Esta Easociación, que trabaja activamente por el adelanto general de sus co-aasociados, que verifica sesiones donde se estudia y se aprende, donde se adquiere cultura y se desarrolla el talento sin orgías y sin ambiciones mal sanas, que se dedica a realizar nobles y generosos fines, no cuenta con elementos pecuniarios, puesto que sus miembros todos pertenecen a la noble clase obrera.[38]

Astrea's writings further engage the contruction of new subjectivities and communities, which project a "modern working woman." Directed to a collective participating addressee, the article "Debemos trabajar" ("We Must Work") speaks to "la mujer soltera, digna y trabajadora" ("honorable working, single women") and summons them to seek economic independence and self-sufficiency, to be vigilant for their rights, and to forthrightly support the movimiento feminista (feminist movement):

> La mujer obrera reconociendo sus derechos, alza la frente orgullosa y se afronta a la lucha; la epoca de su degradación ha pasado, ya no es la esclava vendida por unas cuantas monedas, ya no es la sierva, sino la igual del hombre, su compañera. . . . Mucho se ha tratado y escrito contra el movimiento femenista, pero a pesar de los oposicionistas ya en California las mujeres pueden dar su voto como jurado y pueden desempeñar oficinas públicas.
>
> Yerran y mucho, esos espíritus descontentadizos, superficiales e indignos de una buena obra, críticos de aquella mujer, que haciendo a un lado los convencionalismos sociales se dedica a trabajar por algo provechoso o benéfico.[39]

Through the use of pseudonyms evoking justice and the bearer of news, Jovita Idar launched her political ideas in La Crónica about the need for political organization on the part of the Mexican community in the United States for cultural and linguistic nationalism and for working-class women's social, political, and economic emancipation. Although a few such articles have been recovered, her articles on her involvement in the violent phase of the Mexican revolution have not. It is through the recovery of Leonor Villegas de Magnón's autobiography that we learn of Idar's transborder political activism.

While official history of the Mexican Revolution has focused on male political intellectuals and military leaders, *La Rebelde* attempts to highlight the contributions of some women, such as Jovita Idar, Teresa Villarreal, and Teresa Villarreal's sister, teacher-poet Andrea Villarreal, as well as other borderlands heroines. As official history nearly erased the memory of the nurses' involvement in the Mexican Revolution of 1910, especially those from the Texas-Mexico border area, Leonor Villegas de Magnón made it her duty to leave a written record of that participation through her memoirs of the medical relief group she founded in 1914, La Cruz Blanca (the White Cross), comprised of women and men of both sides of the border, Laredo, Texas, and Nuevo Laredo, Tamaulipas. She left two versions of her life story. The first three-hundred-page Spanish text written in the 1920s and titled *La Rebelde* was written for a Mexican audience. After various unsuccessful attempts to have the Mexican government publish what they labeled "novelized memoirs," Villegas de Magnón wrote an English version, titled *The Lady Was a Rebel*, for a United States mainstream audience.[40] Quick strokes attempt to capture brief moments of lives, deeds, social mores, customs, landscapes, and historical events filtered through the memory of Leonor Villegas de Magnón. Ironically, her autobiographical text is written in the third person. She suppresses, even silences at times, the "I" to tell the story of "The Rebel." In the style of revolutionary romanticism, we learn of the Rebel's life, from her birth in 1876 to the death of one of the major figures of the revolution, Venustiano Carranza, in 1920. The first quarter of her story narrates the transformations undergone by the protagonist as she changes from a highly-sensitive child and lonely orphan into a brave woman with an altruistic sense of duty and loyalty.

Similarly significant in this section is the narrator's emphasis on spatial, national, and geneological links, which suggest the obliteration of geopolitical borders. In the English version of her manuscript, Villegas de Magnón alludes to this through the dialogue of Valeriana, La Rebelde's mother: "Come here mother. Look, now I shall have two daughters, one Mexican and one American. And two sons, one Mexican and one American. The Virgin de Guadalupe, my flag, shall keep them unified."[41] By aspiring to make public the story of a woman who rebelled, however tenuously or ardently, against her class origins, religious upbringing, family expectations, political affiliations, and patriarchal social mores, she reveals the multiplicity of selves linked to her sociohistorical context. She depicts a rebel who subsequently escapes, through her own agency, the normal destiny of a bourgeois woman of the borderlands.

In order to give written form to her anecdotes, remembrances, historical and heroic deeds, ventures, treasure stories, and love tales, she inevitably entered into a communicative process that demanded awareness, conscious or intuitive, of herself as a writer, of her narrative text as a medium of unique communication, and of her potential readers as receptors of an ignored part of history.

As Villegas de Magnón experienced La Cruz Blanca's erasure, and sensed its dilution into folklore—following the fate of the revolutionary female image into the mythified *soldadera*, (female soldier), with its accompanying folk songs "La Adelita" and "Marieta"—she unrelentingly sought to reinscribe a "real" image into historical memory through the first Spanish version of her story, *La Rebelde*. Her portrayal of "rebel women" derived from different social classes—from rural, destitute soldiers' companions to middle-class teachers, journalists, propagandists, printers, telegraph operators, nurses and bourgeois socialites—subverts the Mexican social text.[42] Just as subversive is her own self-portrayal as an independent, intelligent, and extremely outspoken woman.

From the outset, the narrative voice establishes an internal distancing, an "articulated connection, a tension, between identity and difference" through the use of the third person.[43] With the construction of this "fictive witness," Villegas de Magnón creates an internal distancing that also expresses personal confrontation. Throughout the entire Spanish manuscript, the subject is referred to as *"la niña"* ("the child"), *"la joven"* ("the young girl"), or *"La Rebelde"* ("The Rebel"). Her proper name is never used. It is this "other" who rebels against the ideology of her bourgeois class, against the boundaries set by society with regard to women's role.

Unlike the memoirs of revolutionary generals, however, *La Rebelde* focuses on the names of the women of the various Cruz Blanca brigades as well as vignettes of women turned spies, female military officers dressed as men, and valiant heroines. Although the temporal structure is that of traditional chronological discourse, Villegas de Magnón interrupts the chronological narration to remind the reader of her purpose in writing her story. After a detailed account of the journey of the revolutionary forces and the Cruz Blanca battling the federal troops from the border area down to Mexico, she disrupts the third-person narration, inserts herself in first person with an outcry against what official history is negating. As the narration describes the events of La Rebelde's thirty-eigthth birthday, June 12, 1914, when she finds herself absorbed in "vague melancholic thoughts," offended at the ingratitude shown toward the Cruz Blanca's work, her first-person narrative discloses the following:

¿Qué acaso ha habido al pie de la tumba del Mártir Madero o del Mártir Carranza, cuando los grandes oradores recuerdan los actos de los héroes y

sus hazañas, quién se acuerde de mencionar la valiosa colaboración de la Cruz Blanca?

Aquellas mujeres abnegadas jamás encontraron en los hospitales de sangre a las esposas de los generales. ¿Dónde estaban? En el extranjero esperando el toque del clarín para recibir, por lo menos una palabra de reconocimiento.

Por eso precisamente escribo esto, para glorificar a las enfermeras patriotas y desinteresadas de entonces. . . .

Todas ellas habían probado ya su lealtad y su eficacia; no dudaba la Rebelde que en su corazón jamás habría traición; por eso cada una se convertía en cabeza ya probada y aprobada.[44]

La Rebelde understood that as U.S. citizens their national alliance was continually being questioned. Her narrative pointed to their deeds as acts of an international social justice, which knew no national boundaries. For her, all border-area participants, regardless of gender, were equally important. Continued interruptions by the narrator in the story line boldly protest calculated omissions by official Mexican history: "*La historia se ha encargado de relatar los hechos, pero se ha olvidado del importante papel de los pueblos de Laredo, Texas, Nuevo Laredo, Tamaulipas y otros fronterizos que en esos momentos se unieron en un fraternal acuerdo.*"[45] Through the discursive mode of memoirs, then, the narrator lists paragraphs of names of those whose lives as labor, political, and revolutionary leaders were dedicated to social change. As such, *La Rebelde* stands as one of the few documents produced between 1910 and 1920 that challenges the stereotypes of Texas-Mexicans held by both Mexican and U.S. dominant societies.

The articulation of gender issues within an environment of revolutionary change published in these newspapers must have encouraged rethinking of women's role in society. Recovery of documents such as these and research of their impact on various communities and on women's social history reveal the history of the development of feminist consciousness in the borderlands. The voices and pens of these women articulate a passionate rebelliousness whose documentation has been long absent from the cultural theaters of both Mexico and the United States.

NOTES

This essay is an expanded and updated version of "The Articulation of Gender in the Borderlands, 1900–1915," published in the anthology *Recovering the U.S. Hispanic Literary Heritage* (Houston: Arte Público Press, 1993). The updates were done as a result of further research conducted in Mexico City during my year on sabbatical funded by the Fulbright Scholars Program.

1. Juan Gómez-Quiñones, *Sembradores Ricardo Flores Magón y el Partido Liberal Mexicano: A Eulogy and Critique* (Los Angeles: University of California, Chicano Studies Center Publications, 1973).

2. Luther E. Ellsworth, *"Informe al Secretario de Estado, Fechado el 12 de Octubre de 1910 en Ciudad Porfirio Díaz, México,"* in *Documents on the Mexican Revolution*, ed. Gene Z. Hanrahan (North Carolina: Documentary Publications, 1910).

3. María de los Angeles Mendieta Alatorre, *La Mujer en la Revolución Mexicana* (Mexico City, México: Biblioteca del Instituto Nacional de Estudios Históricos de la Revolución Mexicana, 1961), 32.

4. Tita Valencia, *"Ricardo Flores Magón y el Periodismo Subversivo Mexicano en EUA,"* *The Americas Review* 17:3/4 (1989): 169–78.

5. José Valadez, *"Más de Cuatrocientos Periódicos en Español se han Editado en Estados Unidos,"* *La Prensa*, February 13, 1938, 1–8; and Richard Griswold del Castillo, "The Mexican Revolution and the Spanish-Language Press in the Borderlands," *Journalism History* 4:2 (1977): 42–47.

6. Gómez-Quiñones writes, "Mobilization of the PLM groups not only antedated legal difficuties but continued despite them throughout 1907 and into the summer of 1908. [. . .] A manifesto published in 1907, by Praxedis Guerrero, alerted the Chicano communities to the continuing militancy of PLM. Aproximately forty to sixty-four groups were involved. Thirty groups were equipped with arms. The date set for this rebellion was June 25, 1908. On June 19 and on June 25, arrests took place as Casas Grandes, Chihuahua, and at El Paso, Tejas" (*Sembradores Ricardos Flores Magón y el Partido Liberal Mexicano*, 35).

7. Gómez-Quiñones, *Sembradores Ricardo Flores Magón y el Partido Liberal Mexicano*, 52–56.

8. I located one issue of *El Obrero* at the Secretaría de Relaciones Exteriores in Mexico City.

9. All translations are mine.

We remember with true enthusiasm the scene that took place in Puebla at Cerdán's [sic] house, where the inhabitants retaliated with bullets against the police, those subservient men who work in favor of despotism in order to make a living. We rejoice that Mexico still has heroines that stand up to challenge the mercenary tyrants. A woman, lacking the strength of a man, yet with a heroic virile soul, killed Police Chief Miguel Cabrera, a degenerate man who committed crimes to obey a despotic government. (Teresa Villarreal, *"El Partido Anti-reeleccionista,"* *El Obrero*, December 15, 1910, 1)

10. You, indifferent depraved men, supporters of the dictatorship's attacks, and you Mexican women, daughters of Mexico, that beautiful native country that has given birth to brave heroes and irreproachable heroines, follow the example of

that woman who has died as the brave die: challenging the tyrants. Let us unite our strengths. (Villarreal, "*El Partido Anti-reeleccionista*," 1)

11. Historically, the presence of Carmen Serdán in public life lasts scarcely four hours. Perhaps it was she who killed Cabrera while he was going to attack Aquiles—the first versions of the incident stated that it had been a woman—because he was left-handed and could not handle weapons very well. She, on the other hand, could have had the sharp aim of those who shoot for the first time. . . . However, very little can be said about those hours. There was a mystery that the Serdán family faithfully kept with the traditional loyalty given to family secrets. (Mendieta Alatorre, *Carmen Serdán* [Mexico: Editorial Bohemia Poblana, 1971], 199)

12. Alatorre, *Carmen Serdán*, 199.

13. We must aspire for the economic improvement of the masses. We want Mexico to stand out as an educated people among the nations of the civilized world. This must be the goal to encourage all of us in the fight against the present dictatorship. We struggle on behalf of civilization and the moral and material progress of the Mexican proletariat." (Villarreal, "*El Partido Anti-reeleccionista*," 4)

14. I have retrieved five issues of *La Voz de la Mujer* from the Silvestre Terrazas Collection at the Bancroft Library and the International Institute of Social History in Amsterdam (IISH), dated July 28, 1907, August 11, 1907, September 6, 1907, and October 27, 1907. I am grateful to Rafael Chabrán for alerting me to the IISH's holdings of *La Voz de la Mujer* and of *Pluma Roja*.

15. *La Voz de la Mujer* appeared in the arena of liberal journalism defending principles of freedom. It contributes to our brothers' ideals in defending oppressed people. Its work is honest and so we speak clearly. We are not servile, and so we reprimand the perverse. We do not fear wakening their anger, and so we denounce their corruption. ("*Unifiquémonos: Trabajemos en Favor de la Junta de San Louis, Mo*," *La Voz de la Mujer*, October 27, 1907, n.p.)

16. Anna Macías, *Against All Odds: The Feminist Movement in Mexico to 1940* (Connecticut: Greenwood Press, 1982), 26.

17. Alatorre, *La Mujer en la Revolución Mexicana*, 33.

18. Anonymous, "*Apocalipcis* [sic] *de la Tiranía*," *La Voz de la Mujer*, July 28, 1907, 3.

19. Anonymous, "*Apocalipcis* [sic] *de la Tiranía*," *La Voz de la Mujer*, July 28, 1907, 3.

20. As a solution/answer to their demands, they are torn from their homes as

they are violently taken to the barracks, a tormenting place for those souls without rights and those who persistantly claim for their dignity, especially when a female member of their REBEL group is the victim of some nasty tyrant. (*"Conviene Prevenirse: Iniciativa," La Voz de la Mujer*, July 28, 1907, 4)

21. Today we face a new dilemma: to take what we need: freedom! This we can only achieve through rebellion. We must rebel! We would rather die before allowing our children to become slaves. We, mothers, wives, sisters and daughters must confont this dilemma. (*"Conviene Prevenirse,"* 4)

22. The same old chorus is nauseating. Daily we see in an unnamed newspaper that calls itself honest, independent, and educational, a defamatory load of attacks against the opposition press to the Mexican government. These attacks have never been justified. Although it uses offensive language against its adversaries, it never justifies itself. Its eloquent rhetoric serves more to hypnotize its readers through sublime worldly concepts than to express truth. (*"La prensa honrada? Redactado por Pseudo-independientes," La Voz de la Mujer*, October 27, 1907, 3)

23. I am grateful to Victor Nelson-Cisneros for sharing the Lopez and Cortéz text, which led to this correspondence.

24. Surely, an accusation such as the one you predict can be made since I appear as the secretary of *La Voz de la Mujer*. I have been forced to do so because our friend Don Lauro [Aguirre] fears that the public may think he is the one who writes the weekly and this made him quite uneasy. Moreover, the ladies that appear as the writers are only big-hearted in working for the cause. They cannot express anything because they are incapable of writing. In this case, I only take their names as a driving force for the cause. I hope that men will feel ashamed when they see women's names in the newspaper and realize the women are taking on jobs men should be holding. I repeat, what is published in *La Voz* is not written by women, yet their devotion expresses more than what goes down on print. (López and Cortés, *El Partido Liberal Mexican* 1906–1908 [Mexico City: Ediciones Antorcha, 1986], 194–95).

25. Emma Pérez, "'*A la Mujer*': A Critique of the Partido Liberal Mexicano's Gender Ideology," in *Between Borders: Essays on Mexicana/Chicana History*, ed. Adelaida R. Del Castillo (Encino, Calif.: Floricanto, 1990), 459–82.

26. At the International Institute of Social History in Amsterdam I was able to locate five numbers of *Pluma Roja*, November 5, 1913, December 14, 1913, February 1, 1914, June 15, 1915, and June 27, 1915.

27. John Hart, *Anarchism and the Mexican Working Class, 1860–1931* (Austin: University of Texas, 1987), 113.

28. *Pluma Roja*, February 1, 1914, 1.

29. *Pluma Roja*, June 27, 1915, 1.

30. Gómez-Quiñones, *Sembradores Ricardos Flores Magón y el Partido Liberal Mexicano*, 27.

31. Macías, *Against All Odds*, 49.

32. According to Jovita Idar's niece, Jovita Idar de López, in a June 22, 1995, interview, these extant issues barely survived being destroyed. Idar de López comments on the incidents that determined the fate of the Idar papers:

> In the 1940s, my aunt Jovita [Idar] had the foresight to send the few issues of *La Crónica* she had in her possession to the University of Texas Library, where they are now housed at the Barker History Library at the University of Texas in Austin. Tragically, there were three fires that destroyed the vast majority of the Idar papers, periodical collections, and documents. In 1956, nine years after the death of Eduardo (Jovita's younger brother), the servant's quarters at his house burned down, destroying his entire collection. Due to his political involvement, many thought the fire had been arson. Jovita's older brother Clemente's house burned down in 1964, also after his death. In 1958, after the death of Jovita's husband, Bartolo Juárez, his second wife burned the contents of an old trunk, which contained Jovita's papers.

33. José Limón, "*El Primer Congreso Mexicanista* (The First Mexican Congress): Precursor to Contemporary Chicanismo," *Aztlan* 5:1/2: 86–106.

34. Mexican children in Texas need an education. Neither our government, nor the U.S. government, can do anything for our children. Therefore, we have no other option but to do it on our own, so we are not discriminated and mistreated by the foreigners around us. (A. V. Negra, "*Por la Raza: La Niñez Mexicana en Texas*," *La Crónica*, August 10, 1911, 1)

35. The national language should be kept, for it is the characteristic seal of the races and peoples. Nations vanish and castes disappear when we forget the national language; We are not against teaching English to our Mexican-Texan children, on the contrary, we say let us not forget to teach them Spanish. Just as arithmetic and grammar are useful to them, so is English for those who live among native speakers of English. ("*Por la Raza: La Conservación del Nacionalismo*," *La Crónica*, August 17, 1911, 1)

36. *La Crónica*, October 19, 1911, 1.

37. [This] group of ladies who constitute this society is one of great significance and much importance. Many orphans will have bread and many women, who while isolated and scattered were only part of the weaker sex, together will be strong and respected. (*La Crónica*, October 19, 1911, 1)

38. This association actively works for the general well-being of its members. It establishes study sessions to acquire culture and develops pure talent without evil ambitions. It dedicates itself to do noble and generous deeds without special financial interests because all of its members belong to the respectable working class. (*La Crónica*, December 7, 1911, 1)

39. Working women recognize their rights, proudly raise their chins, and face the struggle. The times of humiliation have passed, women are no longer slaves sold for a few coins. They are no longer men's servants but their equals, their partners. . . . Much has been said and written against the feminist movement, yet despite the opposition, in California, women can vote in juries and hold public offices. Those disappointed and superficial souls are very wrong. Those critics of women who put social conventions aside to dedicate themselves to work for something worthwhile or beneficial do not deserve a good deed. (Astrea, "*Debemos trabajar,*" *La Crónica*, December 7, 1911, 1)

40. After I spent several years attempting to locate the autobiographical manuscript of *La Rebelde*, the Villegas de Magnón family made available to me the two versions. The English version, *The Rebel*, was published by Arte Público Press in 1994 as part of the Recovering the U.S. Hispanic Literary Heritage Project. The Spanish version, *La Rebelde*, is forthcoming as a copublication by Arte Público Press and the Instituto Nacional de Estudios Históricos de la Revolución Mexicana (INAH) in Mexico City. The following quote in the original English is from *The Rebel*, and the following quotes in the original Spanish are from the manuscript of *La Rebelde*.

41. Villegas de Magnón, *La Rebelde*, 34.

42. It is not until the 1990s, with the celebration of the eightieth anniversary of the initiation of the Constitutionalist struggle, that the Instituto National de Estudios Históricos de la Revolución Mexicana made available valuable historical studies, such as *Mujeres y Revolución, 1900–1917* by Ana Lau and Carmen Ramos, which reveal the versatility of women's roles in the Mexican Revolution.

43. Philippe Lejeune, "Autobiography in the Third Person," *New Literary History* 9:1(1977): 32.

44. When the great orators remember the deeds and feats of the heroes, has there been someone who has remembered to even mention the collaboration of the Cruz Blanca?

Those unselfish women never saw the generals' wives in the hospitals. Where are [those selfless women]? They are abroad awaiting the bugle call to at least receive a word of acknowledgement.

This is precisely why I am writing this, to glorify those patriotic and selfless nurses. . . .

All of them had already proven their loyalty and efficiency. La Rebelde had no doubt that in their hearts there would ever be treason. Every one of them therefore [had become] a proven and approved entity. (Villegas de Magnón, *La Rebelde*)

45. "History has assumed responsibility for documenting the facts, but it has forgotten the important role played by the communities of Laredo, Texas, and Nuevo Laredo, Tamaulipas, and other border cities that united themselves in a fraternal agreement" (Villegas de Magnón, *La Rebelde*).

La Cultura, la Comunidad, la Familia, y la Libertad

GRACIELA I. SÁNCHEZ

Esta mañana, like most Sunday mornings, I went to my parents' home for breakfast. For the *avena con canela hecho por mi mama*, and nowadays, even my papa. He tends to experiment combining oatmeal with Cream of Wheat because he likes the different textures. *Y algunas veces quema la avena* because, as they explain, this too was a way to prepare the *avena*, even considered a delicacy. I don't know if I should believe them, *porque para mi, cuando esta quemada, esta quemada*, and I don't eat it.

As we eat breakfast, *escuchamos la musica y hablamos*. I wait for the stories. Today, the *musica* brings up the stories.[1] We listen to *chotis*, the German schottische *mezclado con nuestra cultura Mexicana*, and my mom describes dancing with *señores viejos* as a little girl. They told her that she was light on her feet. I wonder, does anyone still play this music? Does anyone dance this *baile* anymore? How can we program musicians and dancers to teach this in San Antonio? I become desperate to pull myself into millions of pieces so that I can do all the work that we need to do, *antes que se nos mueran nuestros ancianos*.

Each day, many *viejitos* pass away. Each day, I mourn the loss of their sacred stories and regret having failed to learn all the traditions, not knowing how to create the delicacies of *dulces y comidas*, not understanding the critical role of cultural grounding of our people *hasta los ultimos anos*.

I hear the music again:

Damisela encantadora
Damisela por ti me muero,
Si me miras,
Si me besas,
Damisela seras mi amor[2]

I grew up hearing *esta y muchas otras canciones* on weekends. That's the way Dad would wake up his children, by playing various records—Maria Grever, Agustin Lara, Lobo y Melon.

I need to remember—*Canciones, poesia, tradiciones, cuentos.*

Not as an anthropology project. Not as a ritual prescribed to me by my parents or grandparents, but because it is essential to my survival. And I like how the words feel:

> *Los Maderos de San Juan*
> *Piden queso, piden pan*
> *Los de troque alcantroque*
> *los de trique alcantriqu*
> *los de triqui, triqui, tran*
> *triqui, triqui, triqui, tran*[3]

How they sing.
How they made me move.
But young *chicanitos* aren't suppose to be smart.
They're not supposed to know how to read
in English.
Much less in Spanish.

My parents understood the power of *cultura*. They understood that knowing these poems, songs, and rituals, knowing how to converse and think in the language of our ancestors was important; that knowing about our history, and culture, and traditions would help their children develop a better sense of themselves. We learned to like ourselves. We learned to love each other. We learned to respect ourselves and our neighbors who, as working-class Chicanos living in the barrio, were no better or worse than other people in the city. That was essential to my survival.

And I'm one of the few who has survived.

What other songs, what other memories fight for a place on these pages?

> *Cucurucucu, Paloma.*
> The Alameda Theater and its red velvet curtains.
> Going out with the family, including my *abuelita*, who rarely went out since she had arthritis and was wheelchair bound.
> *Coca Cola Grande, te da mucho mas!*

We grew up in San Antonio; that's where my mom grew up and where Abuelita Teresita, my great-grandmother, was one of the Chili Queens who worked downtown in the market area, selling food to the men who worked in *el mercado* until the businessmen complained and kicked them out. Today, the Chili Queens are a fond memory, and the businessmen who ran *estas mujeres* out of business have a yearly celebration each spring to honor these *mujeres*. But hey, let's forget our racist history because we need to market our Mexican people and culture to the tourists.

And on my dad's side, we were from Chicago, and before that Tampico, and before that, Vera Cruz. We came from the eastern shores of Mexico. White bread and corn tortillas. Fish. Black beans and rice. *Salseror.* African beats and movements. Curly hair. Some dark skinned, like my great-grandmother Abuelita Guadalupe, who smoked a cigar and *algunos negros como my tio Mino.*[4]

Some of us came out looking white, like me.

My mom had to hear: "Oh how pretty—whose child is she?" In other words, she can't be yours—she's white, she's pretty. You're dark and ugly.

My mom—*morena, prieta,* and survivor of a racist society. *Ella, la que me enseño,* the one who continues to teach me to love, even those who I should hate. *Ella la que me enseña,* to forgive. Who teaches me to respect? Who teaches me about challenging authority? *Esta morena,* a small brown woman with straight black hair who passes for Indian, who passes for Asian, who passes for Mexican, who passes for black, but who never passes for white.

Y mi papa—que me enseño a bailar, y cantar, y leer, y pensar en español— who taught me that being different was crucial to our survival as people, because nothing changed when everyone just followed like sheep. He wanted us to challenge. He even let his wife and daughters challenge him. He wanted us to survive.

Pin Pon es un muñeco
De trapo y de carton
Se lava sus manitas con agua y con jabon.
Se desenrueda el pelo
Con peine de marfil
Y aunque se da tirones
No llora y hace asi
Pin Pon dame tu mano
Con un buen apreton
Yo quiero ser tu amigo
Pin pon, Pin pon pin pon[5]

And it was these *gente* who formed me. It was these *cuentos, y tradiciones y valores que me formaron*. These were the people who first taught me about culture and its power, *respeto*, defiance, equality, sharing, community, family, trust, hunger, colonialism, anger, fear, love, being humble, caring, challenging authority, fighting for our rights at all costs, and risking everything in order to live honestly.

I learned about race and racism from the moment I was born. I learned that men could be loving and actually support the women in their lives. I learned the power of affirming one's cultural roots and how easily they could be destroyed. I learned about respecting elders and the importance of intergenerational living. I learned about community and sharing, about hunger and poverty, about trust and *cariño*. And, I learned about being outspoken and being different.

Why did *gente* resist? What caused them to speak out against injustice, hate, humilation, oppression, and destruction? How could people with so little, without political or economic power, risk everything? Simply, they had to. To be silent, to avoid struggle, would mean that their families, *los vecinos, todos alrededor*, would not survive. So they spoke the truth in their own language, they responded to injustices, they fought against the tyranny imposed on them and . . . they suffered the consequences. Lynching, expulsion from their lands, physical pain, loss of language, music, dance, loss of self—all of these are the consequences of resistance, the consequences of survival.

> *Yo soy vicentito, y vengo a cantar*
> *Al niño que llorar, y hacerle callar,*
> *Ni, ni, ni, ni, ni, ni*
> *Ni, so, so, so, so, so*
> *No llores mas bien mio, no llores mas ya no*[6]

ESPERANZA THINKING:
POWER AND COMPLEXITY OF CULTURAL GROUNDING

Fifteen years ago, a group of women dreamed together. We came together as cultural workers, cultural activists. At that time, we wanted to share our limited resources. We wanted to share a space for all of us to meet, talk, and act. We wanted to resist the oppressive policies of this city, this state, this nation, and nations throughout the world. And, one strategy with which to do this was the idea of using art as a tool of political change.

Over fifteen years of work we have come to a much different understanding of cultural activism. Through *muchas discusiones*, Esperanza grew with our shared understandings and experiences. We continue to discuss, get frustrated, dream, and reflect about our visions and our actions.

Our work now is based on a deeper understanding of culture and political change:

Vuela paloma blanca vuela
Dile mi amor
que volvere
Dile que ya no estara tan sola
que nunca mas
me marchare[7]

Este cuento, es como los cuentos de todos ustedes. We need to hear stories of other people as well as our own. In our stories, we tell our joys and fears, how we survive, who we love, how we hate, how we deal with the attacks on our lives, and how we celebrate . . . *todos estos cuentos* are the secret of our survival as *gente*.

In order to resist oppression, we need to remember what our elders, *nuestras antepasados*, taught us. They gave us value and traditions of being good people, of community, of sharing, of respecting, and caring, of *cariño, y compasion, y ternura y dignidad*. From these values we get our strength. And living them, we also shape and recreate them:

Todos me dicen la negra llorona
Negra y cariñosa (repetido)
Yo soy como el chile verde llorana
Picante pero sabrosa (repetido)[8]

Notice. I changed the gender and erased the racist shadows. Subtle but important changes we need to make.

Dice mi Papa, "Hemos olvidado nuestros antepasados por el modernismo y el materialismo." What we do is threatening—our living and teaching values, history, and traditions of *nuestras antepasadas*, our being *Buena Gente*, our recognizing and loving our *Indio, Prieto*, Arab, Jewish, and African features, our many languages, foods, musics, aesthetics, and community responsibilities. By culturally grounding ourselves and our communities, by helping people gain a sense of pride, of self-love, of self-respect, by being *gente* who respect others, work with others, and honor the community, we present a serious challenge to the culture of individualism, an alternative to the culture of violence and domination, and an alternative to the culture of profit over people. The right wing is now explicit in its cultural strategy and its understanding of the power of culture. Domination is much easier if those at the bottom believe in the values of individualism, violence, and profit.

We challenge the fundamental values of white supremacy, sexism, homophobia, and classism that are the basis for everyday oppression in our society.

OUR WORK QUESTIONS THE LEGITIMACY OF POWERFUL PEOPLE AND THEY HAVE TRIED TO SILENCE OR, AT LEAST, TO ISOLATE US

We do threaten the status quo. We work to reveal and weaken the power of violence and exploitation. When we do that, when we speak out and create spaces for people of color, for women, for queer people, for the poor, the homeless, and the undocumented, we do threaten the power of current business, political, religious, and social leaders.

When we speak the truth, it hurts those who benefit from the lies. And, they lash out, wanting to be rid of us, to silence or, at least, to isolate us. The Esperanza Peace and Justice Center has been physically attacked, broken into, and our computers have been stolen. Human feces have been smeared on bras and hung over our cars. We have received threatening phone calls at our homes, and we have been stalked and harassed.

City officials have tried to isolate us. Some gay white men have joined with right-wing activists to attack us and to pressure other arts organizations and Latino organizations to distance themselves from us. Although other arts and Latino organizations in San Antonio are staffed by people who would oppose homophobia, the intensity of the attacks on the Esperanza caused these organizations to fear becoming targets themselves.

We speak the truth and ask the city council members, Who do you represent? And they call us disrespectful, shameful, and lacking civility. They said we have created a "dark cloud over San Antonio." We have "divided the city" (as if the city has not been divided by years and years of racist and classist exploitation).

Sadly, when we speak out, our outspokenness, our boldness, may seem disrespectful to the very people who have taught us the power of truthfulness. Our *antepasados* would not approve, they say. But I believe that honesty with oneself and with others is more valuable and more a part of our history than keeping silent. It is true that the practice of keeping silent has, for generations, been a strategy of survival, of self-protection. Yet *gente* did speak out, and they suffered the consequences. We dishonor those brave voices of the past when we keep silent or, worse yet, join in or accommodate the values of violence and exploitation.

Si se calle el cantor
Calla la vida
Porque la vida, la vida misma es todo un canto
Si se cala el cantor
Muere el espanto, la luz, la alegria y la esperanza[9]

I've been quite scared during past few years because the work is so difficult and the repression is so extreme. The powers that we challenge continue to build up their strength, in part by turning the words and images of liberation to the ends of domination—George W. Bush claims to be the true descendant of Martin Luther King and Caesar Chavez—and in part by promoting and pressuring Latinos to accommodate and assimilate into the culture of violence and to distance themselves from community. Ed Garza was elected mayor in 2001 by refusing to identify as a Latino and refusing to speak Spanish, yet the Hispanic Chamber of Commerce and others have supported and protected him because he is one of their own.

Bush and his relatives and associates have convinced many in the United States that our true enemies are the enemies of capitalism and imperialism. Each day, thousands are dying in our streets because of hunger, disease, and hate, yet we are taught that this is the nation of peace. Immigrants are being shot in the back, enslaved as sex workers, and jailed for no reason. And, we are taught that evil resides in those who reject domination by the United State and its allies. We are told that the struggle for cultural survival of peoples throughout the world is silly, if not insane. We are told that the death of affirmative action is the end of racism.

I am scared because at this time, especially, the work we do is hard and lacks respect, and so very few are willing to take it on. Many of the young Chicanas and African American women and men who have worked at the Esperanza flee to the relative safety of the university, not realizing what they have to lose. Others move on to other cultural groups or more deeply into the individualistic art world. I can understand the fear, but I cannot forget those who refused to run from similar hardships: Emma Tenayuca, Audre Lorde, Manuela Solis Sager, and Dolores Huerta. And sometimes, beaten down by attacks from the outside, we turn anger on each other. We are so used to fighting the enemy, those with power, that we turn against ourselves. We see the shadows and marks of racism, sexism, and homophobia in each other and then refuse to see the rest. Under constant attack from the outside, we fall victim to self-hatred. We can't continue to do this to one another.

We must work with one another. We must continue to offer each other new ways of seeing and invite each other in to share our work. Our work is about social justice, and we must learn to live justly, lovingly. That does not mean that we approve and protect the culture of violence when it is practiced by our allies, but it does mean that we do not turn the violence against each other.

This commitment to change the culture of violence and exploitation explains why, at the Esperanza, we don't throw people away. It explains why we work with whites, African Americans, other Latinos, and Asians, the rich, middle class and poor, the young and old, the queer and straight. It explains why we continue to work with people who, one year ago or fifteen years ago, attacked us, kicked us out of our building, libeled us, stole from us, and called us crazy, racist man-haters.

I hope we can all find ways to protect and strengthen the young activists so that they can remain in *la lucha*. I hope that they, too, can survive by remembering the secrets, the values, the knowledge of those who survived, and can find the methods and strategies to continue to work of those who came before us.

I hope we can find leaders who are strong and wise enough to resist the pressure to accommodate the culture of violence and exploitation. This is a crucial time. *Latino USA*, a program on National Public Radio, enthusiastically reports how more Latinos are running for public offices now than ever before. How have we gotten to this place in history? We assume, perhaps, that when we get our people in, they will make a difference for our community. But our elected and appointed officials, our educated sons (Latinas were not yet running for office) are our *verguenza*. With the exception of Maria Berriozábal, I can think of no other official in the past few years who has dedicated his or her public service to the community. Maria stood alone as an elected official and lost most votes against a council that, like today, is comprised in the majority of people of color. Sadly, the people who have entered electoral politics have tended to be personally ambitious, supported by the white business political elite, and unexamined about the needs of the larger communities of color. Consequently, there was, and continues to be, a split between community and the Latino elected officials. But she won respect from her community.

Salías del templo un dia llorona
Cuando al pasar yo te vi (repetido)
Hermoso huipil llevavas llorona
Que la virgen te cree (repetido)[10]

Cultural domination in public education, the news media, the entertainment industry, and in public funding of the arts continues to choke us. How can diverse artistic and cultural expression occur when the culture still suffers from the murderous disease of colonialism? Centuries of cultural domination have taught us to hate ourselves, to feel dumb, illiterate, and ugly.

So, where do the majority of our *gente* learn to counter this accommodation to violence, this assimilation to the values of profit above people? We must continue to work with others to learn, reclaim, and reform our culture. We need to alter the expectations of our participation. Instead of following Robert's Rules of Order, we need to understand Doña Panchita *y* Doña Chavelita's ways for community. Doña Panchita *y* Doña Chavelita are my grandmother and mother. However, in this context, they represent all the generations of women in my community. We need to strengthen the habit of refusing to accommodate to the culture of violence and refusing to assimilate the rules of domination.

And, following the teachings of Doña Panchita *y* Doña Chavelita, we must tell the truth about the work we're doing, and so we must tell people that we're going to challenge homophobia. We're going to challenge racism, but not merely by resisting its many forms and by speaking the words "race" and "racism" and naming the injury. We're also going to call out sexism and misogyny; we're going to *dar la palabra to mujeres, y jovenes, to jotas y jotos, to trabajadores, e imigrantes.*

As we challenge corporate and mainstream structures, we recognize that we will suffer the consequences. We have no choice. But we do have choices about how we treat each other. As my mother told me when I asked her how she has been able to survive, "When I was young, it hurt, but I had a home, which was my haven. I was surrounded by love." So our movement and the institutions we build, our friends, allies, and ourselves, must recognize that we need to be surrounded with love, *cariño y respeto*, in order to live fully and to continue the revolutionary work that we do.

Our work is about telling our stories, valuing our lives, and understanding the social, economic, and political power structures that maintain us in our roles so that our communities can devise their strategies and solutions to resolve their problems. It's not as simple as challenging people or simply loving each other. Movement building should be about helping to sustain our institutions, about people committed to struggle for justice and finding ways to sustain energy, because we're under attack all the time. How do we learn from each other, learn to see one another, cherish the complexity of our differences, and give each other the love we need to survive?

Doña Panchita knew her neighbors, spoke to them, lobbied for them. She helped birth them and also to laid them to rest. And, Doña Panchita did not work alone. Community was at the core of all her work, at how decisions were arrived at, at how solutions were decided.

Our work has never been about grassroots-inspired organizing but about the theory, and poetry, and fiction, and song of Gloria Anzaldúa, Audre Lorde, Barbara Smith, Cherríe Moraga, Pat Parker, Mercedes Sosa, and Doña Panchita *y* Doña Chavelita.

We have to write our own rules, develop our own language, find new ways to inform and support others in our community. We need to find ways to fund our projects and to create institutions that give voice to those wounded by oppression and domination, that allow us to make decisions for ourselves, that allow us to self-define, to believe in ourselves. We have to do this out of respect for ourselves, out of respect for our communities and for the survival of our *gente*.

Hay de mi Llorona
Llorona del azul celeste
Y aunque me cueste la vida Llorona
No dejare de querete[11]

NOTES

1. The songs and poems in this paper are those I learned growing up. For a couple of years, my father taught his six children and a few neighborhood friends traditional Mexican/Latino songs. I've included stanzas of some of those songs throughout the text because they are part of my life, my memories. Some of these songs do not have any specific meaning within the text, but when performed, the melodies are soothing and grounding to me.

2. Charming Damisela
   Damisela I give my life for you
   If you look at me, if you kiss me,
   Damisela you will be my love

Ernesto Ecuona, "*Damisela Encantadora*," a cuban song heard while I was growing up as sung by Juan Arvizu, *El Tenor de la Voz de Seda*, RCA Victor Mexicana, 1962 and 1996, Bertelsmann de Mexico, S.A. De C.V., trans. by author.

3. The fools of the town of San Juan
   Ask for bread and ask for cheese

"*Los Maderos de San Juan*," a children's rhyme that I memorized when I was first learning to read. While I was being taught to read English in school, I was still unsure about so many words that surrounded me at home and in the streets of my neighborhood. I learned to read in Spanish by asking my parents how certain words were pronounced.

When I discovered this poetry book at home and found this rhyme, I started memorizing it because I loved the way the words sounded together (trans. by author).

4. Others, like my Uncle Mino, who could pass for black (trans. by author).

5. Pin Pon is a puppet
Of cloth and cardboard
S/he washes her little hands with water and soap
She untangles her hair
With an ivory comb
And even with pulling and tugging
She doesn't cry or grimace
Pin Pon give me a strong handshake
I want to be your friend
Pin Pon, Pin Pon, Pin Pon

"*Pin Pon*" is a traditional Mexican children's song (trans. by author).

6. I am a crowd follower
And I come to sing
To the baby Jesus who cries and help put him to sleep
Ni, ni, ni, ni, ni, ni
Ni, so, so, so, so, so
Don't cry my little one, don't cry anymore

"*Yo Soy Vicentito*" is a Spanish Christmas carol (*Villancico*) (trans. by author) *Villancico* and others were taught by my father to his children. My mother made sure that my sister and I sang this song as a duet during the Christmas season, both at church and during the *Posadas*.

7. Fly white dove, fly
Tell my love that I shall return
Tell her that she will no longer be so lonely
That I will never leave her again

This untitled traditional Mexican love song that my father taught me became famous during the 1940s and 1950s. When I asked my father why he taught us these songs, he explained that they needed to be easy enough for young children to learn, and they had to be pleasant to the ear (trans. by author).

8. Everyone, Llorona calls me the Black One
Black and affectionate
I'm like the green chile, Llorona
Spicy but delicious

"*La Llorona*," a traditional Mexican *huapango*, was recorded by many artists, including Chavela Vargas (recorded in Madrid, 1999, distributed by Warner Music, Mexico) and Lila Downs (La Sandunga, Aries Music Ent., June 1999). The original refrain, "*Todos me dicen el negro Llorona, El negro*," suggests a male voice. "*Negro pero cariñoso*" translates into "black but loving."

9. If the singer dies, life dies
   Because life itself is a song
   If the singer dies, terror dies
   As does light, happiness and hope

Horacio Guarany, "*Si Se Calla El Cantor*," a song made famous by Mercedes Sosa, an Argentinian Nueva Cancion singer (*Mercedes Sosa: 30 Años*, 1993, Polygram Latino U.S., a division of Polygram Records, Inc., trans. by author).

10. You were coming out of the church, Llorona
    When I saw you passing by
    You were wearing a beautiful *huipil* (a woman's chemise), Llorona,
    You looked so beautiful that I thought you were the Virgin

"*La Llorona*" (trans. by author).

11. Oh my Llorona
    Llorona from the blue skies
    Even if it takes my life away Llorona
    I will never stop loving you

"*La Llorona*" (trans. by author).

Performance Artist María Elena Gaitán

Mapping a Continent without Borders
(*Epics of* Gente Atravesada, Traviesa, y Entremetida)

YOLANDA BROYLES-GONZÁLEZ

THE ONE WOMAN-SHOW: POST-*MOVIMIENTO* WOMEN'S VOICES

A survey of Chicana/o theater topography from the mid-twentieth to the twenty-first centuries—from the Chicana/o civil rights movement to the present—reveals three major performance strands. The first is the 1950s and 1960s working-class itinerant tent-shows (*carpas*) and then dozens of *movimiento* (civil rights movement) collectives, virtually all of them now defunct. Performance collectives featured low-budget and highly-mobile oral creations conceived through the collective improvisational process, stored in the memory through oral tradition, and performed anywhere possible: the streets, the fields, classrooms, or stages. These highly-topical creations ranged from the usually male-centered one-act *actos* (skits) to the full-length epics, such as Teatro Campesino's *Gran Carpa de la Familia Rasquachi*.[1] A second strand is the mostly post-*movimiento*, individually-authored dramatized literary works characteristic of Chicanas/os "breaking into print."[2] These individually-authored works mark the move from an alternative theatrical movement into the establishment mainstream of proscenium theater, ranging from small theaters to the high-tech, monied performance venues. Examples range from Cherríe Moraga's plays from as early as the 1980s, such as her *Giving Up the Ghost* (1984), to Teatro Campesino/Luis Valdez's *Zoot Suit* (1978–1979), and the Latino Theater Group's *August 29* (1990).[3] A third distinguishable strand is the more contemporary proliferation of one-woman (or one-man) performance pieces presented anywhere possible, some existing earlier in the *Raza* (Chicana/o) movement of the 1980s. These early solo performances include the relatively rare one-woman, multi-voiced poetry performances, such as Carmen Tafolla's *Los Courts* and Denise Chávez's *Novena Narrativa*.[4]

Although these three strands are distinct and historically specific, there is some degree of kinship, exchange, and even a causal relationship among the three. The shoestring collectives emerged in times of intense social movements during the 1960s and 1970s, while the high-tech, individually-authored performance pieces arose with the emergence of a Chicana/o middle class. Today's one-woman performance creations show much kinship with the creations of the struggling itinerant 1960s collectives that could perform virtually anywhere, but, when feasible, today's women performance artists also incorporate high-tech elements. The historical specificity of the contemporary one-woman show's emergence has to do with the rise of women and gay/lesbian liberation movements as much as with the alienation so many women, gays, and lesbians faced in the *movimiento teatro* (and other political) collectives.[5] There is even a causal relationship between the collapse of the male-centered, misogynist, and often homophobic collectives and the rise of women's and men's solo performance art. Collectives characteristically featured an entrenched male leadership, and as an extension of the sexist leadership, *movimiento* theater collectives also featured performance pieces with universalized maleness as the center of all dramatized human experience. Many of today's Chicana one-woman shows grew from the negative patriarchal legacy of the civil rights movement. Veteran women activists carry deep scars and have waged protracted battles to manifest their voices. The one-woman show has experienced a boom in the last fifteen years and yet has received little critical attention, although one of Los Angeles's major live mainstream theaters venues, the Mark Taper Forum, acknowledged the strong presence of solo performers during an evening showcase titled "Diva L.A."[6]

In terms of their visibility and numbers, these women solo performers have come to represent contemporary Chicana/o theater, just as the dozens of alternative theater collectives—the now defunct *Teatristas*—represented the *Raza* movement during the 1960s through the 1970s. Although the staging of individually-authored plays in proscenium theater houses has dramatically increased, performances still remain sporadic at best. In contrast, one-woman shows are more visible and more immediate in their response to the issues of the day. The performances have the freedom to be radically countercultural and creative because they are neither tied to the censorship and aesthetic expectations of theatrical institutions, nor are they tied to dominating men. That freedom has allowed strong women's voices to finally be heard. Solo performance artists enjoy great independence, flexibility, and mobility, and space for the performances can be found almost anywhere. However, the price exacted for that independence is economic instability and a hard life on the road. María Elena Gaitán, for example, could not dedicate herself full time to performance until her son was grown and financially independent.

In the short space allotted me here, I want to examine the contributions of performance artist Gaitán, who is among the most notable and active contemporary performers of one-woman shows touring the United States and other countries. Over one decade she has created and performed five one-woman shows. Each of these shows has gone through a process of evolution, growth, and transformation over time. Thus, each show is the sum of many different recycled versions. In chronological order they are: *Chola con Cello: A Home Girl In The Philharmonic* (1992), *De Jarocha a Pocha* (1995), *Aztlan Africa: Songs of Affinity* (1998), *The Adventures of Connie Chancla* (1999), *The Teta Show* (2003), and a number of stand-up comedy shows.[7]

Gaitán's formal training and life experience provided rich preparation for her performance work. She is a woman of many lives, born to a musician mother from Monterrey, Nuevo León, México, and a working-class father, a Tejano of many generations. Her musician mother later became a high school teacher in East Los Angeles and codesigned the first bilingual education program for the Los Angeles Unified School District. Her father broke the color line by winning election to the Del Rio, Texas, city council and an appointment as a boxing commissioner for the state of Texas. Gaitán was born in 1949 and raised in East Los Angeles. She trained classically as a cellist, and as a child won various local and state scholarships, performed at age fifteen with the Pasadena Symphony, and won a scholarship to the California Institute of the Arts School of Music. Later she studied at California State University in Los Angeles. In her late teens she abandoned the cello—which had been such an important part of her "voice"—and dedicated herself to civil rights activism, working with the United Farm Workers of America as well as with Centro de Acción Social Autonomo Hermandad Mexicana (CASA).[8] In 1980 she graduated from the court interpreter's program at the University of California in Los Angles and began working as a certified court interpreter. She raised her son, Octavio Tizóc, alone, and she became the first Chicana ever appointed to the Los Angeles County Office of Education, serving also as its outspoken vice president.

Gaitán emerged as a performer in the context of the 1992 Los Angeles riots triggered by the acquittal of four Los Angeles policemen who brutally beat an unarmed Aftrican American, Rodney King. Los Angeles was in flames; hundreds were arrested. Gaitán was reborn from those warm ashes as a performance artist. What emerged was her continued political commitment to her community, as well as her commitment to establish her voice as an Indigenous Chicana woman and her desire to develop her artistic authority in new ways.

Gaitán fully assumes the power potential of the one-woman show. She is not beholding to any of the established theatrical institutions, which tend to tokenize, trivialize, and censor *Raza* performance art, allowing only for what she calls "an occasional Beaner Night at the Mark Taper Forum."[9] Her perfor-

María Elena Gaitán in comedic performance. Photo courtesy of Gia Rowland.

mances are politically and aesthetically motivated. Her political concerns arise from the social crisis generated in California by the passage of xenophobic and anti-immigrant ballot propositions. *Chola Con Cello*, for example, was a response to California's Proposition 187, passed by voters in 1992. Proposition 187 sought to deny public education to undocumented immigrant children, while also denying prenatal care to undocumented women immigrants. It was followed in 1998 by Proposition 227, which dismantled bilingual education, and then Proposition 209, which dismantled affirmative action. Various other ballot measures primarily targeting youth of color have also been passed.

WATCHING GAITÁN'S AUDIENCE: WHY THIS APPARENT HUNGER?

The starting point of my analysis comes from witnessing and exploring the exchange of energy between performer and audience at a performance of *The Adventures of Connie Chancla*.[10] One March evening in 2001 I drove two hours to the predominantly *Raza* agricultural community of Santa Maria on California's central coast. I wanted to experience a Gaitán performance in a non-university, nonacademic, and non-Los Angeles setting. I wanted to experience Gaitán's performance with regular working-class people. She was performing at Santa Maria High School, an accessible and familiar space for poor working families. There was great anticipation in the long line that waited for the doors to open.

Once the performance began, the packed house quickly became captivated by the striking persona/narrator of Connie Chancla and participated in the history lesson she gave with an attentiveness that often broke into audience comments and bouts of laughter. In *The Adventures of Connie Chancla*, one of the most ambitious performance undertakings of recent years, Gaitán reconstructs the hemispheric history of the Americas through the collective millenarian history of the "Chancla People," and delivers it through the outspoken persona of Connie Chancla. All of her historical narrative, beginning with precolonial Indigenous history, is enhanced with the help of dozens of slides and with musical performances. The revolutionary ways in which she reconstructs borderlands history is underscored by the imposing eccentricity of her persona. She wears a huge green wig with giant braids, a black smock with white polka dots, and glittery make-up. The history lesson she delivers is hilarious and spiced with expletives.

After the performance ended and the applause and cheering were over, Gaitán reappeared and came down from the stage. An interesting dynamic ensued: Although audience members were exiting and had their backs to the stage, when they felt Gaitán's presence, they made an about-face and headed toward her. I was touched to see person after person (80 percent were young women) stand with Gaitán while a family member took a photo. I wondered, What are they wanting to capture? What did Gaitán give them? The aftersession, photos, and conversations lasted almost an hour.

One avenue for understanding the appeal of Gaitán's performance presence has to do with the affirmation the show gives *Raza* women who comprise the nonexclusive center of her historical vision. Gaitán opens new visual, spiritual, physical, and intellectual women's spaces between the official histories and young audiences who are force-fed those histories. That is what I call *entremeter*, meaning "to come between" and "to speak without being asked," or "to interrupt impudently." *Entremeter* also carries the connotation of "voicing" and breaking decorum, breaking the established ongoing rules of his-story, interrupting and inserting new elements, and breaking onto the scene. Gaitán says of herself, "I've fought for my own space. It didn't come from an agent or an institution."[11] Gaitán's *entremetida* stance involves the resistance of creating a distance between audiences and standard Eurocentric, male-centered histories. She thus opens a new liberatory space for *Raza* women. *The Adventures of Connie Chancla* begins and ends with an abundant display of womanist images. Photographs make the officially "invisibilized" agents of history visible by highlighting facets of the multiple identities of women in the Americas *sin fronteras* (without borders).

The audience hungers for those sustaining images, for those self-affirming spaces that she opens up. Wherever she performs *Connie Chancla*, Gaitán reverses the erasure of *Raza* women within the borderlands, school curricula, and the media. As a parent of two adolescent children, I constantly struggle with this curricular gynocide and culturcide. University curricula are not much better—save for the occasional Chicana studies course. Looking for *la Chicana Indígena* in public school textbooks is an exercise in futility. Thus, the curriculum of erasure and social marginalization is the daily bread for *Raza* women in the schools. By virtue of its mobility and accessibility, not to mention the utter inaccessibility of most printed academic materials on *Raza* women, Gaitán's *Connie Chancla* provides a liberated gender zone for teen *Raza* women (and, of course, young men). It is perhaps the only such performance of an alternative herstory now performed in community centers, schools, church basements, and college campuses, and witnessed by thousands of *Raza* youth.

Another aspect of Gaitán's performance is compelling. Her truths are explosive, spoken vividly in explicit terms. They have the quality of a *limpia* or a *grito*—a ritual purification. Her humor and rowdiness, her reckoning with received knowledge—such as that provided by official U.S. male-centered histories—shatter academic space. She is a crosswise woman (*atravesada*); she crosses conventions, borders, and hierarchies with wisdom. *Atraviesa las reglas de hablar y decir, atraviesa la historia y sus fronteras nacionales* (She crosses linguistic conventions, received histories, and national boundaries). Gaitán is unequivocally, openly, and defiantly committed to speaking the truth to empower others.

In her performance piece *Chola con Cello: A Home Girl in the Philharmonic* she affirms human and artistic freedom by combining, and thus reconfiguring, disparate elements of creative cultural possibility: the home girl in the philharmonic, bilinguality, and the breaking of gender expectations with the cello—all while eschewing oppression. These are her words as she first encounters the audience:

> Thank you. Thank you. *¿Como están todos* tonight, eh? You know, I've always had to fight for my *pinchi* rights . . . even to play the cello. It's hard being a Chicana. Even the Homies used to get on my case. Oh, and then I had an aunt who hated me to play the cello. She used to go: "*Ay, Sufrida, ¿porqué tienes que tocar ese instrumento tan grandote?* Such a big instrument . . . between your legs . . . in front of all the people. Ay, how embarrassing!!" *Pinchi vieja neurótica ignorante.* Thank God I never listened to her *¿verdad?* Oh, and then the peoples in classical music, they didn't like me neither, eh. Imagine, a Home Girl in the Philharmonic. . . . You got a bunch of *pinchi gente tapada* in there.[12]

Gaitán's performance venues are all in alternative spaces. Since the beginning of her performance career Gaitán has refused to perform in the kinds of institutions that silence truth, that make mincemeat out of truth, that exchange paychecks for discretion. It is significant that Gaitán has made a commitment to her social truths that require her to work as a migrant. Gaitán reclaims submerged identities in her performances town by town, campus by campus, high school by high school, neighborhood by neighborhood. I can understand her public appeal: She holds up a mirror of affirmation and performs a ritual of collective self-definition and remembrance in a society that systematically cultivates historical amnesia and oppressive boundaries.

CHICANA *INDÍGENA* VOICE

Gaitán came of age in California during the *Raza* civil rights movement of the 1960s and 1970s. Although the *Raza* movement was a rich, empowering, and tumultuous experience, those struggles also left many wounds and many unvoiced concerns, particularly about gender and sexuality. I discuss some of that sexism as well as women's creative responses to it in my book *El Teatro Campesino: Theater in the Chicano Movement.*[13] Women's truths, history, bodies, and powers were often suppressed through physical violence during that period. It is no coincidence that Chicana women's expressive culture did not experience a flowering until the *movimiento* had collapsed from its own internal contradictions, most notably its misogyny and homophobia. As an activist, Gaitán experienced male violence firsthand, within the very organizations that sought social justice. Her own voice—along with her cello playing—were in many ways muted and only flourished through the subsequent voices she has cultivated as a performance artist. Hers is the mature, emancipated post-*movimiento* woman's solo voice. She enjoys complete artistic control over her neo-*rasquachi* performances, and she deploys her control in part to obliterate patriarchal and nationalist agendas while advancing a womanist political vision by placing at centerstage a strong Indigenous Chicana voice. In her own words, "The absence of indigenous women's voices everywhere in my life is a big issue for me. I put that *India* voice in the center of my work. I represent the *India* voice." [14]

Gaitán's performances mark the continuation of the longstanding Indigenous *rasquachi* aesthetic practiced by Indigenous collectives since the beginning of time and into the 1960s and 1970s. Although I cannot offer a complete discussion of the traditional *rasquachismo* here, I do want to highlight some of its key elements. The *rasquachi* aesthetic is the inventiveness driven by necessity: not only economic necessity, but also by the need to resist, to speak out, and to address the burning issues of the day. *Rasquachismo* makes the most out of very limited performance resources and, thus, is not ensnared in the cumbersome machinery of theatrical productions, their aesthetics, and their politics. Although some may consider *rasquachismo* unsophisticated—because it lacks the full trappings of a proscenium theater—it is highly sophisticated in terms of its instant creativity, its appropriation and inventive mixture of diverse cultural elements, its mobility, subversive topicality, radical satirical humor, and improvisational capacity. It does not require ten weeks of rehearsal and a playwright with a year's grant or residency. Its constitutive elements are typically derived from a wide range of readily available cultural resources.

Through *The Adventures of Connie Chancla*, Gaitán unearths and exposes the officially obscured and invisible history of *Raza* peoples, especially of *Raza* working-class women. Gaitán calls these women "the Chancla people," and this performance is a clan history of Native *Raza* peoples who experience daily the effects of poverty and colonization. The *chancla*, a worn and torn shoe, is a symbol of working-class *Raza* who, like the *chancla*, are unpretentious and always on the move.

The protagonist's name and identity also symbolically mark the union of two forms of colonization in the Americas: that in English (Connie instead of Consuelo) and that in Spanish (Chancla). Trilinguality (Spanish, English, and Nahuatl) is spoken throughout. The realities of female Nativeness—in all their hybrid forms—continually resurface throughout the performance. Indigenous women and gender relations are centered within the hilarious his-

María Elena Gaitán in "The Adventures of Connie Chancla." Photo courtesy of Misha Erwitt.

torical discourse of Connie Chancla's character. As a barrio historian, Connie Chancla foregrounds the strength, beauty, historical trauma, and survival of Native Chicana women, while taking issue with the various faces of colonial misogyny. In the scene called "Malinche maligned," or example, Gaitán establishes a powerful Chancla womanist historical lineage. Connie Chancla names these *antepasadas* (forebearers), including "Malin-Chancla," "Greatgrandma Chencha Chancla," "Greatgrandmas China Chancla and Chole Chancla," as well as "Grandma Lupe and Lupe's best friend Darlene." These are the Native Chicana women of the mythical Native homeland, Aztlán. The concept of Aztlán emerges as representation and remembrance of the Chicana/o Native borderlands populated by very strong women.

Barrio historian Connie Chancla adeptly unfolds a rich panoramic exploration of *Raza* history. She functions as a woman elder speaking *historia* (history).[15] Although Gaitán follows in the *rasquachi* footsteps of *movimiento teatristas*, hers is a nouveau high-tech *rasquachismo*. Her use of various media, including spoken word, video, taped and live musical performance, and slides allows for quick movement between multiple lines of thought and performance textures. She does not pursue any extended dramatic stories but rather weaves ideas, imagery, and musical performance into a *trenza* (braid).

The first strand begins with a dozen or so slides of women, which she accompanies one-by-one with a live cello performance. These initial Native American images relate directly, by the end of the show, to the slides of historical and contemporary *Raza* women. She introduces the Chancla people's Native Chicana genealogy before colonization, including reference to naked bodies ("We were once the Happy Naked Chanclas") as well as reference to "The Centrality of the Drum."[16]

A second interwoven strand reconstructs the arrival of colonization and the resistance of the Chancla peoples. Connie Chancla highlights the Chancla peoples' struggles, resilience, and self-affirmation in the face of colonization. She does so, for example, by reminding us of anticolonial struggles, such as the rebellion led by California Tonga tribal Native Toypurina, who helped organize the uprising against Mission San Gabriel in California in 1785. Another example is her many references to the soil of culture as the "wounded borderlands." Euroamerican colonial hubris and landmass appropriation are exposed and decried, when she states, "At Mount Rushmore . . . they carved the faces of their own gringo forefathers into the sacred rocks of the Chancla people." Connie Chancla describes the social dynamic of de-Indianization while celebrating contemporary Native survival.[17]

A third strand involves the intermittent discussion of the ongoing effects of the U.S.-Mexican War and the Treaty of Guadalupe Hidalgo. The Chanclas become *"Pochas Chanclas"* (*"pocha"* is used to denote bicultural Chicanas). Here Connie Chancla sets forth quick-paced cultural commentaries concerning sexual and body politics, including *pocha* fashion, tattoos, makeup, and cuisine. She also comments on lowriders and makes brief references to Chancla men. Connie Chancla deals with contemporary politics by lining up and berating male establishment politicians, including Clinton, Bush, and Henry Cisneros (former mayor of San Antonio and Clinton cabinet member). She also includes local politicians from the towns where she performs.

Although the show's title, *The Adventures of Connie Chancla*, features an individual, it is not a performance about any single individual. The piece is a radical departure from the individualistic *bildungs*-trajectory conventionally signaled by such titles. In the course of the performance we come to see the Connie Chancla figure as a collective identity, not an individual identity.

GENTE ATRAVESADA: CROSSWISE PEOPLE OF THE LAND

The borderlands figure prominently in the historical narration of Connie Chancla. *La línea divisoria* is the wound the nation-states inflicted upon the land. Connie Chancla repeatedly refers to the borderland as "the wounded borderlands" and "the wounded border," and includes a reference to the fact that "the land has memory."[18] Thus, Connie Chancla envisions the borderlands not just as an abstract political intersection of nations or armchair academic paradigms concerning cultural hybridity, but as a living unified Indigenous land base.

The land is memory, and it is also contemporary reality. Current notions of land ownership as real estate obscure the fact that people are part of the land. Connie Chancla reminds us that the land carries the very lifeblood of immigrants who suffer the violence of contemporary immigration policy. *The Adventures of Connie Chancla* reaches one of its climaxes in the sustained video display of the brutal 1996 Riverside, California, police beating of immigrant Alicia Sotero Vazquez and, symbolically, of all poor *Raza* women.[19] The footage is looped and runs for several minutes. Connie Chancla interrupts her commentary and accompanies the visual images of this brutal beating with cello music. History comes close-up and is woman-centered as the arresting police repeatedly smash Alicia Sotero Vazquez's face into the side of a car. As spectators we are similarly captured, as the scene moves into slow motion. We are terrified as we witness U.S.-Mexican borderland atrocities visited upon an Indigenous woman's body. Chicanas/os history is created at the place where two nation-states collide.

Gaitán then underscores the transnational brutalization of women with a cello performance, a sweet legato piece that provides a disconcerting harmony to the disharmony of the assault on Native women. The cello sings to the oppressive and exploitative national political history played out on the bodies of women and men who try to cross: *gente que atraviesa, gente atravesada*. Gaitán comments on the music, "For me, the music is a spiritual place from which to view the atrocity, a place from which the viewer can see the terrible thing. The music opens up the heart."[20] Alicia Sotero Vazquez is an example of Gloria Anzaldúa's proverbial woman whose home "is this thin edge of barbwire."[21] That woman crosses the border to look for work and survival in the militarized border zone. At one point Connie Chancla states, "The border has become a painful place where the Chancla people are being hunted and shot like deer."[22]

The persona of Connie Chancla deserves some attention. She is the classical *pelada* (working-class comedic figure), the *payasa* (clown), the trickster, the *atravesada*, thinking, speaking, and historicizing at cross-purposes with the nation-states and their powerholders. The Chancla people are *gente atravesada* who cross and transgress the neat categories of nation, its borders, hierarchies, and narratives. Gaitán as Connie Chancla performs the border as a terrain of diverse interlocking cultural movements, clashes, and cultural harmonies. People and languages meet, intertwine, converge, clash, and evolve at a fast pace and on a daily basis. Bilinguality and trilinguality are a fact of *Raza* life. *La linea divisoria* (the U.S.-Mexico border) is the place of greatest interaction, the place where the transnational and supranational is most evident and active.

The persona of Connie Chancla is *atravesada* in its several meanings: *atravesada* carries the sense of crisscrossing and of connecting two things that might be considered detached. By spanning the borderlands, Connie Chancla reunites separated meanings created by the imagined communities of nation-states. She remakes Aztlán, the North-South connection enacted in ancient pilgrimages by *Raza* ancestors. Native American wisdom reminds us that all oppositions are contingent and complementary. Everything will always contain its (marked or unmarked) opposite, whether we perceive it or not, want it or not. Connie Chancla continually reminds us of these oppositional complementarities. Indeed, Connie Chancla performs her powerful decolonial consciousness from within the belly of the colonial beast.

Atravesada also implies a sense of transgression, of confrontation, of challenging, of trespassing, of being out of official boundaries. Connie Chancla is the consummate *atravesada* who wipes out patriarchal national narratives. Anzaldúa refers to "*los atravesados*" as "the squint-eyed, the perverse, the queer, the troublesome, the mongrel, the mulatto, the half-breed, the half dead: in short, those who cross over, pass over, or go through the confines of the 'normal.'"[23] *The Adventures of Connie Chancla* extend that meaning in various directions. She performs multiple challenges to any neat and oppressive categories and social hierarchies that are often taken for granted in our daily lives: hierarchies of gender, culture, race, sexuality, of nations, of power relations, and of environmental degradations, all of which enable human rights violations. Her historical discourse exposes the colonial power relations that have naturalized national boundaries and hierarchies. She denaturalizes and transgresses the official history of social elites while proclaiming the marginalized histories of the border crossers.

With her bold vocabulary, expletives, and womanist truths, Gaitán is radically out of official bounds as she establishes for us the outlines of formerly occluded and eclipsed *indígena* womanist territories, images, histories, faces, meanings. She then reconfigures histories in utterly hilarious terms: Connie Chancla's historical discourse provokes incessant laughter. Only cultural histories in print have to be serious in order to deflect "*el que dirán*" of institutional (academically disciplined) histories.[24] But for barrio historians, truth can be packaged *a como de lugar* (by any means possible).

RECONSTITUTING *TRAVESURA*: GAITAN'S NEO-*RASQUACHISMO*

The historical medium for Connie Chancla is comedy. When the *atravesada* is grotesquely comical, then she is a *traviesa*, a trickster. Laughter is the ingredient the magically changes everything, which turns the *atravesada* into a *traviesa*, the trickster who shocks us out of the complacency of seriousness. Connie Chancla's attire is shocking and patently *traviesa*: her huge green wig with bright flowers, her shirt with huge polka dots, and, yes, lots of makeup and glitter on her face. She is an extravagant *traviesa atravesada pelada*. My reference to Connie Chancla as a trickster or clown (the *pelada* or *payasa*) bears further elaboration. The personage of Connie Chancla fits squarely within the Indigenous tradition of the sacred clowns who are present in the context of most ritual performance as a constant complement to seriousness. The clown or trickster, in fact, functions to dispel the seriousness of the sacred (here of the anointed histories) and to violate established ceremonial boundaries and conventions.

Ritual sacred clowns shake people out of their complacency, and Gaitán's performance is visually, emotionally, intellectually, physically, and spiritually jarring. Her discussion of "*La mentira sistematica*" or of "fake chi-chis" and "real chi-chis," and her critique of the term "*puta*" jars people into reconsidering the history they are taught. For example, when she ridicules the notion of colonizer priests helping "the poor dumb Indians," she is wakening and changing people's consciousness.[25] Audiences are made to feel uncomfortable and irritated. Connie Chancla subverts the established master colonial histories. An audience member may disagree with her, but that person has been forced to look at history differently. Clowns enact the unspeakable. There are no boundaries or borders that laughter cannot tumble. Gaitán draws us into this place of laughter, where it can assist us in leaping over oppressive social boundaries and in imagining freedom.

Gaitán often refers to her artistic preparation and process as "hunting and gathering." She hunts for and gathers ideas, images, costumes, slides, music, musicians, and more on an ongoing basis. Her performance pieces evolve further in the course of each new presentation and all presentations, held together by the central comic stock figure of the Connie Chancla *pelada* figure, the clown whose vision comes from the bottom up.

WHAT BORDERLANDS ARE THESE?

Given the flood of borderlands writing triggered by Anzaldúa's *borderlands/La Frontera*, it is important to explain Connie Chancla's borderlands. The borderlands boom that followed Anzaldúa has made some buzz words obligatory; among them are words like hybridity, *mestizaje*, fusion, acculturation, syncretism, and multiple identities. All cultures on the planet are hybrid, and everyone is a mestizo because there is no cultural purity. However, specification is needed about the nature of the mix. We need to ask: How does Gaitán define borderlands in her performances? The space and cultural dynamic she unfolds is not a simple mixture of contiguous cultures. The borderlands are the crossroads where colonization interact with the Indigenous on a daily basis. In *The Adventures of Connie Chancla* cultural elements are shown to be appropriated from colonizers and then Indianized as they are assimilated into the Mesoamerican Indigenous cultural and historical matrix. Thus, even the appropriated elements affirm the presence of Native American identity, of hybridity, of resistance and survival. Culturally speaking, the origins of appropriated cultural elements cease to be important; what is important is who controls them and the deeper underlying Native cultural strata that those elements express. For Connie Chancla, the cultural geography and civilization of the borderlands remains Native in spite of multiple colonial presences. She is the embodiment of the longstanding Indigenous civilizations of this continent, whose struggles for survival and self-affirmation continue.

The work of borderlands syncretism could be said to constitute one of the great humanistic feats of the Americas. It is the capacity of colonized peoples to absorb, transform, and integrate colonial cultural features into the Native cultural matrix. María Elena Gaitan's performance work forms part of contemporary strategic Native humanism performed by Chicana nation. Grounded in an Indigenous matrix, she constructs new decolonial womanist histories and visions for rethinking and recreating the Americas.

An earlier version of this paper was presented at the Gender on the Borderlands conference sponsored by St. Mary's University, San Antonio, Texas, July 13–14, 2001. I presented an earlier draft in Mexico at the June 2001 international conference of the Hemispheric Institute of Performance and Politics.

1. *La Gran Carpa* was collectively authored by the *Teatro Campesino* ensemble. It was rewritten four different times between 1972 and 1979. It toured throughout the United States and Europe, and was presented in hundreds of venues. *El Teatro Campesino* was based in San Juan Bautista, California, and toured widely until its demise in 1981.

2. Chicana/o culture is rooted in the oral tradition of Native American cultures. It is only after the Civil Rights Movement of the 1960s that Chicanas/os gained the first appreciable access to universities, theaters, and publishing. This access allowed them to "break into print."

3. Cherríe L. Moraga, *Heroes and Saints & Other Plays: Giving Up the Ghost, Shadow of a Man, Heroes and Saints* (Albuquerque: University of New Mexico Press, 2001); and Luis Valdez, *Zoot Suit and Other Plays* (Houston: Arte Publico Press, 1992).

4. Carmen Tafolla, "Lost Courts (5 Voices)" in *Five Poets of Aztlan*, ed. Santiago Daydi-Tolson (New York: Bilingual Press, 1985); and Denise Chavez, "Novena Narrativas y Ofrendas Nuevomexicanas," *The Americas Review* 15:304 (1987): 85–100.

5. Cherríe Moraga does a brilliant retrospective critique of the *movimiento* from a radical lesbian feminist perspective in "Queer Aztlan: The Re-formation of Chicano Tribe" in her book *The Last Generation: Prose & Poetry* (Boston: South End Press, 1993).

6. Most theater research has tended to privilege the full-length play and the multi-character shorter plays. Significant Latina research includes the first such anthology of plays, *Shattering the Myth: Plays by Hispanic Women*, ed. Linda Feyder (Houston: Arte Público Press, 1992), followed by other anthologies, such as *Puro Teatro: A Latina Anthology*, ed. Alberto Sandoval-Sánchez and Nancy Saporta Sternbach (Tucson: University of Arizona Press, 2000) and its accompanying volume of critical studies titled *Stages of Life: Transcultural Performance and Identity in U.S. Latina Theater*, ed. Alberto Sandoval-Sánchez and Nancy Saporta Sternbach (Tucson: University of Arizona Press, 2001). I would also refer readers to the eloquent and groundbreaking volume by José Esteban Muñoz, *Disidentification: Queers of Color and the Performance of Politics* (Minneapolis: University of Minnesota Press, 1999), written at the intersection of sexuality, race, and politics. Another important anthology is *Out of the Fringe: Contemporary Latina/Latino Theatre and Performance*, ed. Caridad Svich and María Teresa Marrero (New York: Consortium, 2000). In terms of criticism, Alicia Arrizón's incisive in-depth study *Latina Performance: Traversing the Stage* (Bloomington: Indiana University Press, 1999) does include a discussion of two one-woman pieces. Elizabeth C. Ramírez very

briefly discusses four women performance artists in her book *Chicanas/Latinas in American Theatre: A History of Performance* (Bloomington: Indiana University Press, 2000), 126–28. The only publication that mentions the work of María Elena Gaitán (if only in highly tokenized form) is *Corpus Delecti: Performance Art of the Americas*, ed. Coco Fusco (London: Routledge, 2000). In his *Chicano Drama: Performance, Society, and Myth* (New York: Cambridge University Press, 2001), Jorge Huerta gives a vivid overview of the individually-authored dramatic literature produced in the last two decades of the twentieth-century, but does not treat performance art.

Some of the contemporary Chicana solo performers who foreground women's visions and voices include (in alphabetical order): Adelina Anthony, Nao Bustamante, Denise Chávez, Olivia Chumacero, Elvira and Hortensia Colorado, Consuelo Flores, Rosa María Escalante, Laura Esparza, María Elena Fernández, María Elena Gaitán, Linda Gamboa, Marisela Norte, Monica Palacios, Ruby Nelda Pérez, Diane Rodríguez, Paulina Sahagún, Raquel Salinas, and Silviana Wood. Other Latinas (across various borders) include Coco Fusco, Marga Gómez, Astrid Hadad, Carmelita Tropicana, and Jesusa Rodríguez. I would also include here the spoken-word performances known as "slams," whose performers feature a whole new generation of women.

7. All of Gaitán's plays are unpublished. *De Jarocha a Pocha* was created under very difficult circumstances in collaboration with two men, which Gaitán refers to as "an abortion."

8. *Centro de Acción Social Autonomo or CASA Hermandad Mexicana* was directed by Bert Corona. In response to the anti-immigrant hysteria of the late 1960s and 1970s, Bert Corona and Soledad "Chole" Alatorre established CASA in Los Angeles. Additional chapters were later founded in five other cities. The organization helped conceptualize the protection of undocumented workers as a civil and human rights issue. At one time CASA claimed a membership of over two thousand undocumented workers. CASA dissolved by the late 1970s.

9. This quote speaks to the exclusion and then tokenization of *Raza* performance in mainstream Euroamerican-dominated theater houses such as the Los Angeles Mark Taper forum. María Elena Gaitán, interview with Yolanda Broyles-González, Santa Barbara, California, November 11, 2000.

10. *The Adventures of Connie Chancla*, a multimedia performance piece commissioned in 1998 by UCLA's César Chávez Center for the Interdisciplinary Study of Chicanas and Chicanos to commemorate the one-hundred-fiftieth anniversary of the Treaty of Guadalupe Hidalgo. The 1848 treaty marked the official end of the U.S. war of aggression against Mexico, a war that shifted the meanings of north and south, a war by which the United states annexed over half of Mexico, including present day California, Utah, Texas, New Mexico, Colorado, and Arizona.

11. Gaitán, interview with author.

12. Gaitán, *Chola con Cello: A Home Girl in the Philharmonic*, 1999.

13. Yolanda Broyles-Gonzalez, *El Teatro Campesino: Theater in the Chicano Movement* (Austin: University of Texas Press, 1994).

14. Gaitán, interview with author.

15. I write extensively about Chicana history as *historia* in my book *Lydia Mendoza's Life in Music: Norteño Tejano Legacies /La Historia de Lydia Mendoza*: (New York: Oxford University Press, 2001).

16. Gaitán, *The Adventures of Connie Chancla*, 1999.

17. Gaitán, *The Adventures of Connie Chancla*. For more information on the Toypurina uprising, see *Indians, Franciscans, and Spanish Colonization: The Impact of the Mission System on California Indians*, ed. Robert H. Jackson and Edward Castillo (Albuquerque: University of New Mexico Press, 1996).

18. Gaitán, *The Adventures of Connie Chancla*.

19. In 1996, Riverside, California, police chased a small truck carrying undocumented workers. Once apprehended and in front of television cameras, the police severely beat the immigrants. This blatant violation of their civil and human rights did not receive the same publicity as the Rodney King beating.

20. Gaitán, interview with author.

21. Gloria Anzaldúa, *Borderlands/La Frontera: The New Mestiza* (San Francisco: Spinsters/Aunt Lute, 1987), 13.

22. Gaitán, interview with author.

23. Anzaldúa, *Borderlands/La Frontera*, 3.

24. With regard to what is accepted as history, I refer you to Emma Pérez's powerful contribution, *The Decolonial Imaginary: Writing Chicanas into History*, (Bloomington: Indiana University Press, 1999).

25. Gaitán, *The Adventures of Connie Chancla*.

Borderlands Critical Subjectivity in Recent Chicana Art

JUDITH L. HUACUJA

Graphic expressions of gender politics can be found in the most recent efforts of Chicana artist groups such as L.A. Coyotas, Mujeres de Maíz, and Las Comadres Artistas. While many of these artists' prints and posters illustrate shared experiences of racial and gendered oppression, their mutual emphasis on women's bodies—veiled, masked, shrouded, or denuded—makes this body of work distinctive. The works' focus on the surface of bodies is meant to particularize the effects of hegemonic powers as they literally wear their difference on their persons. The artists' work represents the forging of an activist consciousness rooted in the lived cultural experiences of marginalized people. As border region artists, they work to re-member their bodies and to depict assertive active subjects reclaiming personal and public terrains.

Turbulent public spaces and the changing social context of living Latino, Mexican American, and Chicano realities within the major border state of California include, in the words of Chicana scholar Antonia Darder, "social marginalization, exploitation, cultural invasion, powerlessness, systemic violence . . . and the experience of having been driven out of the dominant political spaces and relegated to a subordinate position."[1] The ongoing political and artistic activism of Chicanos throughout the past four decades has been waged in the face of overwhelming social inequities in education, labor practices, and political representation. Recent studies on race relations indicate that throughout most of U.S. history, subordinate cultures have received little political legitimacy in governmental structures and in cultural discourses. The authors of one major study find, "However democratic the United States may have been in other respects, with respect to racial and cultural minorities it may be characterized as having been to varying degrees despotic for much of its history."[2]

CLAIMING SPACES

The Chicana artistic groups discussed in this essay have formed specifically in order to educate and activate themselves and other women on methods of overcoming systemic structures of oppression. They struggle against cultural imperialism, racism, and sexism. As they become politically organized, these women use art as a means of making visible what they have come to call the strategies of cultural imperialism. In the words of one of the artists, Patricia Valencia, "We make visible the tactics that disempower us: the usurpation of natural resources and land, the destruction of economic and agricultural self-sufficiency, the irrelevant and foreign educational environments, the interference with generational transmission of spiritual knowledge, the devaluing of language, of labor, of women and of youth."[3] Community and social justice constitutes the thesis of their art.

For example, community justice concerns are well represented in Yolanda Lopez's *Woman's Work is Never Done: Dolores Huerta*, 1995 (fig. 1). The poster commemorates the efforts of Delores Huerta, cofounder and first vice president of The United Farms Workers Union (UFW), and the efforts of other female laborers to organize in protest against unsafe working conditions and unjust wages in California's abundant agricultural regions. Huerta's work with the self-help group known as the Community Service Organization represents a legacy of Latina/Chicana social activism that reaches back to the 1950s. Yolanda Lopez's art pictures a class of women at risk for being marginalized, women who because of their migrant-labor status are relegated to a borderlands means of existence. Fearful of detection by immigration authorities, the women are forced to maintain a nearly-invisible profile while working in the United States. This profile of seclusion allows U.S. agricultural industries to benefit from migrant labor while dishonoring wage, labor, and health laws.

In Yolanda Lopez's print, female agricultural workers wear heavy veils, gloves, and masks in a futile effort to protect their bodies from harsh and even lethal chemicals used in agriculture. The shrouds render these women anonymous. The risk is that we, the viewers, read the images of these women as unidentifiable, insignificant, or as nonentities. However, in the background of the poster we see Huerta raising a banner for workers' rights. One of the workers, in solidarity with all the women, raises her arm to signify that all are in support of the union. On hats and shirtsleeves, they bear the UFW logo. In this instance, women work to resist the capitalist tendency to employ bodies as machine parts, useful only for the maximization of commodity production. In their fight for justice in the workplace, the women transform burdensome protective attire into proof of the atrocities visited upon their bodies.

Theorist Michel Foucault points to the ways in which institutions such as corporate agriculture and mass media craft positions of strength or of disem-

Figure 1: Yolanda Lopez, *Homenaje a Dolores Huerta: Woman's Work is Never Done*, 1995, silkscreen print.

powerment through representations, pictures, and stories that human subjects occupy. More recently, social scientists have also argued that representations, stories, and works of art are discursive objects that carry with them the possibility of upsetting subject positions. They argue that representations have the power to convey "efficacy beliefs," that is, beliefs that "shape expectations about one's own actions, the affective and unconscious dimensions to our sense of agency."[4]

Following the maxim that "agency is a feminist belief about human fulfillment," Yolanda Lopez presents women as agents of change who by wearing their union logos become the advance guard in promoting women's and workers' rights.[5] In Lopez's print depicting women with heavy scarves over their mouths, the women might be perceived as being gagged, for they appear at institutional sites that control who may and may not participate in serious acts of speech. However, Lopez, Huerta, and the women in this poster engage in activism that "encourages women to believe they can act in the collective best interest exactly because it is collective. . . . The individual and the collective are implicated in one another, and therefore the personal becomes political."[6]

Yolanda Lopez's art identifies the specific and collectivist efforts of Chicana women. Often, these images do more than picture bodies; they work to engage audiences in creating social change. To bring about change within the community, one must involve community. Many Chicana artists/activists ensure that audiences participate in the design, implementation, and analysis of the art project. Some of these artists model their activism through community-based collectives, such as L.A. Coyotes, Mujeres de Maíz, and Las Comadres Artistas. These collectives organized collaborative workshops to deal with issues of relevance within the neighborhood (such as economic development, toxic waste, and the effects of the North American Free Trade Agreement (NAFTA), as well as to initiate cultural projects such as music, dance, street theater, and art programs. Gaining the input of community participants serves to broaden the perspectives represented in the artwork and to ensure the fullest expression of community needs.

Collective needs and community issues are well represented in Alma Lopez's *California Fashions Slaves*, 1997 (fig. 2). The print depicts a lineage of workers who also have contributed significantly to California's productivity and wealth. These are women who labor in Los Angeles sweatshops, and who—as time permits—struggle to organize themselves toward better working conditions. A common definition of a sweatshop is a workplace where workers are subject to extreme exploitation, including the absence of a living wage or benefits, poor working conditions, and arbitrary discipline, such as verbal and physical abuse. In the United States these conditions exist in many low-wage industries that employ immigrants, such as the garment industry.[7] In a sense, these laborers put together the clothes that mask any common humanity; clothes that often segregate wearers into identifiable class distinctions. In her print, Lopez portrays fashions as both enslaving and exemplifying the borders and separations experienced by Mexican American and immigrant women. Fashions also help perpetuate economically and socially unjust conditions. In Los Angeles, the affluent fashion capital, generations of immigrant women labor for unconscionably low wages under unsafe circumstances.

In *California Fashions Slaves* the artist points to border issues exemplified by the notion of Manifest Destiny, the nineteenth-century belief in a divine right of Euroamerican settlers to take land from earlier groups. A map of the 1848 Treaty of Guadalupe Hidalgo reminds viewers of the broken guarantee of full citizenship rights made by U.S. officials to the original Mexican occupants

Figure 2: Alma Lopez, *California Fashions Slaves*, 1997, digital print.

of lands from Texas to California. Manifest Destiny usurps not only land, but continues today to claim low-wage labor from disenfranchised bodies as one of global capitalism's assumed economic rights. When translated out of an economic perspective of low-wage labor, the worker's body is criminalized by governing agencies—witness the mass media-sponsored aerial photograph of the *migra* chase scene in the lower left field of the digital image.[8] A border patrol vehicle pursues a dark-skinned individual as she is made to flee from the vibrant urban domain that is Los Angeles toward the remote parched south that is Mexico's border region. Alma Lopez's composite image illustrates the many interventions and ruptures suffered, yet also the generational legacy of activism forged by Latina women.

In their efforts to resist the cultural problem of racism and patriarchy, contemporary Chicana artists have developed their own specific strategies for an engaged art practice. Their socially-engaged cultural practices work to offset the effects of racism that denigrate individuals and stimulate self-hatred and alienation for both perpetrator and victim. Against the influences of racism, the artists use their art to help build a shared sense of an empowered identity bent on stamping out internalized oppression and domination. In response to the oppressions of patriarchy, these Chicana artists use the power of cultural forms to reproduce themselves—to make visible—their bodies and their surrounding social structures. This visibility is crucial to a politics of affirmation because it is, in Gail Pheterson's words, an opportunity of "being oneself fully, openly, undefensively and expressively. . . . [Such] visibility for an oppressed group contradicts self-concealment, isolation, subservience, and dominant denial or avoidance of oppressed persons."[9]

The strategies these artists have developed to broaden an activist base include decolonizing the female subject by supplying knowledge that is rooted in the lived cultural experiences of the marginalized community and denaturalizing an oppressive visual culture by picturing "othered" Chicano subjectivities, such as gay and lesbian bodies.[10] These artists blend histories in order to picture a mestizo-, hybrid-, or border-consciousness. Borderlands artists work to re-member their bodies and to embody an activist presence that claims political spaces. Through their work these artists cross-reference and transgress multiple ethnicities.

Alma Lopez's *Ixta*, 1999 (fig. 3) explores the power of the gaze—its readiness to perceive criminal acts in Chicana and Latina bodies and dress. Chicana cultural activism and commitment to equal political legitimacy at times require a contravention across hermetic gender and sexual boundaries as well as borders enforced by patriarchal and ethnic-based nationalisms. Lopez's images reflect the multiple, complex political and personal realities of Chicana feminists today while forcing such transgressions. Audience reception of her poster *Ixta* has been diverse. Viewers have read this as a tragic display of gang violence or as a sorrowful lament on the criminalization of *chola* (urban Chicano) culture. For the artist who made this work, the romantic story of Ixta and Popo as doomed Mexican lovers is translated to endow a sense of heroic love for the much-disparaged Chicana lesbian lovers adorned in their late-twentieth-century garb.

The issue of the gaze, desire, and disavowal are made visible in Ixta and her partner as they wear the transgressive signs of lesbian youthful beauty, *chola* makeup, dark skin, and other Indigenous physical traits. Alma Lopez's attempt to tell many different, at times conflicting, stories—the social ostracizing of lesbian love, the physical endangerment faced by Chicano youth, and the criminalization of youth culture based on attire and skin color—asserts that Chicano culture is neither monolithic nor essentialist in nature. There are, in fact, many Chicana cultures with a multiplicity of concerns that speak out for a diversity of issues and that negotiate varied relations of power within, as well as across, communities.

It is important to note that Alma Lopez stages the sacrificial pieta across the ancient Aztec stone sculpture that depicts the goddess Coyolxauhqui.[11] Since the 1980s, Chicana artists, writers, and critics have emphasized Coyolxauhqui as the symbol of identity reclamation. For feminists, she represents recovery of

Figure 3: Alma Lopez, *Ixta*, 1999, digital print.

the physical and intellectual body, earlier mutilated by sexist attitudes against women's pleasure and power. For Mexicanas and Chicanas, she embodies the Indigenous concept of spirituality dismembered by colonizing powers. According to ancient Aztec mythology, Coyolxauhqui was daughter of the earth goddess Coatlique and sister of Huitzilopochtli, the sun warrior with whom she was to share power. Unwilling to share his power, Huitzilopochtli mutilated his sister Coyolxauhqui and threw her body to the base of Coatlique's temple at Coatepec. As depicted in the Mexica sculpture, Coyolxauhqui's body has been mutilated by her brother and torn asunder. In Lopez's image, her body becomes a space re-membered as a site for the testing of desire's limits, a terrain for sacrifice and re-making, a place of empathetic engagement.

Alma Lopez and the other artists of the collective known as L.A. Coyotas developed from their collective research an in-depth understanding of Chicana theorist Gloria Anzaldúa's call to re-member the body. Anzaldúa's symbolic reconstitution of the female body seeks to heal the wounds of degradation wrought by racist and sexist actions. In numerous writings, Anzaldúa urges Chicanas to bring forth the memory of the fragmented body of Coyolxauhqui, which serves as a metaphor for the historical *indigena/mestiza* body. Anzaldúa refers to personal struggles undertaken through the creative process of self-reflection as a kind of dismemberment, or fragmentation of the body that can prompt new introspection and renewed awareness. The writer asserts that only after a stage of breaking apart or of alienation can the artist enter into a new consciousness and experience life differently. Empathy, an empowering tool for social change, can be wrought out of experiences of marginalization. Anzaldúa "urges us to piece together the corpse and give it life, to demand that the 'exiled body and exiled emotions be re-membered.'" [12]

Decolonizing the borderlands has forced a rejection of assimilation. Across the borderlands, artists are reconstituting Indigenous symbols and belief systems, visioning syncretic icons that speak of diaspora, exile, and gender struggles. For example, Margaret Alarcon's *Virgin Liberada*, 1997 (fig. 4) alludes to the Virgin Mary in a fashion similar to Ester Hernandez's widely popular print titled *The Virgin de Guadalupe defendiendo los derechos de la gente* (*The Virgin of Guadalupe Defending the Rights of the People*). Hernandez's Virgin depicts a warrior saint engaged in martial arts who physically challenges oppression, thereby rejecting a demure posture or a humble position. However, Alarcon's version of Guadalupe goes beyond breaking out of the physical constraints of saintliness. She entirely disrobes herself of Catholic propriety. Denuding herself of Western-European conventions, this Virgin's liberation from the Spanish Roman Catholic manifestation represents a decolonizing of the Indigenous and Chicana mind and spirit.

Alarcon's Virgin reveals the ancient goddess of central Mexico suppressed by Spanish colonizers during the sixteenth century. Tonantzin, one of the most significant of the Indigenous goddesses, reclaims her sacred aureole from Mary. Tonantzin also recovers her ancient Aztec place-sign that designates her temple

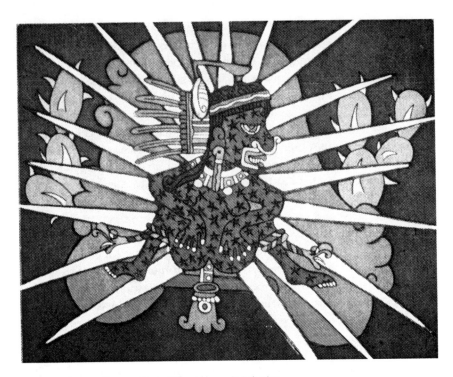

Figure 4: Margaret Alarcon, *Virgin Liberada*, 1997, digital print.

site at Tepeyac, previously obscured by the Catholic story describing Mary's appearance on this hill of Tepeyac. Through the Catholic stories, Tonantzin "Mother of Our People, Mother of the Gods" had become subsumed by the appearance of Mary. However, it was Tonantzin who first wore the garb of the Mexican heaven, a blue mantle dotted with golden stars.

Tonantzin, as with many Aztec deities, manifests numerous aspects and personages, including that of Metzli. In pre-Christian Mexico, the moon was an Indian emblem of Metzli, goddess of agriculture. The goddess was originally patroness of fertility, sexuality, and well-being. Mary's veil of stars conceals her sexuality in a highly codified structure of modesty and purity. However, Tonantzin's stars become synonymous with, indeed a structural part of, her very being. She is nude, powerful, and in the birthing position (Indigenous texts describe childbirth in this squatting position).[13] By raising the vibrancy of Tonantzin, Alarcon's image reinvokes a heritage of power and sexuality suppressed since the time of the conquest.

Much recent Chicana art references the effects of cultural mixing that has occurred since the conquest. The graphic art of Patricia Valencia titled *There*

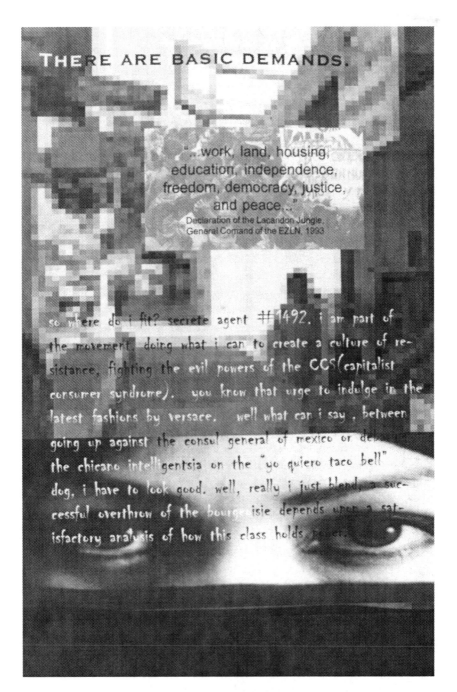

Figure 5: Patricia Valencia, *There are Basic Demands*, 1999, digital print.

are Basic Demands, 1999 (fig. 5) is one page from a series of graphics that are distributed throughout barrio streets in Los Angeles. This particular image portrays the artist as "agent 1492." 1492 refers to the year colonialism first enacted *mestizaje* (European and Indigenous ethnic mixing) in the Americas. As agent 1492, she is a *mestiza* cultural hybrid, reacting against assimilation by producing a culture of resistance against global capitalism and its consumerist effects upon her body. Fashions subvert her priorities. Text incorporated in the graphic art testifies to her struggle to resist the objectification of women's bodies. Indeed, this poster reads, "The urge to indulge in the latest fashions [is intimately related to the] analysis of how this class holds power." [14]

Valencia depicts the bold, direct gaze of the eyes. She images the power of the intellect to behold. The background she views has been digitally disrupted. She gives foregrounded clarity only to the object of her intent—a bit of text juxtaposed over Zapatista fighters that proclaims "work, land, housing, independence, freedom, democracy, justice, and peace." The text signals her allegiance with the Zapatista movement, the struggle for land and social justice being waged in Chiapas, Mexico. The effects of global capitalism have rendered communication instantaneous between the Zapatista leaders and supporters across the globe. Valencia celebrates their cause as an internationally viable movement towards human rights.

Valencia is part of the artists' collective known as Mujeres de Maíz (Women of the Corn). [15] With the primary goal of forging bonds among creative women of color, Mujeres de Maíz is an open collective that serves the local community of Los Angeles. It participates in a global network of solidarity with Latin American and Mexican women. Mujeres de Maíz taps the local by producing a quarterly grassroots magazine and by staging multimedia performances, visual art exhibits, and poetry readings throughout various neighborhoods in Los Angeles. It maintains global connections via Internet communiqués, email newsgroups, and alliances with groups such as the Zapatista women's contingent in Chiapas, Mexico. [16]

Nicole Limon's *Sangre de Maíz: Bullet Rituals in Chiapas*, 1999 (fig. 6) also signifies solidarity with Zapatista resistance. Limon is affiliated with the Comadres Artistas and with El Teatro Espejo (Theater of Hope), both of Sacramento, California. Her poster announces the performance she cowrote with Andrea Porras, a theater piece that documents death and oppression ongoing to this day in Mexico. Her performance and the poster propose an international activist alliance in solidarity with the women of Mexico. For more than three decades, such international alliances have worked to support the emancipatory struggles of oppressed groups around the world. Intervention from solidarity groups, such as Limon's, includes education about the subor-

Figure 6: Nicole Limon, *Sangre de Maiz: Bullet Rituals in Chiapas*, 1999, digital print.

dinate culture, as well as publication of military abuses within the offending country. The Mexican Indigenous peoples' call for liberation has resulted in a vast movement of solidarity in Europe and in North and South America that puts pressure on the Mexican government to end human-rights and land-ownership abuses.

The women of Mujeres de Maíz, as the name refers, emphasize ancestral connections to the Indigenous peoples of the Mesoamerican region today called Guatemala and Mexico. In Valencia's more specific terms, "This path we see as a blood line, a connection to women who have resisted and struggled for what they believed in, whether that was their family or a revolution."[17] For Limon's group, Sangre de Maíz (Blood of the Corn) signifies the sanctity of life represented by the precious body fluid and the spilling of that blood at the hands of the military.

L.A. Coyotas and Mujeres de Maíz have traveled to and studied with women's *communidades* in Chiapas. The women make these trips in order to "create a deeper understanding of the causes and effects of colonization, imperialism, racism and sexism as it develops even across cultures and borders."[18] Both groups, through their art, allude to the colonizing powers of global capitalism. The women point to the strident materialism in which they find themselves implicated. However, as Chandra Mohanty argues, it is the "daily strategies and ideologies of global capitalism [that] make visible the common interests of Third World women workers [and that] can serve as the basis for organizing across racial and ethnic differences and national boundaries."[19]

These study groups also interrogate body-related issues such as self-image, sexuality, addiction, and physical abuse. Through the dialogue fostered by the collective, the women found they lived a veiled reality. They were conscious of their attempts to deflect the power of the gaze that objectifies and limits their activities as women. In Limon's case, the veil protects the identity of the individual, thereby allowing her to freely take part in the revolutionary cause. The veil symbolizes her solidarity with the Chiapas movement. In representing herself as a fighter (through the simple use of a red bandanna), Limon exemplifies Cherrie Moraga's assertion that "women of color are more like urban guerrillas trained through everyday battle with the state apparatus."[20] Here, women display the power of the returned gaze, as fully active agents.

In many of the selected illustrations, women have chosen the veil as a means of focusing attention on their power. No longer simply objects to be gazed upon, they take up strong subject positions, challenging who speaks and what gets said about the subject. If these artists are sensitive to colonizing strategies that usurp power by speaking for subordinated subjects, how is it that they, as privileged U.S. citizens, might speak for disempowered populations in Mexico?

This raises the question of who authorizes another as a legitimate speaking subject. Stuart Hall has pointed out that identity is neither transparent nor unproblematic, that "we should think of identity as a production which is never complete, which is constituted inside, not outside representation, and which can stake no claim of authenticity."[21]

Hall goes on to argue the distinction between political identity that fights to end injustice and the many nuanced cultural identities in between. It is political identity that requires conscious, specific commitments. Angie Chabram, quoting Hall, asserts, "It may be necessary to momentarily abandon the multiplicity of cultural identities for 'more simple ones around which political lines have been drawn."[22] These women forego rigid territorial identities in support of a broad-based and politically relevant human-rights alliance. They seek new identities appropriate for their political practice.

The art-making practices of the women of Mujeres de Maíz, Las Comadres Artistas, and L.A. Coyotas are informed by third-world feminist theory. Their understanding of new "subject configurations" is well explained by theorist Chela Sandoval's statement:

What U.S. third world feminism demands is a new subjectivity, a political revision that denies any one ideology as the final answer, while instead positing a tactical, indeed a performative, subjectivity with the capacity to de- and re-center depending upon the kinds of oppression to be confronted, depending upon the history of the moment. This is what is required in the shift from enacting a hegemonic oppositional theory and practice to engaging in differential social movement, as performed, however unrecognized, over the last thirty years under U. S. third world feminist praxis.[23]

A tactical subjectivity repositions itself regarding individual and collective identities in order to perform multi-ethnic coalitions. White laborers, Latina lesbians, and Chicana intellectuals re-position their work at times to locate a tactical unity—especially around issues of the body and its shared experiences of oppression. Many Chicana artists do this by answering Anzaldúa's calls for woman's exiled body and exiled emotions to be re-membered, as Margaret Alarcon does in her poster titled *Tezcatlipoca*, 1998 (fig. 7). Here, the Aztec god/goddess of smoke, fire, and water is depicted. Attention is focused on the ancient Mesoamerican deity's eyes as a means to know this subject. He/she cannot be fully known because no physical body is manifest, yet fire, passion, and light emanate from within a deeply textured surface that veils Tezcatlipoca. Layers of thick felt create the actual material; *amate* (fig bark) paper resembles luscious wool that provide warmth and healing to the entity behind the fabrics.[24]

Figure 7: Margaret Alarcon, *Tezcatlipoca*, 1998, pastel and acrylic on bark paper, offset prints.

Tezcatlipoca's eyes and brilliant glow denote an active agent who, in her craftiness, is darkly subversive, political, and revolutionary. She is embodied, yet disembodied. She wears a mask as the sign of a tactical subjectivity, fully present and grounded in the material, historical realities of the late-twentieth century. Iconographically, Tezcatlipoca is identified in part by the banded eyes. The eyes connote looking inward, self-scrutiny, and knowing one's self. She follows her gaze inward; she travels a path toward enlightenment and transformation. For contemporary Chicanas, Tezcatlipoca enacts Chela Sandoval's call for a "commitment to the process of metamorphosis itself: the activity of the trickster who practices subjectivity-as-masquerade."[25] The Chicana feminist/ artist/activist/trickster knows well this kind of activity that "allows movement through and over dominant systems of resistance, identity, race, gender, sex, and national meanings."[26]

These Chicana artists are forging new analyses and political strategies that are, in effect, reinventing progressive feminist and ethnic-based movements in more inclusive and relevant ways. These groups bring together lesbians, American Indian, Asian American, Latina, white, and African American women, and working-class, academic, and grassroots-activist women who are discussing and sharing the intimate connections of their everyday lives. For these Chicana artists, group processes always link art-making with education and political activism. In so doing, their work performs new notions of cultural citizenship defined as "a range of social practices which, taken together, claim and establish a distinct social space for Latinos in this country," a space where difference is seen as a vital resource producing new cultural forms.[27] This coming full circle becomes praxis that forges community action and social change. Their rich encounters continue a legacy of community activism by educating others about successful struggles for social and economic justice.

NOTES

1. Antonia Darder, "Introduction," in *Culture and Difference: Critical Perspectives on the Bicultural Experience in the United Sates*, ed. Antonia Darder (Westport, Conn.: Bergin & Garvey, 1995), 3.

2. Michael Omi and Howard Winant, *Racial Formation in the United States: From the 1960s to the 1980s* (New York: Routledge, 1986), 55.

3. Patricia Valencia, interview with the author, August 9, 1999, Los Angeles, Calif.

4. Daniel Miller and Christopher Tilley, "Introduction," in *Ideology, Power, and Prehistory*, ed. Daniel Miller and Christopher Tilley (New York: Cambridge University Press, 1984), 14.

5. Judith Kegan Gardiner, "Introduction," in *Provoking Agents: Gender and Agency*

in Theory and Practice, ed. Judith Kegan Gardiner (Urbana: University of Illinois Press, 1995), 13.

6. Gardiner, "Introduction," 6.

7. Recent studies conducted by the U.S. Department of Labor found that 67 percent of Los Angeles garment factories and 63 percent of New York garment factories violate minimum-wage and overtime laws. Ninety-eight percent of Los Angeles garment factories have workplace health and safety problems serious enough to lead to severe injuries or death. In the United States, the 1990 Census showed that garment workers in Los Angeles earned about $7,200 annually (figures from Sweat Shop Organizing web site, *http://www.sweatshopwatch.org/swatch/questions.html#sweatshops*, September 2001).

8. *La migra* translates as immigration police.

9. Gail Pheterson, "Alliance Between Women: Overcoming Internalized Oppression and Internalized Domination," in *Bridges of Power: Women's Multicultural Alliances*, ed. Lisa Albrecht and Rose M. Brewer (Philadelphia: New Society Publishers, 1990), 35.

10. See Gloria Anzaldúa, *Borderlands/La Frontera: The New Mestiza* (San Francisco: Spinsters/Aunt Lute Books, 1987); and Nilda Peraza, Marcia Tucker, and Kinshasha Conwill, eds., *The Decade Show: Frameworks of Identity in the 1980s* (New York: Museum of Contemporary Hispanic Art, New Museum of Contemporary Art, The Studio Museum of Harlem, 1990).

11. "The Coyolxauhqui Stone" (1400 A.D.), a giant monolith found at the Great Temple of Tenochtitlan, is currently located at the Museo del Templo Mayor, Mexico.

12. Alma Lopez, interview with the author, August 9, 1999, Los Angeles, Calif. Lopez quotes Gloria Anzaldúa.

13. Catha Paquette, Latin American art historian, identified the image borrowed by the artist as Metzli in a conversation with the author, September 1999, Santa Barbara, Calif.

14. Text on Patricia Valenecia's graphic *There are Basic Demands*, 1999.

15. The group was "born out of the need for women of color to communicate collectively for empowerment; to bridge the communication gap among women and men, younger and older generations, academia and the community" (Patricia Valencia, "Mujeres de Maíz," unpublished paper written for a presentation at the University of California, Los Angeles, 1997, 1).

16. Valencia, "Mujeres de Maíz," 2.

17. Valencia, "Mujeres de Maíz," 1.

18. Valencia, "Mujeres de Maíz," 1.

19. Jacqui M. Alexander and Chandra Talpade Mohanty, "Introduction: Genealogies, Legacies, Movements," in *Feminist Genealogies, Colonial Legacies, Democratic Futures*, ed. Jacqui M. Alexander and Chandra Talpade Mohanty (New York: Routledge, 1997), 13.

20. Chela Sandoval, quoting Cherrie Moraga, in "Feminist Forms of Agency and Oppositional Consciousness: U. S. Third World Feminist Criticism," in Gardiner, *Provoking Agents*," 217.

21. Stuart Hall, "Speaking for the Subject," lecture delivered at University of California, Santa Barbara, May 26, 1989, quoted by Angie Chabram and Rosalinda Fregoso in "Chicana/o Cultural Representations: Reframing Alternative Critical Discourses," *Cultural Studies* 4:3 (1990): 210.

22. Chabram and Fregoso, quoting Hall, "Chicana/o Cultural Representations," 210.

23. Sandoval, "Feminist Forms of Agency and Oppositional Consciousness," 218.

24. The artist reproduced this art as a series of posters for distribution at various feminist art events in L.A. The events brought together a wide range of social justice organizations committed to feminist change.

25. Sandoval, "Feminist Forms of Agency and Oppositional Consciousness," 218.

26. Sandoval, "Feminist Forms of Agency and Oppositional Consciousness," 218.

27. William V. Flores and Rita Benmayor, "Introduction: Constructing Cultural Citizenship," in *Latino Cultural Citizenship: Claiming Identity, Space, and Rights*, ed. William V. Flores and Rita Benmayor (Boston: Beacon Press, 1997), 1.

Queering the Borderlands

The Challenges of Excavating the Invisible and Unheard

EMMA PÉREZ

I begin with a passage from my novel in progress titled *Forgetting the Alamo, Or Blood Memory*. I write fiction not only because I have a passion for literature, but also because I am frustrated with history's texts and archives. I've always wanted to find in the archives a queer vaquera from the mid-nineteenth century whose adventures include fighting Anglo squatters and seducing willing señoritas. Impatience led me to create a *tejana* baby butch, named Micaela Campos, who must avenge her father's death at the battle of San Jacinto, just a month after the fall of the Alamo:

> By dusk she came upon the ranch and the land that her father had settled. Eleven *sitios*. Nearly forty-nine thousand acres. A lot of land for a young boy whose people had inched their way up the valley two centuries prior, moving slowly at first from the central valley then north each time the rivers shifted, each time they shifted further north to boundless prairies crossing rivers and streams. Monclova had been home for awhile, two hundred years felt like plenty of time, so they picked up and moved north crossing el Rio Bravo, traveled some more, and stopped and settled in for what they thought would be another two hundred. They came in groups. Tlascaletecas and Otomi with the Spanish and the Spanish with the Mexicans and the Mexicans with Apache, mixing into a brown race journeying through land expansive with blood-red horizons, until they stopped and looked around and settled into what was already in their blood. Movement. Settlement and movement. Back and forth they trekked, rivers and streams blending and inter-breeding with tribes and making families and villages from beginning to end of deserts and plains and groves. Tribes of families and villages of mud-huts sank into the landscape where buried vessels and bones became the soil and the clay and the water.[1]

I began with this passage in order to inscribe a gaze on the borderlands that is geographic and spatial, mobile and impermanent. The borderlands have been imprinted by bodies that traverse the region, just as bodies have been transformed by the laws and customs in the regions we call borderlands. In the *History of Sexuality*, Michel Foucault challenges us to look closely at bodies and how they are engraved and transformed through laws, customs, and moralities imposed upon them through centuries.[2] He is not as direct about coloniality, but we can still borrow from a critique that exemplifies how land is imprinted and policed by those traversing and claiming it as they would claim a body—both becoming property for the colonizers. Native Americans became as much the property of the Spanish as did the land that came to be known as the Spanish borderlands.

To unravel colonialist ideology, I put forth my notion of decolonizing history embedded in a theoretical construct that I name the decolonial imaginary. This new category can help us rethink history in a way that makes agency for those on the margins transformative. Colonial, for my purposes here, can be defined simply as the rulers versus the ruled, without forgetting that those colonized may also become like the rulers and assimilate into a colonial mind-set. This colonial mind-set believes in a normative language, race, culture, gender, class, and sexuality. The colonial imaginary is a way of thinking about national histories and identities that must be disputed if contradictions are ever to be understood, much less resolved. When conceptualized in certain ways, the naming of things already leaves something out, leaves something unsaid, leaves silences and gaps that must be uncovered. The history of the United States has been circumscribed by an imagination steeped in unchallenged notions. This means that even the most radical of histories are influenced by the very colonial imaginary against which they rebel.[3] I argue that the colonial imaginary still determines many of our efforts to revise the past, to reinscribe the nation with fresh stories in which so many new voices unite to carve new disidentities, to quote Deena González and José Esteban Munoz.[4] If we are dividing the stories from our past into categories such as colonial relations, postcolonial relations, and so on, then I propose a decolonial imaginary as a rupturing space, the alternative to that which is written in history.[5] How do we contest the past to revise it in a manner that tells more of our stories? In other words, how do we decolonize our history? To decolonize our history and our historical imaginations, we must uncover the voices from the past that honor multiple experiences, instead of falling prey to that which is easy—allowing the white colonial heteronormative gaze to reconstruct and interpret our past.

In my own work, I have attempted to address colonial relations, of land and bodies, particularly of women, particularly of Chicanas in the Southwest. I argue that a colonial imaginary hovers above us always as we interpret our past and present. I argue that we must move into the decolonial imaginary to decolonize all relations of power, whether gendered or sexual or racial or classed.[6]

In my study of Chicanas, I've put forth the notion of the decolonial imaginary as a means not only of finding women who have been so hidden from history, but also as a way of honoring their agency, which is often lost. The premise that Mexican women are passive wives who follow their men had to be contested. Now, I'm asking, how is the decolonial imaginary useful for lesbian history and queer studies? If we have inherited a colonial white heteronormative way of seeing and knowing, then we must retrain ourselves to confront and rearrange a mind-set that privileges certain relationships. A colonial white heteronormative gaze, for example, will interpret widows only as heterosexual women mourning husbands. In his book, *Disidentifications: Queers of Color and the Performance of Politics*, Munoz argues that queers of color are left out of representation in a space "colonized by the logics of white normativity and heteronormativity." For Munoz, disidentification is the third mode of dealing with dominant ideology, one that neither opts to assimilate within such a structure nor strictly opposes it; rather, disidentification is a strategy.[7] For me, disidentification is that strategy of survival that occurs within a decolonial imaginary. In other words, the queer-of-color gaze is a gaze that sees, acts, reinterprets, and mocks all at once in order to survive and to reconstitute a world where s/he is not seen by the white colonial heteronormative mind. As my queer vaquera baby butch gazes upon the land that her family settled upon, she is refashioning that space, re-establishing her relationship to that land as a *tejana* and as a queer who will no longer have rights to land and history. She will be erased by the white colonial heteronormative mind. And so, we will make her up or locate documents to uncover a history of sexuality on the borderlands that is hidden from the untrained eye.

How do we train the eye to see with a decolonial queer gaze that disidentifies from the normative in order to survive? The history of sexuality on and in the borderlands looks heteronormative to many historians who scrutinize marriage records, divorce records, and even court cases on adultery. To disidentify is to look beyond white colonial heteronormativity to interpret documents differently.

Historians have explored race, class, gender, ethnicity, and nation, region; however, sexuality, and more specifically, queer history, has only recently joined the ranks of serious scrutiny. Generally, historians of sexuality in the United States and Europe have offered key books and articles that examine the lives of women and men in New York, Buffalo, London, San Francisco, and even the South. For example, historians like Martin Duberman, Martha Vicinus, George Chauncy Jr., Elizabeth Lapovsky Kennedy, Madeline D. Davis, Lillian Faderman, Randolph Trumbach, Lisa Duggan, and John Howard uncover queer histories in the United States and Britain while the Southwest borderlands is quite nearly untouched.[8] Historical studies that focus upon Chicanas/os and Mexicans of the Southwest primarily highlight immigrant and labor studies, social histories of communities, and biographies of heroes or heroines. The study of gender and sexuality, however, are central in works by Deena González, *Refusing the Favor: The Spanish Mexican Women of Santa Fe, 1820–1880*; Ramón Gutiérrez, *When Jesus Came, the Corn Mothers Went Away: Marriage, Sexuality, and Power in New Mexico, 1500–1846*; and Antonia Castaneda, "Sexual Violence in the Politics and Policies of Conquest: Amerindian Women and the Spanish Conquest of Alta California."[9] Queer histories of the Southwest and of the U.S.-Mexico borderlands are that much more marginal; however, there are as many questions as there are sources for interrogation. Cultural and literary texts, newspapers, police records, widows' wills, court dockets, medical records, texts by sexologists, religious tracts, as well as *corridos*—all of these and more must be reinterpreted with a decolonial queer gaze so we may interrogate representations of sexual deviants and track ideologies about sex and sexuality.

We must begin by asking, For whom and by whom has sexuality been defined? Who was having sex with whom when laws began to police the practice of sex? Foucault contends that discourses of sex and sexuality, specifically the history of those discourses in Europe, were transformed from somewhat more libratory in the eighteenth century to far more repressive in the nineteenth century. Victorian England made a space in which deviant sexualities could be repressed on the one hand and could proliferate on the other.[10] The mixed scheme of moralities spread through the Western world, and the borderlands between Mexico and the United States were no exception, particularly after the U.S.-Mexico War of 1846–48, when droves of white Anglo Saxon Protestants brought with them a white colonial heteronormative ideology. Sexuality, then, cannot be defined without attention to epochs and centuries, each of which imprinted borderland queers in its own way. Racialized sexualities on the geographic border we know as El Paso del Norte has its own underpinning, however.

An examination of the late-nineteenth and early-twentieth centuries on the border of El Paso/Juárez offers one window into twenty-first-century lesbian and queer identities. (I use each term of identity cautiously, given that each identity is charged with its own politics and history. While "queer" has for many become the overarching identity for all who are nonheteronormative, "lesbian" is sustained as the self-identity for women who choose to be with other women—physically, psychically, and politically.) The late-nineteenth and early-twentieth centuries are key for a couple of reasons. One reason is that the late-nineteenth century is encoded with Victorian values of repressive sexuality. Sex acts became policed in ways they had not been before. In her book *Queering the Color Line: Race and the Invention of Homosexuality in American Culture*, Siobhan B. Somerville argues that "it is not historical coincidence that the classification of bodies as either homosexual or heterosexual emerged at the same time that the United States was aggressively constructing and policing the boundaries between black and white bodies."[11] Somerville refers to the 1896 Supreme Court case, *Plessy v. Ferguson*, which established a "separate but equal clause" that legalized the segregation of blacks from whites. I would further note that in the Southwest, in these geographic borderlands, *Plessy v. Ferguson* sanctioned the segregation of brown from white.

Moreover, I would take her premise and argue further that it is not historical coincidence that the classifications of homosexual and heterosexual appeared at the same time that the United States began aggressively policing the borders between the United States and Mexico. The change from the Texas Rangers, who policed Indian and Mexican territory in the nineteenth century, to the Border Patrol, created in 1924 to police the border between the United States and Mexico, occurred at the moment when a new form of anti-Mexican sentiment emerged throughout the nation. The sentiment was linked to anti-immigrant acts that would become laws against non-Northern-Europeans. As the borders in Texas, California, Arizona, and New Mexico were pushed against by too many Mexicans crossing the Rio Bravo, trekking back and forth through land they had crossed for centuries and paying little attention to anything but rising river banks, the borders become more and more closed and only opened up when a labor shortage demanded cheap laborers. Meanwhile, a brown race was legislated against from fear that it could potentially infect the purportedly pure, white race in the United States. Eugenicists and sexologists, according to Somerville, worked hand in hand.[12] Consequently, the border was closed as a result of scientific racism clouded by a white colonial heteronormative gaze looking across a river to see racial and sexual impurities. Throughout the 1880s, 1890s, and even as late as the 1900s, Mexicans crossed from Juárez to El Paso and back again with ease. Not until 1917 did a law impose requirements on those crossing a political border. A head tax of eight dollars per person and the ability to read restricted the crossings.[13] I would ask, How did the emergent and rigid policing of the border between the United States and Mexico in the early twentieth century reinforce a white colonial heteronormative way of seeing and knowing that fused race with sex? Further investigation will illustrate that the ideologies constructed around race and sex were linked to justify who was undesirable as a citizen in the United States. Immoral and deviant behavior included anything that was not a heterosexual marriage between a woman and man. In the El Paso of 1891, adultery could lead to the arrest of both man and woman. Of course, someone would have to file a complaint to have them arrested, usually an unhappy third party. The courts listened and adjudicated many cases of adultery in which Mexican women and men were thrown into jail because they "unlawfully live together and have carnal intercourse" outside of marriage.[14]

Another way of tackling primary research for an "invisible" group is to study the category of "deviance" and how deviant behavior has become a politicized queer identity in the twenty-first century. It is not a coincidence that Chicana lesbian historian Deena González unearthed the lives of widows, or women who lived alone during the nineteenth century.[15] González was already thinking outside and beyond a heteronormative interpretation when she perused nineteenth-century documents.

Oral interviews and ethnography are the methods available to those who do not want to ferret through pre-twentieth-century tracts to find queer histories. For the late twentieth century, activist-scholar Yolanda Retter has conducted extensive research on the lesbian communities of Los Angeles from the 1970s through to the 1990s, relying on oral interviews, as did Kennedy and Davis. Chicana lesbian historian Yolanda Chávez Leyva has also conducted a series of oral interviews on the lives of Chicana lesbian activists in Tucson, Arizona. Sociologist Deborah Vargas has interrogated queer audience responses to *tejana* singer/performer Selena and the drag artists posing as Selena. Theorist and historian Maylei Blackwell has interviewed a Chicana feminist activist from the 1970s who was ostracized from the Chicano movement because she was a feminist, meaning a lesbian to many homophobic Chicanos in the early movement.[16]

Chicana lesbian cultural critics Luz Calvo, Catriona Esquibel, Sandra Soto, Yvonne Yarbro-Bejarano, and others continue to problemetize how we think of queers in, on, and of many borders.[17] The border *reyna*, Gloria Anzaldúa, could not have known the impact her book of poetry and essays would have on the field called borderlands, which was initially coined the "Spanish Borderlands" in the early twentieth century by University of California historian Herbert Eugene Bolton.[18] Studies by queer cultural critics and theoreticians influenced by Anzaldúa's work continue to proliferate. Creative writers have also been theorizing the borderlands and its deviant, non-normative population for the last few decades. In her historical novel, El Paso border writer Alicia Gaspar de Alba's queering of Sor Juana Inez de la Cruz has caused consternation among those who cannot imagine a nun having sex with another woman. Many of Gaspar de Alba's short stories are reflections of the border twin cities El Paso and Juárez. Other border queer writers, like John Rechy and Arturo Islas, also from El Paso, construct powerful narratives in which their protagonists confront heteronormative sexuality.[19]

Historical research on and of borderland queers is not as abundant. Part of the problem is that the queer gaze has only recently become sanctioned. Queer history, after all, is a new, growing field. Despite the practice of queering our daily lives, academic institutions and disciplines have discouraged that "oh so disturbing" queer gaze. Our epistemological shift, however, has already begun to challenge rhetoric and ideologies about racialized sexualities. To queer the border is to look at the usual documents with another critical eye, a nonwhite, noncolonial, nonheteronormative eye. A decolonial queer gaze would permit scholars to interrogate medical texts, newspapers, court records, wills, novels, and *corridos* with that fresh critical eye. Graduate students at the University of Texas at El Paso (UTEP) are scrutinizing some of these records in order to construct the queer history of the border. In the History Department, I offered for the first time a graduate seminar on "Gender and Sexuality on the Border," in which queer history was explored. In the seminar, graduate students conducted research on El Paso/Juárez, tracking gay, lesbian, and queer histories through the centuries. Because the majority of historical studies on gender and sexuality ignore the geographic border between the United States and Mexico, these graduate students and I realized that it is difficult to assess how to pursue research on queers in this region. We also concluded that "queer" history included anyone who was considered "deviant," therefore we expanded whom we studied and how we conducted our studies. We found ourselves "queering" the documents. This was a daunting task; however, the students were creative as they challenged white heteronormative sexualities in studies that explored, for example, Juárez transvestites in their work place, prostitution in the late nineteenth and early twentieth centuries, lesbian oral histories of the El Paso community, gay and lesbian activists of El Paso, and Mexican American women's agency in the *colonias* of El Paso. Some of these studies are ongoing. UTEP's Ph.D. program in Borderlands History, the only one of its kind in the nation, is regionally specific to the United States and Mexico, and therefore is drawing students of color who are Chicana/o and Mexican nationals. A core faculty in the department is training students whose research interests include gender/sexuality/race/ethnicity in the borderlands, the Mexican Revolution, histories of Colonial Mexico, the Southwest, Latin America and Spain, as well as comparative world borders.

But what about the gaps and silences? I know that nineteenth-century *te-*

janas lived and roamed the "wild West" and probably knew how to handle a six-shooter and ride a horse, and I'm sure there were those who passed as men and those who loved women. As much as I would love to stumble upon diaries, journals, and letters written by queer vaqueras of the nineteenth century, I must challenge my own desire for the usual archival material and the usual way of seeing, as well as honor that which women scholars before me have uncovered. While I'll not always find the voices of the subaltern, the women, the queers of color, I will have access to a world of documents rich with ideologies that enforce white, colonial heteronormativity. A white heteronormative imaginary has defined how researchers and historians as well as cultural critics have chosen to ignore or negate the populations who are on the margins, outside of normative behavior, outside of twentieth-century nuclear white heterosexual family systems. I am arguing for a decolonial queer gaze that allows for different possibilities and interpretations of what exists in the gaps and silences but is often not seen or heard. I am arguing for decolonial queer interpretations that obligate us to see and hear beyond a heteronormative imaginary. I am arguing for decolonial gendered history to take us into our future studies with perspectives that do not deny, dismiss, or negate what is unfamiliar, but instead honors the differences between and among us.

NOTES

1. Emma Pérez, *Forgetting the Alamo, Or Blood Memory*, forthcoming.

2. Michel Foucault, *The History of Sexuality, Vol. I: An Introduction* (New York: Pantheon, 1978).

3. Emma Pérez, *The Decolonial Imaginary: Writing Chicanas into History* (Bloomington: Indiana University Press, 1999), 5–7.

4. Deena González, *Refusing the Favor: The Spanish Mexican Women of Santa Fe, 1820–1880* (New York: Oxford University Press, 1999); and José Esteban Munoz, *Disidentifications: Queers of Color and the Performance of Politics* (Minneapolis: University of Minnesota Press, 1999).

5. Pérez, *The Decolonial Imaginary*, 6.

6. Pérez, *The Decolonial Imaginary*.

7. Munoz, *Disidentifications*, xii, 11.

8. Martin Duberman, Martha Vicinus, and George Chauncey Jr., eds., *Hidden from History: Reclaiming the Gay and Lesbian Past* (New York: New American Library, 1989); George Chauncey Jr., *Gay New York: Gender, Urban Culture, and the Making of the Gay Male World: 1890–1940* (New York: Basic Books, 1994); Elizabeth Lapovsky Kennedy and Madeline D. Davis, *Boots of Leather, Slippers of Gold: The History of a Lesbian Community* (New York: Routledge University Press, 1993); Lillian Faderman, *Odd Girls*

and *Twilight Lovers: A History of Lesbian Life in Twentieth Century America* (New York: Columbia University Press, 1991); Randolph Trumbach, *Sex and the Gender Revolution: Heterosexuality and the Third Gender in Enlightenment London*, (Chicago: Chicago University Press, 1998); Lisa Duggan, *Sapphic Slashers: Sex, Violence, and American Modernity* (Durham: Duke University Press, 2000); and John Howard, *Men Like That: A Southern Queer History* (Chicago: Chicago University Press, 1999). Also worth noting is the San Francisco Lesbian and Gay History Project compiled by Liz Stevens and Estelle B. Freedman, which was produced as a video, *She Even Chewed Tobacco* (New York History Project, 1983). Susan Lee Johnson refers to one of the more prominent lesbians featured in the pictorial collection, a mixed-race Mexican-Anglo woman, Elvira Virginia Mugarrieta, also known as "Babe Bean," and Jack Garland, born in Stockton, California, in 1870. See Susan Lee Johnson, "'A Memory Sweet to Soldiers': The Significance of Gender," in *A New Significance: Re-envisioning the History of the American West*, ed. Clyde A. Milner II (New York: Oxford University Press, 1996), 255–78.

9. González, *Refusing the Favor*; Ramón Gutiérrez, *When Jesus Came, the Corn Mothers Went Away: Marriage, Sexuality, and Power in New Mexico, 1500–1846* (Stanford: Stanford University Press, 1991); and Antonia Castañeda, "Sexual Violence in the Politics and Policies of Conquest: Amerindian Women and the Spanish Conquest of Alta California," in *Building with Our Hands: New Directions in Chicana Studies*, ed. Adela de la Torre and Beatriz M. Pesquera (Berkeley: University of California Press, 1993), 15–33.

10. Foucault, *The History of Sexuality*, 3–4.

11. Siobhan B. Somerville, *Queering the Color Line: Race and the Invention of Homosexuality in American Culture* (Durham: Duke University Press, 2000), 3.

12. Sommerville, *Queering the Color Line*, 31.

13. For fundamental background to the history of the Southwest, the making of the U.S.-Mexico border, and subsequent immigration laws, refer to Rodolfo Acuna, *Occupied America: A History of Chicanos*, 3rd ed. (New York: Harper and Row, 1988); Juan Gómez-Quinones, *Roots of Chicano Politics, 1600–1940* (Albuquerque: University of New Mexico Press, 1994); David Gutiérrez, *Walls and Mirrors: Mexican Americans, Mexican Immigrants, and the Politics of Ethnicity* (Berkeley: University of California Press, 1995); and Vicki L. Ruiz, *From Out of the Shadows: Mexican Women in Twentieth Century America* (New York: Oxford University Press, 1998).

14. El Paso County Court Records, 1881–1920, *The State of Texas v. Guadalupe Vega and Margarita R. Pérez*, adultery, April 17, 1841, 887, University of Texas, El Paso Special Collections.

15. Deena González, "The Widowed Women of Santa Fe: Assessments on the Lives of an Unmarried Population, 1850–1880," in *On Their Own: Widows and Widowhood in the American Southwest, 1848–1939*, ed. Arlene Scadron (Champaign: University of Illinois Press, 1989).

16. Yolanda Retter, "On the Side of Angels: Lesbian Activism in Los Angeles, 1970–90" (Ph.D. diss., University of New Mexico, 1999); Yolanda Chávez Leyva, "Listening to the Silences in Latina/Chicana Lesbian History," in *Living Chicana Theory*, ed. Carla Trujillo (Berkeley: Third Woman Press, 1998); Deborah Vargas, "Cruzando Fronteras: Selena, Tejano Public Culture and the Politics of Cross-Over" (paper presented at the annual meeting of the American Studies Association, Washington, D.C., October 1997); and Maylei Blackwell, "Contested Histories and Retrofitted Memory: Chicana Feminist Subjectivities between and beyond Nationalist Imaginaries—An Oral History of the Hijas de Cuauhtémoc" (paper presented as qualifying essay, History of Consciousness: University of California, Santa Cruz, May 1997).

17. Luz Calvo, "Postcolonial Queer Fantasies" (Ph.D. diss., University of California, Santa Cruz, 2000); Catriona Esquibel, *With Her Machete in Her Hand* (Austin: University of Texas Press, forthcoming); Sandra Soto, "Sexing Aztlán: Subjectivity, Desire and the Challenge of Racialized Sexuality in Chicana/o Literature" (Ph.D. diss., University of Texas, Austin, 2001); and Yvonne Yarbro-Bejarano, *The Wounded Heart: Writing on Cherríe Moraga* (Austin: University of Texas Press, 2001).

18. Gloria Anzaldúa, *Borderlands/La Frontera: The New Mestiza* (San Francisco: Spinsters/Aunt Lute, 1987); and Herbert Eugene Bolton, *The Spanish Borderlands: A Chronicle of Old Florida and the Southwest* (New Haven: Yale University Press, 1921).

19. Alicia Gaspar de Alba, *Sor Juana's Second Dream: A Novel* (Albuquerque: University of New Mexico Press, 1999); Alicia Gaspar de Alba, *The Mystery of Survival and Other Stories* (Arizona: Bilingual Press, 1993); John Rechy, *City of Night* (New York: Grove Press, 1963); and Arturo Islas, *No* (New York: Avon Books, 1991).

rasgos asiaticos

VIRGINIA GRISE

My maternal great-grandmother, great-grandfather, and grandfather were born in Canton, China. They all migrated to Mexico at different times *y ahora descansan en campo santos* in Monterrey and Tampico, Mexico. Though there have been books and articles written about the Chinese and Asian presence in Latin America, there are very few written about the Chinese in Mexico. Two years ago, my research partner Marco Iñiguez and I went to Monterrey to conduct a series of oral interviews with family members, their *colegas*, and friends. Each interview introduced me to another family and another world, and I soon discovered that this project was bigger than my family or me. The *paisanos*, those born in China, are dying, and with them, their stories. Telling our stories is a radical act. Memory is a form of resistance.

rasgos asiaticos, a forty-minute multi-media performance piece, is a collection of different voices, artifacts, and memories based on research and oral interviews conducted in Monterrey and Tampico. The performance is an installation of different *altares* that include original photos, letters, papers, and a collection of Chinese records from the 1920s. I use the music, photos, and stories to weave a history of three generations of women—grandmother, mother, and daughter—as they explore shared stories of identity, violence, and love. *rasgos asiaticos* moves in and out of these three voices throughout the piece but is performed by a single artist.

The excerpt below is a small piece of the larger work and was developed in workshops with playwright/poet sharon bridgforth, writer/director Daniel Alexander Jones, and director Adelina Anthony. I have performed it as a staged reading at the Esperanza Peace & Justice Center in San Antonio, Texas, the Mexican American Cultural Center (Red Salmon Arts) in Austin, Texas, and at Project Reach, New York, New York. An earlier version was also published in *La Voz de Esperanza*.

rasgos asiaticos

I.

Mother

Your grandfather Manuel Yee was a successful businessman, my mother used to say. He and your tío Andrés had the best puestos in all of Mercado Colón, the old marketplace, the one they tore down in the fifties—green shoot and bean sprout merchants in the mercado in Monterrey—titles and deeds signed in the name of their Mexican wives half their age. The fruits and vegetables they sold were from Tampico, adopted home of your great-grandmother, and they would buy from Angel, Carolina, and don Carlos Lee en el Mercado Asbastos. The Chinos from the lodgia masónica wouldn't buy their produce from anywhere else. Rafael Lee owned a yerbería next to your grandfather's puesto and Luis Wong owned the Zapatería Justicia. And we lived in a big red two-story house en el centro.

Daughter

but that's not the Mexico I knew

My grandmother
lived in a gray cinderblock house
en la colonia central
behind the bus station
calle Simón Bolivar
the metro cuts through the middle of the neighborhood
and all the houses shake when the train passes by

Do you remember when your grandmother was indian? my sister once asked
me. *She was indian*
before she was chinese she tried to explain

and I tried to imagine my grandmother
doña María
with trensas

The author's grandmother, mother, and father (María de Jesus Yee Cortez, Emma Lesi Yee Cortez, and Manuel Yee) at Emma's *quinceañera* at the Salon Versailles, Monterrey, Mexico, on May 5, 1959.

Grandmother

gray cinder-block house with dirt floors   when the light creeps through the windows in the living room it's like magic the way the dust floats in the rays of sunshine but mostly it's dark and you choke on the dirt   I feel like I can't breathe sometimes   earth in my throat   and I imagine   the desert y sé   I know that I have to go   I never wanted to stay here   tengo que irme

en la secondaria my mother pulls me out of school so that I can work   my father died and we need the money so I work cleaning houses like my mother and her mother   I want to be a doctor but my mother says that women aren't doctors anyway and I wish I was a man   I would have rather stayed in school with Margarita sitting next to me   she makes me laugh but my mother says I should be more serious and I wonder if I will ever see Margarita again   tengo que irme

the ladies I clean for treat me nice and sometimes they even give me food   I sit at their kitchen table and imagine living in their homes   their houses are never gray   their floors are not made of dirt but of white ceramic tile with designs on it.   I wish I could sit down and that they would clean for me but I never get to sit very long tengo que irme   I have to go to work

when I go home and tell my mother that the ladies feed me she gets mad and tells me to tell them no thank you that I'm not hungry   she says that they never ask her to sit at the table and that they just feel sorry for me because I'm a little girl   but I'm not a little girl so the next time they try to give me food I should look down and say very politely no thank you   así es   women do not choose do not ask do not want   but I will   sometimes I wish I were born into another body not my own not the one I was born into   so when the ladies ask me if I want something to eat   I look at them in the eyes and say sí por favor because I am hungry and because I know my mother is right   they feel sorry for me because I am young   and I know I will not be young forever   tengo que irme

I do not want to stay in that gray house   so every night when I come home from work I put some of the money I make underneath the mattress I know that one day I will save enough and will leave   tengo que irme

the walk from my house to el centro is long and I don't like to take the bus so I wake up early   earlier than my mother and I go to the mercado   the one she says not to go to by myself   and I buy fresh fruit from Andrés because he always gives me a pilón   cositas he has hidden in his puesto   dulce, pan, pasteles   his puesto is in front of the flower stand and I like the way it smells like brightness   tengo que irme

II.

Mother

Your tío, Andrés Wah Ginko, was my tío too. You see, he wasn't my blood uncle. In fact, he was older than my mother. Andresito was my father's companion who joined him in the journey from Canton to Tampico, but they didn't stay there long. They moved to Monterrey, where they lived together. When my father married my mother, Andrés didn't leave the home, and when my father died, Andrés moved with my mother to the home of her birth.

He gave candy to the neighborhood children, cooked fish soup with chile, and when you got sick, he fed you warm rice and milk. Andrés hung a picture of the Virgen of Guadalupe in his puesto at the market. The other Chinese merchants said that it was to attract Mexican clients, but your tío abuelo hung a picture of the Virgen in his bedroom too.

Daughter

when Andrés died
my family collected all of his belongings
his clothes
letters from his daughter in china
poetry written in symbols
history
taken outside
burned in a bonfire behind the house

it's a mexican tradition my mother said *we have to let the spirit of your
uncle rest*

before the ceremony
my blood uncle
my mother's brother
took a stack of mud covered records from the pile
wrapped them in a plastic soriana bag
and saved them from the fire

dust covered memories
hidden underneath
el chino's bed
talk-story

etched in
the grooves of old records
words I don't understand
memories I can't forget

it's a mexican tradition my mother said *we have to let the spirit of your
uncle rest*
mi espíritu left in gray ash in quietude red embers of olvido . . .

III.

Grandmother

I have to go I say   to work I tell him   my first husband the one I never talk about
to the movies? I like the movies so I say yes but after work   after the movies
he walks me home and the next day he walks me to work   gives me flowers   bright yellow flowers   I give them to the lady when I get to work so
that my mother won't know   I walk home alone that night and imagine that
I have a big house with white tile and yellow flowers in a vase   every morning he meets me after I go to the market and buy my fruit from Andrés   every morning for three months he meets me and walks me to work   my first
husband   the one I never talk about   tengo que irme
     one night I lift my mattress where I hide my money take it and like the light
in the morning I creep out of the window quietly out of my gray house and I
meet him on the corner underneath a bright street lamp underneath a dark
sky   I was indian before I was Chinese   I wore a white lace dress and my
hair in dos trensas rested on my chest.   he bought me that dress and a bou-
quet of flowers   my first husband the one I never talk about   tengo que irme
     his house doesn't have white tile and he stops giving me flowers   he starts
coming home late   he spends his nights at the bars then he starts hitting
me   I left my gray house for the smell of brightness and I won't go home
to hear my mother say she was right so I take the money from underneath
my mattress again and leave   tengo que irme
     in the church I kneel make the sign of the cross and ask the father what
I should do   I have one suitcase in my hand and my money pinned to the
inside of my dress   go back home to your husband he says   a woman didn't
live by herself in those days but I will   tengo que irme
     I never saw jesus again and he never looked for me   he was not a very good
husband my first husband the one I never talk about   I move into a small apartment on top of the cigar factory worse than my mother's home   my apart-

The author's mother (left) working at *el mercado*, Colon, Mexico, in the 1950s.

ment has cockroaches and the smell of the cigar factory gets caught inside my chest   I start to cough   I am coughing and every night I pray even though I do not go to church anymore   tonight I pray for forgiveness tomorrow when I go to the market I will ask Andrés if he needs a wife   I hear that it is hard for Chinese men to find wives in Mexico and I'm tired of the cockroaches ay dios mío señor I am sorry   tengo que irme

in the morning I walk slowly   I don't go to work that day   Andrés has a wife and a daughter   they live in china   I feel shame in my chest where the coughing hurts and I look at my feet but Andrés smiles and says that I should not worry   he invites me to his home in el centro   en una casa con cinco recámaras   dos baños   una cocina   cuántas personas viven aqui   le preguntó   dos   yo y manuel   Andrés feeds me   I sit in his kitchen and I feel like I'm a little girl again imagining this home mine   he explains to me that he lives with his companion Manuel and because they're chinamen they can't own anything   the house   their puesto en el mercado   and that he has a wife but Manuel he doesn't   will I stay he asks   tengo que irme

I lie in the bathtub and pray   I'm sorry mi'ja but I never wanted children not with him and I know you are inside of me and can feel what I'm thinking so I might as well say it   I do not want you   Manuel found out that today I went to see doña Teresa to ask her for hierbas the kind that would make you go away   he threatened to kick me out   I know you are inside of me and can feel what I'm thinking   I'm sorry   Andrés said he will help take care of you   take you to the market everyday   show you how to run the business because one day he'll be too old   I know that you are inside of me and can feel what I'm thinking   I'm sorry   I just want to be alone   I'm sorry tengo que irme   I have to go . . .

Only Strong Women Stayed

Women Workers and the National Floral Workers Strike, 1968–1969

PRISCILLA FALCON

On July 1, 1968, after months of organizing, the women-led National Floral Workers Organization (NFWO) went out on strike against the Kitayama Corporation's floral operations in Brighton, Colorado. One of the first floral-workers' strikes in which the organizers and the majority of the workers were Chicanas and Mexicanas, the strike quickly became a rallying point for the Denver-based Chicano Crusade for Justice, and the United Mexican American Students (UMAS) and Students for a Democratic Society (SDS) activists at the University of Colorado at Boulder.

The story of this strike, which has yet to be fully told within the historical context of Chicanas' struggle for justice, is part of a work in progress. The following account is drawn from oral interviews by the author with Guadalupe (Lupe) Briseno, then president of the NFWO and the "sparkplug" of the strike. Texas-born Lupe and her husband Jose Hernandez Briseno had worked as migrant laborers in Colorado for a number of years while raising their four children. When their youngest child was old enough to go to school, Lupe Briseno sought work:

> I found employment at Kitayama Brothers Company, in Brighton, Colorado. I went to work at the Carnation and Rose plant and recognized many women whom I had met in 1957 when we moved into the area. My friends, these women I had known, were now middle-aged, in their thirties and forties, sad and beaten down. They had no *animo*. . . . I looked around, and I asked what is going [on] here. The women told me how they were mistreated and taken advantage of by [the company and its managers]. I told them that workers are not to be treated without respect.[1]

Kitayama Brothers, a partnership in Brighton and in Union City, California, was one of the most influential members of the National Association of Florists (NAF). In 1966, Ray Kitayama located the sixty-unit greenhouse opera-

Lupe Briseno. Photo courtesy of Briseno personal archives, Brighton, Colorado.

tions two miles north of Brighton in Weld County, claiming to have moved into the area because of its need for industry. However, the Mexican women of the NFWO believed that the carnation and rose factory was located near Brighton in order to have access to cheap Mexican labor.

When Lupe Briseno began working at the plant, conditions in the greenhouses were very bad. The women were tired of the long hours and poor work-ing conditions, the lack of sanitary eating areas and the low wages. The women worked inside the nurseries on uncovered floors where dirt turned to mud, with the constant high humidity year around that produced several inches of water daily. During the winter months the humidity had the effect of produc-ing a continual misty rain. Under these conditions, slipping and falling were regular occurrences. Colds, flues, pneumonia, coughs, allergies, arthritis pain, and inflamed sinuses were common health problems suffered by workers. The women were not provided protective clothing or coverings of any kind to pre-vent them from getting wet or injured. Every day the women came to work dry and went home wet after working nine- to ten-hour days, including Saturdays and sometimes Sundays, with no overtime pay. The women were allowed one fifteen-minute work break in the morning and a half-hour lunch, and only a few were allowed a ten-minute break during the afternoon. One drinking fountain and two bathrooms served over one hundred workers. The women acquired no seniority rights.[2] Briseno later said:

> When I first walked into that greenhouse, and I see my friends . . . older than I am . . . crying because of the abuse that is going on in that plant. How can that be? We are Americans. We are born here, and it doesn't mat-ter, even if you are not born here, you are not supposed to be treated the way. . . . I was a housewife. This was the first job I got out of the house, and then to find out . . . that I was going to be working under those conditions . . . to be treated like animals . . . to be called names, and men could come up and say dirty jokes in the presence of women, mak-ing vulgar signs, talking dirty in loud voices, disrespecting all the women. I just can't take it, and I told the other women, "You don't have to cry; get off your knees and do something about it." And everyone decided together . . . we can do something about it.
>
> I called the women and men together to begin to think about how we could solve our problems at Kitayama's. I suggested two things: one that we organize, and two, that we support each other. I told the women that once the managers find out, things will get rough. Secretly we passed the word for women and men to organize themselves, and most were all for it. We called the first meeting, and many of the workers showed up, flower-cutters, maintenance [workers], drivers, and other employees. [But some-how the managers and owner Ray Kitiyama found out and came to the meeting to dissuade us.] [These intimidating tactics] only made me and the women more determined to fight for our rights. We all agreed that,

"We can't accept this. . . . It has to change." After this, the women and men became more careful, and they set a second meeting in Brighton, [and again their meeting was intruded upon]. Myself, the women, and men were offended . . . and concluded that we are not toddlers, we are grown men and women, and we can meet whenever we want. During this time the pressure was on [us], and some of the men were afraid of losing their jobs; they had families to support, and so they left. Now, only the strong women stayed.

We asked ourselves, Shall we quit or stay? And all the women said, No we will stay. The next day we go to work, and the first thing we see is police. Police at the gate, police inside the plant, police at the exits, police everywhere. Myself, the women, and the [other] workers had never seen anything like this—it was a police state. We were scared, we had done nothing wrong, we had violated no laws, we had hurt no one. Why was this happening to us? Some people started to cry, to vomit; some got diarrhea; most were intimidated. This was like being in the middle of war or something you read about in a book . . . or something that happens in another country, but not in America.

When things like this happen, you get angry. I'll never tolerate it; this has to change for our future . . . for our children, and for all human beings. For me, it is hard to see abuse. . . . We're all human beings . . . we are all here to work, . . . *no es verguneza trabajar* . . . to work any kind of work. We must respect all work—carnation workers, field workers, all labor, no matter what kind of labor. So, I called a meeting because we now knew that there were no laws to protect us. . . . The teamsters were invited because the truck drivers delivering the flowers to the airport needed to be involved. We called a meeting which was held at the Good Americans Organization/Paco Sanchez building. The teamsters were there, and the women from [the] Kitayama Carnation and Rose plant and [there was] support from the community—the building was packed. At this meeting we formed the National Florist Workers Organization. We wanted a union. . . . We wanted protection and power. [Mr. Ray] showed up again at this meeting. . . . [We felt intimidated, but] this time we were not scared because we had . . . *mas valor*. . . . We had our families, husbands, the teamsters, and community supporters. We were not going to be sacred away any more.

Briseno and the NFWO members spent several months working to set the groundwork for organizing a union. Strike preparation was divided into four steps. Step one outlined ways to organize the employees to support a union. The NFWO worked to prepare and plan a course of action once the union proposals were either accepted or rejected by the company. The NFWO had in place picket captains and assignments for each member willing to walk the picket line. Finally, the union worked to draw up a proposal and demands to be presented to Ray Kitayama. Step two involved preparations to be made before calling the strike and setting up the picket line. Picket captains were selected and written schedules for members were finalized. Picket signs were designed and produced by the women. The slogans read: "Unfair to Labor," "Deduct Income Taxes," "We Want Decent Wages," "We Want Seniority," and "We Want Job Rights"; the most prominent were red flags with the Aztec eagle in the center and the lettering NFWO-UFWOC, indicating NFWO's affiliation with the well-know United Farm Workers of California. Step three involved discussions of who the NFWO should approach for public political support. They decided on four public groups: local community organizations, churches, labor unions, and university student organizations. Each of these would have a variety of resources that NFWO might then have access to, thereby facilitating the strike campaign. One of the major concerns for the NFWO was obtaining legal council prior to the formation of the union and calling for a strike. They sought to be advised of their rights at every step of the way. The NFWO also engaged in their own investigation of the Kitayama Corporation before they called for public contract investigations. This involved documenting information on the production and shipment of flowers—how they were handled, by whom, where, and in what quantity. Step four concerned issues of wage and ranking scales. According to the NFWO, the more delicate the operation of work to be performed, the more wages the workers performing that work should receive. Seniority, medical benefits, and federal income tax and state income tax deduction from payroll were also deemed necessities. Briseno and the women of the NFWO argued that it was a great hardship when they had to pay taxes in one lump sum at the end of the year. The women also requested organized breaks each morning and afternoon following every three hours of work and the improvement of working conditions, for example, in spreading gravel or building planks over water pools that continually accumulated, sanitary eating areas, and access to bathrooms. Finally, they sought recognition of NFWO/UFWOC as the sole bargaining agent for their place of employment, empowered to negotiate wages, benefits, and working conditions.[3]

Belief in these proposals and demands would lead Briseno and NFWO into direct confrontation with Ray Kitayama and his management staff. Lupe Briseno was willing to sacrifice body and soul for recognition of the union and improvement of the working environment for all workers. By June of 1968, the

Lupe Briseno and supporters of the National Florist Workers Organization, 1968. Photo courtesy of Briseno personal archives, Brighton, Colorado.

NFWO had nearly seventy members, all of whom had signed the union card. Briseno recalled:

> After the meeting, the work of the union began. We went back to work, to each section of the Kitayama Carnation plant to talk to the workers about the union. Mr. Ray was not happy with me, and so, one Saturday in May after work I went home and was fixing supper when Mr. Ray and his assistant showed up at my door with my cutting knife, my hat, my drinking jar, and my gloves. He told me, . . . "You are fired."
>
> It was an honor that he took the trouble to come all the way to my house to fire me! I told Mr. Ray, "This [is] not the end of it! If we win, we win; if we lose, we lose; but, we'll give you a good fight!" The women talked, voted, and went on strike.

As Briseno and others were taking the legal steps necessary to form a union, they turned first to Teamsters Local 452 that represented the truck drivers who transported Kitayama flowers. But in early 1968, the Teamsters National Legal Research Department told them that the employees at Kitayama were classified as "farmworkers" and therefore were not subject to the National Labor Rela-

Lupe Briseno and two supporters of the National Florist Workers Organization, 1968. Photo courtesy of Briseno personal archives, Brighton, Colorado.

tions Act and National Labor Relations Board protection laws. Briseno then wrote directly to Cesar Chavez of the UFWOC in Delano, California, telling him that forty-five women had signed up with the NFWO and asking for guidance in their unionizing efforts. In June, after the National Labor Relations Board (NLRB) issued its ruling on their status and refused jurisdiction, the women requested that their group, the NFWO, be accepted with affiliate status by the UFWOC-AFL-CIO. Larry Itliong, assistant director of UFWOC/AFL-CIO, confirmed that affiliate status would be provided to the NFWO.[4]

One might argue that being officially classified as farmworkers by the NLRB was a strategic loss for the floral workers, but one might also see it as an emotional advantage. Specifically, denial of NLRB jurisdiction, and thus the legal right to organize, meant that the workers had little hope of obtaining recourse against Kitayama's union-busting efforts. On the other hand, affiliation with the United Farm Workers Union, led by Cesar Chavez and Dolores Huerta, then at the height of its national fame, was an invaluable source of strength, solidarity, and support.

On June 28, members of the NFWO voted to go on strike against Kitayama. The vote was unanimous, and the date selected was July 1, 1968. Briseno recalled:

> You know, the strike continued. For several months union supporters were outside the greenhouses picketing. Supporters were inside the plant organizing for a union. Mr. Ray hired young Anglo kids and others to break the strike, [and] he raised the pay so they would work, but soon they left the job.
>
> We attempted to negotiate with Mr. Ray, but he would not listen to us because we were women. We heard from friends, family, and farmworkers that some of the farmers in the area were attempting to improve conditions for the workers, because they did not want any trouble from the farmworkers. From what we were told, some farmers were fixing up the sheds that the farmworkers were living in.
>
> After months of day-after-day picketing, the NFWO gained support from the surrounding communities [of] Fort Lupton, Boulder, Denver. Mr. Ray wanted the union to go away . . . but we were not going anywhere. Nuns from the Catholic Church, teachers . . . the AFL-CIO, [and] Chicano students from University of Colorado at Boulder supported us, as well as the Crusade for Justice. But during those long days and nights, the picket lines grew smaller and smaller . . . and . . . being on the picket line on an isolated country road can be a dangerous thing. People were living on donations, and things were scarce. The families on the picket lines were seen as troublemakers. They couldn't get jobs in the area. Business people remembered your face being in the paper, in marches, and pickets. We were being blackballed.
>
> As the weeks went by, it became harder and harder for the women to stay on the picket line all day. The families were poor; they had bills to pay and needed to put food on the table and dress their kids. So many women went to work the beets, cucumbers, or in the Kunner packing factory. They would come to picket before they went to work, and after they got off of work, and then on weekends. I was on the picket line mostly every day.
>
> Working every day on the picket line was my job. I got no money, but that's not why I was there two hundred and twenty-one days. I knew we needed a union—the women needed a union; the community needed some protection. Walking the picket line sounds so simple, but it is not. Ray Kitayama had his armed guards. . . . The Weld County Sheriff's were always intimidating people, writing down license plate numbers.

Lupe Briseno and friends on the picket line at Kitayama Rose and Carnation plant, 1968. Photo courtesy of Briseno personal archives, Brighton, Colorado.

The scabs crossed the picket line sometimes. It was too hot, and then the weather changed and it became too cold. Then you begin to get arrested: They provoke you, and threaten you, and when you go to court, the courts don't see it your way. The courts try to pressure you to quit. I don't think the law is there for all of us, only for those who have money. The workers have very few rights. The courts and laws let the companies mistreat the workers. Like the National Labor Relations laws, why couldn't they protect us? Just so Kitayama could make a few more dollars off our backs? The courts believed that we, the National Florist Workers Organization, were provoking everything, and that's not true. In fact, Ray Kitayama's guards carried weapons; we didn't, and yet we were accused of being violent. The National Floral Workers Organization believed in Cesar Chavez's philosophy of nonviolence, and so it was our job to walk the picket line peaceful—summer and winter—holding our banners, *huelga* flags, and signs. We talked to the people who crossed the picket, and I would say, You see me here; why do you cross the picket line? . . . Do you like the way Kitayama is treating you? . . . Do you want your children to work like you do? . . . But some people don't see it like that, and that's why things don't work good sometimes.

As the strike continued, violence escalated:

Several women were on the picket line, like Mary Padilla, Rachael Sandoval, Martha del Real, myself, and others were also there. We had been doing this for about twenty-eight weeks, and the organization had been discussing and planning a large demonstration. The NFWO had support from Fort Lupton, Denver, Boulder, and several colleges and university campuses. The NFWO had been planning the march to bring an awareness to the people of what we are doing.

Tears began to form in Lupe's eyes as she continued: "People who have never been on a strike don't know how much sacrifice we made. . . . We were nonviolent; Kitayama and the police were violent." Tears flowed softly down Lupe's cheeks as she painfully recalled:

We were doing things as peaceful as possible, but somehow it came to the attention of Chuck Boomer, the supervisor inside the greenhouse. I'm sure he was the supervisor on the roses section. I think he was fed-up with seeing me on the picket line every day. One day in January, like the previous two-hundred-three days, I was setting up my picket signs, United Farm Workers flags, and getting myself ready at the picket line.

Tears came to Lupe's eyes, her voice cracked as she continued:

And, there are no people on the line but me. Well, overnight it had snowed a little, and in the morning, the icy wind was blowing. There I was, I had just finished putting my sign into the dirt by the road, and I was walking to take up my post near the cement sidewalk close to the entrance to the plant, so I could see the cars and talk to the employees as they went into work. At that point, Chuck came out and said, "I'm so fed-up to see you here; you

Left to right: Mary Padilla, Martha de Real, Lupe Briseno, Rachel Sandoval. A Weld County sheriff's deputy approaches with tear gas, Februar 15, 1969. Photo courtesy of Briseno personal archives, Brighton, Colorado.

shouldn't be on the picket line," and he shoved me. At that moment, I fell on my knees, and I thought I had hurt myself. . . . I got up somehow, and I picked up my *huelga* flag of the United Farm Workers, and I told Chuck, "This is not the end; we will stay here as long as we need to."

I then went to the G.I. Forum, and from there I made a call to the Crusade for Justice, [to] Corky Gonzales in Denver, and in twenty minutes Corky was there, and he said this guy will remember us. By Saturday, the Crusade, University of Colorado students, [the] SDS, community people, G.I. Forum—many people came to protest what had happened to me. Everyone was picketing, marching, and then somehow Chuck Boomer came to the gate to taunt the protestors. The next thing I knew Chuck Boomer was laying on the ground, knocked-out. The next day Ricardo Romero was arrested for assault on Chuck Boomer. He was released from Weld County jail, and a court date [was] set for April 24.

That's the way it happened. It happened almost forty years ago, but I can see it right before my eyes. . . . I didn't get to see Chuck get hit, but I did see him on the ground. You know we get blamed for violence, but they provoke the violence, they hurt us everyday—not just one day—as we fight for our rights.

On February 15, 1969, Lupe Briseno, Rachael Sandoval, Mary Padilla, Martha del Real and Mary Sailes chained themselves to the gates of the Kitayama plant as a last form of nonviolent protest. Within the hour, Weld County sheriffs arrived. Deputy D. B. Rutz flanked by two deputies turned on a tear gas machine and sprayed a snow-white layer of gas over the women, who instantly fell to the ground chained together, coughing and weeping. This is how Lupe remembers the last day of the strike:

> January of 1969 had been a very hard month for us because of the aggressive behavior from the guards and employees of Kitayama against the women on the picket line. I had filed complaints of assault and battery against Chuck Boomer and petty theft against George Brinkmann for stealing picket signs. So the National Floral Workers Organization decided in February that it was too dangerous for me to be on the picket line alone all day. On the seventh of February, Kitayama had succeeded in obtaining a temporary injunction by the order of Judge Hugh Arnold, Weld County Court.
>
> We, the women of National Florist Workers Organization, got together that following week to plan our strategy for ending the picket. We had meetings all week to get ready for Saturday, February 15.
>
> Mary Padilla, Rachael Sandoval (who was six months pregnant at the time), Martha del Real, Mary Sailes (who was Martha's aunt), and myself arrived at Kitayamas' about six a.m. In the early morning, the car lights were barely visible because of the heavy fog and mist. It was eerie. Well, that was the day we were going to chain ourselves to the gates of Kitayama. We all said, This is it. . . . We are gong to call if off, and this is how we will end our picketing. Everything had been planned out the week before; our final action was to be nonviolent protest.
>
> But we did not expect violence from the police. We decided to chain ourselves because the courts gave us no alternative. The week before they had issued a temporary injunction to stop the picketing; they were not on our side. We wanted the community to know about our struggle. We wanted to prevent the scabs from coming into work—that was the main thing. Mary, Rachael, Martha, Mary, and myself got ready because the workers would be arriving by seven a.m. We didn't know anything about the police. All five of us went to the fence and gate. We got the logging chain we had bought and wrapped it around our waists, and the men helped tie it with wire to prevent it from slipping. Meanwhile, Ramon Navarro and Jim Garcia were responsible for weaving the chain through the fence and placing padlocks on each end. After this, both supporters and workers began arriving. We could see lights moving up the road to

Kitayama's; it was very foggy that morning. Then, suddenly, a figure appeared in the road, stopping the workers cars and routing them to an alternative road behind the greenhouses.

The foreman and guard at Kitayama were running back and forth between the fence, where we were chained, and Ray's two-story house. We knew what was coming next. We heard sirens wailing in the distance, but the fog was so dense we couldn't see them coming until there were one hundred feet from our chains. The Weld County sheriff deputies arrived . . . jumped out of their cars, and approached the gate where we were chained. All I could hear was the boom-boom-boom of their boots as they walked past us under the chain wearing gas masks and . . . carrying something like a long machine-gun rifle. The men across the street—my husband Jose, Rachael's husband Sam, Mary Padilla's husband Gavino. Jim and Ramon ran across the street when they saw the Weld County sheriff deputies with this strange tear-gassing machine. Jose said, "They are going to try and kill you guys. Forget it, let's go," and the rest of the husbands tried to persuade us to leave. Rachael, Mary, Martha, Mary and myself, we said, "No, that's okay. We are right; they are wrong. They have workers in chains every day, only the workers don't realize this." We know that the police were attempting to scare us, who had no weapons, no guns. We were protesting with the only thing we had—our lives. We said to each other, "This is our way to do the fight; we will not leave." We didn't want to reach this point, but Kitayama, and the courts, and laws were not on our side. We didn't want to be tear-gassed. . . . We were chained, and we were not going to move. The chain was very thick, and after the men locked us up, I got the key and threw it away. We had our minds made up, nothing was going to change our plan.

Shortly after this, I guess it was Kitayama who gave the order to cut the chain. [The deputies] proceeded cutting the chain, which was attached to the main gate. It fell away. But the chain around the women's waist remained tight, so in effect, we were still chained together.

At that instant . . . three [deputies] wearing gas masks advanced on us women, and when they were face to face [one deputy] turned on the machine and sprayed a snow-white layer of gas over us. We were in shock, and some of us fell to the ground to get away from the tear gas. . . . We were coughing and weeping. The men, our husbands, and supporters ran up to help us out of the chains. They cut the wires holding the chain around us and gave us handkerchiefs. Rachael was pregnant, and we were worried about her. I still have the chain and the lock to prove it, for my kids and grandkids. . . . This is a part of history.

We wanted to show the workers that we believed in our rights, that we were nonviolent, and despite the injunction, we still believed in the union. We wanted the workers, the community, and our families to know that we were doing this for them, for ourselves, and our children. We wanted them not to cross the picket line. We had expected that the Weld County sheriffs would have arrested us, but instead they tear-gassed us. The week before, the court had given us an injunction; for months they had not listened to us. Kitayama did not want to negotiate with us, so what options do they give us?

Conditions on the picket line had become very dangerous . . . so this was the only way we can say, We're going to leave the picketing, but we're still going to give you a good fight, Ray Kitayama, and that is why we chose to chain ourselves. The only thing we have power over is our mind and body. . . . We didn't move. . . . They moved us out. . . . They cut our chain and tear-gassed—oh what big men they are.

Through our veil of tears, you could not see our broken hearts. We all believe that we have to get off our knees. We don't have to take abusive treatment. No one is supposed to have this kind of treatment. That was the end of the picket line. The conditions improved at the Kitayama Carnation and Rose plant, although we did not get a union. We were women of integrity, pride, and conviction. We went on strike because we wanted to be treated with dignity and to improve the working conditions and obtain better wages. You know, maybe we who went on strike didn't get the benefits of what we were fighting for, but other people did and that's good. We completed what we started.

Finally, as Lupe reflected:

Since then, my family and I have never crossed a picket line . . . because it [respecting the picket line] is the only way to gain something together, to make the work place better. We have always supported the farm-work struggle of our brother Cesar Chavez. Juanita and Alfredo Herrera were sent from California by Chavez to organize in Colorado. We supported their work because we know what it is like to be on the frontlines. You remember struggle. You remember how many people have suffered and died to change America. The struggle to overcome low wages, lack of medicines for children and families, lack of food for young people, increasing poverty. I don't know what it's going to take to change people to support struggles—we need to pay attention to all that is happening around us. I ask, My God, my God, why is oppression and racism still happening? People are not violent, but they are put into violent conditions. . . . They are put up against the wall. What do you do? You just can't close the door and forget about it, you stay on it and you change it—that is the honorable way, that is the right way, that is the way of human beings.

NOTES

1. The information in this article is based primarily on an interview I had with Lupe Briseno on September 2, 2001. The interview took place at her home in Brighton, Colorado. I have known Lupe Briseno for more than thirty years, as we are both participated in the Chicano movement in northern Colorado.

2. "*Viva la Huelga*: Battle for Labor Dignity," Colorado Labor Council, AFL-CIO, July 19, 1968, Briseno personal archives, Brighton, Colorado, hereafter cited as BPA; "Picket Line Formed at Kitayama Flowers, *Brighton Blade*, BPA, July 3, 1968, 2; Nancy Beezley, "Teachers Join Picket Line at Brighton Greenhouses," *Colorado Daily* (Boulder, Colorado), BPA, July 24, 1968, 1.

3. Guadalupe Briseno, interview with author, September 2, 2001.

4. "Boycotts and Strikes: Council in Accordance with Rules Enunciated by AFL-CIO is Declaring Two Boycotts: Against Capitol Life Insurance Company and Kitayama Brothers," Colorado Labor Countil, AFL-CIO, July 12, 1968; Jim Garcia to Cesar Chavez, April 17, 1968, BPA; "*Huelga Campesina en Colorado*," El Malcriado: La Voz del Campesino (Delano, California) 11:1 (1968): 1.

Una Historia de Una de Muchas Marías

MARÍA ANTONIETTA BERRIOZÁBAL

La profesora me dice, write about who you are. I have been intimidated about sharing my writings, especially in a scholarly journal. My language may not be appropriate for the form required. Why is it, I ask myself, that I am able to speak anywhere, to anyone, in any setting and do just fine thinking on my feet but fear sharing my writing? I think it is because my story is not only my story. It is also the story of those who came before me.

My story does not start with my birth. My life's journey began so very long ago. From childhood days, I received a gift: I learned the story of my family of origin. I guard it, precious as the universe itself. It is my universe.

Apolinar Rodriguez and Sixta Arredondo, my parents, crossed the Mexican-U.S. border separately with their parents during the Mexican Revolution of 1910. Maria Rodriguez, my great-grandmother, crossed with her children Sebastiana and Felix and her baby grandson Apolinar in 1910. Theresa Torres Arredondo and Melecio Arrendondo crossed with Pepita, Blas, and Sixta, who was then four years old. That is the beginning of my story. Because I am a fortunate woman to still have my parents at ages ninety-three and ninety-two respectively, my parents' stories are still being written. Their storytelling continues as I care for my *mama y papa*.

When my family crossed there was no border. Family members had been going back and forth from the interior of Mexico to Texas for many years. In the case of my mother, her family traveled on burros from their little town of Doctor Arroyo near Monterrey in the state of Nuevo Leon. They took a train from Monterrey to Nuevo Laredo and took another train into San Antonio, Texas. Her father literally walked on the railroad tracks—*el camino de fierro*—part of the way when he came alone on an exploratory trip. My mother recalls being mounted on a burro packed high with *carne seca*, a dried meat that the travelers carried to eat on the way. The story of how her burro almost fell into an

Felix Rodriguez Sr. and Sebastiana Ramirez Rodriguez with their children, Lockhart, Texas, 1922.

embankment with her still on it was one of the most repeated stories of my childhood.

Both the Arredondo and Rodriguez families joined relatives and friends who had come before them to work the vast landholdings of German immigrants near Lockhart, Texas. These Mexican immigrants were sharecroppers and they came to work the land. As my parents even just recently recounted, all that was necessary was that the new family have "*manos.*" The German landowner only had to know two words in Spanish, "*Quantas manos?*" The hands of even the children counted because they could work in the cotton, corn, and sugarcane fields.

The Mexican families created a community when they arrived. These families brought their stories, religious practices, music and dance, healing practices, foods, and the work of their hands. They brought a language and a culture. The first beautiful art pieces that I saw as a child were my grandmother's *bordados* and *tejidos*, embroidered and crocheted articles such as tablecoths and pillow cases. To this date, my mother can recite from memory the poetry she learned as a child. Her songs filled our house with music.

Apolinar and Sixta were not allowed to attend any public school as very young children. Texas public schools in those years were only for white children. Apolinar was fortunate to arrive in the small community of Martindale where there was a Catholic church that sponsored a school with classes taught in Spanish. Sixta had to wait for any education until public schools in Texas accepted her. By then, however, she was a young lady and was taken out of school to help in the fields. "*Como me dolio salir de la escuela. Me gustaba tanto,*" are the feelings she has expressed as long as I can remember; she loved school so much that leaving hurt her. But even in the brief time both my parents had in a formal education setting, they learned to read and write in Spanish and English. They also learned some of U.S. culture, like Christmas carols that we sing at home to this day.

The life that families like mine had to endure in those years was difficult and painful. The housing made available in the midst of the fields was pathetic. They cared for their sick with home remedies and herbs that the women planted. They suffered the humiliation and pain of discrimination. The combination of discrimination and poverty is lethal. It was so not only for my parents' families but also for all Mexicans and blacks. This manifested itself in the early deaths of family members. My *abuelito* Felix died in his forties from tuberculosis, as did two of his sons. My *abuelita* Sebastiana and my father nursed them. My father took over as the man of the house after his father died. The story of how my uncles and grandfather died is recorded not only in my mind but also in my bone marrow. It will never leave me. Because of the need for quarantine the family built a small shed away from the main house. I have always had the image of my handsome young father at the age of twenty-six and twenty-seven walking out to that shed to feed and care for his loved ones. I can see my grandmother *con su rebozo* that she always wore listening to the horrible, unending coughing that ended only when death came.

My mother also suffered through the illness of a loved one. My *abuelita* Teresita had asthma, another ailment that could not be treated. Some weeks ago when my mother was sick she was repeating a story I heard often as a child. Sometimes my grandmother would be sick with fever, coughing, and struggling for breath all night. My mother would sit by her bedside all night long. My grandmother died of pneumonia at the age of sixty-seven. My mother also lost a young brother whose appendix burst.

I grew up with many, many stories, including those that were funny and joyous. Growing up in the open air—*libre al interpiere* (in nature)—was a gift. Families could grow vegetables if time allowed after the fieldwork. They could have cows, chickens, goats, and horses. The main message of many stories was what it is to be *familia*. In the joy and in the sorrow *familia* is what counts. Always there was pride in being who we were. "*Somos mejicanos. Venimos de una cultura digna.*" But the most powerful message of my childhood was the importance of faith and service. "*Hay un Dios y El nos cuida. Hay que tener fe y servir al projimo.*" We must have faith and be of service to our neighbor.

Faith. Hard work. Responsibility. Education. Family. Community. Although my acceptance of these values has been an evolutionary process, they continue to be the main anchors of my life. I have always marveled at how the messages were transmitted. Most of my learning did not come from my parents directly telling me to do things. I heard plenty of stories and they had powerful messages, but these stories did not teach me all I learned either. What shaped my life was how my parents treated us as children. We were respected. Our opinions were valued. "*Andele, mija puede*" ("Look! My daughter can do it"), my father would say as he handed some *papel importante* to me. He trusted that I could handle whatever transaction the important paper demanded. My mother would say with pride, "*Hay, mira nomas lo que hizo la nina*" ("Oh! Just look at what our little girl did"), as I completed some task assigned to me at home or something I decided to take on myself. To a young girl these were mighty affirmations.

When my parents left the fields they settled in San Antonio. The only work my father could find was construction work, mostly as an unskilled laborer. My mother worked at home all her life, raised six children, and stretched the dollar as no other I have ever known. She had the gift of being able to feed us and dress us on a shoestring budget.

My father's weekly paycheck went directly to my mother. She was in charge of groceries and other needs. I marvel to this day at the miracle of how they made ends meet. When I was a teenager, my father was earning the most he had ever earned. He earned fifty dollars a week, and we children were all in Catholic schools, which required paying tuition. I do not recall ever being hungry or missing a meal.

But not all was rosy. Poverty takes a toll on a family, on a child. These scars last a lifetime, and they are transmitted from generation to generation. The economic systems dependent on labor penalize the working poor. Racism and discrimination affect everyone, and these abide everywhere, even in the best institutions. The institutions that had an impact on my family and shaped my life were the school and the church. I am grateful for the education I received in my early school years, yet I had to work, had to heal wounds inflicted by thoughtless or even mean-spirited teachers.

I also learned about discrimination within the environment of the church. As a very young child, I observed the Spanish priests treating wealthy and well-dressed parishioners with deference. Even so, regardless of the messengers who were sent my way, it was the traditions of Catholic social justice that had the most profound influences on my life. Putting faith into action was a value that I took seriously.

Most of my childhood was spent on Picoso Street. When we purchased our house with a loan from my father's brothers, the house had two rooms and an

Felix and María Antonietta stand next to their mother, Sixta Rodriguez, who holds Louis. They stand in front of the first home owned by Apolinar and Sixta Rodriguez in San Antonio, Texas. The photograph was taken around 1944.

outdoor toilet. We were four children then. As the two youngest ones came, my father built some more rooms. The school we all attended was across the street from our house. The church was only half a block away. The Gonzalez store was on the corner. The bus stop was half a block away. With no car to take us beyond our little barrio, an area no larger than two blocks was our whole life.

Christ the King Catholic School was run by the Cordi Marian Sisters and was our educational home from kindergarten until the eighth grade. The Mexican nuns who ran the school had been chased out of Mexico during the war against the Cristeros. Although many of my memories of grade school are very painful, the nuns prepared us well for high school. The pain came from watching schoolyard bullies who would beat up on my brothers. I would defend them at times, running after the oppressors and sometimes scratching a face while hanging onto a neck. Other painful experiences were the nuns' own internalized oppression that manifested itself in favoring the fair-skinned and well-dressed children. Also, they did not respect my parents as I thought they should be respected. I eventually came to understand that these nuns had been victims of racism and discrimination in their own journeys. Oppression begets oppression.

Christ the King Church itself provided most of our entertainment. The church's liturgical calendar offers many interesting opportunities for little kids. *Semana Santa*, or Holy Week, provided the longest celebrations. On Holy Thursday we would get holy bread and see the priest washing some people's feet, and it was a highlight of the year. That Thursday you could stay around the church almost all day long because the congregation would be invited to the adoration of the Blessed Sacrament, which lasted until about noon on Friday.

I most remember my grandmother Sebastiana from this time. She belonged to all the organizations, so she was present for each group's prayer hour. She would merely change ribbons, *distintivos*, on her chest after each hour. One of the strongest memories I have of my paternal grandmother was her self-confidence and unabashed way of worshipping. In the middle of some really quiet moment during an adoration time she would suddenly get up and start singing. She reached really high notes. I can still hear her:

> *Alabado sea el Santisimo,*
> *Sacramento del altar,*
> *En el cielo y en la tierra*
> *Aqui y en todo lugar.*[1]

I would be watching from the back and would at first be embarrassed, but then the ladies around her and then all the people who were in the church would get up and join her. Wow! That was impressive.

My grandmother was active in all the ladies' societies of the parish. She held offices in most and was president of several. This would amaze me as a child. How could my *abuelita* be *presidenta*? She could not write, so how could she do it, I wondered. She was a real leader. The people of the church respected her. She would organize fundraisers such as making and selling *tamales* or *bunuelos*. Until a couple of years before she died at the age of ninety-two, she managed the *manita* at the many church *jamaicas*, or festivals. The *manita* was a small wheel that sat on a table. The smallest children would pay a nickel or so, spin the wheel, and get a prize. The wonderful thing about the *manita* was that it was the only game where you would always win. So my grandmother was quite popular with the younger set. The older I get, the more I feel my grandmother walks with me in what I do.

Aunts and uncles from both sides of my family were members of assorted organizations at the church. The young women were *Hijas de Maria* or Children of Mary. The men were *Caballeros de Cristo Rey*, literally Gentlemen of Christ the King. My father belonged to this group. But my poor mother with six kids never belonged to anything. When I was about twelve she tried to join the Legion of Mary, but it meant that she would have to leave the house at dinnertime. She went a couple of times, but it did not work. For one, I made a big deal of not wanting to cook supper because I did not want to make flour tortillas. I couldn't make them. I rebelled and told my father that a young woman did not need to know how to make tortillas. I told him it was not necessary for life. My father and mother never asked me to make them again. My mom quit the Legion after only several meetings.

High school took me out of *mi barrio* for the first time. I graduated from Providence High School under the tutelage of the Sisters of Divine Providence. My experience in high school was a lot better than in grade school. In high school the sisters respected me. Some of them acted as advisors and took me under their wing. It was at Providence that I met *Americanas* for the first time. Most of the students at the high school were Anglo girls, but I do not recall any problems. They had pretty clothes to wear on days we did not wear uniforms, but then some of the Mexican American girls also had really pretty clothes. I think that class, more than race, was an issue at our school. My experience at Providence was good. I can still sing the school song:

Oh, Providence, our beacon
Through life's weary storm.
We will love you forever.
Our haven from harm.

I was a good student, but I would have been an excellent student if had I studied more. I barely studied and made good grades. But I was impatient to get out of school. I had to go about my mission.

When I was fourteen years old I developed "my mission": to help my parents with household expenses so that my three brothers and two sisters could finish high school and go to college. Upon graduation I started working part time as a secretary to the commanding officer of The Salvation Army in San Antonio, typing Christmas envelopes for one dollar an hour. That job lasted six years.

My first bosses at the Salvation Army were more like parents than supervisors, and they taught me a lot. When a racist Salvation Army officer came from East Texas, though, I was in trouble. I had to leave a job that I grew to love as no other I have ever had. After six years, I had taken on more responsibilities than those of a secretary. The new boss brought his own staff and found a way to ease me out. In front of the entire staff, he falsely accused me of spreading rumors about him. He added that he would sue me for libel. As a naïve young woman, I was frightened and devastated. Yet, my coworkers remained silent.

I had grown to love my job with the Salvation Army, but I left my job on that same day.

HemisFair '68, a world's fair held in San Antonio, was in the planning stages in 1966 when I joined its legal staff as the secretary to the general counsel. I was exposed to the politics of San Antonio and of Texas in that position. I started to learn how the political and business establishments rule a city. I learned how they use the political process to accomplish their ends. I developed a keen interest in politics. I began to see that if I got involved in this system and learned about the people who ran it, I could use these tools to help my community. This job led me to a new job as executive secretary to the county judge of Bexar County. I stayed for about six years and was again immersed in government and politics.

During all these work years I attended school at night. I involved myself in neighborhood issues and was very active in my parish. I worked with other young Latinas to organize the Mexican American Business and Professional Women's Club of San Antonio in 1972. This was one of the first such organizations in the country. We organized out of need. As young Mexican American working women, most of us were solitary pioneers in the places where we worked. Very frankly, I was lonely for a support system, but the fledgling feminist movement was not a place where I felt comfortable. Others felt the same, and the women I met through our organization not only provided support, but also instructed me, inspired me, and provided a channel for my incredible energy. At this time I also became active in Democratic Party politics and other community organizations.

By 1971 all my siblings had obtained their college education. One of my brothers was an attorney, another was on his way to becoming one, and my other brother got a degree in economics. All graduated from St. Mary's University in San Antonio. My two sisters obtained teaching degrees at Our Lady of the Lake College in San Antonio (now named Our Lady of the Lake University). I was thirty years old and had spent thirteen years of my life helping my family and my community. It was a very happy time of my life.

The next year I met a wonderful man who would be my partner for my life. Manuel Berriozábal and I were married in 1975. Our first project as a married couple was to help me complete my college education. I did so in May 1979, twenty years to the day of my graduation from high school.

With diploma in hand it was easy to land my first professional position. In 1980 I directed the San Antonio District Census Office with a workforce of over fourteen hundred employees. Managing this gigantic effort took me to every corner of my city and was a highlight in my life. But the job also showed me the faults of a federal bureaucratic system that insisted on creating one-size-fits-all efforts that allowed poor people and minorities to fall through the cracks. The Decennial count was a clear example. I had to use every contact I had ever developed in community groups, churches, politics, and government to assure that we minimized an undercount of urban residents.

The census experience, a supportive family, and politically astute friends all helped me to make a decision to run for public office when I completed the census work. In the fall of 1980 I announced my candidacy for councilwoman of District One at the doorsteps of my parents' home in the neighborhood where I had grown up. Our campaign was one of the most insightful experiences of my life. Clearly, we were thought to be political underdogs. "Maria is a nice lady but she will never make it," was the prediction of the day. "Nobody knows her." But a surprise was in store.

The effects of the Chicano movement, the elimination of at-large elections, and a growing neighborhood association movement made it a great opportunity for leaders like myself to get elected. We had cut our political teeth at the neighborhood level. Our issues had remained the issues of our *comunidad*.

In the spring of 1981 I was elected the first Latina councilwoman in the history of San Antonio. In that same election, Henry C. Cisneros was the first Latino in contemporary times to be elected mayor of a large American city. I credit the work of hundreds of women and men over decades for the foundation that made it possible for both of us to win elective office. Many sacrificed to open those doors, and Cisneros and I were privileged to walk in.

I took the values of my childhood, the dreams of my family, and the history of a people to my work. The democratic principles I had studied in college became guidelines for my service, along with the values of Catholic social justice. My job was cut out for me. My inner-city district was mostly Mexican American, generally working class, and poor. My constituents lived in twenty-four distinctive neighborhoods, including seven apartments for the elderly and three of the largest public housing projects in the city. Downtown San Antonio was smack in the middle of my district.

Very soon my vision for my position began to clash with the competition for scarce resources in the recession of the 1980s, the return to federalism of Ronald Reagan, the enormous power wielded by the business establishment, and the reality of local politics. The clash continued for the whole decade that I served. A Hispanic male political leader told me once that I would not get ahead in politics because I emphasized the "soft" issues. While I never thought that sustainable development, affordable housing, investment in youth and elderly programs, care for the environment, and neighborhood revitalization were soft issues, I understood the remark and know that many people also held his viewpoint. I kept my focus on those priorities but they were definitely not

Councilwoman María Antonietta Berriozábal speaking in front of the state capitol building in Austin, Texas, on March 24, 1984, at a rally commemorating the tenth anniversary of the assassination of Archbishop Oscar Romero. Photo by Susan Klein.

the priorities for everyone in San Antonio in those years. Near my heart always was the basic duty of government to be fair and inclusive, and to protect the civil rights of all people. These were critical values, especially in the communities that I represented because of a history of politics of exclusion.

My work was a joy during those ten years in office because of the devoted service of a small staff, interns, volunteers, neighborhood leaders, and friends. Having others use my platform for their voices, providing a space at city hall for the average citizen, providing instruction on how to fight city hall, and using the bully pulpit that elective office provided made of my decade of service a deeply satisfying experience.

By 1990 I had decided that the only way to solve the long-term problems our community faced was to hold the higher position that encompasses the entire city. I decided to run for mayor of San Antonio. I used my record of ten years in my campaign, including the major votes I had lost: the building of a major sports stadium, construction of a water reservoir that was a waste of money, continuous zoning changes for development over our sole source of water, annexation, and tax abatements. These were the accomplishments that the Cisneros administration celebrated. In my view, however, these were expensive, short-term actions that burdened the poor and working class. They did not assist in solving long-term economic or social problems we had in San Antonio. In contrast, my consistent theme was the investment in human capital as a major thrust for economic and community development in San Antonio.

Standing on these principles and with the help of over one thousand volunteers, in the spring of 1991 I led a field of eleven candidates with 30 percent of the vote while incumbent two-term mayor Lila Cockrell, who had succeeded Cineros, came in third. I had enough votes to go into a runoff election with a fellow councilperson who was quite wealthy. I lost the runoff election with 47 percent of the vote. We were outspent and did not have even one of the major business interests in the city with us. Many prominent Hispanic leaders worked against us, too, and so we saw this percentage as an outstanding victory, even though we lost the election. This was the first time a Latina had run for mayor of a large city in the United States.

I left public office then, but continued to work on the same issues as a private citizen. I have served on many boards and commissions and have volunteered my time as speaker, presenter, and participant in countless events. During the Clinton administration I was appointed U.S. Representative to the Interamerican Commission on Women of the Organization of American States agency.

My work with this commission led to an appointment as a member of the U.S. Official Delegation to the Fourth World Conference on Women in Beijing, China, in 1995, where I was privileged to meet women from throughout the world. At that conference I received a great affirmation of my trajectory in politics. My belief was that what the world needs today is leaders who will not be afraid to focus on the "soft" issues previously discussed, because they truly are the major issues of the day. The women I met in Beijing understood this. They had seen the same needs in South Africa, in the Indigenous communities of South and Central America, and in other parts of the southern hemisphere. The needs were even greater in some of the Middle Eastern countries and China. In Beijing I saw myself as part of a worldwide movement of women who are making contributions in their communities and in their countries. The work may be the formation of workers rights movements, rural development, or civil rights efforts. The unifying factor in Beijing was that these were women working for women. Out of the Beijing conference came the first international declaration that Women's Rights are Human Rights. I was part of the writing and the consensus building of that document. It will be many years before this great statement is understood. But in Beijing we started the discussion. After this experience I feel that I am part of a huge movement of women all over the planet working for a more inclusive, compassionate, and just world. Being on the same path with such incredible women gives more meaning to my life.

Recently I have returned to the place where I started my life. I am spending much time as caregiver to my parents. Accompanying them on their last journey takes me to my early years. My father keeps repeating how proud he is of his children and grandchildren. He tells me that we should be proud of what we have accomplished because of where we started.

I spend time with my mother listening to her stories and thinking about how I spent time with her when I was a very little girl. "What did you tell me?" I ask her. She does not remember, but she is quick to tell me what I looked like. She describes the dresses she made for me, including details like what buttons and ribbons she sewed on them. She also recalls the sad experiences of her life. One that she cannot forget is the asthma of my oldest brother. There was no cure and no money to take him to doctors. She cries as she describes his wheezing, crying, and inability to breathe at the age of eight months. There is nothing as painful, she says, as seeing a baby so sick and not being able to do anything to help. Miraculously, my brother grew out of his illness when he was twelve.

In this the sixtieth year of my life I find I turn to my interior as never before. Being with my parents takes me back not only to my childhood but also into the lives of my ancestors. I realize every day how much we are connected with the past. I realize how utterly necessary it is that we know where we came from. As we hear it often said, if we do not know where we have been we cannot know where we are going. Simply said, our world has gotten very complicated. A good way to keep our composure about us is to anchor ourselves in our history, both individually and as a community. We must understand that we stand on the shoulders of those who came before us. It is only through this understanding that we each will know how much we need to do so that some day others will be able to say the same about us.

"What are you doing now, María?" is the question I often get asked.[2] It is not an easy question to answer. What I am doing is preparing myself for the next part of my life. That will be the time that I become part of the oldest generation, and I want to do that well. This takes preparation. I have been given time and opportunity to travel this road with my elders, to study, to reflect, to read, and to write. I want to continue traveling that road. After I say goodbye to them, I want to keep that road open so that others may travel behind me.

NOTES

1. The translation of this passage is: Adored be the Blessed Sacrament of the altar, in heaven and on earth, here and in all places.

2. Since I wrote this piece, my role as caregiver for my parents has expanded as they become frailer. In addition, recent months have brought one of the most difficult

times of my life. The turmoil has been great because the struggle involves my beloved husband. At an age when many have retired, my husband Manuel Berriozábal is still building upon a long career of unselfish commitment to education. He is a mathematician at the University of Texas at San Antonio, and is founder and Executive Director of San Antonio PREP, TexPREP, and Proyecto Access—award winning pre-college math and science enrichment summer programs conducted at more than thirty college campuses in Texas, eight other states, and Puerto Rico. These programs target minority students and women. In his work, he has had to struggle with unexpected, unjust, and most painful issues, and this latest journey has forced me to search deeper for meaning. This has affirmed my belief in the interconnectedness of our human family. I have found sustenance in the love and support of family and friends, and have also found myself in solidarity with the global struggles that have caused so much grieving for humanity today. All our stories are one.

Rosita Fernández

La Rosa de San Antonio

DEBORAH R. VARGAS

The romantic and historic city of San Antonio is more beautiful when at night one hears the sweet voice of the "first lady of song" from San Antonio. She is the diminutive Rosita Fernández. Her very special style with romantic songs is recognized in many places, from Hollywood, where she had a starring role in Walt Disney's *Sancho the Homing Steer*, to México and New York, where she has had great success on television and in the best clubs. Often, Rosita's voice has delighted United States President Lyndon B. Johnson, and on his renowned ranch, she has performed for the president of México and for other European dignitaries. In her travels, Rosita has always received the finest attentions, but she always returns to her adoptive city, San Antonio, Texas. Rosita and San Antonio are inseparable.

Walter Jurmann, *San Antonio (Ciudad De Encantos)*, Rosita Fernández, Miramar Music MR-502.

Rosita Fernández has performed publicly for more than sixty years and has continually negotiated her representation and iconography as "Rosita," "San Antonio's Rose," "La Rosa de San Antonio," and "San Antonio's 'First Lady of Song'"—the latter name bestowed upon her by Lady Bird Johnson. Rosita navigated through varied musical expressions, audiences, and gendered expectations throughout her career, all the while maintaining her desire to be a public performer, to earn a living, and to make a home in San Antonio. As a Mexicana public performer in Texas, the ability to carve out a livelihood as a public performer was quite a feat, particularly in the earlier decades of the twentieth century.[1] Rosita's negotiations of racialized representations, language, gender, and class as a Mexicana public figure in San Antonio reveal the complexity and tensions that exist for Tejana (Texas-Mexican female) singers within a hegemonic Anglo-Texan public sphere.

The brief biographical overview presented below of Rosita Fernández's life and career reveals intricate ways in which she negotiated aspects of her career and personal life. Moreover, this overview validates a Mexican American woman singer's life story that has gone unrecognized and under-explored.[2]

Rosita Fernández was born in Monterrey, Mexico, in 1918, to Petra San Miguel and Cesar Fernandez. Around 1924, she and her family migrated through Laredo into Texas, eventually settling in San Antonio at the age of nine.[3]

When Rosita and her family crossed the U.S.-Texas border into Laredo, they did not find it to be as explicit a demarcation between the United States and Mexico as it is today:

La frontera no existía. Era muy fácil. Mi papá y mamá con tanta familia, pues cuando nos imigraron nos pasamos por acá por Laredo, Tejas. Lo que cobraban entonces era cinco dólares por persona y tres y medio o cuatro por los chiquios . . . era mucho más facil.[4]

The border didn't exist. It was very easy. My father and mother with so much family, well, when we immigrated, we came through Laredo, Texas. What they charged then was five pesos per person and three-fifty or four for the little ones. It was very much easier.

Rosita described San Antonio in the 1930s and 1940s as *"un Mexico chiquito"* (a little Mexico). Her entrance into San Antonio's public cultural sphere was within a vibrant urban landscape. Her statement is validated by the demographics of the time. During the 1930s and 1940s, Texas had the largest Mexican presence of any state in the South. Also, according to the 1930 U.S. Census, over 60 percent of the Mexican residents in Texas were born in the United States. Within the context of racial segregation and economic subordination of Mexicanos in Texas, a vibrant culture of Spanish-language song and cultural ambience was expressed whenever Rosita and other Mexicano singers and musicians stepped into the South Texas public sphere.[5]

For Rosita, San Antonio has always been home—a place that represented the possibility for extending the cultural legacy of Mexico she so strongly embraced and desired in her cultural production. Although no longer having strong ties to the land where she was born, her love and respect of Mexico was absolute, as was her love of Texas. Throughout my oral history interviews with Rosita there was a consistent reference to San Antonio as home because this was the place where she grew up and where her talents flourished and were transformed.

Rosita's musical career involved constant play between dual languages and between audiences of varied ethnicities and social classes. On radio and in live performances, publics ranged from working-class Mexicanos to middle-class Anglo-Texans. It is this fluidity across culture, time, and geography, as well as the staunch and ever-present marking of *Mexicanidad* upon Texas land, that have been foremost in Rosita's cultural work and in her philosophy about what her performances have contributed to public culture.

SIX DECADES OF PUBLIC PERFORMANCE

Las Carpas

Rosita credits her love of music and singing to her mother's family. Rosita recalls her mother's joy when she heard Rosita's voice on the radio for the first time. Her mother, Patrita San Miguel de Fernández, loved singing and sang to the family when Rosita was young. Rosita recalled, "Oh mama was very happy, because she had a voice too. All the San Miguel's on my mother's side had pretty voices. Every time we would go by my mama and papa's house, and she was singing, he [papa] would come to the door and say 'your mama is singing,' and we would wait until she would finish." [6]

In the late 1920s Rosita began traveling as the lead singer with the Trio San Miguel, a singing group comprised of her uncles Santiago, Sotero, and Fernando, performing in *carpas* (tent shows) along the migrant path throughout south and central Texas, including Robstown, Falfurrias, Alice, San Antonio, and San Marcos (fig. 1). At that time, Tejana/o singers like Rosita could find work in *carpas* such as La Carpa Cubana or Stout Jackson's El Teatro Carpa. In fact, San Antonio was the home base of many *carpa* companies. [7] Initially, *carpas* were primarily a site for showing movies, sometimes charging a bit extra to include a variety show.

Besides *carpas*, *teatros* (Spanish-language theaters) provided another venue for Tejano/Mexicano public entertainment, and both served as important sites for the symbolic construction of class identities, with more of the middle-class population participating in the arena of *el teatro*. Spanish-language theater in Texas extends as far back as 1884, when Mexican actors performed at the Salón Teatro del Mercado, and Spanish-language theatrical companies traveled widely in the early 1900s. As many as twenty-five Mexican-based and local touring companies entertained Tejano audiences by 1910. These Mexican theater companies performed throughout south Texas, establishing theatrical circuits from Rio Grande City and Brownsville throughout central Texas. [8]

Figure 1: Rosita Fernández in one of her earliest professional photos with her uncles' El Trio San Miguel. From left to right: Santiago, Sotero, and Fernando (man at farthest right unidentified). Photo courtesy of the University of Texas at San Antonio Archives, Library, University of Texas at San Antonio.

Stout Jackson's El Teatro Carpa was one of the most popular *carpas*. Jackson initially created an entertainment niche in south Texas by seizing the opportunity to make money screening Spanish-language films in big circus tents. He would travel to Mexico frequently to buy Mexican movies and eventually would host some of the finest Mexican entertainers of the time, including Cantinflas, Dolores Del Rio, Tin Tan, Jorge Negrete, and Pedro Almendariz.[9] Rosita and Trio San Miguel worked almost exclusively for Jackson's El Teatro Carpa.[10] Although she was quite young to be traveling without her mother, Rosita later said that performing with her uncles provided her security and safeguarded her reputation as a young woman on a public stage. She also recalled the racism and discrimination she faced as a young woman performer: "It was hard because of the social barriers against Mexican Americans and other minorities I remember when I would perform with my uncles in the surrounding towns. We could not even go into the restaurants to eat when we were hungry."[11]

Records

Rosita made her first 78-rpm single with the Trio San Miguel in 1931. Rosita was one of the first Mexican American women in Texas to record during the early part of the twentieth century. Rosita's recording career included solo performances as well as duets, such as those she recorded with her sister and with Laura Hernandez, as "Rosita y Laura" in the mid-1940s.[12]

Many of her earliest recordings were with her sister Berta as "Duo Fernández," "Las Diniamicas Estrellitas," and "Las Hermanas Fernández." For example, on August 9, 1934, the Duo Fernández recorded "Tres Dolonias" and "Traigo un Sentimiento" for Bluebird Records at the Texas Hotel. In 1937, Hermanas Fernández recorded "Aburrida me Voy" and "Me Tocó Perder" for Decca Records, in Dallas, Texas. Also in 1937, Rosita recorded "Elevo al Cielo" and "El Ranchero Afamado" with the Trio San Miguel on Vocalin (Brunswick Record Corporation). On average, the trio and duets were paid twenty-five dollars per song. In all, duet and solo recordings included those with local Tejano record labels, such as Discos Ideal and Discos Falcon, as well as with national recording labels, such as Brunswick, Vocalin, Decca, Blue Bird, and RCA Victor.[13]

Rosita was also accompanied by some of the most legendary Tejano *orquestas* (Texas-Mexican orchestras). Rosita performed with the Beto Villa orchestra and the Eduardo Martinez orchestra for over five decades.[14]

Rosita's last recording was a self-produced compact disc, *La Legendaria: San Antonio's First Lady of Song, La Rosa de San Antonio*. She demonstrated the influence of Augustin Lara, Mexico's most notable composer of boleros (music written in the rhythm of the bolero dance) in her selection of such songs as "Granada" and "Maria Bonita." Rosita often said that boleros were her favorite songs.[15] Rosita ends the compact disc with a remake of Bob Wills's "San Antonio Rose," exemplifying the complexity of how she negotiated race and gender within a public sphere shaped by Anglo-Texan popular song. Rosita takes one of the most popular Texan songs, imbued with a legacy of racism and sexualization of Mexicanas, and changes the lyrics (also translating them into Spanish) in order to express her love for the city of San Antonio.

Radio and Television

Rosita's preference was to appear on stage and before a live audience. She was drawn to radio in the 1930s and 1940s because it offered a similar engagement with music in a live space. Radio performance also meant steadier work and more pay. In 1932, at the age of fourteen, she made her radio debut after winning a radio station talent contest locally sponsored by Gebhart Chili. She earned two dollars per week performing on thirty-minute shows and singing Frito Lay corn chip jingles seven days a week.[16] In 1936, she and her sister Berta sang at the Texas Centennial celebration featured on live radio broadcasts. Years later, it became quite common to see advertisements in the San Antonio newspaper promoting Rosita's appearances on shows broadcast on WOAI, an affiliate of NBC and the Texas Quality Network. These included "Music of the Americas" and "New Spanish Trail." WOAI radio programs, with Rosita playing a key role, were some of the first commercial radio broadcasts in the country. She was eventually featured on several regional radio shows of the 1930s into the 1950s. During that time, the voice of Rosita Fernández was what the San Antonio public heard on commercially-sponsored radio, advertising products ranging from Pearl Beer to White Wing Flour Tortillas.[17]

It is important to note that in early days of radio when Rosita sang, full-time Spanish-language radio did not yet exist, and there were no radio stations owned by Tejanos/Mexicanos. Thus, programming was geared primarily toward the English-speaking Anglo public. It was common for local business sponsors to buy blocks of time from radio brokers to advertise products to the Spanish-speaking audience. Changes in demographics and the popularity of radio in the post-WWII era resulted in changes to broadcast policies that created a context of possibility for diversity in station ownership and programming content. Rosita's career in radio encompassed these critical periods in radio as negotiations over language, minority ownership, broadcast policies, and audience programming were transformed.

During the 1940s, KCOR radio began to offer just four hours of Spanish-language programming. Rosita recalled experiences appearing on radio, including when she and her sister Berta won a contest sponsored to find talent for the Spanish language radio program, "La Hora Anáuhuac": "First there was a Spanish program out of an Anglo station, La Hora Anáuhuac. . . . They would buy one or two hours from the main station, like KTSA now. They would rent the two hours, the one or two hours, and we would perform." Rosita's husband Raul Almaguer recalled: "The most important sponsors of Mexican music programs on English-language radio on WOAI were Frito Lay and Gebhart Chili Powder." In 1947, KCOR became San Antonio's first twenty-four-hour Spanish-language radio station.[18]

Eventually Mexicano/Tejano artists would appear on Spanish-language radio programs designed for a Spanish-speaking public, but Rosita began her career on WOAI as the only woman singing in Spanish to a primarily English-speaking or Anglo audience. These experiences taught her to negotiate language and song while singing to both English-speaking, and later, Spanish-speaking publics. Rosita and her husband recalled how he would translate familiar English-language tunes into Spanish so that "American" radio audiences would find the music more appealing: "My husband would translate songs that were in English to Spanish. . . . and he would translate all my songs, most of them, translate to English."[19]

Raul recalled how he would translate popular tunes of the time for Anglo audiences on the radio: "[Songs] like 'The Tennessee Waltz,' 'Slow Poke,' [and] 'I Came to Your Wedding' were very well liked. . . . I'm the only one in my family that did not know music, but I am the only one in my family that wrote songs that were recorded by Rosita." Rosita described the experience of singing to two different publics this way:

> *Cantaba un poco en ingles para complacer a todo . . . a tanto el americano como el mexicano y el mexicano también fue muy acostumbrado a la música americana pero más en español porque alli era . . . a mi me gustaba muchísimo claro. Pero lo mismo en el americano y así canté en los dos idiomas.*[20]

> I sang a bit in English in order to please the American just as the Mexicano, and the Mexicano also was accustomed to American music but preferred more the music in Spanish because that's what . . . That is what I enjoyed very much. But equally in American, and this is how I came to sing in both languages.

Her wide popularity on radio and on records enabled her to make the transition to other media. Having connected with San Antonio's English-speaking and Spanish-speaking publics through song, radio shows, and commercial jingles, Rosita became a visible presence as well. For instance, it was common to see Rosita asking the public to purchase Amigos Tortillas in print advertising bearing the slogan, "These are my favorite tortillas, says Rosita, San Antonio's own star of radio, stage, and television."[21]

In October 1949, Rosita was chosen to perform live on the first local television program in San Antonio, broadcast from the White Plaza Hotel by WOAI-TV, an affiliate of WOAI radio (fig. 2). Rosita recalled the early days of television when there was no technology for manipulating camera angles and varied shots: "They had a very, very small studio. I remember they used to do all sorts of tricks. They would hang a mirror . . . as if the camera was up on top focusing down."[22] Eventually, Rosita performed on a weekly basis for several subsequent television programs on KTSA-TV and KCOR-TV, and at one point she was working simultaneously on three different television stations and eleven radio stations.

Figure 2: Rosita Fernández appearing live in San Antonio's first televised broadcast for WOAI television. Photo courtesy of the University of Texas at San Antonio Archives, Library, University of Texas at San Antonio.

Rosita made a conscious choice to move away from recording and touring in the early 1960s. As she stated in an interview, "I decided, even though I knew I could make more money if I toured, that I wanted to stay close to my family and not have to travel." She noted that, "Xavier Cugat, Sammy Kay, Herman Waldman, and Tex Beneki each made me an offer to go on tour all over with them, but I turned them down. At that time my children were small, and I always felt they needed me."[23]

Figure 3: Rosita Fernández performing at El Teatro Alameda, San Antonio. Photo courtesy of the University of Texas at San Antonio Archives, Library, University of Texas at San Antonio.

It was challenging for Rosita to balance her desire to perform in public with her priorities as mother and wife. Her husband insisted that Rosita quit the music business completely so that she could dedicate herself to their children: "She became ill, actually ill, and I swallowed my ego and realized I was hurting our marriage and hurting her," recalled Raul after realizing that he should support Rosita's love for public performance.[24]

One of Rosita's favorite places to sing in the 1950s and 1960s was El Teatro Alameda (the Alameda Theatre) in downtown San Antonio. Built in 1949 as one of the grandest movie palaces in the country, it was the premier performance space for Mexicano/Spanish-speaking entertainment in San Antonio. The Teatro Alameda held nearly three thousand seats and featured the most popular Tejano and Mexican artists of the time (fig. 3).

In 1957 Rosita began her involvement with the Arneson River Theater on the San Antonio Riverwalk. She helped to initiate Fiesta Noche Del Rio, a nightly entertainment ensemble that included performance and music. She also sang for conferences and conventions held in San Antonio. This allowed her to stay near her family and to have a more stable life while performing. Her decision to continue singing in public while maintaining her role as mother and wife signaled a transition from being a recording and radio personality to becoming an ambassador for the city of San Antonio. Rosita felt fortunate to have the opportunities to perform at the Arneson River Theater and for contracted shows with the city tourist industry:

> *Luego nos dió por poner shows, todo en variedad pero variedad mexicana y española. Entonces tenia yo como ochenta y tantos convenciones por año y con eso, era muy bueno. Porque San Antonio era siempre de turismo.*[25]

Then we got this idea to put on shows, variety shows that were diverse but all pertaining to Mexican or Spanish culture. Then I had about eighty or so conventions per year, and that was really good. Because San Antonio usually was a tourist town.

Rosita was quite invested in maintaining the Arneson River Theater as the city's premier live stage/theatre along the Riverwalk because live stage performance reminded her of the *carpas* she had performed at as a young girl. At one point, she helped raise eight hundred thousand dollars for restoration of the Arneson River Theater.[26]

Rosita remained in the limelight of Fiesta Noche del Rio for over twenty-five years, returning periodically to perform at the Arneson for special occasions, where she held some of her most notable performances. For example, she was invited by President Johnson and his wife Lady Bird to perform for them and presidential cabinet members visiting the city (fig. 4). This was when Lady Bird Johnson bestowed on Rosita the title of "San Antonio's 'First Lady of Song'" (a play on the nickname of famous singer Ella Fitzgerald).

As a public personality she garnered high status through her performances at Fiesta Noche Del Rio. It was quite common to see news coverage on her when any notable person came to visit the city. Rosita was arguably San Antonio's cultural ambassador, often invited by the city to sing for, or at least to greet these notables on their arrival. Within the last three decades of her career, she also appeared in several movies that increased her visibility among her fans, including *The Alamo* (1960) and *Sancho the Homing Steer* (1962).[27]

Rosita's Bridge

On September 23, 1982, Mayor Henry Cisneros signed a city resolution proclaiming that the bridge spanning the San Antonio River and leading to the Arneson River Theater, where Rosita performed for so many years, be named "Rosita's Bridge" in honor of her decades as a singer and public performer. The

Figure 4: Rosita Fernández performing live at the Arneson River Theater, San Antonio Riverwalk, for President Lyndon B. Johnson, his wife, Lady Bird, and cabinet members. Photo courtesy of the University of Texas at San Antonio Archives, Library, University of Texas at San Antonio.

city resolution states that Rosita "has been an ambassador of good will in every section of our City, throughout the country, and in Mexico." Cisneros wrote to her, "I am very proud to be able to inform you officially that the City Council recently voted to name the bridge which spans the San Antonio River in front of the Arneson Theatre 'Rosita's Bridge.' We are looking forward to coordinating with you to set a date for the ceremonies officially designating the bridge and honoring you as you so richly deserve. Best wishes! Henry." [28]

For Rosita, the dedication of the bridge was the city's most public recognition of her contributions of song and performance. The city's gesture also held a symbolic connection between her cultural work and place, between song and San Antonio. Rosita recalled in a television special marking the fortieth anniversary of WOAI-TV's (and Rosita's) first broadcast that, in fact, her connection to the Riverwalk went all the way back to her childhood. She recalled that her father was employed to work on the Riverwalk as part of the Works Projects Administration (WPA) in San Antonio during the Great Depression. The naming of "Rosita's Bridge" meant coming full circle, a connection between making a home in San Antonio, her father's work on one of the city's most recognized landmarks, and establishing her livelihood on that very site.

Rosita explained what the naming of a bridge in her honor meant to her: "We usually think of bridges as things to transport people from one side to the other side . . . but Rosita's Bridge . . . I think it stands for uniting two sides . . . two cultures . . . the Mexicano and the Anglo-American." [29]

For Rosita, the symbolism of her bridge was not in its function to bring people together, but rather the cultural space created for the engagement of difference. Rosita's cultural labor represents a metaphoric cultural circuit, translating and transporting lo Mexicano and lo Americano into a newly imagined "third space" for Mexicana cultural production in Texas. "Rosita's Bridge" symbolizes mediation between/across borders and the ever-present negotiation Tejana cultural producers exercise, what Emma Pérez refers to as "third space performative acts," persistently working within the here and the there. [30]

"LA CHINA POBLANA"

By the age of eighty-five, Rosita had garnered most regional music accolades. She had been inducted into the San Antonio Musicians Hall of Fame, the San Antonio Women's Hall of Fame, and the Tejano Music Hall of Fame. On May 5, 2001, I attended the acquisition ceremony of Rosita's dress "La China Poblana" by the Smithsonian Institution (fig. 5). [31] The acquisition ceremony, held at the Alameda Theatre in downtown San Antonio, was in many ways a "coming home" for Rosita, who had appeared so often on stage in that historic theater.

During her speech at the acquisition ceremony, Rosita recalled spending hours working with her mother and sisters to make costumes: "It was truly a family event to sit and sew the details of the dress. . . . I recall my sisters and mother taking so much time. Gracias a dios. Mamacita, ella se dedicaba mucho para cocer (Thank God. Mamacita, she dedicated so much towards sewing)." Rosita considered what she wore—its style and color—central to her presentation as a singer. It was, in many ways, her musical "instrument": "Para nosotros [mujeres] era el vestuario. Quiero decir la mitad de tu atuación (For us [women], it was the costume. What I mean to say is that, it was half of the performance)." [32]

Rosita chose to donate "La China Poblana" because it is Mexico's national costume. [33] She wore the dress to her most special engagements, performances at Fiesta Noche del Rio and to events where she was recognized with an award. This dress, more than any other, represents many of Rosita's travels and key public appearances throughout her career. Rosita's choice of this particular

Figure 5: Rosita Fernández wearing "*La China Poblana.*" Photo courtesy of Rosita Fernández.

dress certainly raises questions about metaphoric blurring of national borders between the United States and Mexico, especially in its acquisition by the Smithsonian, "the nation's museum." It also signifies quite profoundly a material marker of Mexicano presence reinforced by the Mexican *dicho* occasionally expressed to me by Rosita, "*Acqui estamos y no nos vamos* (Here we are, and we will not leave)."

Rosita's Fernández's cultural work took her outside social class, race, and language characteristics commonly associated with Texas-Mexican music and singers. To be sure, her cultural work may be described as racially "ambiguous" because it does not fit seamlessly within the subordinate Texan narratives of Mexicanos or within the male-centered history of Texas-Mexican music that has ignored most of her contributions. The ambiguity of her cultural work stands explicitly at the crossroads of Anglo-Texan hegemony, as well as Texas-Mexican sexism. This complexity launches critical questions pertaining to systems of power Tejana/Mexicana-American women performance artists strategically contest, negotiate, and live daily on the borderlands of gender and culture. The larger study of these questions further theorizes them in relation to Rosita's Fernández's life and the cultural spaces that she and her generation of Mexicana/Tejana performers carved out for themselves, and for future generations.

NOTES

1. The terms "Texas-Mexican," "Mexicana" and "Mexican American" are used interchangeably to define someone of Mexican descent born and/or raised in Texas. The term "Mexican" is used later in the article in reference to Mexican traditional costume and culture.

2. Excellent biographies on Lydia Mendoza are Yolanda Broyles-González's *Lydia Mendoza's Life in Music: Norteño Tejano Legacies* (New York: Oxford University Press, 2001); and Chris Strachwitz and James Nicolopulos, *Lydia Mendoza: A Family Autobiography* (Houston, Tex.: Arté Publico Press, 1993). For scholarship on Tejana singers in the twentieth century see Deborah R. Vargas, "*Las Tracalers*: Texas-Mexican Women, Music, and Place," (Ph.D. diss., University of California, Santa Cruz, 2003); and Maryann Villareal, "*Cantantes y Cantineras*: Mexican American Communities and the Mapping of Public Space" (Ph.D. diss., University of Arizona, 2003).

3. Rosita Fernández, interview with author, San Antonio, Texas, August 18, 1999.

4. Text of Rosita Fernández's interviews appear throughout this essay in the language spoken. When Spanish is spoken, English translations follow in text. Fernández, interview.

5. Fernández, interview. David Montejano, *Anglos and Mexicans in the Making of Texas, 1836–1986* (Austin: University of Texas Press, 1987); and Neil Foley, *The White Scourge: Mexicans, Blacks, and Poor Whites in Texas Cotton Culture* (Berkeley: University of California Press, 1997).

6. Fernández, interview.

7. Aside from Rosita, other Tejana singers performed in *carpas* around south Texas, including Lydia Mendoza and Las Hermanas Gongora (Strachwitz and Nicolopulos, *Lydia Mendoza*; and Teresa Paloma Acosta and Ruthie Winegarten, *Las Tejanas: 300 Years of History* [Austin: The University of Texas Press, 2003]). Rosita Fernández, interview with author, San Antonio, Texas, May 5, 2000; and Peter Haney, "Fantasía and Disobedient Daughters: Undressing Genres and Reinventing Traditions in the Mexican American Carpa," *Journal of American Folklore* 112 (1999): 437–49.

8. Acosta and Winegarten, *Las Tejanas*, 298–99.

9. Fernández, interview, August 18, 1999.

10. Jackson was commonly referred to as "the Strongman," and was a popular circus performer of his time. After retiring from the circus, he entered the entertainment business in the Coastal Bend area, primarily showing Mexican movies in makeshift tents he created. Jackson's *carpas* were located in Alice, Robstown, and Kingsville. Rosita and Raul Almaguer became good friends with Jackson, and they later asked him to be their first child's godfather (Fernández, interview, August 18, 1999; and Haney, "Fantasía and Disobedient Daughters").

11. "Fernández Chose Family Over Fame, Fortune," *San Antonio Express-News*, May 31, 1990, 2D.

12. Carmen Hernandez, Laura's sister, part of the famed Tejana sister duet Carmen y Laura, recorded the first record for Discos Ideal in Alice, Texas. Discos Ideal was the first Tejano owned and operated label to emerge.

13. Fernández, interview, August 18, 1999.

14. Manuel Peña, *The Mexican American Orquesta: Music, Culture, and the Dialectic of Conflict* (Austin: University of Texas Press, 1999); Fernández, interview, August 18, 1999; and Acosta and Winegarten, *Las Tejanas*, 294.

15. Rosita Fernández, interview with Ruthie Wiengarten (San Antonio, Texas, April 29, 1997), Rosita Fernández Papers, MS 18, University of Texas Archives, University of Texas at San Antonio.

16. Fernández, interview with Wiengarten.

17. Years later, Rosita would also appear in print media advertising, including newspapers. She also appeared on a calendar for White Wing Flour Tortillas, as well as in local television commercials.

18. Rosita recalled that Joe Davila, producer of "La Hora Anáhuac," was one of the original Spanish-language radio pioneers. Another Spanish-language radio pioneer in San Antonio was Raul Cortez, Sr., who started KCOR radio, the first all-Spanish-

language radio station in the city (Fernández, interview, August 18, 1999). Rosita and Raul were married in San Antonio in 1938. Raul played a significant role in various aspects of Rosita's career, including acting as the English and Spanish language translator for many of Rosita's tunes. Fernández, interview, August 18, 1999; and Elizabeth McIlhaney, "Rosita Celebrates 50th Anniversary as Performer," *San Antonio Light*, May 30, 1980, 3.

19. Rosita took evening English language classes as a teenager, although she never formally completed high school. She met her future husband, Raul Almaguer, while taking these evening classes (Fernández, interview, May 5, 2000).

20. Fernández, interview, August 18, 1999.

21. Print advertisement in Rosita Fernández Archives, University of Texas at San Antonio Institute of Texan Cultures.

22. Fernández, interview, August 18, 1999.

23. Fernández, interview, August 18, 1999; and "Fernández Chose Family Over Fame, Fortune," 1–2D.

24. McIlhaney, "Rosita Celebrates 50th Anniversary as a Performer."

25. Fernández, interview, August 18, 1999.

26. Fernández, interview, August 18, 1999; and Fernández, interview, May 5, 2000. In my conversations with Peter Haney, we discussed similarities and differences between *carpas* in Texas during the early part of the twentieth century and live open-theater performances in Mexico that extended to south Texas. For example, La Carpa Cubana traveled extensively from Mexico throughout south Texas. Fernández, interview, August 18, 1999; and "Singer Shunning Retirement," *South Side Sun*, March 7, 1991, 1, 13.

27. Juan Seguin's story is especially significant in the history of San Antonio. As a Mexicano, Juan Seguin fought on the side of the defenders of the Alamo and was rejected by Mexican nationalists as a traitor, but he was still seen as subordinate by Anglo-Texans because he was of Mexican descent. For an excellent analysis of the made-for-television movie *Seguin*, see Rosa Linda Fregoso, "Seguin: The Same Side of the Alamo," in *Chicano Cinema: Research, Reviews, and Resources*, ed. Gary Keller (Binghamton, N.Y.: Bilingual Review/Press, 1985), 146–52. Rosita had a minor appearance in *The Alamo* (United Artists, Hollywood, Calif., 1960), with John Wayne. *The Alamo* premiered in San Antonio. Rosita played the wife of the lead male character in *Sancho the Homing Steer* (Walt Disney Productions, Burbank, Calif.), a 1962 made-for-television movie based on the novel *The Texas Longhorns*, written by J. Frank Dobie. My future writing on Rosita will explore her appearance in these movies along with a critical exploration of the narratives' reinscription of Anglo-Texan hegemony.

28. City of San Antonio Resolution Number 82-41-56, passed and approved by Mayor Henry Cisneros on September 23, 1982; and Mayor Henry Cisneros to Rosita Fernández, n.d. (Rosita Fernández Archives, University of Texas Institute of Texan Cultures).

29. Fernández, interview, May 5, 2000.

30. Emma Pérez, *The Decolonial Imaginary: Writing Chicanas into History* (Bloomington: Indiana University Press, 1999). See also Gloria Anzaldúa, *Borderlands/La Frontera: The New Mestiza* (San Francisco: Spinsters/Aunt Lute Books, 1987).

31. Two costumes from the personal collections of Rosita Fernández and Lydia Mendoza were acquired by the Smithsonian Institution on May 5, 2001. The Mendoza costume was included in a traveling exhibit "Corridos," sponsored by the Smithsonian, and on exhibit through 2002. Fernandez's costume was featured, along with costumes belonging to Celia Cruz and Selena, in a Smithsonian Institute exhibit, "Moda y Musica: Stage, Fashion, and Style," in November 2001.

32. Rosita Fernández, speech, Smithsonian Institute acquisition ceremony, May 5, 2001; and Fernández, interview, August 18, 1999.

33. The traditional colors of "*La China Poblana*" dress are red, white, and green, the colors of the Mexican flag. Rosita's dress is black with orange-gold trim and has an eagle detailed in sequins on the front.

Esperanza v. City of San Antonio

Politics, Power, and Culture

AMY KASTELY

I first visited San Antonio, Texas, in 1958, when I was seven. I remember a downtown with many houses and lots of people sitting outside on porches and stoops. My older cousin explained that the people we passed on the street were speaking Spanish. Crisp, spicy smells and lively music came from the homes and restaurants. I wanted to dance. My white relatives lived in a house that was air-conditioned and cold, even when it was hot outside. Everybody at my aunt's house was white except a man who mowed the lawn. My aunt took my cousin and me to the Alamo, and we learned that the Mexicans killed everyone. I was afraid.

I moved to San Antonio in 1993. The downtown neighborhoods have been replaced by huge buildings surrounded by manicured grass and cement, hotels, and restaurants for tourists. You rarely hear Spanish spoken in these downtown streets.[1] Songs such as "La Bamba" and other "crossover songs" boom from shops selling Alamo T-shirts and ceramic Mexican hat dancers. Burger King offers breakfast tacos. The people in my aunt's neighborhood, on the near-Northside of town, are still mainly white, but most will tell you that San Antonio is fully integrated and culturally diverse. Many white San Antonians will explain how racial equality has come to the city without the conflicts experienced in other cities. Indeed, many white San Antonians experience diversity as living near several Latino families in suburban neighborhoods, working with Latinos as professionals or trained staff, and having a favorite Mexican restaurant, staffed by working-class Chicanos and Mexicanos. Some may also interact in similar ways with black Americans and Asian Americans.

Remarkably, in San Antonio, the largest city in the United States with a majority Latino population—the "capital" of Mexican-America—few white people experience genuine cultural difference. Although different cultures exist in San Antonio, the city and its business leaders have successfully corralled genuine diversity and replaced it with a commodified, "feel good" version of cultural difference.

I do not mean to say that authentic cultural diversity must be painful. However, unmediated exposure to another culture will force one to realize that other intelligent, healthy, well-meaning, and clear-thinking adults perceive the world very differently and value aspects of the world very differently. And in the United States, unmediated exposure to minority cultures will require one to see the destructive effects of cultural imperialism and forced assimilation. These experiences can be painful. In *The Color of Fear*, filmmaker Lee Mun Wah asks David, a white man, what it would mean for him if he were to believe what the men of color were telling him about racism. With a trembling voice, David responds, "Oh, that's very saddening. You don't want to believe man can be so cruel to himself or to his own kind. I do not want to accept that it has to be that way or maybe it is." [2] For many white people in the United States, it would be very upsetting and disturbing to experience genuine cultural difference. This disturbing feeling will not sell hotel rooms and investment packages.

As Arturo Madrid observes, the dominant view in the United States embraces diversity as "desirable in principle, not in practice. Long live diversity . . . as long as it conforms to my standards, my mind set, my view of life, my sense of order." [3] This is the kind of "cultural diversity" that sells airplane tickets, hotel rooms, and restaurant seats. This is the "cultural diversity" embraced by San Antonio's wealthiest business leaders and promoted by city policies.

But it is not easy to hide genuine cultural difference, particularly when members of a "minority" culture constitute a majority of the population, as in San Antonio. [4] Historically, public and parochial schools have subjected Chicanos and Mexicanos to mandatory assimilation. In the Westside barrio of San Antonio, for example, high schools have followed an "Americanization" curriculum since the 1930s. [5] This curriculum focuses on the skills of culture-crossing. Even today, the city's children are taught a highly-filtered version of San Antonio's history in which Chicanos, Mexicanos, and black Americans are portrayed as moving with easy acceptance into the highest places of San Antonio's professional, religious, and social life. In the 1960s, while downtown Chicano, Mexicano, and black neighborhoods were replaced with tourist facilities, poor and working-class neighborhoods of color were isolated in the Westside, Southside, and Eastside. Placement of highways and bus lines ensure that most middle-class people never see the neighborhoods where most working-class Chicanos, Mexicanos, and black Americans live. Police violence is routine in San Antonio and is particularly prevalent when police intervention is used to keep poor people out of the downtown area and off the streets. As a result, downtown streets cannot be used for traditional community activities and street commerce, except for the few strolling *helado* and *raspas* (ice cream and snow cone) vendors that are allowed to continue selling—quaint or exotic remnants of a once-active street life.[6]

City leaders work hard to promote a comfortable concept of cultural diversity in which all San Antonians share a love of "Tacos, Tequila, and Tenderloin," and celebrate Juneteenth and Cinco de Mayo along with the Fourth of July, Columbus Day, and, for a full week, the victory of Anglos over Mexicans at the Battle of San Jancinto. According to the 2002 San Antonio Visitors Bureau promotion, "San Antonio has always been a crossroads and a meeting place. Sounds and flavors of Native Americans, Old Mexico, Germans, the Wild West, African-Americans and the Deep South mingle and merge."[7] There is no mention of the genocide of Native Americans in this region, of lands taken, nor of forced segregation of Mexican and black Americans. There is no mention of the use of military force to subdue Mexican and black workers in the 1930s, or of the city's refusal to install sanitation equipment, flood protection, and health care facilities to brown and black neighborhoods during the 1950s and 60s.

In 1989 the city of San Antonio created a Department of Arts and Cultural Affairs (DACA) to administer grants to arts and cultural organizations and projects from money generated by the Hotel Occupancy Tax and other funds granted to the city by the National Endowment for the Arts and the Texas Commission on the Arts. DACA was short-lived. The decision to create a separate department had been made as a reform effort, to remove cultural arts funding from political influence and to extend public funding to community-based organizations that had never been included before. Working in the spirit of reform, the first DACA director, Eduardo Díaz, and his staff sought to fund numerous Latino and black arts and cultural organizations, to require the large European-oriented arts organizations to diversify their staffs and programming, and even to encourage the revival of cultural arts and practices that had been weakened by years of exploitation.

DACA's open recognition of the dominance of Anglo and other European-based cultural arts in San Antonio's major arts organizations was angrily criticized by many city leaders. Tourist industry leaders, conservative arts leaders, and others in city government denounced DACA's explicit focus on race and ethnicity as "divisive" and "exclusionary." Others spoke in favor of DACA's commitment and called for an even more profound commitment to cultural justice.

One critical moment came in 1994, when DACA recommended a 5 percent reduction in funding to five organizations, including, most notably, the San Antonio Museum of Art, because these organizations had failed to take reasonable steps toward developing an ethnically-diverse programming staff. At the Museum of Art, despite repeated promises to diversify, every department head and every programming curator was white. City and tourist industry leaders responded that the museum was incorporating cultural diversity in its programming, citing the "Chicano Art: Resistance and Affirmation" and "The Harmon and Harriet Kelley Collection of African American Art" exhibits.[8] The Esperanza Peace and Justice Center, a community-based center for cultural arts and activism, led a coalition of individuals and organizations, the Coalition for Cultural Diversity, formed to support and extend DACA's diversity initiatives.[9] A coaliton statement identified the heart of the dispute over DACA: "The issue, so often distorted, is not about some ill-defined notion of 'cultural diversity,' but about who gets to decide what 'cultural diversity' is." [10]

The 1994 cultural diversity debate ended with the DACA director refusing to implement the 5 percent reduction.[11] In the wake of this victory for "non-divisive" cultural diversity, business and city leaders sought greater control over the city's arts and cultural funding and sought to focus funding on the promotion of cultural expression that would be attractive and comfortable for "the whole city" (which many people understood as a code word meaning class-privileged Anglos) and "tourists" (which many understood as indicating Anglo and Hispanic middle-class travelers). In addition, the city eventually fired the DACA director, dissolved its status as a city department, and replaced it with a much smaller, less autonomous Office of Cultural Affairs (OCA). Recognizing its vulnerability, OCA abandoned the earlier commitment to cultural diversity in favor of a funding program based on the model of "cultural tourism" that included evaluation of an organization requesting funding based in part on its attractiveness to tourists.

During this debate, city officials identified Esperanza as a group that would challenge the ways in which city funding favored Anglo interests and discriminated against Chicano and African American communities. Esperanza could mobilize hundreds of people for public protest, letter writing campaigns, and petition signing. Esperanza was, and is, committed to cultural rights—the right to maintain and participate in one's cultural tradition and the corresponding obligation of government to protect and nurture the cultural traditions of all people. For city officials—particularly those concerned with public election—Esperanza was a troublemaker. For the next three years, city officials worked to silence the debate over cultural diversity, and defunding Esperanza was one piece of this effort. In 1995 some members of the city council argued for complete defunding, but could not muster a majority vote for more than incremental defunding.[12]

Esperanza was created in 1987 by a group of young Chicana women, some queer and some straight, who dreamed of a place for community-based organizers, activists, and cultural artists to meet, discuss, and act against all forms of social, political, and economic oppression. Most of the women grew up in working-class San Antonio and wanted to do progressive political work in their hometown.

For fifteen years, women of color have led, worked, and shaped Esperanza as a vital cultural arts and activist organization. Today, Esperanza is alive with women and men, old and young; Latinos/as, black Americans, Asians, Native Americans, and whites; queer and straight; working class, poor, and middle class. The organization is feminist, politically progressive, outspoken, and deeply rooted in San Antonio. Esperanza is run by a very hardworking volunteer board, a full-time paid staff of only four people, scores of volunteers, and hundreds of participants and supporters. As a community of people working for and within larger communities, we are committed to multi-issue work for social justice, and to long struggle for change in the world and in ourselves.

Esperanza has organized hundreds of programs, *platicas* (community discussions), classes, and activities that have explored complex issues and enlarged understanding of diverse cultures and histories. The organization has been active in women's reproductive choice, human rights, and the rights of Spanish-speaking workers. Esperanza has organized antiwar protests, low-cost housing actions, and demonstrations against the Klu Klux Klan. Esperanza has presented the work of hundreds of artists and cultural workers, particularly those who have been ignored or silenced in mainstream arenas. Individually, the women and men of Esperanza have done the work at home. They have talked, challenged, and learned with their own families and with neighborhood friends. With great courage, they have strived to live the changes they advocate and to empower the people they love.

Throughout its history, Esperanza has worked hard to maintain a cooperative relationship with city government, recognizing that city officials are not the source of oppression against the people of San Antonio, although they have often been the agents of oppression. Yet, in 1994 and thereafter, as Esperanza articulated and organized in favor of genuine cultural diversity, this work threatened the deep entanglement of the city with the tourist and development industries.

Emboldened by the success of the anti-affirmative action movement, some—both in and out of city government—decried Esperanza for raising issues of race, ethnicity, class, and sexuality in connection with public funding.

Esperanza and its leadership, particularly Graciela Sánchez (Esperanza's long-time executive director), Gloria Ramirez (current chair of the board of directors and longtime editor of the newsjournal *La Voz de Esperanza*), and Michael Marínez, (activist artist and longtime Esperanza volunteer), were demonized by the news media and hounded by anonymous threats.[13]

Howard Peak, who had been a new city council member during the 1994 DACA controversy, was elected mayor in 1997. Peak, trained as an urban planner and closely tied to San Antonio builders and developers, believed that city officials must promote the city's tourist and development industries. He also felt that cultural diversity could advance these goals, but only in its "feel good" form. Toward this end, Peak sought to silence and isolate Esperanza as the principal voice for cultural rights. As we discovered later in litigation, it was Peak who guided the defunding of Esperanza. Peak encouraged the involvement of right-wing organizers by personally appearing on conservative radio talk shows, garnered support for the defunding from a network of conservative white gay men, and secured the unanimous agreement of the city council in a closed meeting at City Hall late in the evening before the defunding vote.[14] Throughout, Peak's position was that Esperanza's social justice programming and its vision of cultural diversity were political, that art is not political, and therefore Esperanza did not qualify for "arts" funding.

COMMUNITY RESPONSE: TODOS SOMOS ESPERANZA

The Esperanza community deliberated for almost a year about how to respond to the 1997 defunding. It was difficult to survive. In addition to the city funding, the city withheld state funding, some local private foundations rejected funding applications because of the adverse publicity, and some individual donors were frightened off. The Esperanza board, staff, and community worked hard to keep the organization strong.

The politics of the defunding were difficult to address. In 1997 Esperanza was attacked by an unusual alliance among city officials, conservative white gay men, and the Christian Right. We had been defunded by an eleven-member city council that had six Mexican American members and one black American member. We knew that many people, both Anglos and Latinos, would assume that Latino and black council members would not discriminate against a group that promoted the rights of people of color. And further, the media and city officials had emphasized Experanza's cosponsorship of a lesbian and gay film festival, Out At the Movies, as the reason for the defunding, thereby driving a wedge between Esperanza and other progressive arts and social justice organizations who were frightened by the political strength of the right wing and by the fury of the homophobic attacks.

We knew both the power of the homophobic wedge and irony of its role in city politics. Not only were the mayor and city council willing to fund the Alamo Gay Men's Chorale, but Dennis Poplin, coordinator for the Lesbian & Gay Media Project—producers of Out at the Movies and the only organization to receive public funds for the film festival—was advised by the city's arts department officials that the Media Project would be funded if it broke its association with Esperanza.[15] The more we learned of the actual events leading to the defunding, the more clear it became that Esperanza's cosponsorship of the Lesbian & Gay Film Festival was being used by city officials to fuel right-wing protests against Esperanza and to drive a wedge between the center and other Latino and African American organizations.

Esperanza responded by joining with other arts organizations to create the Arte es Vida campaign. The campaign focused on the importance of art to the lives of individuals and communities, and asked people to send postcards to the city council to express their support for public funding for the arts. As a direct result of this campaign, arts funding rose in the city council's list of priorities from forty-second in 1997 to tenth in 1998.

Meanwhile, during 1997 and 1998 Esperanza participants met in a series of weekly and then monthly meetings. People worked hard in these meetings to analyze the defunding in the context of ongoing political struggles in San Antonio. María Berriozábal shared insights from her ten-year experience on the city council and took members on an "economic tour" to emphasize the lasting social, economic, and cultural effects of city government decisions. Petra Mata and Viola Casares talked about their experiences in organizing Fuerza Unida and the frustrations they endured in their lawsuit against Levi Strauss.[16] Dulce Benavidez shared the lessons she learned as organizer of the San Antonio Lesbian and Gay Assembly. Linda Morales and Terry Ramos spoke of their experiences as AFL-CIO organizers working with Boeing employees. Mike Sánchez reported on his discussions with members of the carpenters' union, and numerous others shared their experiences and insights.

The Esperanza community was cautious about the possibility of filing suit against the City of San Antonio, in part because the Civil Rights Movement in the 1960s lost some community momentum when legal action was taken. Through discussions, the Esperanza community decided to file a lawsuit only if the legal claim would not distort the truth of the defunding and would support a focused organizing and community education campaign.

It was important to pursue the issue of cultural rights and to engage others in discussions of the power of culture and art in the historical survival of our communities and in our daily lives. Regardless of the outcome of the legal case, it would provide a focus for these discussions and illuminate the connections between cultural dominance and other forms of oppression.

We filed a federal lawsuit alleging an unconstitutional targeting of Esperanza.[17] We also undertook the Todos Somos Esperanza campaign utlizing door-to-door organizing, small house parties throughout the city, street theater, and a variety of formal and informal discussions and programs focusing on the importance of culture to the survival of oppressed communities and the obligation of government to respect the cultural expression of all of the city's communities.

Central to the defunding of Esperanza was the city's lack of support for authentic cultural expression in Chicano and black communities, its insistence on production for the tourist industry, and its pervasive commitment to European-derived cultural norms and practices. The lawsuit alleged that the mayor and city council responded to Esperanza's advocacy for cultural rights by targeting it for defunding. This targeting was successful because of the power of homophobic attacks against Esperanza. In both public and private justifications for the defunding, the mayor insisted on the idea that art and politics were distinct. This idea of "art for art's sake" is itself a product of fairly recent European American, middle- and upper-class cultural thought, and is quite different from the understanding of art in Mexican American communities and throughout Latin America. The city's insistence on a separation between art and politics is an insistence on European American culture and Anglo-centered cultural diversity.

Distinguished art historian Tomás Ybarra Frausto, who appeared as an expert witness, explained:

Latin American art was born out of political struggle. As countless academics and artists have written, Latin American art for the last hundred and fifty years has been predominantly characterized by intense social concern. While much of European art has focused on the individual experience or on experience between the genders, the most important works of Latin American literature and much of its painting are concerned with social phenomena and political ideals. Art has been a critical vehicle for exploring social and national identity, political violence, racial and national integration both in Latin America and by Latinos in the United States.[18]

The lawyers working with Esperanza were challenged to shape claims and arguments that would accurately reflect the complexity of the defunding, including the racial and ethnic dimensions. This was difficult because the law of racial discrimination was severely limited by Reagan-era decisions. Further, the right to free speech, the center of First Amendment law, has been defined and elaborated as an individualistic, even class-based privilege. The words to describe genuine cultural diversity and a group's right of cultural integrity barely exists in First Amendment law.

When we researched the legal precedents, we were tempted to tell the defunding story as a simple case of antigay governmental action because that claim had been successfully raised before. That was, indeed, the advice offered by national groups such as the American Civil Liberties Union (ACLU). As lawyers, we are shaped by the law's structures, and so it was difficult to find ways to speak about Esperanza's experience. In addition, we knew that the formalities and practicalities of a courtroom trial would not allow us to tell the entire history of the Esperanza defunding. Every legal case requires that reality be simplified. We worried that if we simplified the story enough to prove our case, we would risk losing the complex truth.

Moreover, the core group of three lawyers who worked to shape the claims— Carol Bertsch, Mary Kenney, and I—are all white. Although Carmen Rumbaut, a Cubana, and Chicanas Elvia Arriola and Ilene Garcia provided helpful guidance at the beginning, and the trial team included Chicanas Isabel de la Riva, Denise Mejia, and Judy Saenz, (together with Lynn Coyle, a white attorney), most of the analysis, research, and drafting was done by white lawyers. We did not see the issues of race and ethnicity as clearly as other members of the Esperanza community. Because of this, we had difficulty knowing how to analyze the information we were collecting and how to present the evidence we had discovered. Esperanza and its lawyers solved this problem by making sure that Esperanza staff and community members were involved with every step in the legal decision-making.

As the lawyers worked with the Esperanza community to shape the lawsuit to reflect the actual story of the defunding and to define the racial and ethnic significance of the city's arts funding decisions, we came to understand the power of grassroots discussions of law and justice. Through the sometimes-painful process of listening, agreeing, and disagreeing, we came to a much deeper understanding of race and ethnicity, and the many differences among us. The community focused the lawsuit on issues of respect and cultural integrity, and held to this focus throughout the litigation.

The participation of Esperanza community members in decisions regarding legal strategy is very different from traditional lawyering practice, but Esperanza lawyers embraced it as an important part of our work. Yet, as we tried to bring in other attorneys to help us on the case, most resisted our decision-making process as unprofessional. As a result, Esperanza lawyers experienced a level of distancing and disrespect that was unfamiliar. This was particularly clear when we attempted to work with young white lawyers from the national ACLU. Although we were older and more experienced lawyers than they, and although we had been working on the case without them for two years, the young lawyers treated us as if we simply did not understand the law or the legal process. They were not comfortable in the cramped, mosquito-infested law office we had set up at Esperanza and repeatedly suggested that we should bring in a big firm attorney, who they thought could better "handle" the case. They resisted the Esperanza community's participation in legal decisions and disagreed with legal claims we shaped to reflect Esperanza's experiences and politics. Repeatedly, they spoke as if we simply had not thought enough about the case and did not understand the world. After a few months, the Esperanza board of directors and the ACLU agreed that the national organization should withdraw from the case.

After reflecting on this failed collaboration, I see that Esperanza staff and lawyers were treated as brown and black people are often treated by white Americans. Somehow, white Americans assume, without conscious thought, that they are the moral judges of people of color.[19] We assume, without thought, that we can assess and measure the thoughts and perceptions of others. "Yes, that is reasonable," we say, or, "No, your fear is unfounded." And we assume, without thought, that people of color who graciously or gently express disagreement with our evaluations are simply misinformed or misunderstanding some aspect of our conclusions. This unseen assumption often presents people of color with the unhappy choice between being "confrontational" and being patronized. If people of color are not confrontational, white people tend not to hear them, and if they are confrontational, we tend to dismiss them as "too angry."

The ACLU lawyers treated Esperanza lawyers as if we were brown or black, primarily because we did not distance ourselves from our clients. Positioned as merely part of the Esperanza community, we became legal outsiders, in need of education and guidance. I am glad for this experience, for it helps me to understand the tremendous pressure on lawyers of all races to separate themselves from poor, working-class, lesbian or gay, and brown or black clients. Sadly, lawyers too often give in to these pressures.

THE ALCHEMY OF CULTURAL RIGHTS

The Todos Somos Esperanza campaign brought the issues of cultural diversity and public funding for cultural arts to discussions throughout the city. The campaign was most intense during the four years between the defunding and

Judge Orlando Garcia's decision in favor of Esperanza. During this time thousands of people engaged in or with *cafecitos, platicas*, street theater, yard signs, community meetings, bumper stickers, a community mock trial, and a evening vigil at the federal courthouse. The issues raised by the defunding were actively discussed by people in their homes, on the streets, in community meetings, and at neighborhood gatherings.

At these gatherings, people talked about the power of culture. The Chicano community has survived because of its careful maintenance of its language and cultural practices. The black community has survived because of its conscious commitment to nurture cultural identity and traditions. Dance, song, and verse have held the pain and joys of life. They have taught the lessons of survival despite political domination, theft, rape, and betrayal.[20]

The vitality and visibility of the Todos Somos Esperanza campaign was crucial to the success of the lawsuit. The discussions engendered by this campaign informed the legal strategy at every stage of the litigation. During the trial, the courtroom was packed with Esperanza supporters: old people and youth, gay and straight, women and men, brown, black, and white people.

We were lucky to have been assigned to Judge Orlando Garcia (assignment of judges is done randomly). Garcia was raised in San Antonio and served as a state legislator prior to his appointment as a federal judge. Although reputed to be tough on lawyers, he is also known as intelligent, skillful, and hardworking. It was helpful that Garcia has a deep understanding of San Antonio and the importance of culture to the Mexican American community. At the beginning of the trial, the first witness, Eduardo Diaz, used the word "*quinceañera*" and quickly translated for himself, "that means a fifteenth birthday celebration." Judge Garcia smiled and instructed the witness, "This is San Antonio," he said, "I don't think you have to translate."[21]

The next witness, Esperanza Executive Director Graciela Sánchez, identified herself as a lesbian and a woman who had grown up working class in San Antonio's Westside barrio. Graciela used numerous Spanish words as she testified about the work of Esperanza, speaking in a bilingual weave that is familiar among Chicanos in San Antonio. Judge Garcia listened closely, and the courtroom filled with the power of Spanish spoken openly, without translation, in the formal atmosphere of federal court. The audience was completely silent in recognition of the moment. Sánchez testified to the judge and to her family, friends, and allies. The determined, engaged presence of community members was essential as a testament to that moment.

Later in the trial, the crowded courtroom witnessed as Mayor Peak testified to his belief that art and politics are necessarily distinct. When asked whether a program like MujerArtes, in which low-income women learn to tell their stories through the art of ceramics, is a "political" program, Peak responded that it could be, "depending on the program and what the purpose is, and what the people are that go through that program."[22] At that moment, a collective gasp arose from the back of the courtroom as members of the community reacted to the unexamined racism in the mayor's statement.

With members of the Esperanza community present for the trial, the focus on issues of cultural integrity and genuine cultural diversity remained at the center of the legal strategy. And the visible interest of community members in the lawsuit brought home to the judge the importance of the case. Following the trial and months of careful thought and research, Judge Garcia issued an eighty-five-page decision in favor of Esperanza, finding that the city had violated the First and Fourteenth Amendments of the United States Constitution, as well as the Texas Open Meetings Act. The Judge ordered the city to refrain from favoring or disfavoring grant recipients on the basis of their views on culture and cultural diversity, and required the city to compensate Esperanza for lost funding.

There is an alchemy to rights, as Patricia Williams teaches.[23] The concept and content of rights is nothing more than a manifestation of political power—a slogan invented by one European group in struggle with another.[24] Yet when communities use the concept and commit to the belief that they, too, are entitled, the obtuse logic of law can sometimes benefit the less powerful. If people believe that their cultural practices should be respected and protected by city government, if people yearn for a vital, liberating cultural diversity despite the multifaceted pressures of assimilation and accommodation, then legal decision-makers may begin to recognize and protect these values and activities.

Alchemy happened in the Todos Somos Esperanza campaign. Liberating cultural diversity existed for moments at Esperanza and other community-based venues. It is glimpsed in honest public discussions. In the Esperanza case, a place was found within First Amendment law that could protect and engender cultural rights. As we come to see the importance of culture in our lives, we grow closer to Indigenous peoples throughout the world who are fighting for cultural and political autonomy. Within international law, a human right of cultural integrity is increasingly recognized. This right requires that the cultural identities of minority groups be preserved and developed and that nations support the economic, social, political, and cultural institutions necessary to ensure the survival of minority groups.[25]

The United States has actively opposed efforts for international recognition of cultural rights over the past several decades.[26] Our government has tended to see cultural rights as inconsistent with global capitalist development and international trade.[27] The present regime in Washington shows no willingness to alter this policy. Sadly, U.S. rejection of international cultural rights is just one of many ways that the U.S. government now stands against the deep yearnings of people around the world to maintain something of their own values and cultural practices in the face of U.S. economic and cultural domination.

Esperanza v. City of San Anotonio and the Todos Somos Esperanza campaign engaged many in the struggle to understand and enact dynamic and liberating cultural diversity. Together we forged a vision of cultural rights and a place for such rights in U.S. domestic law. Similar work is being done by others in the United States and throughout the world. This work is important, and it suggests the possibility of more fully understanding ourselves and others. If we can imagine cultural diversity, if we can see the deep and precious significance within different cultures throughout the world, perhaps we can understand our own fears in the face of such difference. If we can do that, perhaps we can then understand the anger and fear directed against us.

NOTES

1. This is true even though 41.9 percent of the people in San Antonio speak Spanish in their homes (U.S. Census Bureau, *2000 Census* [Demographic Surveys Division, Washington D.C., 2002,]), available at *http:www.census.gov*.

2. Lee Mun Wah, *The Color of Fear*, video, 90 min., StirFry Productions, 1995.

3. Arturo Madrid, "Diversity and Its Discontents," in *Racial and Ethnic Diversity in Higher Education*, ed. Caroline Sotello Viernes Turner, et al. (Needham Heights, Mass.: Simon & Schuster Custom Pub., 1996), 526.

4. The 2000 Census reported 59.4 percent of the population of San Antonio as Hispanic, 30.8 percent as white, and 6.8 percent African American (U.S. Census Bureau, *2001 Supplemental Survey* [Demographic Surveys Division, Washington D.C., 2002,]), available at *http:www.census.gov/acs/www/Products/Profiles/Single/2001/SS01/Tabular/160/16000US48650001.htm*.

5. This curriculum is discussed in Eugene E. Garcia, *Hispanic Education in the United States: Raíces y Alas* (Lanham, Mass.: Rowman & Littlefield, 2001), 49–55.

6. A U.S. Department of Justice study found that the leading jurisdictions in number of complaints filed in federal court alleging police use of excessive force were New Orleans, Louisiana; Los Angeles, California; Jefferson Parish, Louisiana; San Antonio, Texas; Houston, Texas; and El Paso, Texas (United States Department of Justice Report, Crime Control Digest 26:1 [June 1, 1992]). See also Macarena Hernandez, "Video's Violence Angers Viewers in S.A.: Blacks Say Scene Familiar to Them," *San Antonio Express-News*, July 11, 2002, 10A; and John Gutierrez-Mier, "Protest Targets Police Abuse: Groups Say Incidents Rising," *San Antonio Express-News*, Dec. 2, 1999, 3B. The loss of street vendors is examined in Regina Austin, "'An Honest Living': Street Vendors, Municipal Regulation, and the Black Public Sphere," *Yale Law Journal* 103 (1994): 2119.

7. San Antonio Visitors Bureau, *Welcome to San Antonio*, *http://sanantoniovisit .com/visitors/com_history.asp*, accessed on October 10, 2002.

8. Dan R. Goddard, "Definition of Diversity at Center of Arts Battle," *San Antonio Express-News*, August 6, 1994; and "Editorial," *San Antonio Express-News*, August 11, 1994, 16A.

9. I joined the Board of Directors of the Esperanza Peace and Justice Center in 1996 and was lead attorney in the case of *Esperanza et al. v. City of San Antonio et al.*

10. Mike Greenberg, "Coalition Seeks Arts Funding Cut for Groups Failing Diversity Test," *San Antonio Express-News*, August 30, 1994, 16A.

11. Mike Greenberg, "Arts Board, Director Still Split on Diversity," *San Antonio Express-News*, September 1, 1994, 16A.

12. That year, funding was cut from Esperanza's MujerArtes collective and the Center's Visiones de Esperanza: Inner-City Youth Media Project.

13. The Esperanza building suffered repeated break-ins. Threats were written on the walls, and in one episode, human feces were smeared on the building and hung in a bra from a tree. Esperanza members were followed and received threatening phone calls at their homes, and their cars were scratched and damaged.

14. These events were cited in the testimony of City Director Terry Brechtel, Mayor Howard Peak, City Council Member Jeff Webster, City Council Member Tim Bannwolf, and City Council Member Ed Garza in *Esperanza v. City of San Antonio*, trial transcript, United States District Court for the Western District of Texas CA No. SA-98-CA-0696-OG, 102; and in the Declaration of Graciela Sánchez, 65.

15. Testimony of Dennis Poplin, trial transcript, *Esperanza v. City of San Antonio.*

16. The history of Fuerza Unida and its struggle against Levi Strauss is reported at *http://www.accd.edu/pac/lrc/chicanaleaders/fuerzaunida.htm.*

17. Two smaller, unincorporated organizations for which Esperanza served as fiscal agent were defunded along with the Esperanza and were coplaintiffs in the lawsuit. These were the San Antonio Lesbian & Gay Media Project and V~N, an artists' networking organization.

18. Affidavit of Tomás Ybarra-Frausto, para. 8, in Plaintiff's Motion for Summary Judgement, Exhibits, July 14, 1999, *Esperanza v. City of San Antonio.*

19. Marilyn Frye explores this idea in her book, *Willful Virgin: Essays in Feminism, 1976–1992*, (Freedom, Calif.: Crossing Press, 1992), 153.

20. Valarie Boyd's wonderful biography *Wrapped in Rainbows: The Life of Zora Neale Hurston* (New York: Scribner, 2003) records the complexity of black cultural survival in Hurston's vision and practices.

21. Testimony of Eduardo Díaz, *Esperanza v. City of San Antonio*, 59.

22. Testimony of Howard Peak, *Esperanza v. City of San Antonio*, 429.

23. Patricia Williams, *The Alchemy of Race and Rights* (Cambridge, Mass.: Harvard University Press, 1991).

24. This was a basic insight of the Critical Legal Studies movement of the 1970s and 80s (Costas Douzinas, Peter Goodrich, and Yifat Hachamovitch, eds., *Politics, Postmodernity and Critical Legal Studies: The Legality of the Contingent* [New York: Routledge, 1994]).

25. See, for example, Halina Niec, "Cultural Rights: At the End of the World Decade for Cultural Development" (background paper for UNESCO, 1996), available at *http://www.unesco-sweden.org/Conference/Papers/paper2.htm*; and Terri Janke, "Report on Australian Indigenous Cultural and Intellectual Property Rights" (Australian Institute of Aboriginal and Torres Strait Islander Studies and the Aboriginal and Torres Strait Islander Commission, 1999), available at *http://www.icip.lawnet.com.au/index.html*.

26. The United States is the lone industrialized nation that has refused to ratify the United Nations's International Covenant on Economic, Social, and Cultural Rights (see *http://www.hri.ca/fortherecord2002/vol6/usarr.htm*). Also see Philip Alston, "U.S. Ratification of the Covenant on Economic, Social, and Cultural Rights: The Need for an Entirely New Strategy," *American Journal of International Law* 84 (1990): 365.

27. This view is reflected in a recent United Nations report that states: "The most fundamental flaw reflected in the approach of the independent expert is the idea that economic, social, and cultural rights are entitlements that require correlated legal duties and obligations" ("Report of the Open-Ended Working Group on the Right to Development," United Nations Doc. E/CN.4/2001/26, 45–46; and by Padideh Ala'I, who writes: "The United States has been, for the most part, opposed to the recognition of economic, social, and cultural rights as 'rights,'" ("A Human Rights Critique of the WTO: Some Preliminary Observations," *George Washington International Law Review*, 33 [2001]: 545–46).

Carolina Munguía and Emma Tenayuca

The Politics of Benevolence and Radical Reform[1]

GABRIELA GONZÁLEZ

There should exist something greater . . . that will speak higher of us as women, wives, and as Mexicans—that is the betterment of our people—all for country and home.

> Carolina Munguía to members of Círculo Cultural "Isabel la Católica," January 8, 1939

Everyone felt we [Communists] were trying to take over the government. What we were trying to do was organize labor, organize the unemployed, so they would have their rights.

> Emma Tenayuca, quoted in the *San Antonio Express-News*, March 6, 1988

On August 25, 1938, labor leader and Texas Communist Party chair Emma Tenayuca barely escaped with her life as she and other party leaders attempted to hold a meeting at the San Antonio Municipal Auditorium. Outside the auditorium, a large anticommunist mob prepared to storm the building. Inside, police guided party members to a secret tunnel. Everyone escaped safely, but that climactic day marked the end of Tenayuca's public career in radical reform politics. Two days after the Municipal Auditorium riot, but a world away, the ladies of the Círculo Cultural "Isabel, la Católica," led by their president, Señora Carolina Munguía, held their bimonthly meeting at the San Antonio Latin American Center. The members of this female benevolence organization delved into a full agenda consisting of a report on securing free legal aid for the poor; a discussion on sending delegates to a conference at the Mexican Library; plans for an upcoming art exhibit sponsored by the Círculo; and, acknowledgments for charitable services provided by the organization. Tenayuca and Munguía shared a vision—to help *la Raza* (the Mexican-origin community)—but they chose to do so in different ways.[1]

Chicana community politics in Depression-era San Antonio reflected a diversity of ideas and strategies. Responses to the challenges of racial discrimination and severe poverty in the city's West Side barrio, the historic Mexican American neighborhood, ran the gamut from the conservative politics of benevolence as expressed by Carolina Munguía's passionate summons to Mexican-origin women to work for *la Raza* in their capacity as "women, wives, and Mexicans," doing it "all for country and home," to Emma Tenayuca's radical reform politics as reflected in her equally compelling revelation on how Communism served as a means to "organize labor, organize the unemployed so they would have rights." [2]

Munguía and Tenayuca's community activism provides a study in contrasts. For Munguía, the politics of benevolence defined the gender and class parameters within which she could negotiate individual and community improvements for *la Raza*. As a middle-class, married Mexican woman with children, she took wife and mother as her primary roles in life. As a maternalist with Methodist influences, she expanded these primary roles into the community, providing Mexican-origin women with tools for self-improvement and a mandate to uplift their families and community. Tenayuca, though married during the height of her political activism, did not organize around the mantle of domesticity. She married Homer Brooks on October 19, 1937, and divorced him on April 14, 1941. Tenayuca did not have children during her activist career, but in 1952 she gave birth to a son in San Francisco. During her activist career, Tenayuca turned to the Communist Party and organized as a worker, not as a mother. The politics of radical reform often placed her at odds with gender and class conventions. [3]

The history of Chicana community politics is replete with examples of women pursuing all manners of organizational strategies, and that diversity highlights the creative ways in which people on the margins have empowered themselves. Munguía worked within a tradition of benevolent reform that included women's clubs and, to some extent, women's auxiliary groups such as Ladies League of United Latin American Citizens (LULAC). Before the 1930s, the politics of benevolence often informed the work of Mexican mutual-aid societies. Radical reform also has its antecedents. The Magonista anarcho-syndicalist movement and other radical movements of the late nineteenth and early twentieth centuries in Mexico inspired Tenayuca and others. During the Mexican Revolution, radical reformers, such as Sara Estela Ramírez, Jovita Idar, and Leonor Villegas de Magnón, struggled to effect social and political change across national boundaries. Tenayuca's contemporaries included Manuela Solis Sager in Texas, Josefina Fierro in California, and Luisa Moreno, who organized workers in several states. However, the path from Chicana's lived experience to historical inclusion has been arduous because traditional masculinist and Eurocentric histories have either excluded these stories or included them only at the points of contact.[4]

Writing Chicanas into history, according to historian Emma Pérez, requires a different set of methodological tools. Pérez posits "decolonial imaginary" and "differential consciousness" as theoretical tools for uncovering the hidden voices of Chicanas—voices that have been relegated to passivity, into the silences of interstitial spaces. Chicana agency is thus enacted through third-space feminism. In other words, the third space, or the interstitial space, is where marginality is converted into empowerment by human agency. Pérez issues a challenge for Chicanas to claim ownership by writing their own decolonizing histories on their own terms with themselves as subjects. To that end, she credits Chicana scholars Antonia Castañeda, Vicki Ruiz, Cynthia Orozco, Deena Gonzalez, and others for their recovery projects and their gendered analysis.[5] This essay contributes to the study of the interstitial spaces from which Mexican-origin women, such as Carolina Munguía and Emma Tenayuca, have formulated strategies of negotiation and resistance.

"ALL FOR HOME AND COUNTRY":
CAROLINA MUNGUÍA AND THE WORK OF BENEVOLENCE

Carolina Munguía knew about negotiation and resistance through her community activism. For example, according to her daughter, Elvira Cisneros, Munguía attended a Parent Teacher Association (PTA) meeting at her sons' school, Crockett Elementary and was shocked and angered to learn that she was the only Mexican-origin mother present. The language barrier kept Spanish-speaking mothers away, and the school had done nothing to address this issue. Munguía met with the principal to discuss the matter and volunteered to initiate a Spanish-speaking PTA at Crockett, thereby resisting the exclusion of Mexican-origin mothers as she negotiated with the school system to support her idea of creating a Spanish-language affiliate of the PTA.[6]

The self-confidence and poise with which Carolina Munguía resisted Anglo society's complacency and negotiated solutions for such discriminatory practices by working through the system stemmed, in part, from her privileged background. She was born Carolina Malpica to a wealthy *hacendado* (landowning) family in Puebla, Mexico, on January 14, 1891. The Porfiriato, the thirty-year rule of Mexican dictator Porfirio Díaz, was in midcourse, and Malpica's father was among those who benefited from Díaz's economic development policies. Such privilege allowed Patricio Malpica to provide his daughter with the best education available to Mexican women at the time.

Carolina Munguía with her children, 1926. Clockwise from left, Ralph, Guillermo (wearing sailor suit), Ruben, and Elvira (in mother's arms). Romulo, Henry, and Estela had not yet been born. Photo courtesy of Mrs. Elvira Cisneros.

Educated at the Instituto Normal Metodista, Malpica acquired her teaching credentials and elements of the value system of the Protestant middle class. As a proud Mexican, she combined her educational influences with a cultural nationalism tailored to the tastes of the privileged classes. The young woman became a successful teacher and administrator until her marriage to Rómulo Munguía in 1916 ended her career. Carolina Munguía did not resent this shift, for she adhered to the principle of female domesticity. Her husband's political involvement during the Mexican civil war eventually led to the family's exile in the mid-1920s. In San Antonio, Texas, Señora Munguía, then a mother of four, immersed herself in community activities designed to uplift less fortunate Mexican-origin women through a dual strategy of cultural redemption and female benevolence.[7]

Taken at face value, this dual strategy was simply a means to the end of community uplift. However, examining these ideas in the context of Munguía's background and in the context of Depression-era San Antonio, we begin to unravel the class implications involved in cultural redemption and the gender ideologies that informed female benevolence. The study of Munguía's activism reveals how shared ethnicity and gender brought together women from diverse socioeconomic and educational backgrounds to work for *la Raza*.

CÍRCULO CULTURAL "ISABEL, LA CATÓLICA"

On June 12, 1938, Carolina Munguía, "influenced by the social and cultural redemption labors so successfully sponsored by the Counsel General of Mexico," formed a female voluntary association to help lower middle-class and working-class Mexican-origin women in San Antonio. Under the slogan *"Toda Por la Patria y el Hogar"* ("All for country and home"), Munguía founded the Círculo Social Femenino, "México" (Female Social Circle, Mexico). Later changed to Círculo Cultural "Isabel, la Católica" (Cultural Circle, "Isabella, the Catholic"), the organization was a vehicle for cultural redemption and female benevolence. Social and cultural redemption worked to restore the culture of *la patria* (México) in the face of the growing pressure of Americanization and dilution of a Mexican identity. It promoted a common ethnic identity to unify Mexicans across class lines in a struggle for survival amid racial discrimination and devastating poverty. To Mexican cultural nationalists like Munguía, West Side San Antonio was in a state of economic and cultural decline. The society's statement of principle read: "The main objective of this society is to procure the moral and intellectual improvement of 'women of modest means' so as to benefit the community."[8] The Círculo was operated by women for the benefit of women, and as the statement indicates, the self-improvement of women translated as community betterment. This self-help ideology recognized women's centrality in community uplift.

The members of the Círculo Cultural met twice a month on Sunday afternoons in a hall at the Mexican Library. Although the names of forty-six women appear on the organization roster, an average of twenty to twenty-five people attended the meetings. Munguía, assisted by six officers, served as president of the society during the sixteen months of the organization's existence.

Beyond conducting housekeeping tasks and listening to self-improvement/educational speeches, the members of Círculo Cultural engaged in a number of benevolent activities, such as taking in donations for the needy, supporting the *Fiestas Patrias* (Mexican holiday celebrations), helping the Mexican consulate and the Mexican Clinic, organizing cultural events, and raising money for charitable projects. In Munguía's view, women, as transmitters of cultural values and caregivers, were in a position to advance Mexican culture and provide for the needs of others. Community edification was the desired end, and the means was encouragement of moral and intellectual improvement of its members. Munguía worked diligently to "redeem" club members for the cause.

CULTURAL NEGOTIATION AND CULTURAL NATIONALISM

Munguía carried out her goals through a system of cultural negotiation and cultural nationalism. Few lower-middle-class women belonged to the organization; most members belonged to the working class. They were women of limited means and, like most people of color during that time, they were isolated from mainstream institutions. Munguía sought to help them by expanding their social horizons and providing for their needs. As their cultural negotiator, she was trying to help the women adapt to a foreign, often hostile world. She contributed to the survival of working-class women in her club by securing resources for them. Her benevolent work included procuring the services of two Mexican-origin lawyers so that the women would have someone to turn to for questions regarding U.S. laws. She also sought the services of doctors, nurses, and teachers for their benefit, often serving as the contact between the club and the Euroamerican community. She also informed members of educational opportunities, such as free sewing and English classes.[9]

While cultural negotiation benefited members by expanding their social networks and resources, cultural nationalism promoted Mexican ethnicity. Cultural nationalism celebrated ethnic pride and unity, and tended to obscure class differences. That Munguía exercised cultural nationalism is evident from letters she sent out to Mexican governors asking them to donate a representative handicraft from their state for an art exhibition. The implication here is not so much that Munguía was trying to preserve Mexican culture, but that she was advancing a particular vision of Mexican culture. To the working classes on the West Side who had been in San Antonio long enough to know about violent encounters with Texas Rangers, Mexican culture was reflected in *corridos* (folk songs) about the *rinches malvados* (evil rangers). For more recent arrivals, *corridos* about "*Adelitas* [Mexican women warriors] in Revolutionary Mexico" represented Mexican culture. Mexican culture for West Side residents was also expressed through the commingling of Spanish and English, and that usage created a new form of communication, the Tex-Mex style. Yet, by categorizing these Mexican Americans as being in a state of cultural abandonment, Munguía essentially negated their experiences and imposed her own understanding of culture on them. Munguía probably did not see it as an imposition but rather as an intervention designed to help a predominantly rural and formally uneducated people survive in an urban, capitalist, and Anglo-dominated world. In that sense, her redemption work forged a subtle form of resistance based on the celebration of Mexican culture at a time when it was denigrated by Euroamericans.[10]

Although Munguía's assumption that all Mexican-origin women had the same cultural needs was no doubt incorrect, she nevertheless succeeded in attracting them to the club. In addition to affirming Mexican art and culture, all minutes and correspondence were written in Spanish. The society's theme song was the *Mixteca*, a popular song expressing sorrow brought on by life away from Mexico; Munguía periodically delivered talks on issues related to Mexico; and the *Fiestas Patrias*, *Cinco de Mayo*, and *Dieciséis*, were regularly observed.[11]

The society's association with the other members of the *Colonia Mexicana* (ethnic-Mexican community) also served to foster ethnic pride. Círculo Cultural sent delegates to the Mexican Clinic and la Asociación de la Biblioteca Mexicana (The Mexican Library Association), a Mexican consulate project. They also made donations to the campaigns of young Mexican women running for queen of the *Fiestas Patrias*. Society members made honorary members of a former consul, two lawyers, and a teacher—all of Mexican-origin—in appreciation for past assistance and future support. The lawyers provided free legal advice and the teacher taught art classes for the children of members and participated in the arts and crafts exhibition.[12]

Their successful undertaking of activities designed to foster ethnic pride and unity suggests that class differences did not interfere with Munguía's plans to promote cultural nationalism. However, there is some evidence to suggest that class differences did cause a few problems for the club. In her letter of

Parent-Teacher Association for Crockett Elementary School. Carolina Munguía sits third from left, next to the principal, Mr. Hirsch. Munguía served as head of the Spanish-speaking Department, District 5 of the San Antonio PTA in 1940 and 1941. Photo courtesy of Mrs. Elvira Cisneros.

January 8, 1939, to the members, she wrote: "As to the moral part of our society, with great sincerity I tell you that I am not satisfied, for knowing each other that we are from different parts of the city, it seems that we do not understand each other. We do not trust each other." After Munguía wrote the letter, the club continued to operate for ten months, and then the minutes ended abruptly. Munguía's son, Ruben, speculated that perhaps the society broke up because World War II was fast approaching. Four Munguía sons joined the service, and Carolina become active in the American Red Cross. She was also active in the PTA.[13]

FEMALE BENEVOLENCE

The second component of Carolina Munguía's quest for community uplift was female benevolence. Munguía believed that as women, members were in a unique position to help others. Combined with self-help, female benevolence had the potential of achieving the community improvements that she sought, but answering the challenge given to them as "women, wives, and Mexicans" had to be done a certain way. Carolina Munguía's daughter described her mother as the type of person who did not believe in "banging on doors" to achieve goals. Munguía seemed to believe that Mexicans and Mexican Americans could be accepted by mainstream society only by becoming more "respectable." For Munguía, acceptance did not mean assimilation, but simply fair and equal treatment. In part, her feelings can be explained by her family's experience. The Munguía family's success in the United States was evident in the house they owned in the then very "respectable" neighborhood called Prospect Hill. They also owned a business. However, unlike the majority of Mexican exiles, the Munguía family arrived with significant resources. Rómulo Munguía, a self-taught intellectual and political thinker, had experience in the printing business, and Carolina's education and teaching experience prepared her to take on leadership roles within her new community.[14]

Munguía's concept of proper gender roles based on her own upbringing doubtlessly influenced her activism. Munguía and club members observed traditional gender roles. For instance, with the exception of one member, there is no evidence that the members in this society worked for wages outside the home. They worked at home raising families, and they helped their community through traditional female means—benevolence. The notion of "lady-like" behavior was encoded in the group's bylaws. For example, the need to maintain peace and preserve harmonious relations seemed to have been important, and the club had a rule forbidding the general discussion of any subject that could seriously disrupt order.[15]

Central to the idea that women bore moral responsibility for society were two measures of personal conduct: a woman's personal integrity and a woman's interpersonal relationships. To address the first, Munguía delivered talks or invited guest speakers to discuss issues such as vice and its threat to *el honor de la mujer* (a woman's honor). Morality in interpersonal relationships meant getting along with others. The rules were designed to foster this type of morality, and Munguía safeguarded the club from too much divisiveness. Despite a few minor incidents, the members of Círculo Cultural worked well together by using gender and ethnicity to bridge class differences, and although the club disbanded after sixteen months, no evidence exists that such differences undermined their unity.[16]

EMMA TENAYUCA, THE PEOPLE'S RADICAL REFORMER

While Carolina Munguía organized benevolence on the basis of gender and ethnicity, U.S. native-born Emma Tenayuca organized female and male workers around issues of labor and the economy. Born on December 21, 1916, in San Antonio, Texas, Emma Tenayuca was the first daughter of eleven children born to Sam Tenayuca and Benita Hernandez Zepeda. Emma claimed that her father was Indian and that her mother descended from Spanish land grantees in East Texas. She received her first political lessons as a child in the home of her maternal grandparents, the Zepedas, who were registered voters and took an interest in local and state politics. Major economic crisis contributed to the development of Tenayuca's early political experiences as she witnessed how the Great Depression worsened the living conditions of Mexican-origin people in San Antonio. During this time, when many Americans began to question the strength and wisdom of the capitalist system, Tenayuca, then a teenager, began to venture into labor organizing, where she sought the radical reform of a system that victimized Mexican-origin people. While Carolina Munguía's activism followed Methodist community service teachings, and her successes can be largely explained by the fact that benevolence fell within traditional gender roles and middle-class notions of "respectability," the work of radical reformer Emma Tenayuca requires a different explanation. Tenayuca's early identity formation, the sociopolitical environment in which she worked, and her adult experiences help to explain why she called for economic, political, and social change in the 1930s.[17]

Raised by her politically-active grandparents, Tenayuca developed an understanding of politics as a young girl while listening to various "soapbox" speakers from one or another faction of the Mexican Revolution on Sunday outings to the Plaza del Zacate (Milam Square). Tenayuca remembered San Antonio as "a center of Carranzista, Maderista, and Villista activity," where she first learned about the anarcho–syndicalist Magonista movement and their newspaper, *Regeneración*. There she first saw the exiled mass of humanity from Mexico lining up for low-paying jobs in faraway fields. At a young age, Tenayuca began to see the connections between exploitative systems in Mexico and the United States. Moreover, she took note of how the group victimized by capitalism was the same on both sides of the border: dark-skinned peasants and working-class people.[18]

The issue of race concerned Tenayuca from the time of her youth. Some members of her own family ostracized Tenayuca's father because he was, as they put it, *puro Indio* (pure Indian). Sam Teneyuca responded to these attacks, Emma recalled, stating that "if he knew he had Spanish blood he would cut open his veins." While she had the opportunity to claim social status derived from her mother's links to a Spanish colonial past, Tenayuca chose to identify, not with the privileged few, but with her father. Speaking about her parents in relation to her participation in the Finck Cigar Strike in 1933 (employees of the company had gone out on strike because the company had reneged on its pledge to pay the minimum wage as specified by the National Recovery Administration [NRA]), and her subsequent arrest, she declared, "I was picked up too [arrested by the police]. . . . My father applauded me. My mother thought I was just wasting my time. Typical Spanish reaction." There were clear antagonisms between Mexicans claiming a Spanish ancestry and those defined outside the parameters of whiteness—the ones designated as *Indios*. Still, as noted by Emma Tenayuca herself, light-skinned Mexicans often married dark-skinned Mexicans, creating the *mestizaje* that she identified with and embraced.[19]

THE ROAD LESS TRAVELED

Tenayuca's introduction into the world of organized politics began as she entered high school. As she later recalled:

> During my first year in high school, I joined the Ladies LULAC auxil-iary. . . . When the matter of discrimination really started to dawn on me was during the course of the Depression when I saw the poverty. . . . I attended their meetings. I noticed that their policy [sic] and I followed it for awhile, was one of Americanization. . . . I delivered a talk on "I Am an American," or something like that.[20]

Her association with LULAC was short-lived because Tenayuca disagreed with the group's original policy of distancing itself from Mexicans of foreign birth. Early LULAC policies encouraged U.S. Mexicans to distinguish themselves from Mexicans of foreign birth and to combat the stereotype of "the dirty Mexican" by presenting themselves in the best possible light. Her family had been in Texas for centuries, and so Tenayuca's claims to citizenship were solid. She could have stayed in LULAC and become complacent about their policy, but instead, she criticized LULAC for failing to see that Anglo America treated all Mexicans and Mexican-origin people as second-class citizens. She said, "And this is what really made me rebel against the LULACs. No matter how clean you were, how well-scrubbed your neck was, if you had a name like Garcia, it was bad."[21] For Tenayuca, Mexicans needed to unite, not divide on the basis of citizenship, class, or educational status.

Tenayuca also joined a reading group at Brakenridge High School. Like other youth groups during the 1930s, they read works by Marx and Tolstoy, kept abreast of current events, and discussed society's inequities in a student newspaper. As she put it, "All of us were affected by the Depression. We became aware that there were some aspects of the free enterprise system which were highly vulnerable." She graduated from high school in 1934, and her social consciousness continued to develop.[22]

Emma Tenayuca standing on the steps of the San Antonio City Hall, with upraised fist, surrounded by people with banners, San Antonio, Texas, ca. 1938. Photo courtesy of The University of Texas Institute of Texan Cultures at San Antonio, no. 1541-D.

Tenayuca's early organizing experiences happened almost spontaneously. According to her niece, Sharyll Soto Teneyuca, her aunt participated in the Finck Cigar Strike mainly for social justice and humanitarian reasons. Soto Teneyuca commented:

> I don't think she [her aunt] ever set out to be an organizer or even an activist. She was compelled to do something about the human suffering she witnessed. She was ware of human injustice—even as a child she had been aware of it. Because of her deep compassion, she couldn't ignore it. It happened that she was a gifted speaker and organizer, and could mobilize workers. She was able to communicate to people that by working together, they could change their condition.[23]

The condition of Mexican-origin workers in San Antonio during the 1930s was deplorable, and when they attempted to effect change, they were often met with strong opposition. For example, the local sheriff, Albert West, made a comment about using his new boots to kick the Finck Cigar strikers—all women. Then, a prominent San Antonio leader casually commented on how easy it was to break a strike by calling the immigration authorities. Indeed, immigration officials often got involved, although some of the strikers were born in the United States. Tenayuca, motivated by what she described as "an underlying faith in the American idea of freedom and fairness," could not sit by and watch such injustices. She went down to the Finck Cigar strikers' picket line to show support and was arrested for her efforts.[24]

While helping the Finck Cigar strikers, Tenayuca noticed the complicity of the Catholic Church. Like her own family, Finck, she noted, was Catholic:

> That guy used the priests. I didn't have one worker tell me, I had several workers tell me that the priests, and this was Father Clem Casey and some of the others, expressed an attitude that every union is a communist union. They backed Finck to the hilt. I was told that even in the confessional box they had been advised not to join.[25]

Like the local machine-run government, the Catholic Church, she learned, could not be relied upon to uphold and defend workers' rights. For solutions to poverty and discrimination, Tenayuca turned to the Communist Party. In 1935, Emma Tenayuca joined the Young Communist League; she dropped out in 1936 to join the Communist Party.[26]

Led by Earl Browder, the U.S. Communist Party of the late 1930s pursued a Popular Front strategy designed to mainstream the party into American political life. Popular Front supporters organized against fascism at home and abroad, often reminding Americans of the similarities between Franco's and Hitler's fascism in Europe and racism and ethnocentrism in the United States They supported the progressive Franklin D. Roosevelt's administration, the struggle for black equality, the right of workers to organize, and a vision of a multi-ethnic nation. Like other Popular Front advocates, Tenayuca placed faith in the socialistic aspects of New Deal liberalism, supporting the FDR administration's efforts to reform and regulate business practices and to create an economic safety net for Americans through legislation, such as the Social Security Act (1935) and the Wagner Labor Relations Act (1935) that facilitated labor organizing.[27]

After the Finck Cigar Strike of 1933, Tenayuca continued to organize workers. She joined the Workers Alliance of America, serving as a member of its executive committee by 1937 and as general secretary of ten Alliance chapters in San Antonio. The Workers Alliance, a national federation, was a part of the movement of the unemployed that sought to assist the jobless. The San Antonio branch included about ten thousand workers and met on Sundays. As a member of the San Antonio Workers Alliance, Tenayuca wrote letters to national Works Prgress Administration (WPA) officials, calling for reform in the Texas Relief Commission (TRC). The TRC often turned down unemployed Mexican-origin workers who applied for WPA work, sending them instead to work in out-of-town fields for starvation wages and forcing them to pull their children out of school early. Tenayuca also participated in a number of demonstrations to pressure local authorities on behalf of laid-off WPA workers. The police arrested Tenayuca, among others. As a result of their activism, members of the Workers Alliance were harassed and their headquarters ransacked by the police. The Alliance also focused on helping workers organize without harassment from immigration officials who used the threat of deportation to silence workers. Out of all of the projects that the San Antonio Alliance branch worked on, the most famous was the Pecan Shellers Strike of 1938.[28]

THE PECAN SHELLERS STRIKE

During the 1930s, Texas controlled about 40 percent of the nation's pecan production. San Antonio stood at the center of this industry because half of the Texas pecan crop was grown within a two-hundred-fifty-mile radius of the city. Southern Pecan Shelling Company owner Julius Seligman initiated a contracting system whereby he provided contractors with whole pecans on credit for about $.10 a pound and then bought the processed nuts back for $.30 to $.36. The contractors furnished the building, electricity, and water needed to process the pecans, and they dealt with labor management issues. This arrangement proved exploitative. It was common to find one hundred pickers sitting around a long table in a space of only twenty-five feet by forty feet, working under poor illumination. Because there was no ventilation, the brown dust from the pecans hung heavy in the air, leading many to draw a connection between the polluted air and the high rate of tuberculosis among pecan-shelling families. Sanitary facilities in a typical sweatshop consisted of one toilet for workers of both sexes. Workers received pitiful wages in this female-dominated industry. The average annual family income of shellers was $251. An individual might make a weekly salary of $2.73. Because pecan shelling was a seasonal business, workers often supplemented their incomes with migratory fieldwork.[29]

Ironically, it was not these abysmal conditions that led to the creation of the first pecan shellers' union in 1933. According to Tenayuca, Seligman hired Magdaleno Rodriguez to organize the Pecan Shelling Workers' Union because the Pecan King was afraid that smaller operators might undercut him by paying workers less than he could. "He admitted to taking money from Seligman," Tenayuca declared when asked about Rodriguez's association with Seligman.

Some believed that Rodriguez was also connected to Chief of Police Owen Kilday's political machine. By 1937, Rodriguez no longer led the union, which had virtually disappeared. Remnants of the union reorganized as the Texas Pecan Shelling Workers' Union, and the Communist Party brought in Albert Gonsen, a Chicano from New Mexico, to lead it. That same year the United Cannery and Agricultural Packing and Allied Workers of America (UCAPAWA), a CIO union, offered the San Antonio pecan shellers a temporary charter. The understanding was that the union would expand to include other groups working with agricultural workers. One such group was the Workers Alliance, and Emma Tenayuca, as director, seemed poised to play a leadership role in the strike that was about to erupt.[30]

On January 31, 1938, the Southern Pecan Shelling Company's contractors announced a pay cut from six cents to seven cents per pound to five cents to six cents per pound. Wages for pecan crackers were cut from fifty cents to forty cents per one hundred pounds. A spontaneous walkout involving twelve thousand strikers ensued. The Gonsen faction of the CIO Pecan Shellers' Union stayed away, but UCAPAWA supported the strikers. Tenayuca emerged as a leader of the strikers. The strike lasted three months, during which strikers dealt with opposition from the San Antonio political machine. Over one thousand picketers were arrested, tear gas was used several times, the police and fire departments were drafted for "riot duty," and both Mayor C. K. Quin and Police Chief Kilday refused to acknowledge the strike.[31] Kilday, in particular, used the local media to red-bait Tenayuca and the strikers. The *San Antonio Light* reported:

> Mrs. [Emma Tenayuca] Brooks, the wife of Homer Brooks, former Communist candidate for governor, was taken into custody at another West side factory. Chief Kilday said he ordered her arrested because he "did not intend to let any Reds mix up in the strike."[32]

Kilday continued his harassment, emphasizing the Communist angle. The *San Antonio Light* reported, "Kilday took the position that actually there was no strike. . . . The police chief, in a prepared statement, declared that the entire strike was a Communist movement and that it was without standing with the Committee for Industrial Organization." Red-baiting became the favored tactic of those who sought to silence demands for social and economic justice.[33]

The gross mistreatment of the strikers attracted national attention, and Texas Governor James V. Allred ordered the Industrial Commission of Texas to investigate violations of civil liberties. Assistant State Attorney Everett Looney served as chairman of the investigative body. On February 14, 1938, Looney called a public meeting in San Antonio. The San Antonio Ministerial

Association testified that pecan shellers received a mere $2.50 per week. Several ministers, as well as some journalists, reported that the strikers "had behaved peacefully, although the police had taken their picket signs away from them." Looney also heard from strikers who told of arrests and beatings at the hands of police officers. Ultimately, the Commission hearings determined that Kilday's police department had overstepped its authority. Unfortunately for the strikers, the Commission could not enforce its own ruling, and a local judge failed to grant an injunction against the police that would have permitted picketing.[34]

Violations of civil liberties by the police occurred in an environment marked by strong anticommunist and anti-unionist sentiment. City officials, as well as representatives from the National Catholic Welfare Council, attacked the strike, characterizing it as communist-inspired and therefore illegitimate. Tenayuca became the target of much of this vitriol because she was a Communist, a labor leader, and the wife of a former Communist Party gubernatorial candidate. The attacks against Tenayuca because of her Communist Party affiliation came from the labor movement as well. Rebecca Taylor, president of the San Antonio International Ladies' Garment Workers' Union (ILGWU), refused to help the strikers because Tenayuca was one of the leaders. Furthermore, Taylor drove around with police, pointing out which union activists might be Communists. Soon UCAPAWA made it clear that in order to maintain their support, Emma Tenayuca needed to step down as strike leader. Even after removal from a leadership role, Tenayuca continued to put out circulars and organize pickets. This turn of events was not surprising in light of the CIO's, and more generally the Left's, position on Communists within their ranks during the 1930s. Union leaders were willing and often eager to receive assistance from Communists as long as they kept their political and ideological identities hidden. By 1938, Emma Tenayuca's reputation as an outspoken Communist made her not only the target of reactionaries, but also a potential liability for the Left, which hoped to achieve revolutionary changes in American society by attempting to mainstream its radical programs. Removing Tenayuca from a visible leadership role seemed the safer route for the union.[35]

UCAPAWA president Donald Henderson took charge of the strike with advice from CIO leader Luisa Moreno. Henderson, Moreno, and George Lambert, the UCAPAWA representative in San Antonio, negotiated the strike settlement. This turn of events bothered Tenayuca because the national labor leaders failed to promote local grassroots leadership. Over thirty years later, Tenayuca, examining the factors that had prevented the organization of Mexican workers, wrote that one such factor had been the "inability of out-of-state union organizer to recognize the particular needs of Mexican workers

The wedding of Emma Tenayuca and Homer Brooks, San Antonio, Texas, ca. 1938. Photo courtesy of the University of Texas Institute of Texan Cultures at San Antonio, no. 1662-A.

especially with [sic] in relation to building leadership." Nevertheless, in 1938, the CIO did manage to secure the initial wage of seven cents to eight cents per pound of pecans for shellers, which increased when the Fair Labor Standards Act was passed by Congress that same year. This act established a minimum wage of twenty-five cents an hour for pecan shellers. The settlement came about after the governor persuaded Julius Seligmann to negotiate and the union to arbitrate. Soon after, however, the pecan-shelling industry turned to mechanization, and as many as ten thousand pecan shellers lost their jobs. With World War II on the horizon and a whole new array of war-related industries opening up, few people missed the pecan-shelling business that had been looked upon as employment of the last resort, even in its heyday. The significance of the Pecan Shellers' Strike is not the short-lived pay increase but the political galvanization of workers and a community. The role that Tenayuca played in this transformation, as a Mexican American woman taking to the streets and demanding radical reforms, represented an attack on the racial, class, and gendered caste system holding up the edifice of San Antonio's political machine.[36]

Emma Tenayuca paid a heavy price for her high profile as a labor leader and her Communist Party affiliation. Tenayuca was the chairperson of the Texas State Committee of the Communist Party from 1938 to 1941, and her husband, Homer Brooks, served as the president. Tenayuca's political identity eventually led to her self-exile from San Antonio.[37]

In 1939 a riot erupted at the Municipal Auditorium after people found out that San Antonio Mayor Maury Maverick, a strong advocate of civil liberties and former New Deal congressman (1935–38), allowed Communist Party members to meet there. The American Legion knew in advance about the Communist Party's request for permission to use the auditorium. Outrage erupted when the mayor's office granted the party the permit. *San Antonio Express-News* columnist and the mayor's son Maury Maverick Jr. recalled, "The organizations attacking him (his father) included the Catholic Church, the Ku Klux Klan, the Elks, the Breakfast Club, all veterans' organizations, and the Texas Pioneers. . . . San Antonio's newspapers joined in condemning." According to Claude Stanush, a reporter at the scene of the riot, the American Legion and other organizations demanded that Mayor Maverick rescind this permit, but he refused on the grounds that everyone had a right to freedom of speech.[38]

On August 25, 1939, the day of the controversial meeting, a crowd five thousand strong gathered outside the auditorium. Inside the building, Tenayuca, Homer Brooks, and Elizabeth Benson attempted to start a meeting with one hundred fifty party supporters in the audience. The mayor ordered police officers and firemen to create a barrier between the crowd and the auditorium in anticipation of trouble. The crowd grew tense when Catholic priest M. A. Valenta and American Legion leader Clem Smith did their part to stir the unstable throng. Suddenly, violence erupted when the crowd heard Communist Party members singing the "Star-Spangled Banner." Reporters and photographers witnessed in horror as the crowd turned into a mindless mob, throwing rocks and bricks at the building, breaking windows and injuring people, including police officers, as they charged forward. While all of this occurred outside the building, police officers guided those inside to safety using a tunnel that extended from the auditorium to the San Antonio River nearby. The mob eventually broke through the police barrier and charged the auditorium. Finding it empty, they unleashed their anger on the auditorium itself, slashing curtains and seats with knives. Newspapers estimated the damage done by the mob at between three thousand dollars and five thousand dollars. After disrupting the Communist meeting, about thirty-five hundred people held an "Americanism" meeting in the main room of the auditorium, where they denounced the mayor and the Communist Party. The rest of the mob, with Klan members among them, next moved on to the mayor's home. Fortunately, police had hidden the mayor and his family. Maury Maverick Jr. recalled that night, writing, "On the night of the riot, the police hid my parents and me for fear that we would be murdered. The next morning a police escort took us home. Throughout the day, people would drive by shouting insults." That frightful night ended at city hall where the frustrated mob burned the mayor in effigy.[39]

That night cost Maury Maverick his political career. Maverick served as mayor from 1939 to 1941. He ran for reelection but was defeated. In a newspaper interview years later, Tenayuca was asked if she had any regrets looking back at her activist career. She said she had only one. She regretted that the progressive Maverick's political career ended the night of the riot. She also pointed out that she had not been in favor of holding the Communist Party meeting at the auditorium, but her husband had insisted it be held there. "I didn't want to hold the meeting, but I wasn't listened to," Tenayuca was quoted as saying in a 1990 *San Antonio Express-News* article. In a 1986 article, she expressed her misgivings about the Communist gathering, stating, "It was just a very bad time to organize a Communist meeting. Coming right on the heels of the non-aggression pact [Soviet-German Non-Aggression Pact reached in 1939], there was a lot of anger in this country. You could almost expect this type of reaction."[40]

Mayor Maverick was not the only one whose public career ended that day. Besides receiving death threats, Tenayuca was also blacklisted in San Antonio, forcing her to move to Houston in 1940, where she worked various office jobs. In order to secure employment, Tenayuca assumed a new identity as Emma B. Giraud and, politically speaking, went underground. During the 1940s and 1950s, under the pressures of the second Red Scare, hundreds of Communists resigned themselves to a life of self-exile and underground political activism.[41]

For the next ten years, Tenayuca faced numerous challenges. She and Brooks divorced in 1941. That same year she contracted tuberculosis and was unable to participate in Communist Party activities for several months. Although she remained the branch organizer of the Harrisburg District in Houston, she was not reelected as chair of the Texas State Committee of the Communist Party. After recuperating in 1942, Tenayuca resumed her party work, traveling from Houston to San Antonio every other weekend to help organize a Communist Party branch in her hometown. By this time, the Federal Bureau of Investigation (FBI) had established an elaborate information-gathering network around Tenayuca and her associates. Her FBI file dates back to 1939, and it is evident that agents infiltrated CPUSA meetings, acquiring information about Tenayuca from her employers, school registrars, and classmates, and through interference with the U.S. mail, eavesdropping from the apartment next door to hers, and general observations. Tenayuca's file also indicates the rather sporadic nature of her 1940s Communist involvement during this period, when Emma Tenayuca held various jobs and attended the University of Houston and Sinclair Business School in Houston. These time commitments, plus illness, made it difficult for her to take on a greater role in the party. Nevertheless, the FBI considered Emma Tenayuca a potential threat to the interests of the United States, and as early as July 1941, placed her under consideration for custodial detention in the event of a national emergency. Tenayuca must have been unaware of her FBI file, because in 1942, in an effort to contribute to the U.S. war against fascism, she applied to the Women's Army Auxiliary Corps (WAACs), denying any current involvement in CPUSA politics. She was provisionally accepted but later rejected with no official reason provided. Clearly, the U.S. government's knowledge of her past and current Communist Party work played a role in their decision to reject her application. Tenayuca attempted to keep her ongoing involvement a secret, but to no avail; yet, in Tenayuca's mind, there existed no incompatibility between Communism and the struggle of democracy against fascism. Years later, she reflected on how, given the anticommunist climate, she suspected even then that her party involvement influenced top military officials to reject her application.[42]

In 1945 Emma Tenayuca moved to Los Angeles where she attended a few party meetings. In 1946 she requested to be released from the CPUSA and moved to San Francisco. According to an FBI agent who interviewed Tenayuca in San Francisco on April 20, 1953, "Tenayuca stated that the main reason for her dropping out of the CP was that she became disillusioned with CP work." Tenayuca's disenchantment with the Communist Party had started as early as 1939. The Soviet-German Non-Aggression Pact upset her. As she recalled, "I don't think there was a Communist in the country who wasn't puzzled." Still, she continued to believe that the party offered the best avenue for social change. By the mid-1940s, however, she concluded that the party had lost touch with the powerless and decided to leave it.[43]

Tenayuca never returned to labor organizing and decided instead to continue her studies. She earned a bachelor's degree from San Francisco State University and became a reading teacher. She returned to San Antonio in 1968, earned a master's degree from Our Lady of the Lake University, and continued teaching until her retirement in 1982. Although she no longer organized workers, she never stopped caring about their plight. Throughout her life she kept abreast of worker-related issues, clipping newspaper articles, reading books, and helping young scholars interested in American labor history. Many of these scholars expressed a particular interest in her achievements as a woman in the labor movement. Thus, even though subjected to harassment during the 1930s and 1940s because of her association with the CPUSA and exiled from the community she loved most, Tenayuca eventually enjoyed the admiration of Chicano/a movement activists and subsequent generations of Chicanos/as.[44]

"THE MEXICAN QUESTION IN THE SOUTHWEST"

Why did Emma Tenayuca's political beliefs provoke such tremendous negative reaction during the 1930s? An examination of "The Mexican Question in the Southwest," a political essay she coauthored with Homer Brooks, offers insights regarding Tenayuca's politics. In this essay, published in *The Communist* in March 1939, Tenayuca and Brooks presented a program for social change similar to that proposed by the Congress of Spanish-Speaking People in 1939 at its founding national convention in Los Angeles. That movement, calling for "Mexican unification," as the authors characterized it, was based on struggles against economic discrimination, educational and cultural inequality, and social oppression (mainly Jim Crow social and legal policies and political repression). The Congress also demanded that the citizenship rights of U.S.-born Mexicans be respected and the citizenship process for non-U.S.-born Mexicans be facilitated. Two radical positions supported by Tenayuca and Brooks as well as by the Congress included a call to unify with other oppressed groups, namely African Americans, and support for the undocumented. The logic for the latter position was that Mexican workers, regardless of citizenship, had earned a place in American society by virtue of their countless economic contributions toward the development of the U.S. Southwest.[45]

In the final section of "The Mexican Question" essay, titled "The Significance of the Mexican Rights Movement," Tenayuca and Brooks point out that the rise of a Mexican people's movement was crucial to the progressive movement of Euroamericans in the Southwest, and that there were serious international implications surrounding racial discrimination. The "Good Neighbor" policy of the U.S. with Latin American nations needed to begin at home in order to ring true abroad. Moreover, with an impending war, it behooved the United States to treat all Mexicans better, lest Nazi propaganda turn them away from an anti-fascist path.[46]

Nowhere in their essay did Tenayuca and Brooks advocate violent revolution between Mexicans and whites or between the bourgeoisie and the proletariat. In fact, they called for the unity of all Americans as one nation and simply demanded the social justice implied in fundamentally American political precepts. Their views fell in line with 1930s Popular Front positions in that Tenayuca and Brooks identified the enemy as fascism and supported progressive New Deal reforms. Furthermore, like other Popular Front advocates, Tenayuca and Brooks dedicated themselves to transforming the dream of a culturally plural society into a reality.[47]

Identity and experience shaped both Carolina Munguía and Emma Tenayuca. Each pursued her goal of community betterment in ways that reflected her distinct vision of what was possible for women to accomplish. The outcomes also reflect the different paths chosen. Munguía was never ostracized for her work with *la Raza* and ended her days as a respected community activist in 1977, while Tenayuca suffered from decades of blacklisting and harassment in Texas—though she, too, enjoyed the respect and esteem of many San Antonians toward the end of her life, receiving many tributes at the time of her death in 1999. While she called for reform, rather than revolution, Tenayuca's demands carried certain revolutionary implications, especially in conservative South Texas. For one, Tenayuca defended the rights of Mexican-origin peoples, regardless of citizenship status. Moreover, in a nation that still defined Americanism in terms of whiteness, a struggle for the rights of people considered "nonwhite" was radical in the 1930s. Second, Tenayuca never strayed from her working-class, grassroots origins. Tenayuca worked for *toda la gente* (all of the people) not for *la gente decente* (the decent people). This attitude, no doubt, offended people with middle-class sensibilities, Anglo or Mexican, who defined themselves in contrast to *gente corriente*—those who failed to adhere to middle-class notions of respectability and female domesticity. Finally, and perhaps most radically, Emma Tenayuca broke with both Mexican and Euroamerican gender conventions on both the personal and professional levels. In her personal life, she carried herself with great confidence, speaking her mind and living her life without many inhibitions. The fact that she married an Anglo American man with strong Communist ties illustrates her willingness to act unconventionally on an intimate level. A few years later, this marriage ended, and as a divorcee, she once again operated outside the accepted social conventions. After her activist career ended, Tenayuca continued to defy convention by raising a son on her own during the 1950s and 1960s. As a public person, she organized men and women, formed coalitions across ethnic lines, stormed the mayor's office, led a historic strike, banged on the doors of politicians, and stirred up large crowds with inspirational speeches that earned her the nickname *La Pasionaria* (the passionate one). Together these actions comprised the radical reformist politics of Emma Tenayuca.[48]

In contrast, Carolina Munguía adhered to gender conventions by practicing the politics of benevolence. Munguía personified the popular ideal of middle-class respectability. From a privileged background, she was well-versed in languages, music, art, and the social graces. As expected, she gave up her career upon marriage. Married only once, her marriage lasted until death and produced seven children. The energetic Munguía threw herself into child rearing and found time for the community service encouraged by her faith tradition. But unlike Tenayuca, her idea of social betterment had more to do with an individual's moral and intellectual edification than structural changes in the environment. Munguía believed that self-improvement, along with charitable assistance, provided the best course for women of Mexican origin. This is not to say that Munguía failed to recognize the poverty and racism that defined people's lives in the barrio. Rather, her deeply ingrained ideas about women's proper sphere and roles created a circumscribed vision of what women could do in the struggle against these oppressive forces.

Emma Tenayuca and Carolina Munguía pursued different organizational strategies, and yet, the politics of benevolence and the politics of radical reform both involved cultural and political negotiations. Tenayuca and Munguía operated at the crossroads of gender, class, race-ethnic, and national boundaries. As different as their political strategies and tactics were, both women's historical possibilities were shaped by transnational realities of the Mexican Revolution, widespread poverty, labor exploitation, and racial discrimination of Mexicans in South Texas.

NOTES

I would like to thank Antonia I. Castañeda, Estelle B. Freedman, Albert M. Camarillo, Linda K. Schott, Ruthe Winegarten, Rogelio Landeros Jr, and Sharyll Soto Teneyuca for reading drafts of this article and providing me with valuable comments. I would also like to thank the staffs at Texas Woman's University, the Benson Latin American Library at the University of Texas in Austin, and the Institute of Texan Cultures in San Antonio for their assistance, and the Munguía and Teneyuca families for their tireless efforts to preserve the memory of their loved ones who now take their much deserved place in history. *Mil Gracias!*

1. Allan Turner, "A Night that Changed San Antonio," *Houston Chronicle*, December 14, 1986, 46; and Minutes, Círculo Cultural "Isabel la Católica," San Antonio, August 27, 1939 (hereafter cited as CCIC Minutes), Romulo Munguía Collection, Nettie Lee Benson Library Manuscripts Collection, University of Texas, Austin (hereafter cited as Munguía MS).

2. Carolina Malpica de Munguía to the members of the Círculo Cultural "Isabel la

Católica," San Antonio, January 8, 1939, Munguía MS; and Jeannie Kever, "Women: Tenayuca Spent Years as a Strike Leader," *San Antonio Light*, March 6, 1988, J6.

3. Like her middle-class Euroamerican and African American counterparts, Carolina Munguía subscribed to maternalism, an exalted concept of motherhood that created a public space for civic participation by women by assigning them the influential role of social motherhood, that is, the right and obligation to influence government and society on matters relating to the social welfare of their families, particularly children. Estelle B. Freedman provides an excellent study of reform strategies of redemption and maternalist politics in *Maternal Justice: Miriam Van Waters and the Female Reform Tradition* (Chicago: The University of Chicago Press, 1996), 352–54. Despite the similarities, Munguía's maternalist inclinations derived their origins in Mexico, not the United States. She was raised and educated during the Porfirio Díaz regime, which intended to mold Mexico into a unified, modern nation-state. Secretary of Education Justo Sierra, the architect of Mexico's public school system, targeted women in particular, because he saw them as the primary transmitters of cultural values and as such it was imperative that they be educated to serve their nation. Julia Tuñon Pablos, *Mujeres en México: Una Historia Olvidada* (Mexico: Planeta, 1987), 86. Although baptized in the Catholic Church, Munguía was educated by Methodist missionaries stationed in Puebla, Mexico. Munguía's strong sense of community and moral obligation stemmed from her protestant upbringing. Throughout her life, she made time for community-related projects. See Cynthia E. Orozco, "Carolina Malpica Munguía," in *The Handbook of Texas* (Austin: Texas State Historical Association, 2003), online at *www.tsha .utexas.edu*. Telephone conversation with Sharyll Soto Teneyuca, April 30, 2003; "Emma Tenayuca, 1916–1999: Labor Organizer's Firebrand Activism Recalled," *San Antonio Express-News*, July 24, 1999.

Although publicly and, in many ways, privately, Emma Tenayuca's life reflected feminist sensibilities, and even though she can rightly be claimed as an important predecessor to the Chicana feminist movement both as a source of inspiration and as an early Mexican American woman leader, I do not use the term "feminist" in reference to her for two reasons. First, it was not a term that she used to describe herself, either in the 1930s or any time thereafter, nor did she consciously develop a feminist theory or praxis. Her focus was Mexican-origin workers, both men and women. Second, there is some evidence that sheds light on a potentially more complex personal reality. In a *Time* magazine article about Emma Tenayuca's labor organizing in Texas, the author writes, "Since her husband, Homer Brooks, former Communist nominee for Governor of Texas, lives in Houston, their marital life is confined to irregular weekends, but Emma Tenayuca declares pertly, 'I love my husband and am a good cook'" ("La Pasionaria de Texas," *Time*, February 28, 1938, 17). A biography of Emma Tenayuca that will no doubt shed light on these complexities has been undertaken by her niece, San Antonio attorney Sharyll Soto Teneyuca and writer Carmen Tafolla.

4. For critiques of male-identified and Euro-centered histories, see Antonia Castañeda, "Women of Color and the Rewriting of Western History: The Discourse, Politics, and Deconlonization of History," *Pacific Historical Review* 61 (1992): 501–33; and Cynthia E. Orozco, "Beyond Machismo, la Familia, and Ladies Auxiliaries: A History of Mexican Origin Women in Voluntary Association and Politics, 1870–1990," *Renato Rosaldo Lecture Series* 10 (1992/1993): 37–77, and "Sexing the Colonial Imaginary: (En)gendering Chicano History, Theory, and Consciousness," in *The Decolonial Imaginary: Writing Chicanas into History*, ed. Emma Pérez (Bloomington: Indiana University Press, 1999), 3–27.

5. Orozco, "Sexing the Colonial Imaginary," 3–27.

6. Elvira Cisneros, interview with author, April 28, 1994.

7. Carolina Malpica did graduate work in English (Orozco, "Carolina Malpica Munguía").

8. CCIC Minutes, San Antonio, June 12, 1938, Munguía MS. For purposes of simplicity, I hereafter refer to this organization as Círculo Cultural. "Reglamentos del Círculo Cultural 'Isabel la Católica,'" June 12, 1938, Munguía MS. Before her work with the Círculo Cultural, Carolina Munguía labored to uplift the community from what she perceived to be social and cultural decay through the media. According to her daughter, Munguía abhorred the custom of mixing the English and Spanish languages in conversation. She attributed the debasement of the Spanish language to the fact that Mexicans born and raised in the United States were less able to access Mexican culture. In an attempt to take care of what she believed to be a deficiency, she established a radio program called "La Estrella" on KONO in 1932. The Spanish program was designed to educate listeners on subjects such as literature, music, geography, and Mexican culture (Elvira Cisneros, interview with author, San Antonio, November 19, 1995; and Orozco, "Carolina Malpica Munguía").

9. Cisneros, interview, November 19, 1995. CCIC Minutes, January 22, 1939, July 31, 1938, August 21, 1938, September 4, 1938, February 5, 1939, and November 22, 1938, Munguía MS.

10. The implication is that working-class Mexicans in Texas were in a state of economic and cultural abandonment created by multiple forces, among them the ravages of revolution in Mexico, a legacy of severe poverty in their native land, severe poverty in their new American home, and racial discrimination. Carolina Munguía asked Mexican officials to do their part to improve the cultural landscape of their compatriots by participating in the club's art exhibition. In Mexico, middle-class people also sought to impose their value system upon the working class (William E. French, *A Peaceful and Working People: Manners, Morals, and Class Formation in Northern Mexico* [Albuquerque: University of New Mexico Press, 1996]).

11. Carolina Munguía to the Governor of San Luis Potosí, Mexico, May 1, 1939, Munguía MS. Other Mexican states that were sent letters were Querétaro, Sinaloa, Oaxaca,

Baja California, Michoacán, Coahuila, Nuevo León, Colima, Puebla, Guanajuato, and Hidalgo.

12. CCIC Minutes, July 7, 1938, July 31, 1938, July 21, 1938, September 4, 1938, September 18, 1938, February 5, 1939, and February 19, 1939, Munguía MS.

13. Carolina Munguía to the members of the Círculo Cultural, San Antonio, January 8, 1939, Munguía MS. Ruben Munguía, interview with the author, May 6, 1994.

14. Cisneros, interview, April 28, 1994.

15. "Reglamentos del Círculo Cultural 'Isabel la Católica,'" June 12, 1938.

16. "Reglamentos del Círculo Cultural 'Isabel la Católica,'" June 12, 1938, and October 2, 1938. Carolina Munguía to the members of the Círculo Cultural, San Antonio, January 8, 1939. Class divisions seemed anathema to Munguía. She sought to bridge such divisions through cultural nationalism. Aware of the vast material differences between the *gente humilde* (the poor) and the *gente comoda* (comfortable classes) like herself, Munguía, nevertheless, reasoned that the only division that counted was the one between the *gente decente* (the decent people—the high society of reason, manners, and culture) and the *gente corriente* (the common or crude people—the mass society of emotions, ill manners, and no culture). In a society where motherhood was still considered a woman's highest calling, the female litmus test for respectability revolved around domesticity. Immersed in these ideas, Munguía's activism reflected a middle-class ideology similar to that of many nineteenth-century Euroamerican and African American female activists.

17. "Emma Tenayuca" Texas Women's Biographical vertical files, The Woman's Collection, Texas Woman's University, Denton, Texas, hereafter cited as "Tenayuca" vertical files. Emma Tenayuca, interview with Gerry Poyo, February 21, 1987, Institute of Texan Cultures Oral History Program, The University of Texas at San Antonio.

18. Tenayuca, interview with Poyo. "Living History: Emma Tenayuca Tells Her Story," *The Texas Observer: A Journal of Free Voices*, October 28, 1983, 8.

19. Emma Tenayuca, "Interview with Emilio Zamora with the Participation of Oralia Cortez," June 1986, San Antonio, Texas, Emma Tenayuca MSS 420, box 11, folder 5, The Woman's Collection, Texas Woman's University, Denton Texas, hereafter cited as Tenayuca MSS 420. Tenayuca, interview with Poyo; Jan Jarboe Russell, "The Voice that Shook San Antonio," *The Texas Observer*, August 20, 1999.

20. Tenayuca, "Interview with Emilio Zamora."

21. Tenayuca, "Interview with Emilio Zamora." David Montejano, *Anglos and Mexicans in the Making of Texas, 1836–1986* (Austin: University of Texas Press, 1987), 232.

22. "Living History," 9. "Emma Tenayuca, 1916–1999"; "Tenayuca," vertical files; Tenayuca, "Interview"; Julia Kirk Blackwelder, *Women of the Depression: Caste and Culture in San Antonio, 1929–1939* (College Station: Texas A&M University Press, 1984), 103–4.

23. Sharyll Soto Teneyuca, telephone conversation with author, May 7, 2003. The author has her permission to quote.

24. "Living History," 9.

25. Tenayuca, "Interview with Emilio Zamora."

26. FBI report, December 6, 1941, Houston, Texas, Department of Justice, Federal Bureau of Investigation, Freedom of Information and Privacy Acts, Subject Emma Beatrice Tenayuca, hereafter cited as Tenayuca's FBI file. I thank Professor Albert Camarillo for bringing this important source to my attention.

27. Mark Naison, "Remaking America: Communists and Liberals in the Popular Front," in *New Studies in the Politics and Culture of U.S. Communism*, ed. Michael E. Brown, et al. (New York: Monthly Review Press, 1993), 45–70.

28. Roberto R. Calderón and Emilio Zamora, "Manuela Solis Sager and Emma B. Tenayuca: A Tribute," in *Between Borders: Essays on Mexicana/Chicana History*, ed. Adelaida R. Castillo (Encino, Calif.: Floricanto Press, 1990), 272. The Workers Alliance often helped resolve relief grievances, fought for more relief, sought less degrading relief practices, stopped evictions, fought against WPA cuts, and struggled against the exploitation of WPA workers. "The Unemployed Movements of the 1930s," in Mari Jo Buhle, Paul Buhle, and Dan Georgakas, eds. *Encyclopedia of the American Left* (Urbana: University of Illinois Press, 1990), 796; Tenayuca, interview with Poyo, 24. Tenayuca believed that the Texas Relief Commission was operating as a cheap labor agency for Anglo farmers. She noted that many of the Mexican-origin workers denied WPA work and relegated to the fields had no experience in agricultural work and some even possessed other types of skills. Tenayuca also despaired at the slow investigative process whereby Mexican-origin workers were told to wait for the caseworker evaluating their case to visit them. Many were still waiting for the caseworker to show up at the time of Tenayuca's letters. Instead of this prolonged process, Tenayuca asked that the WPA order granting unemployed Midwesterners WPA work prior to an investigation for relief status be extended to all states (Emma Tenayuca, Secretary of Workers Alliance in San Antonio to Mr. Harry L. Hopkins, WPA Administrator, November 15, 1937; and Emma Tenayuca, Secretary of Workers Alliance in San Antonio to Mr. Aubrey Williams, Deputy WPA Administrator, January 13, 1938 and January 19 1938 ["General Correspondence: Friends and Associates," Tenayuca MSS. 420, box 5, folder 42]). "Living History," 9–10; and Tenayuca, interview with Poyo, 31.

29. Richard Croxdale, "The 1938 San Antonio Pecan Sheller's Strike," in *Women in the Texas Workforce: Yesterday and Today*, ed. Richard Croxdale and Melissa Hield (Austin: People's History in Texas, Inc., 1979), 24, 25. "Tenayuca" vertical files. Selden Menefee and Orin C. Cassmore, *The Pecan Shellers of San Antonio* (Washington, D.C.: Government Printing Office (GPO), 1940), 6, 10.

30. Tenayuca, "Interview with Emilio Zamora." Croxdale, "The 1938 San Antonio Pecan Sheller's Strike," 26, 27. Menefee and Cassmore, authors of a study on the pecan

shellers in San Antonio conducted by the WPA, did not make the claim that Seligman hired Rodriguez; however, their study did corroborate Tenayuca's claim that there was a close relationship between the two. The study further confirmed Tenayuca's claim that Rodriguez received financial support from Seligman because the union helped to "prevent small operators from undercutting the piecework scale paid by the larger companies" (Menefee and Cassmore, *The Pecan Shellers of San Antonio*, 16–17).

31. Menefee and Cassmore, *The Pecan Shellers of San Antonio*, 17. Others who opposed the strike included the American Chamber of Commerce, the Mexican Chamber of Commerce, LULAC, and the Catholic Church. One church official offered to help strikers on the condition that they reject CIO leadership, which some conflated with communism. Strikers decided to stick with the CIO (Richard A. Garcia, *Rise of the Mexican American Middle Class: San Antonio, 1929–1941* [College Station: Texas A&M University Press, 1991]).

32. "Pecan Plant Workers Strike," *San Antonio Light*, January 31, 1938, 1.

33. "Pecan Strike Heads Offer to Quit," *San Antonio Light*, February 3, 1938, 1, 4. Redbaiting came from a national source as well. In a *Time* magazine article on Emma Tenayuca and the Pecan Shellers' Strike, the writer characterized Tenayuca as "little Emma Tenayuca, a slim, vivacious labor organizer with black eyes and a Red philosophy . . . [who] from her office at the local Workers Alliance . . . continued to pull strings with the assistance of her "gang," some 300 devoted followers whom she deploys with a masterly hand in picket lines or mass meeting" ("*La Pasionaria de Texas*," *Time*, February 28, 1938, 17).

34. Menefee and Cassmore, *The Pecan Shellers of San Antonio*, 18. "S.A. Strikers Tell Police Beatings," *San Antonio Light*, February 15, 1938, 1; and Blackwelder, *Women of the Depression*, 143.

35. Croxdale, "The 1938 San Antonio Pecan Sheller's Strike," 28. Tenayuca, interview with Poyo; "Living History" 13; Turner, "A Night That Changed Lives, San Antonio." Homer Brooks ran unsuccessfully for governor of Texas in 1936. Naison, "Remaking America," 49.

36. Emma Tenayuca to Mrs. Jimenez, July 31, 1973, part of the "Texas Women in History" exhibit documents found in The Women's Collection, Texas Woman's University, Denton, Texas. Croxdale, "The 1938 San Antonio Pecan Sheller's Strike," 31–32.

37. Tenayuca FBI file; and Calderon and Zamora, "Manuela Solis Sager and Emma Tenayuca: A Tribute," 274.

38. Ernie Villarreal, "San Antonio Landmark Site of Riot in 1939," *Texas Public Radio Newsroom*, aired August 24, 2001. Legionnaires were outraged because the mayor had granted the Communists permission to meet in a building that had been dedicated to San Antonio's fallen World War I heroes. Maury Maverick, "One San Antonio Maverick Sticks by Another," *San Antonio Express-News*, August 1, 1999, 3H.

39. Kever, "Women"; and Jan Jarboe, "S.A.'s Linen Needs Airing," *San Antonio*

Express-News, March 3, 1985. Turner, "A Night that Changed San Antonio," 1. A number of photographs of Father M. A. Valenta and Clem Smith place them at the Municipal Auditorium on August 25, 1939. Villarreal, "San Antonio Landmark Site of Riot in 1939." Gus. T. Jones to Director, Federal Bureau of Investigation, August 26, 1939, Tenayuca's FBI file. Maury Maverick, "Tenayuca's Lessons Are Worth Another Look," *San Antonio Express-News*, September 26, 1999, 3G. *The San Antonio Light* Collection at the Institute of Texan Cultures in San Antonio contains a black and white photograph (2223-VV) of Maury Maverick hanged in effigy at City Hall dated August 25, 1939.

40. Marina Pisano, "Labor Leader's Legacy Endures: Former Union Organizer Living a Quiet Life—Sort Of," *San Antonio Express-News*, February 1, 1990, 3; and Turner, "A Night that Changed San Antonio," 46.

41. "Tenayuca, 1916–1999." R. J. Abbaticchio Jr to Director FBI, September 8, 1941, Tenayuca's FBI file. Maurice Isserman, *If I Had a Hammer: The Death of the Old Left and the Birth of the New Left* (Urbana: University of Illinois Press, 1993), 7–8.

42. "Divorce Decree, 1941, from Homer Brooks, and Restoration of Her Maiden Name," Tenayuca MSS. 420, box 7, folder 6. SAC, San Francisco to Director, FBI, 20 April 1953, Tenayuca's FBI file. FBI report, December 6, 1941, Tenayuca's FBI file. FBI reports, May 6, 1942, and Special Agent in Charge (SAC), San Francisco to Director, FBI, April 20, 1953, Tenayuca's FBI file. Evidence for these claims can be found throughout the Emma Tenayuca FBI file, which extends from 1939 to 1953. In 1953, the FBI ended its surveillance of Tenayuca, adding only one other document to her file in 1968. This document simply recorded her new address in San Antonio, Texas. Robert L. Sikes, 2nd Lieut., Assistant Recruiting Officer, to Miss Emma B. Giraud, December 29, 1942; Charles D. Apple, Assistant Recruiting and Induction Officer to Miss Emma Teneyuca, January 8, 1943; Stanley Kock, Colonel, Cavalry, Recruiting and Induction Officer to Mrs. Emma Teneyuca, January 29, 1943, Tenayuca MSS. 420, box 1, folder 9; and "Emma Tenayuca, 1916–1999."

43. SAC, San Francisco to Director, FBI, April 20, 1953, Tenayuca's FBI file. Isserman, *If I Had a Hammer*, 3–34; and Turner, "A Night that Changed San Antonio," 46.

44. Turner, "A Night that Changed San Antonio," 46. "Emma Tenayuca, 1916–1999." Nomination form for the Texas Women's Hall of Fame, Tenayuca MSS. 420, box 5, folder 22. Some of the scholars who corresponded or received assistance from Emma Tenayuca include Teresa Palomo Acosta, Irene Blea, Roberto Calderon, Martha Cotera, Julia Curry, Juan Gómez-Quiñones, Margarita Melville, Cynthia E. Orozco, Jerry Poyo, Carmen Tafolla, Zaragosa Vargas, Ruthe Winegarten, and Emilio Zamora. She also assisted high school students with their projects. Tenayuca also continued to keep up with local, state, and national politics, supporting the San Antonio mayoral campaigns of Henry G. Cisneros and the Texas gubernatorial campaign of Ann Richards. For more information, see "General Correspondence: Friends and Associates," Tenayuca MSS. 420, boxes 3–5.

45. The Congress of Spanish-Speaking Peoples was a national Chicano civil rights organization founded in 1938–1939 by labor activist Luisa Moreno. Its membership included students, teachers, politicians, and unionists. According to scholars Matt S. Meier and Feliciano Rivera, the activist position of the Congress drew the attention of FBI investigators. Historian Mario T. García characterizes the Congress as a Popular Front organization and a "working-class movement in coalition with progressive liberals" led by the leftist element of the Mexican American generation (Meier and Rivera, *Dictionary of Mexican American History* [Westport, Conn.: Greenwood Press, 1981], 102; and Mario T. García, *Mexican Americans: Leadership, Ideology, and Identity, 1930–1960* [New Haven: Yale University Press, 1989], 145–46). Emma Tenayuca and Homer Brooks, "The Mexican Question in the Southwest," *The Communist*, March 1939, 264, 265–66.

46. Tenayuca and Brooks, "The Mexican Question in the Southwest," 267–68.

47. "Popular Front," in *Encyclopedia of the American Left*, ed. Paul Buhle and Dan Georgakas (Urbana: University of Illinois Press, 1990), 796; and Tenayuca, interview with Poyo, 24.

48. Dawn Letson, comp., "Emma Tenayuca: A Guide to the Collection," Tenayuca MSS. 420.

María and Emma

MARÍA ANTONIETTA BERRIOZÁBAL

Emma Tenayuca, labor leader, teacher, intellectual, and activist, died on July 23, 1999, in San Antonio, Texas. At the wake for Emma, the Tenuyca family invited María Antonietta Berriozábal to lead the community in praying the rosary, that the voices of her family and community may accompany her soul's journey to the other side. María Antonietta reworked the liturgy of the traditional "Five Joyful Mysteries of the Rosary," to reveal, reflect, and celebrate Emma Tenayuca's life.
   Susan Armitage, Editor

At Emma Tenayuca's wake I incorporated Emma's gifts to humanity during the traditional rosary that is recited at such an occasion.
   María Antonietta Berriozábal

1. THE ANNUNCIATION

Mary: An angel came to Mary and told her she would bear a son and that he would be the long-awaited Messiah. Mary did not question how this would happen. She simply said yes.
Emma: Emma said yes to difficult challenges many times. A woman of great faith, she did not question how things would be accomplished or who would listen or if her work would be fruitful. She simply did what she felt had to be done. She did it with courage, tenacity and a great love for her people.

2. THE VISITATION

Mary: While pregnant, Mary traveled a long distance to visit her cousin Elizabeth, who at an advanced age was going to have a child.
Emma: Emma did not let obstacles stop her from doing what she felt needed

to be done. Confronted with powerful business interests in the pecan shelling business, for example, she helped the workers by giving them information, organizing them and helping them use their own voices. Most of the workers were women, some old and some young. Emma, like Mary, understood that women are powerful instruments for the peace that can only be achieved through justice.

3. MARY GAVE BIRTH TO A SON AND IT WAS HER GIFT TO THE WORLD.

Emma: Emma gave the world her own gifts of understanding and unselfishness. She could have had a comfortable life as a very young woman, yet she chose to use the inquisitive mind that God gave her to analyze the world around her. She saw injustices and she spoke out against them. Emma birthed hope.

4. THE PRESENTATION IN THE TEMPLE

Mary: Mary followed Jewish law and took her little son to present him to the elders in the temple. This was a structure of power and Mary entered it and dedicated her son's life to service.
Emma: Emma at a very young age was unafraid to enter structures of power and advocate on behalf of those who could not use their own voices. Her intelligence, her gifted use of words, and her passion were given in service to those who were most in need.

5. THE FINDING IN THE TEMPLE

Mary: One day Mary and Joseph were in a public place and they lost Jesus, only to later find him in the temple speaking his truth to the priests who were there. As any mother, Mary rejoiced when she found him. But when she saw him she understood that this young man was destined to use his voice, and she knew that he would suffer for this. The Bible tells us that she kept these things in her heart.
Emma: Emma prepared herself not only with a formal education but she also was self-taught through her extensive reading. Emma was wise. We can wonder if Emma knew as a young woman what the future held for her? Did she know that in many ways she, too, would be crucified with ridicule, prejudice, racism, and violence? We do not know.

What we do know is that it is obvious that she found joy in her work. She found that joy that comes only from giving from one's deepest self. She found the joy that the world does not understand. She found the joy that only comes from giving and loving deeply.

San Antonio, Tejas
July 1999

La Pasionaria

to Emma

La Pasionaria we called her,
bloom of passion,
because she was our passion
because she was our corazón—
defendiendo a los pobres, speaking out
at a time when neither Mexicans nor women
were expected to speak out at all.

But there she was—
Raising up her fist for justice,
raising up her voice for truth

filled always with a passion
for life and for compassion,
a passion to empower the people
a passion to protect the poor.

A fire of heart and tongue.

And so she raised her fist and her voice
'til the passion had spread like a firestorm,
and the world was changed.

Such unflinching commitment to the truth
stirs fear and panic in some—
and love in others,
empowered by that truth.

She was jailed and jailed and jailed again—
but it could not stop the passion.
A passion to empower the people.
A passion to protect the poor.

While pecan-shellers worked in dark halls,
in clouds of brown dust that filled lungs
and brought a plague of tuberculosis,
while children missed school to work
twelve hour days at rough-hewn tables
where no cool breeze or sunlight ever reached,
while people's fingers were bleeding,
and their pockets were still empty,
and their children were still hungry . . .
she would not be silent.

Years later she would say to me,

"If I had had any hatred in those years,
I wouldn't have lasted at all.
Hatred is self-destructive . . .
you have to have Love for a cause."

No, Emma had no time for hatred.
no time for bitterness.
no time for regret.
She only had time for action,
for raising her fist
for raising her voice,
and searching always for the truth.

She read voraciously,
a one-woman university,
a one-scholar library.

"Have you read Dostoevsky?"
"Have you read Thorstein Veblen?"
"Have you read Barrera-Muñoz?"
"Have you read Sophocles?"
"Take this book."
"Take this book."
"Take this book."

A passion to empower the people,
A passion to protect the poor.

Her black piercing eyes would educate us:

"I cannot go along with this extreme nationalism.
There IS a common goal for all of us—but it is not
isolationism, it is the right for human justice

"The use of the Media to add superficiality
to the relationships between male and female
in America. . . ."

"Count the number of women in managerial positions
in our City Government. . . ."

"No ruling class can oppress another people without
some members of the oppressed people within their structure
cooperating. SOME of us have accommodated ourselves
rather well. . . ."

"Some of the leadership of the Mexican people
will come from the middle class but they must embrace
the aspirations and the desires of the people."

"Have you looked at the position of women in
Plato's *Republic*?"

"Take this book."

Emma had a mind like a razor blade
but a heart that could fit
compassion for everyone—
even those who had no compassion for her.

§

Your mark was made, Emma
but it wasn't made in stone.

Your mark was made, Emma
but it wasn't headlined in the books
that tried to erase your name from history.

Your mark was made
but it wasn't pleasantly applauded on the naming
of streets and of public libraries
where the books you so loved were shelved
without noticing the heroine in our midst.

Your mark was made.
Your mark was made
on the course of history
y en el corazón del pueblo.

Your mark
was made
on our lives,
on all of us
who are
still
following you.

The first draft of *"La Pasionaria"* was read at the funeral of Emma Tenayuca in San Fernando Cathedral on July 27, 1999. In 1938, at the age of twenty-one, Emma Tenayuca organized twelve thousand pecan shellers in a strike, which boosted wages to five cents per pound. It was the first major successful action in the struggle for economic and social justice for Mexican Americans. A powerful and courageous orator, she feared neither jail nor public censure. She devoted her later years to teaching and helping migrant students learn to read. Carmen Tafolla is at work with Tenayuca's niece on a biography of Emma Tenayuca.

Mujeres de San Antonio

Murals of Emma Tenayuca, Corazones de la Comunidad, and Rosita Fernández

THERESA A. YBÁÑEZ

There is a muralist from San Francisco by the name of Juana Alicia. She inspired me to paint the murals that I painted in San Antonio. I became familiar with her work while living in the Bay Area. Her collaborative work on the Women's Building on Eighteenth and Valencia is a masterpiece on historical women of color. Her mural that wraps around the Cesar Chavez Elementary school in its bright, vibrant colors illustrate the value of letters and learning. What struck me about Juana Alicia's art is how it focuses on women, how she uses color, and the size of her art (huge). I thought, "I want to do murals like hers, and focus them on Chicana women of San Antonio."

When I returned to San Antonio I went to Southtown Neighborhood Association in the area where I lived, and which is also the neighborhood where I grew up. I told the director that I had a dream of creating murals on several of the walls of buildings on South Presa Street and South St. Mary's corridor. Thus began the series of murals collectively named *Mujeres de San Antonio*.

The women depicted in the three murals are all native San Antonians who contributed to their communities through their activism, art, and vision. The first mural was created in 1995. It honored one of my heroes, Emma Tenayuca, a civil rights leader and labor organizer. I am a painter who usually works alone in my studio, but with this project I had to collaborate with friends, other artists, people from the community, and people waiting for their clothes to wash (the mural is on the wall of a laundromat).

The second mural was created in 1999. After the Tenayuca mural was completed, I thought that I would love to see the whole building wrapped in a mural. Again, the neighborhood association funded the project and *Corazones de la Comunidad* was completed. In this mural I portrayed four more heroes: Lydia Mendoza, a singer/songwriter; María Antonietta Berriozábal, a community activist/politician/educator; Bambi Cardenas, a politician/educator; and Manuela Sager, a community activist/hell-raiser. On the east and west sides of the laundromat I painted men and women washing and folding *rebozos/* shawls. There are also *dichos/*sayings about washing clothes and a brief history about *rebozos* written by Sandra Cisneros.

In this same year I created *La Rosa de San Antoino—Rosita Fernández*. This mural is on the same street as the other two and was also funded by the South-town Neighborhood Association. Unfortunately, the wall was/is not in very good condition, but we went ahead and painted the otherwise gang graffitied/ *placazo*(ed) wall.

I am hoping that in 2004 that I will find another wall on South Presa Street to paint for my next mural. I would paint the Hernandez Sisters and *Las Carpas/*Tent Shows. The Hernandez Sisters were Mexican American acrobats in the 1940s. I can imagine a two-story mural with the *hermanas* somersaulting or flying in the air. *Espero, que en* the future this mural will come to be. Since the others were dreamed up and then became a reality, it can happen. The reality of documenting and educating every day through the power of art about women who would otherwise be forgotten is the importance of these murals. A community needs help in remembering their history, so what better way than through art?

Rosita Fernández, mural painted on the exterior west wall of the Eagles Nest Café, on the corner of Carolina and South Presa Street, San Antonio, Texas (photo by Joan Fredericks).

Emma Tenayuca, mural painted on the exterior east wall of the Quick Wash Laundromat, South Presa Street, San Antonio, Texas (photo by Joan Fredericks).

Emma Tenayuca, mural painted on the exterior east wall of the Quick Wash Laundromat, South Presa Street, San Antonio, Texas (photo by Joan Fredericks).

María Antonietta Berriozábal, one of the four women included in the *Corazones de San Antonio* mural, painted on the exterior west wall of the Quick Wash Laundromat, South Presa Street, San Antonio, Texas (photo by Joan Fredericks).

Corazones de San Antonio, detail (photo by Joan Fredericks).

Globalization and Its Discontents

Exposing the Underside

EVELYN HU-DEHART

In recent years, we have been treated to a sense of déjá vu of the sixties. Great numbers of mostly young people, men and women, mostly white, middle-class college students, have descended on major American cities such as Seattle and Washington, D.C., as well as their own campuses to protest a new and virulent form of injustice.[1] Only this time, instead of protesting against war or racism, they raised their voices against something called "globalization." Specifically, they named the related evils to be exposed and reformed, if not destroyed, as the World Trade Organization (WTO), which seeks to remove all barriers to world trade, such as regulations and tariffs erected by nation-states; the Multilateral Agreement on Investment (MAI), which prohibits signatory nations from impeding the flow of money and production facilities across their borders; the International Monetary Fund (IMF) and World Bank, both created by the advanced economies to help poor countries "modernize" with loans and development projects; and sweatshops, the unregulated assembly plants. All of these are linked to globalization.[2]

The concern boiling over into outright objection to globalization has been brewing for some time. But if we have to pinpoint a specific event, we can begin with the Zapatista uprising in Mexico in January 1994.[3] On that fateful day, the Indian peasants of Chiapas, Mexico's southernmost province, rose up in rebellion, timing the protest to coincide with the first day of implementation of the North American Free Trade Agreement (NAFTA), eagerly signed by the governments of the United States, Canada, and Mexico to consolidate neoliberal economic policies and practices in the hemisphere. Dubbed the first postmodern uprising because the rebels professed no interest in seizing state power while demonstrating uncanny sophistication in generating and maintaining international media interest in their just cause, the Zapatistas were soon joined by other Indigenous and peasant insurgents in at least six other poverty-stricken states in southern and central Mexico. What all the rural rebels of Mexico have in common is their vociferous objection to one of then-President Salinas's most controversial preparatory moves for NAFTA, the undoing of Article 27 of the constitution of the Mexican Revolution, which had created thousands of pueblos with inalienable community landholdings called *ejidos*, the centerpiece of Mexico's postrevolutionary land reform and the primary symbol of social justice for peasants. Much to the shock of observers in Mexico and abroad, Salinas violated an unspoken, sacrosanct principle that even his most corrupt and venal predecessors had upheld for decades when he allowed the communal landholdings to be broken up, sold off, and privatized.[4] The breakup of the *ejidos* indicated just how far Salinas and Mexico's elite in the official ruling party Partido Revolucionario Institucional (PRI) were willing to go to mortgage Mexico's most vulnerable citizens to neoliberalism's New World Order, also known as globalization. For more than eighty years, peasants were assured of at least a minimum safety net; now, even this threadbare net was yanked out from under them, leaving Mexico's eighty-plus million population, half of whom were living in poverty, to sink deeper into misery. During the ten years of neoliberal policies that preceded the formal implementation of NAFTA in 1994, more than two million new rural poor were produced in the countryside.[5] Nowhere is the poverty more visible or entrenched than in Chiapas, Mexico's poorest state, where the insurrection has been converted into an "armed critique" of Salinas's neoliberal policies. In a nutshell, neoliberalism is designed to "modernize" Mexico through international economic integration based on export-oriented production and removal of all trade barriers, protective tariffs, and central government regulation of the economy. To demonstrate his commitment to the free market, Salinas also had to maximize privatization of Mexico's wealth, her resources, and infrastructure. Not even communally owned *ejido* land was immune to this onslaught.[6] Obviously, the peasants of Chiapas understood the meaning of globalization, at least as far as their well-being was concerned, sooner than many of us in the sophisticated First World, and they registered their opposition to globalization in no uncertain terms.

In fact, well before NAFTA, Mexico had been a test site and launching pad of the new globalization along its extensive northern border shared with the advanced economy of the United States, far away from the southern border zone that the Zapatistas shared with two even poorer countries, Guatemala and Belize. Indeed, for the alert observer of late-capitalist globalization, the Border Industrialization Project (BIP), which spawned the ubiquitous assembly plants called *maquiladoras*, is the prototype of export-zone production that now dominates the manufacturing landscape all over the Pacific Rim and was the forerunner of the notorious sweatshops seemingly resurrected from the ash heap of early capitalist America.

One recent report counts twenty-seven hundred *maquiladoras* in Mexico, which now, after the enactment of NAFTA, spread from the northern border zone deep into the Yucatán of southern Mexico, where labor is more stable and 25 percent cheaper. In addition to North American corporate owners, other large *maquiladora* owners came from Japan, South Korea, Taiwan, Hong Kong, and assorted European countries, such as Germany.[7] Always in search of cheaper labor, usually embodied by women and children, similar assembly plants have penetrated Central America and parts of the Caribbean.[8] The "giant sucking sound" that presidential candidate Ross Perot heard was that of jobs flowing southward as the United States eliminated industrial jobs. This deindustrialization process began in the 1970s in the economically powerful global core, and manufacturing jobs flowed eastward across the Pacific and south to Latin America, while the U.S. labor economy experienced the rapid rise in service employment at both the high- and low-skilled ends. In the United States, the nonmanufacturing labor force came to constitute 84.3 percent of the total hours worked by 1996, or a growth of almost thirty million jobs since 1979.[9]

The ensuing restructured international economy set up "export-processing zones" (EPZs) or "free trade zones"(FTZs) all over the global periphery, where jerry-built factories produce consumer goods—mainly electronics, clothing, shoes, and toys—for export back to the core. In this New World Economy, finance capital from the global core flows unfettered across international borders to locate sources of cheap labor where eager local elites in control of pliant states act as "middlemen" to facilitate what is euphemistically termed global economic integration. Some Asian countries have prospered from early export-based industrialization—notably Japan, Singapore, Taiwan, and Hong Kong before reintegration with China—and have also become exporters of finance capital, setting up assembly plants in poorer Asian countries such as Indonesia, Thailand, and China, as well as in Mexico, Central America, and the Caribbean as mentioned above. Meanwhile, these more prosperous countries have continued to perform middlemen functions for large international capital in their capacity as subcontractors or out-sourcers.[10]

Nothing illustrates the relationship between the transnational U.S. corporation and Asian capital and labor better than Phil Knight's Nike, Inc. The very establishment newspaper *The Washington Post* charges that: "No other company symbolizes the mobilization of American companies overseas more than Nike, Inc. Its thirty-year history in Asia is as close as any one company's story can be to the history of globalization, to the spread of dollars—and marks, and yen—into the poor corners of the earth."[11] Simply put, during the 1970s and 1980s Knight discovered that new computer and fax technology enabled him to export and control the production of his brand-name athletic shoes in Asian countries, where cheap, largely female, labor abounded. By the time he closed down his last U.S. sneaker plants in New Hampshire and Maine, he had discovered the virtues of out-sourcing production. He subcontracted with Asian entrepreneurs from the more affluent Asian countries, such as Taiwan, South Korea, and Hong Kong, to set up assembly plants to manufacture Nike shoes in poorer, and thus labor-cheap, Asian countries such as China, Indonesia, and Vietnam. The subcontractors did all the work of recruiting, training, and disciplining workers, monitoring production, setting wages, and paying workers—in short, handling all aspects of management-labor relations. These Asian subcontractors also took care of dealing with Asian host governments and local officials, greasing palms when necessary. One of Asia's most successful subcontractors was the Tsai family of Hong Kong, whose ninety-seven production lines employing fifty-four thousand workers in China's Pearl River Delta produced forty-five million sneakers in 1995 for Reebock and Adidas, as well as Nike.[12] For a long period of time, the subcontracting system allowed Nike to argue that it had no direct supervision over Asian plants, thus should be absolved from dealing with any problems arising from labor or government relations.

In this global production system, profits are good for the subcontractors, but they are really phenomenal for Nike owner Phil Knight. To expand the worldwide demand for Nike sneakers, he enlisted the alliance of National Basketball Association (NBA) Commissioner David Stern, global media mogul Rupert Murdoch, and most importantly, basketball superstar Michael Jordan. With $20 million in yearly endorsement fees from Knight, Jordan spread his impressive American game to the rest of the world while simultaneously selling the Nike shoes that seemingly propelled him to unparalleled heights. Knight became the sixth wealthiest man in the United States, and Jordan became the most successful global pitchman, but their profits and fame were founded on the labor of legions of faceless, nameless Asian girls and women.

After Jordan's retirement from basketball, Knight signed up Tiger Woods, son of a Thai mother and an African American father, to do for Nike and golf what Jordan had done for Nike and basketball. As a still more perverse turn of globalization, the next global pitchman for Nike is likely to be Yao Ming, China's seven-feet-five-inch gift to the NBA. This first pick of the 2002 NBA draft was signed by the team in Houston, home to America's fifth largest Asian American community. But his real appeal would be transnational, pitching American labels manufactured in Asian sweatshops back to consumers in his densely-packed homeland and all across Asia.

When this global production system first evolved, Knight was rather guileless in explaining his huge profits: "We were . . . good at keeping our manufacturing costs down," he said.[13] How low? In 1992, four Indonesian plants owned by South Korean subcontractors paid young girls as little as $.15 an hour for an eleven-hour day. A pair of shoes that cost less than $5 to make in Asia sold for $150 in the United States.[14] By the late 1990s, Indonesian factories made 70 million pairs of Nike shoes with twenty-five thousand workers, each of them receiving daily wages of $2.23, which covered only 90 percent of basic subsistence needs for one person. Their combined yearly wages did not equal Jordan's endorsement fee.[15] Wages in Vietnam were even lower, at $1.60 for an eight-hour day in 1997.[16]

The Nike shoe captures the essence of the new global consumer product: A particular model can be designed in Nike headquarters in Oregon, and cooperatively developed by technicians in Oregon, South Korea, and Indonesia by putting together fifty-two separate parts made in five countries. It is manufactured by young women hunched over machines and hand tools and glue, working in factories located in Vietnam, Indonesia, or China and owned by someone from Taiwan or Hongkong.[17] Then it is sold all over the world.

In sum, globalization in late capitalism changes relations of production, marked by a labor strategy that stresses minimizing cost and maximizing flexibility. Some have described it as a shift from a Fordist system of production to a "leaner" and more fragmented production process, with greater "spatial mobility" for both capital and labor. From the lowly athletic shoe to the mighty jet planes made by Boeing, the new logic of post-Fordist global production remains the same. After the new jet, the Boeing 777, is designed at U.S. Boeing headquarters, the plane is broken up into modules and each one sent to a different country to be manufactured. For example, the main body is manufactured by Mitsubishi Heavy Industries in Kobe, Japan, using skilled Japanese craftsmen, while other modules are manufactured in twelve other countries. Then all the parts are shipped back to the Boeing plant in Everett, Washington, where the entire plane is assembled.[18] Each one of the modules is out-sourced or subcontracted. Similarly, the Korean-owned Han Young *maquiladora* in Tijuana, Mexico, manufactures truck chassis, which are then shipped duty-free, courtesy of NAFTA, across the border to the Hyundai auto plant in San Diego, California, with the finished product destined for the U.S. market.[19] Finally, and somewhat amazingly, global capital and production in continuous and relentless search for cheap labor, manufacturing flexibility, and spatial mobility have come full circle: The global assembly plant employing low-skilled, low-cost female labor can now be found in abundance in the global core—the United States itself—in the form of hundreds of garment sweatshops scattered throughout southern California, the San Francisco-Oakland area, and in and around New York's garment district and Chinatowns.[20] Although clothing manufacturing has constituted a mainstay of the Mexican *maquiladoras* and fly-by-night assembly plants set up in export-processing zones by Asian subcontractors in the Caribbean, Central America, and all over Asia, the fast-changing designs and fluctuating market demands of the garment business has dictated the need to produce certain styles and quantities of garments close to the retailers, manufacturers, and consumers in the United States. New Asian and Latino immigrants (legal and undocumented) quickly meet the needs both for subcontractors and for workers, doing the same work they would in their home countries had they not migrated to the United States. Nike and other American manufacturers are reluctant to claim responsibility for labor problems in their Asian production, and they have a similar policy at home, arguing they have no control over their subcontractors who own and operate the sweatshops.[21]

While hidden for years from the American consuming public and the media, the revived American sweatshop is no longer a secret, and its exposure is helping to fuel the antiglobalization movement. The raid on the El Monte, California, underground sweatshop in August 1995 freed sixty-seven women and five men, Thai workers smuggled into the country by the Thai-Chinese owners who contracted with several well-known U.S. brand-name manufacturers. Paid only $1.60 per hour, these workers were kept in a modern version of indentured servitude, denied their freedom to leave the barbed-wire compound, forced to pay off their passage, and threatened with retribution against family members back home and rape if they disobeyed their captors.[22] In January 1999, the media exposed another shameful sweatshop situation that resembled El Monte. Hundreds of sweatshops owned by Asians and Asian American subcontractors were found in the U.S. Pacific territory of Saipan, where workers—predominantly young women from the Philippines, China, Thailand and Bangladesh—worked twelve hours daily, seven days weekly, living seven to a room in "dreary barracks surrounded by inward-facing barbed wire."[23]

At the base of this system are the legions of immigrant women workers, Asian and Latina, who have seldom complained because they believe they have no other job options. In converting themselves into an available and flexible labor force almost immediately upon their arrival in the United States, they have enabled the garment industry to keep a critical part of garment production within the United States, right in the manufacturing and retail centers of New York and Los Angeles, where most of these immigrants settle. Those immigrant women absorbed into garment work likely have little formal education and little or no English-language skills, and are deemed to be low-skilled in other areas as well. Research has shown that deficiencies in education and

English-language skills are also the most critical factors in determining immigrant job options in the United States.[24] Many women are compelled to work to supplement family incomes because their equally low-skilled, English-deficient spouses also work in low-paying, often dead-end jobs. It would be wrong to dismiss their contribution to family income as merely "supplementary," for many women earn as much, if not more, than their equally trapped partners.[25] Furthermore, with both partners stuck in these low-wage, dead-end, often seasonal jobs, poverty for many such immigrant families has become a permanent fact of life.[26]

In addition to manufacturing, immigrant women workers from Asia and Latin America are desired in the global core for what might be termed "social reproductive labor."[27] Whether working in domestic, cleaning, janitorial, or food service, or in nursing home or child care, or as prostitutes, sex workers, or mail- or internet-order brides, Third World immigrant women are not just making a living in low-paying, low-status, often demeaning niches that require little English or other skills. In a very crucial way, they, too, are part of the new transnational division of labor, albeit in a less visible and certainly far less acknowledged way. Their paid labor now replaces the previously unremunerated responsibilities of First World women in the social reproduction of daily and family life, both on a daily and intergenerational basis, by relieving professional First World women of much of the burden of the "second shift." Such social reproductive labor has always been associated with women's work and continues to be debased and devalued when "industrialized," that is, performed for payment by Third World women for their largely white and affluent First World "sisters" in a racial division of labor.[28] In sum, "Most white middle class women could hire another woman—a recent immigrant, a working class woman, a woman of color, or all these—to perform much of the hard labor of household tasks," as they fulfill themselves in careers outside the home.[29] To put it bluntly, the "private sphere" responsibilities of class-privileged women are thereby transferred to racially and socially subordinate women.[30]

Although sex work across national boundaries is not new in the world, sex industries have greatly expanded under late capitalist globalization.[31] Preference for Asian women as sex partners—paid or even unpaid, as in the case of military and mail- or internet-order brides—by many American men dates back to the days of America's serial military involvement in Asia, from WW II, through the Korean War, and on to the Vietnam War. "Militarized prostitution" developed around all army bases in Asia while American soldiers on furlough for "rest and relaxation" stimulated the development and growth of sex tourism to countries far beyond the battlegrounds, such as in Thailand.[32] Just as American transnational capital has constructed Third World women as particularly adept at garment assembly work—both "over there" and after migration to the United States—so have American men fetishized these same women as particularly seductive as girlfriends and attentive and submissive as wives, uncorrupted by Western feminist ideas and values. As in Asia, sex work has greatly expanded in the Caribbean as an extension of the lucrative tourist industry, feeding off the familiar, unequal relationships between First and Third world nations.[33]

The *maquiladoras* in Mexico, the export-processing-zone factories in Asia, the garment sweatshops in the United States, the meatpacking plants in the American heartland, the sex work and domestic work of immigrant women— these are the unattractive public faces of the New World Order. Do they represent the trickle-down dividends of globalization by creating jobs, as global cheerleaders would have us believe, or do they represent "lurid examples of random inhumanity" wrought by global capitalism, as its critics charge?[34] What responsibilities do governments and especially the international organizations and policy-setting bodies that facilitate globalization, such as the WTO and IMF, have to ensure minimum wage and workplace standards, including environmental and health regulations? And if these organizations do not address these issues, then who will do so for them? Is globalization only about property rights, or should it also be concerned about human rights?[35] Obviously, there are real winners, or else wealthy corporations and individuals backed up by their powerful governments would not be pushing so aggressively and relentlessly for global policies and regulatory bodies such as the WTO and MAI, but do there have to be legions of permanent losers? These are some of the compelling questions that have galvanized protesters from Chiapas to Seattle to Washington, D.C., who have forced onto the world stage the dark side of globalization.[36] The following are some of the issues and contradictions raised by globalization and its discontents, illustrated by the scenarios described above:

1. Corporate-led globalization depends on intense exploitation of labor, *especially female labor*, exacerbated by the subcontracting system that answers to the logic of a race to the bottom of the wage scale.

To win a contract, the subcontractor must submit the lowest bid, then squeezes the workers to make his profit. Thus, Vietnamese workers in factories under contract to Nike and similar U.S. transnational corporations do not even make a living wage, defined as enough to buy three meals a day, let alone pay rent, health care, and support for a family.[37] Subcontracting works in a particularly oppressive way in the garment industry worldwide, whether in Asia, Mexico, Central America, the Caribbean, or the United States itself. Thus, the antisweatshop movement on college campuses correctly focuses its pressure on the manufacturers and not primarily on the Asian subcontractors, because they understand that U.S. manufacturers pocket the lion's share of profits and call the shots.[38]

The biggest losers in this global assembly line are women—Latina and Asian women—characterized as inherently, innately, and naturally suited for the kind of low-skill labor in light manufacturing, whether in Third World export-processing factories or U.S. electronic assembly plants and sweatshops. This "myth of nimble fingers"—a purely ideological construct—is nothing less than rationalization for low wages, not to mention justification for the perpetuation of the notion of Third World women's intellectual inferiority. It is not just the gendered quality of the international division of labor that is so problematic, but that the gendered division is inferred and inscribed as a permanent hierarchy that is further reinforced by race, class, and nationality differences, as well as denial of immigration and citizenship rights in the case of the smuggled and undocumented.[39]

We are compelled to conclude that Third World women in their home countries and after migration to the United States comprise one continuum in the same gendered, transnational workforce that lies at the base of the extremely exploitative and oppressive global subcontracting system of production.[40] Whether she works in a Nike plant subcontracted to a Taiwanese factory owner in Indonesia or Vietnam, or as a contract worker in an Asian-owned Saipan factory, or in an unregistered, unlicensed underground sweatshop in Los Angeles operated by a Korean immigrant, or in a union shop in New York's Chinatown owned by a newly naturalized Chinese American, she may well be sewing the same style of garment for the same manufacturer, affixing the same name-brand label on the same finished product. How ironic it is that with all its "supposed modernity and wondrous technologies," the "manic logic of capitalism" has reproduced all the old barbarisms associated with early twentieth-century capitalism.[41]

2. Increased trade spurred on by decreased regulation and removal of all barriers does not necessarily produce better jobs.

If anything, removal of regulations only serves to increase the power of the wealthier nations of the North over the poorer nations of the South, which often feel they have little choice but to go along with the dictates of the IMF, the World Bank, the WTO, and, in our hemisphere, NAFTA, and the powerful governments that stand behind these global organizations and policies. Thus, if unregulated, global free trade as we now know it will disproportionately benefit the already wealthy nations to the great disadvantage of the poor nations, enabling a few corporations and individuals to become obscenely rich while furthering the misery of the world's multitudinous poor. Many new studies have demonstrated the growing gap *between* and *within* nations, with the United States providing a notable example of both kinds of inequalities.[42] As some critics point out, contrary to the World Bank's bald assertion that accelerated globalization has produced greater world equality, far from lifting all boats, the rising tide of globalization is "only lifting yachts"![43] Today, the world's richest two hundred people have more wealth than 41 percent of the world's humanity.[44] Increasing the world's productive capacities may be a good thing for all, but it must be accompanied by a broader distribution of wealth.[45]

3. Thus, it cannot be argued that globalization is natural and inevitable, and produces general progress for all.

Rather, it should be made clear that globalization and the global finance system is a "man-made artifact," in the inimitable words of critic William Greider, one of the most trenchant and lucid critics of corporate globalization. It is defined as, "a political regime devised over many years by interested parties to serve their ends," and if man made it, Greider concludes, then man can very well undo it, "because nothing in nature or, for that matter, in economics requires the rest of us to accept a system that is so unjust and mindlessly destructive."[46] In short, globalization is not an inevitable force of history, "but rather the consequence of public policy choices."[47] This is precisely what protesters in Chiapas and Seattle and on our campuses are demanding of their governments and international organizations behind globalization, and of their university administrators: Make *different* public policy choices. Societies and citizens must act to counter the "destructive social convulsions" sown by the unregulated or deregulated market forces of finance capital through so-called free trade, irresponsible investment, speculative lending, and environmental degradation.[48]

4. Immigrants are not only *not* a drain on the U.S. economy, but an absolute necessity.

Why then, has nativism or anti-immigrant hysteria accompanied globalization in the United States and in other parts of the global core, such as Australia and Japan? Immigrant labor is indispensable for the labor-intensive, service-dependent economy of the United States, as well as the resurgent sweatshops of the light-manufacturing sector.[49] Lately, well-educated and professionally-trained immigrant labor is also in great demand in the computer programming sector of the American Silicon Valley.[50] The primary role of the INS is not to stop the flow of immigration to the United States but to regulate the level of that flow and to control the type of immigrants who come in at any given time. In other words, rather than unregulate and deregulate immigration, as is the case with finance capital and trade in manufactured goods, the United States wants to regulate and control the free trade of labor in order to keep wages down and unions out, and thereby protect their high corporate profits, although higher wages and strong unions would ensure a broader distribution of wealth in an expanding world economy.

It is also time for the United States to acknowledge that neoliberal reforms in the Third World, such as Salinas's privatization of *ejido* land, free-trade policies, and IMF-imposed restrictions on social spending, have all created the poverty, that is, forced people from the global south to countries in the global north, including the United States, Australia, Japan, and Western Europe, only to be attacked and maligned as illegal aliens and undesirables, and a drain on society.[51]

When demand for new workers surges in any critical sector of the economy, as periodically happens in the high-tech industries of the Silicon Valley or in the low-tech industries of agriculture in the West and meatpacking in the Midwest, the INS is perfectly capable and willing to look "the other way." In the booming U.S. economy at the end of the twentieth century, with unemployment at just 4 percent and a strong demand for people to take jobs paying $8 per hour or less—which comprise 25 percent of all jobs—documented and undocumented immigrants made up a large share of the available labor pool.[52] Is U.S. immigration policy just an undetected glaring contradiction, or is it part and parcel of another kind of unspoken logic of global capitalism, like the manic logic of the subcontracting system? (After 9/11, national security concerns regulating movement of mostly male foreign nationals from certain countries in Asia and the Middle East have further complicated the immigration equation.) Until very recently, the U.S. labor movement actually fell for the arbitrary line invented by the government and corporate interests to differentiate between legal, thus "good" immigrants, and illegal, thus "bad" immigrants. That canard was finally laid to rest when the Service Employees International Union (SEIU) led its eighty-five hundred janitors who cleaned the high-rise office buildings in downtown Chicago and Los Angeles—many of them "illegal aliens" from Mexico, Central America, and Asia—on successful strikes in those locations.[53] Concretely, current labor leaders such as AFL-CIO's John Sweeney has proclaimed a "new internationalism" for American unions.[54] John Wilhelm, president of the Hotel Employees and Restaurant Employees union (HERE), went one step further in calling for a correction of Labor's previous anti-immigarnt stance. "Immigrants have the right to ask us—which side are we on," he said at the 2000 AFL-CIO convention.[55]

Greider argues passionately that a productive world economy need not produce widespread misery that results from persistent and gross injustices.[56] While public pressure coming from demonstrations across the nation can succeed in uncovering the veil of secrecy surrounding the instruments of corporate globalization and imposing some measure of corporate responsibility on sweatshops, these tactics can only reduce a few of the worst abuses. Ultimately, these protests and their proposed remedies illustrate the conventional liberal argument that globalization is good, just curb its excesses; moreover, it's inevitable, so mend it, don't end it. Former Clinton Labor Secretary Robert Reich expands on this liberal perspective: "The challenge for those of us who believe that free trade and global capital are essentially good things if managed correctly is to avoid the backlash by developing progressive strategies to overcome the widening inequalities and the environmental depredations."[57]

Finally, some protesters and critics of globalization urge us to question the fundamental class relationship between this globalized working class and global capital, interrogate the supposed logic and rationality of the global assembly line, and resist accepting the inevitability of corporate-driven globalization or the permanency of the grossly unequal North-South divide. Our protests and critiques must seek answers to these more fundamental and vexing questions, not just negotiate remedies for abuses and excesses in the existing relationship between workers and capital in the global economy.[58]

I conclude by returning to the peasant rebels of Chiapas, Mexico, who call themselves Zapatistas in honor of the legacy of Emiliano Zapata of the Mexican Revolution. What fate awaits them if they fail to turn back the tide of NAFTA and globalization? After millennia of existence, are these descendants of the once-mighty and brilliant Mayan civilization faced with the untenable options of starving and fading away when they no longer have their traditional land base on which to build a life and community? Or, will they join the legions of Mexican peasants drifting first into provincial capitals, then Mexico City itself, and finally across the border into the core of the global economy that is the United States, trading their labor for low wages and dangerous jobs in the midst of enormous wealth well beyond their reach? Or, do they have a third option, that is, to link their struggle to other resistance movements in the global economy, such as SEIU janitors of Los Angeles striking for better wages, *maquiladora* workers in the Han Young plant of Tijuana seeking to form a union, women garment workers throughout the Pacific Rim, from Indonesia to Saipan to Honduras to California, protesting slave wages and inhumane work conditions? Might these responses signal the emergence of a transnational class struggle, acting together to expose the contradictions of corporate globalization in late capitalism?

There is reason to be hopeful. In fact, when the Zapatistas in southern Mexico demonstrated their opposition to "free trade," they were preceded in resistance to globalization by a group of women, "early victims of NAFTA," just across Mexico's northern border in the Texas city of San Antonio. There, nonunionized Latina women workers laid off by Levi Strauss's plant—which had been moved across the border into Mexican *maquiladoras* for cheaper labor—banded together to form *Fuerza Unida*. Like an earlier group formed in Oakland, California, the Asian Immigrant Women Advocates (AIWA), these grassroots organizations promote immigrant women workers as leaders and advocates for economic justice at home and for themselves, as well as for similarly exploited workers under globalization throughout the world.[59] Networking with other grassroots labor and community advocacy organizations in the United States, around the Pacific Rim, and lately in Europe as well, these and other immigrant women-founded and led groups point the way beyond a simple liberal critique of late capitalist globalization toward a more profound redefinition of global human rights that put working people at the center of the liberation project.

NOTES

1. "Special WTO Issue," *The Nation*, December 6, 1999; and "Special DC Issue," *The Nation*, April 24, 2000.

2. Joel Bleifuss, "Building the Global Economy," *In These Times*, January 11, 1998, 13; William Greider, "Time to Rein in Global Finance," *The Nation*, April 24, 2000, 13–20; Doug Henwood, "Whose Trade?" *The Nation*, December 6, 1999, 11–17; and Evelyn Hu-DeHart, "Women, Work, and Globalization in Late 20th Century Capitalism: Asian Women Immigrants in the U.S.," Working Papers Series (Pullman: Department of Comparative American Cultures, Washington State University, 1999.

3. Evelyn Hu-DeHart, "Latin America in Asia-Pacific Perspective," in *What Is In A Rim? Critical Perspectives on the Pacific Region Idea*, ed. Arif Dirlik, 2d rev. ed. (Lanham, Maryland: Rowman and Littlefield, 1998), 251–82.

4. Greg Campbell, "The New Manifest Destiny: NAFTA and Oil Threaten Future of Chiapas Indians," *Boulder Weekly*, July 4, 1996, 8; "NAFTA and the Chiapas Crisis," *Latin American Labor News* 9 (1993–94): 1, 4; and Andrew Reding, "Rebellion in Mexico," *The Washington Post*, January 11, 1994, and "Chiapas is Mexico: The Imperative of Political Reform," *World Policy Journal* 11:1 (1994): 11–25.

5. Julio Moguel, "Salinas's Failed War on Poverty," in *Free Trade and Economic Re-*

structuring in Latin America, ed. Fred Rosen and Deidre McFadyen (New York: Monthly Review Press, 1995), 209–14.

6. Gerardo Otero, "Mexico's Political Future(s) in a Globalizing Economy," *The Canadian Journal of Sociology and Anthropology* 32:3 (1995): 315–39, and *Neo-Liberalism Revisted: Economic Restructuring and Mexico's Political Future* (Boulder, Colorado: Westview, 1996).

7. Anthony DePalma, "Economic Lessons in a Border Town," *New York Times*, May 23, 1996, C1; Kelly Her, "Mexico's Luring Taiwan Investors," *The Free China Journal*, September 13, 1996, 8; and Barbara Stallings and Gabriel Székely, eds., *Japan, the United States, and Latin America: Toward A Trilateral Relationship in the Western Hemisphere* (Baltimore: The Johns Hopkins University Press, 1993).

8. Mary Beth Sheridan, "Riding Ripples of a Border Boom," *Los Angeles Times*, June 9, 1997, A1, A8.

9. Robert Brenner, "The Economics of Global Turbulence: A Special Report on the World Economy, 1950–98," special issue, *New Left Review* 229 (May/June 1998): 204–5, 210.

10. Annette Fuentes and Barbara Ehrenreich, *Women in the Global Factory* (Boston: South End Press, 1983); and Hu-DeHart, "Women, Work, and Globalization."

11. Quoted by Walter LaFeber in *Michael Jordan and the New Global Capitalism* (New York: W.W. Norton, 1999), 102.

12. LaFeber, *Michael Jordan*, 106.

13. LaFeber, *Michael Jordan*, 104.

14. Thuyen Nguyen, "Nike in Asia: This is Prosperity?" letter, *Wall Street Journal*, June 4, 1997, A19; and LaFeber, *Michael Jordan*, 105.

15. Nguyen, "Nike in Asian"; and LaFeber, *Michael Jordan*, 147.

16. Bob Herbert, "The Sweatshop Lives," *New York Times*, December 28, 1994, A13, "Brutality in Vietnam: Grim Conditions in Nike's Factories," *New York Time*, March 28, 1997, A19, and "Nike's Boot Camps," *New York Times*, March 31, 1994, A11; LaFeber, *Michael Jordan*, 148; and Julie Schmit, "Nike's Image Problem," *USA Today*, October 4, 1999, B1.

17. LaFeber, *Michael Jordan*, 147.

18. William Greider, *One World, Ready or Not: The Manic Logic of Global Capitalism* (New York: Simon & Schuster, 1997), 15.

19. Sam Dillon, "Union Vote in Mexico Illustrates Abuses," *New York Times*, October 13, 1997, A8.

20. Xiaolan Bao, *Holding Up More than Half the Sky: Chinese Women Garment Workers in New York City, 1948–92* (Urbana: University of Illinois Press, 2001); Center for Economic and Social Rights (CESR), "Treated Like Slaves: Donna Karan, Inc. Violates Women Workers' Human Rights," (Brooklyn, N.Y.: CESR, 1999); Hu-DeHart, "Women, Work, and Globalization"; and Miriam Ching Yoon Louie, *Sweatshop War-*

riors: Immigrant Women Workers Take on the Global Factory (Cambridge, Mass.: South End Press, 2001).

21. Bao, *Holding Up More Than Half the Sky*; and Louie, *Sweatshop Warriors*.

22. Julie Su,"El Monte Thai Garment Workers: Slave Sweatshop," in *No Sweat: Fashion, Free Trade, and the Rights of Garment Workers*, ed. Andrew Ross (New York: Verso, 1997), 143–50.

23. *Sweatshop Watch Newsletter* (*http://sweatshopwatch.org*) 1:1 (1995), 4:1 (1998), and 5:1 (1999); and Steven Greenhouse, "18 Mayan Retailers and Apparel Makers Are Accused of Using Sweatshops," *New York Times*, January 14, 1999, A9.

24. International Ladies Garment Workers' Union (ILGWU), *The Chinatown Garment Industry Study* (New York: ILGWU, 1983), 116; and Fung-Yea Huang, *Asian and Hispanic Immigrant Women in the Work Force: Implications of the United States Immigration Policies Since 1965* (New York: Garland, 1965), 28.

25. Morrison G. Won, "Chinese Sweatshops in the United States: A Look at the Garment Industry," in *Peripheral Workers*, ed. Ida Harper Simpson and Richard L. Simpson, *Research in the Sociology of Work* 2 (1983): 267–79.

26. Dean S. Toji and James H. Johnson, "The Working Poor and the Jobless Poor: Asians and Pacific Islander American Poverty," *Amerasia Journal* 18:1 (1992): 83–91.

27. Grace Chang, *Disposable Domestic: Immigrant Women Workers in the Global Economy* (Cambridge, Mass.: South End Press, 2000); Evelyn Nakana Glenn, "From Servitude to Service Work: Historical Continuities in the Racial Division of Paid Reproductive Labor," *Signs: Journal of Women in Culture and Society* 18:1 (1992): 1–43; Pierrette Hondagneu-Sotelo, *Doméstica: Immigrant Workers Cleaning and Caring in the Shadows of Affluence* (Berkeley: University of California Press, 2001); and Rhacel Salazar Parreñas, *Servants of Globalization: Women, Migration and Domestic Work* (Stanford, Calif.: Stanford University Press, 2001).

28. Milyoung Cho, "Overcoming Our Legacy as Cheap Labor, Scabs, and Model Minorities: Asian Activists Fight for Community Empowerment," in *The State of Asian America: Activism and Resistance in the 1990s*, ed. Karin Aguilar-San Juan (Boston, Mass.: South End Press, 1994), 253–73; Glenn, "From Servitude to Service Work"; Saski Sassen-Koob, "Notes on the Incorporation of Third World Women into Wage Labor Through Immigration and Off-Shore Production," *International Migration Review* 18:4 (1984): 1144–67; and Thanh-Dam Truong, "Gender, International Migration and Social Reproduction: Implications for Theory, Policy, Research and Networking," *Asian and Pacific Migration Journal* 5:1 (1996): 27–52.

29. Phyllis Palmer, quoted in Glenn, "From Servitude to Service Work," 7.

30. Parreñas, *Servants of Globalization*.

31. Kamala Kempadoo and Jo Doezema, eds., *Global Sex Workers: Rights, Resistance, and Redefinition* (New York: Routledge, 1998).

32. Alexandra Suh, "Military Prostitution in Asia and the U.S.," in *States of Confine-*

ment: Policing, Detention, and Prisons, ed. Joy James (New York: St. Martin's Press, 2000), 144–58.

33. Kamala Kempadoo, ed., *Sun, Sex, and Gold: Tourism and Sex Work in the Caribbean* (Lanham, Maryland: Rowman and Littlefield, 1999).

34. David Henderson, "The Case for Sweatshops," paid advertisement by the Hoover Institution, Stanford University, *Weekly Standard*, 2000; and Jeffrey Sachs and Paul Krugman, "In Principle: A Case for More 'Sweatshops,'" *New York Times*, Week in Review section, June 22, 1997.

35. Robert Kuttner, "The Seattle Protesters Got It Right," *Business Week*, December 20, 1999, 25.

36. Sarah Anderson and John Cavanagh, "Ten Myths About Globalization," *The Nation*, December 6, 1999, 26–27.

37. Nguyen, "Nike in Asia."

38. Richard Appelbaum and Edna Bonacich, "Choosing Sides in the Campaign Against Sweatshops: The Key Is Enhancing the Power of Workers," *The Chronicle of Higher Education*, April 7, 2000, B4; Mary Beth Marklein, "Making Them Sweat: Students Step Up Pressure to Hold Colleges Acountable for Apparel," *USA Today*, April 13, 2000, 19; David Moberg, "Getting Schooled: Students Are Making Manufacturers Sweat," *In These Times*, December 12, 1999, 20–21; and Martin Van der Werf, "Sweatshop Protests Raise Ethical and Practical Issues," *The Chronicle of Higher Education*, March 5, 1999, 38.

39. Laura Hyun Yi Kang, "Si(gh)ting Asian/American Women as Transnational Labor," *Positions* 5:2 (1997): 403–37.

40. Center for Economic and Social Rights, "Treated Like Slaves"; and Peter Passell, "Unskilled Workers' Short End of the Stick Getting Shorter," *New York Times*, June 14, 1998, A8, reprinted from the *San Francisco Examiner*.

41. Greider, *One World, Ready or Not*, 337–41.

42. William Macklin, "Wealth Distribution Concerns Analysts: Rise of Billionaires in U.S. Frustrates Some Working-Class Citizens," *Sunday Camera* [Boulder], April 30, 2000, 11A; and Mary Williams Walsh, "Latinos Get Left Out of Economic Boom," *Daily Camera* [Boulder], March 25, 2000, 14A, reprinted from the *Los Angeles Times*.

43. "Global Monoculture," paid advertisement, *New York Times*, November 15, 1999, A7.

44. Robert L. Borosage, "The Battle in Seattle," *The Nation*, December 6, 1999, 20.

45. William Greider, "Global Warning. Curbing the Free-Trade Free Fall," *The Nation*, January 13/20, 1997, 11–17.

46. Greider, "Time to Rein In Global Finance."

47. Ethan B. Kapstein, *Sharing the Wealth: Workers and the World Economy* (New York: W.W. Norton, 1999), 8.

48. Greider, "Time to Rein In Global Finance," 12; and Nicholas Kristof and David

E. Sanger, "How U.S. Wooed Asia To Let Cash Flow In," *New York Times*, February 16, 1999, A1.

49. Harold Meyerson, "Liberalism with a New Accent: Immigrants Are Helping to Create a Dynamic, Globally Focused Movement," *The Nation*, October 11, 1999, 15–20.

50. William Branigan, "Visa Program, High-Tech Workers Exploited," *The Washington Post*, July 26, 1998, A1; and Marc Cooper, "Class War at Silicon Valley," *The Nation*, May 27, 1996, 11–16.

51. David Bacon, "Labor's About-Face," *The Nation*, March 20, 2000, 6–7.

52. Louise Lamphere, Alex Stepick, and Guillermo Grenier, eds., *Newcomers in the Workplace: Immigrants and the Restructuring of the U.S. Economy* (Philadelphia: Temple University Press, 1994); Jane Slaughter, "Welcome to the Jungle," *In These Times*, August 22, 1999, 5–6; Louis Uchitelle, "I.N.S. Is Looking the Other Way As Illegal Immigrants Fill Jobs," *New York Times*, March 9, 2000, A1; Louis Freedberg, "Borderline Hypocrisy: Do We Want Them Here, Or Not?" *The Washington Post*, February 6, 2000, B1; and John Markoff, "Influx of New Immigrants Found in Silicon Valley," *New York Times*, January 10, 2000, C2.

53. Steven Greenhouse, "Janitors, Long Paid Little, Demand A Larger Slice," *New York Times*, April 28, 2000, A12.

54. Greider, "AFL-CIO Goes Global," *The Nation*, March 20, 2000, 5–6.

55. As quoted in Bacon, "Labor's About-Face," 7.

56. Greider, "Time to Rein In Global Finance."

57. As quoted in Henwood, "Whose Trade?" 17.

58. Walden Bello, "The End of the Asian Miracle," *The Nation*, January 12/19, 1998, 16–21; William Greider, "Saving the Global Economy," *The Nation*, December 15, 1997, 11–16, "The Global Crisis Deepens: Now What?" *The Nation*, October 19, 1998, 11–16, and "AFL-CIO Goes Global"; Kapstein, *Sharing the Wealth*; and E. San Juan Jr., *Beyond Postcolonial Theory* (New York: St. Martin's Press, 1998).

59. Louie, *Sweatshop Warriors*.

Buscando La Vida

Mexican Immigrant Women's Memories of Home, Yearning, and Border Crossings

MARÍA DE LA LUZ IBARRA

Mexican women are increasingly migrating north, leaving their homes and families behind and looking for private domestic work in U.S. cities. The journey, fraught with danger for those lacking legal entry documents, involves moving across social and cultural divides as well as an international political border. Women bear this dislocation and danger not through unencumbered choice, but within a context of structural constraint. The contemporary movement of Mexican women across borders is rooted in globalization processes—the economic restructuring and crises brought about by unequal relations of power between nations in a capitalist world system.[1] Undocumented Mexican women form part of a labor migration directly tied to changing patterns of capital accumulation that have produced an exodus of at least seven million people from Mexico during the past thirty years.[2]

This "new immigration," including "illegal" crossings, is not unique to the U.S.-Mexico borderlands, but rather is part of a contemporary worldwide experience, one that some scholars describe as unprecedented. Never have there been such massive flows, not only of people, but also of capital, goods, and ideas across national borders over such a short period of time. The rapidity of these flows, in turn, portend important changes to many scholars of global transnational trends.[3] One of the changes most discussed is whether nations will become less diverse as Western "culture" more quickly makes its way into more areas. Arjun Appadurai, one of the principal scholars of "cultural flows" via media, says that the answer is no. He suggests that in this sense transnationalism is good—that it has ushered in a new period of weakened nationalism and deterritorialized citizenship that "has been liberatory in both a spatial and political sense, for all peoples."[4] In coming to this conclusion he and other cultural flow scholars focus on ideas but neglect the grounded experiences and agency of migrants themselves, as well as negative responses to them in migrant-receiving countries.[5]

In the United States, for example, Mexican migration has sparked outrage among nativists and some public officials who fear becoming an "alien nation," both culturally and demographically.[6] Mexican migration is perceived as an incursion into a space imagined as sovereign and "American," and immigrants are seen as a threat to the cultural, racial, and economic make-up of that space. Women are viewed as particularly dangerous because of their reproductive potential.[7] For some, the presence of Mexican immigrants represents the possibility of a "reconquest of the American Southwest," and support measures aimed not only at controlling Mexican entry into the United States, but also in controlling access to social benefits such as health care and education.[8] Here, clearly, demographic change brought about by transnationalism is not celebrated, but rather actively resisted to the detriment of migrants.

And yet, despite these negative repercussions to Mexican migrants, even U.S.-centered scholars interested in the local effects of physical movement across borders tend to portray transnationalism as something overwhelmingly positive. In particular, scholars point to transformatory, oppositional, or transnational identity formation as an example of "resistance," and thus an example of the formation of a "valiant subject."[9] Pierrette Hondagneu-Sotelo, for example, argues that the migration process has created a "gendered transition," wherein Mexican women are positively transformed vis-á-vis Mexican men, and, in essence, women gain more power.[10] Linda Basch and Nina Glick-Schiller, on the other hand, argue that migrants do not just assimilate, but rather confirm nativists' worst fears: they forge and sustain "multi-stranded social relations that link together their societies of origin and settlement" creating a "bi-focal" sense of self.[11] In so doing, these migrants struggle against racism in the United States and class oppression in Mexico—part of what Michael Peter Smith and Luis Eduardo Guarnizo refer to as "transnationalism from below."[12] In a peculiar twist of this resistance in transnationalism argument, Michael Kearney goes so far as to say that poor Mixtec migrants in California have also created autonomous social spheres independent of Mexico or the United States.[13] In short, U.S.-centered transnationalism scholars have persistently focused on the positive aspects of alternative identity and "liberatory" space formation in the lives of migrants.

Less discussed are the "narratives of disillusionment," the accounts of negative changes or effects of transnationalism on individuals.[14] In particular, the effects of moving itself—the clandestine crossings as planned and experienced by individual Mexicanas from a broad range of backgrounds and regions—have been glossed over.[15] This is surprising, considering the recognition that "journeys are rich anthropological veins to be mined and interpreted."[16] It is individual crossings, after all, that leave marks on landscape, bodies, and minds, a circumstance that has long informed Chicano/a poetics.[17] For good reason, a Mexican migrant to Santa Barbara described this journey as "*buscando la vida*" (searching for life).

In this paper I focus on undocumented, single women whose experiences have been little explored in the academic literature. Single women are here defined as those who at the time of the study had never been married, or were widowed or divorced—with or without children. I examine these Mexicanas' narratives of crossing and explore the borderlands that lie somewhere between leaving and arriving. I address memories of home—those places that held women's yearnings to go north. I also address memories of the border—that space where violence shatters illusions and reconstitutes women's sense of themselves. Neither transnationalism nor resistance necessarily results in a more just life or a more positive identity. Women's crossing narratives expose the dark underside of an economic regime that increasingly relies on cheap, flexible, and "illegal" bodies to ensure profits for corporations and comfort for U.S. families who, in the restructured, global economy, hire Mexican women as housecleaners and care providers.[18] (Flaca)

MEMORIES OF HOME

For the Mexicanas who were part of my long-term anthropological study on domestic employment in Santa Barbara, California, "home" meant many different places.[19] The restructuring of Mexico's industry and the consequent economic crisis that have taken place in the last thirty years have had a negative impact on a broad spectrum of people—members of the working and middle classes, living in both rural and urban areas. Likewise, migrants derive from both "traditional" and "new" sending areas and—unlike the previous era of bracero migration between 1942 and 1964—include large numbers of women and children.[20] Consequently, there is now a more complex Mexican migrant profile in the United States.

Recent transnational scholarship reflects these demographic and regional changes and is broader in focus, addressing not only the prototypical rural, working-class male migrant, but also Mexican women.[21] Still missing, however, is an appreciation of the diverse backgrounds of the growing number of single women who are no longer marginal to the migration process, as well as a better understanding of how this diversity helps shape agency in the context of migration.[22]

In this article I draw from interviews with thirty single Mexican women who migrated to the United States between 1985 and 2000. This group is heterogeneous and, as E. Valentine Daniel found among Tamils in Great Britain, their "nostalgia for their home country differed qualitatively," as did their reasons for making the trip to the United States.[23] Most Mexicanas' memories were of rural areas, where they felt that their gendered opportunities were more limited than those of urban dwellers. Thirty-two-year-old Anabel, for example, had grown up in a small agricultural town of fifteen hundred people in Chihuahua, where the majority of women married and had children. While she fondly remembered her tightly-knit female-headed, middle-class family and the importance that her mother and grandmother placed on becoming a mother and wife, she knew from an early age that it was not enough for her. She wanted to be able to choose a life outside of marriage, and that meant "earning her own way." It meant finding a life outside of her village "where everyone knew everybody else's business." Work outside of the home was important to her, and going to the United States would be the only way to fulfill this desire, because even Mexico's urban centers no longer offered the opportunities they once did.

Women from rural areas felt that failed romances not only negatively marked them in their small communities, but also created difficult, long-term repercussions. Thirty-six-year-old Lupe, for example, who came from a working-class farming family, spoke of having fallen madly in love with a "handsome liar," who had given her an "illusion" of a better life. Her erstwhile lover, however, did not come through with his promises of marriage, and instead left her with the responsibility of caring for their two young daughters and with a reputation in her hometown of Jalisco as a woman with few morals. She remembers the judgments placed on her and the "unwelcome advances" on her person. In such a small place, it was impossible to escape. And so she decided to become hard "like a man" and begin to think of herself as someone who would need to be employed in order to meet her obligations. For this, she needed to go someplace where there were opportunities. The United States offered this possibility.

Other women felt that limited social options in rural areas exacerbated the effects of sexual violence. Thirty-five-year-old Cecilia, from a small town outside of Acapulco, Guerrero, recalls that "life was always work" in her working-poor family, and she never conceived of marriage as expanding her possibilities. In fact, her parents' experience "taught" her that marriage meant having to bear large numbers of children, and it meant men were not to be trusted, since her father often drank the family's earnings. At the age of seventeen these already-clear images of life were burned into her person: she was kidnapped and raped by a soldier, who then forced her to become his "wife." In his rural village, a place where she had no support or connections, she was a prisoner for four years, and during that time she gave birth to two children and took care of her kidnapper's elderly mother. She was finally able to execute her escape, a process that implied certain death should she be caught. Until she arrived in the state of Jalisco, where she had family, she sat on the bus in a state of terror. Two years later her husband was spotted in her neighborhood, and she knew then that only by going to the United States could she escape "that man forever." (KIDS?)

For women in urban areas, memories of home also centered on gender and its relation to roles and careers, sexuality, and violence. However, among middle-class urban women, reminiscences were less about a lack of opportunity and more about financial losses. For these women, memories dwell on the shattering effects of economic crisis on their families, and on the consequences of crisis on their class position. Dora—twenty-one years old and one of the youngest women in the group—had memories of home that revolved around a "nice" apartment in the city where she lived with two siblings, her parents, and her grandmother. Dora remembers many family meals and celebrations, good friends coming over prior to attending sporting events, and going to parties, movies, or shopping malls. For Dora, the most immediate and visible sign of financial strife following the country's 1982 economic crisis was her dissolving consumer lifestyle—the lack of luxuries such as shopping and traveling, and later the inability to find temporary life-enriching work. Crossing into the United States—what she described as "travel"—represented her yearnings of holding on to a piece of her disappearing middle-class life.

For other middle-class Mexicanas from cities, memories of home centered on the negative consequences of the economic crisis on their employment and gendered identities. Thirty-one-year-old Teresa, for example, remembered the initial joy of finding a position as a car salesperson at a Nissan plant during the early 1980s in Mexico City. This was a "good," high-paying job with considerable responsibility that allowed her to construct an identity of herself as a self-sufficient, strong, and upwardly-mobile woman. She remembers paying for her own apartment and helping support her boyfriend, who was often unemployed. Memories of home, however, are also clouded by having been laid off when car sales began to decline, and then working in a string of low-paid jobs, experiences that shattered her sense of strong womanhood and of possibility. It also shattered her sense of "reality," and for more than a year after she lost her job, she felt numb and cut off from the world. She yearned to cross the border in order to recompose herself.

For working-class women in cities, reminiscences are different from those of their middle-class counterparts: memories of home are not only about the period of economic crisis, but about long-term material insufficiency. Jacklyn, a twenty-one-year-old Mayan, lovingly remembered her parents' small house in Mérida. There, her grandparents, parents, and siblings lived in four small rooms, a fact that brought tears to her eyes, as she described their poverty and, alongside it, her family's support and kindness to each other. Jacklyn clearly longed for her home, but she also remembered the constant lack of money and, later, her father's failing health and his inability to find a job after being laid off as a municipal street sweeper. These dual images of love and hardship, she said, tugged at her, leaving her unable to sleep some nights as she worried about so many needs in their lives. The United States held the possibility of her being able to help support her family.

The previous vignettes illustrate that Mexicanas' memories of home and nostalgia for it track different places and social possibilities. They also trace intimate details of family life that are not uniform, but rather hold distinct patterns of support, understandings of love, deception, and heartache. The vignettes also sketch yearnings, yearnings to provide material comforts and sustenance in a way that had become familiar, or yearnings to escape conditions, create something new, and find safety for themselves and their families. These diverse yearnings, in the context of structural constraint, are the basis for understanding why so many Mexicanas seek work as domestics in the United States.

CULTURE OF MIGRATION

When describing their different reasons for wanting to leave their homes, of going "in search of a life," Mexicanas clearly spoke about the constraining structural context of limited economic resources and opportunities, and about the constraints of gender and gender relations as potent elements in their memories of home. But women's narratives also make it clear that their yearnings were shaped by a culture of migration present in many communities. Mexicanas who grew up during the 1970s and 1980s heard about others who made the trip to the United States and also saw both men and women migrate. In some cases, women came from families or communities whose members had engaged in international labor migration to the United States for several generations.[24] In other cases, migration was less entrenched but was nonetheless an important part of the experiences of people known to these women. And yet, this culture of migration as perceived by Mexicanas has been ignored in the literature, with one scholar arguing that single Mexican women did not grow up "immersed in a culture that oriented them toward northward migration."[25]

But a culture of migration does include women and subsequently has helped shape their desire to migrate. This "culture" is most evident among migrants from central-western states, because from the late nineteenth century to the present, the majority of Mexican migrants to the United States has come from this region.[26] Not surprisingly, communities in these states have developed rituals to mark both the absence and return of community members, rituals that in turn help recreate the importance of migration to the people who live there. One ritual of absence in the Zamora Valley of Michoacan is the "_ausente hour_" on the radio. In this public service for the benefit of U.S. migrants and their families, letters and messages sent from migrants in the United States are read on the air, and special song requests and dedications are played for wives and sweethearts.[27] This keeps not only the memory, but also the voice and will of the migrant alive. In other rituals, migrants themselves not only mark their absence but their travails and sufferings through votive offerings such as _retablos_, paintings on tin that are left in churches. _Retablos_ document the dangers that migrants face away from home, but also point to religious beliefs that help tie migrants to particular places in Mexico and, in fact, from the point of view of believers, help save their lives.[28]

While these public rituals of absence are important, so are those found in private homes. Mexicans most often remember the absent loved ones with photographs placed on family altars and in places of daily living, such as dining and sleeping areas. The women I interviewed described themselves and other family members looking at these photographs on a regular basis. Their gaze was sometimes accompanied by a fleeting touch of the person's photographic image, including making the religious sign of the cross over them as a protective action. Likewise, Mexicanas remember the collection of photographs that over time record changes in the life cycle of those absent. Mexicanas poignantly describe moments of catharsis in front of these pictures—moments in which tears marked the passing of time. Other markers of absence were the gifts that remained after a migrant's visit—blankets, radios, beds, or a room addition. Twenty-eight-year-old Luz described the boxes of chocolates that her grandmother would hoard—never eating them—because these were a tangible symbol of her son's hard work and love. Others recalled the bittersweet weekly or monthly wait for the phone call that for a few minutes brought them closer to their loved one and then left a deep resonance.

Alongside rituals of absence, which help to reproduce the importance of migration in a community or in a household, there are also public rituals of return that do the same thing. In many communities the celebration of the town's patron saint is one such ritual of return. Douglas Massey and his colleagues write: "On this date, migrants join together to pay the costs of music, church decorations, fireworks, and other diversions. Those who have been able to return participate in the processions and liturgical acts, and in his sermon the priest reaffirms the 'great family' with a patron saint who looks over all."[29] Other rituals are planned and paid for by city residents. In a small city in Jalisco, Lupe remembers the yearly Christmas season's *Noche Mexicana* at the Lion's Club. At this event, male migrants back home on vacation are the guests of honor and are treated to all those "Mexican" things—food, hospitality, entertainment, goods—that are perceived to be missing in the United States. Lupe also describes the clandestine flirting and formal courting by these male migrants, activities that promoted for many young women a sense of the United States as a place not only of economic possibility but of romantic entanglements. As Lupe said, "When I saw him I thought he was very handsome, and I wondered what would it be like to go to the United States with him." This ritual of return for men becomes an opportunity to imagine a life away from home for women.

Rituals of return, like rituals of absence, are likewise not limited to public displays. There are more personal events, such as family gatherings, where banquets of *tamales*, *barbacoa*, or *asado* are prepared in honor of a migrant relative's visit. Likewise, migrants may return to take part in others' important rites of passage, such as a marriage or baptism, and thus reinforce the ties to a place and to people who matter. Other practices that serve to maintain ties between U.S. and Mexican communities are migrants' participation in community improvement projects and politics.[30] In sum, rituals of return solidify the importance of migrants and migration to a community.

In places where a local tradition of migration was less prevalent, personal experiences were important to women who chose migration as an option to improve their lives. In some cases, Mexicanas had migrated to or taken pleasure trips to the United States as younger persons and had good memories of that experience. Margarita, for example, grew up in Mexico City, and as a young woman had attended a three-month art seminar in Los Angles as part of an educational exchange program. When she went back to Mexico, she did so reluctantly, as she liked the American city and the possibilities it held for her. In other cases, women had a girlfriend or a female relative who had gone to the United States. Tere grew up in a rural area of Oaxaca and did not have family members in the United States, but she had a girlfriend who had made the trip. Thus, the United States was at some level a known entity—a real possibility.

The influence of Western culture through the media cannot be underestimated as a source for familiarizing potential migrants with the United States and subsequently making it easier for them to consider moving there.[31] Mexicans are exposed to movies that depict life in the United States, to magazines that favor Western fashions and tastes, and to music that infiltrates the popular imagination. However, Mexicanas do not hold only positive images of the United States. Mexican popular culture in movies, books, and songs also depict life in the north in a more threatening light. Movies like *La India Maria* satirize the dangers faced by undocumented immigrants, while books by writers like Luis Spota call attention to the harsh treatment of Mexicans. In one grating line from a bestseller, Spota writes: *"En Texas ser mexicano no es nacionalidad, sino un oficio. El peor y mas despreciable de todos"* ("In Texas, being Mexican is not a nationality but a job—the worst and most despicable of all").[32] *Ranchera* and *norteño* music tell stories of common people detained and deported, and of the unending search for and daily practice of work in the United States. One of many popular songs by the Tigres del Norte, for example, characterizes the United States as a *"jaula de oro"* ("a golden cage")—a country that simultaneously offers some opportunity for material improvement through work, but also maintains Mexicans in an unequal social position.[33]

Thus, Mexicanas are immersed in a culture of migration that shapes the way they see their world and their possibilities within it. Migration means suffering, but it also means the possibility of personal and family advancement. This fact is one "web of meaning" in a larger complexity of webs that contributes to local Mexican cultures. For men and women, migration is not beyond the bounds of imagination or experience. Imagining crossing the border and imagining being on the "other side," however, are several steps removed from the actual physical process of doing it.

PLANNING TO CROSS THE BORDER

Crossing the border for most women is a pivotal act, one that Leo Chavez considers a rite of passage that marks the transition from one social status to another.[34] He argues that, among other things, this rite involves a process of separation from the country of origin. One neglected aspect of this separation, however, is the everyday practices engaged in by women, which in turn play a role in shaping a culture of migration. To get to the other side of the border requires considerable forethought, effort, and planning. In my sample group, single women most often did not act opportunistically after an invitation to go north; rather, planning was the norm.

Specifically, Mexicanas persuade parents, husbands, or lovers to support their migration; they seek financial help or build up their savings through employment; and they make connections and undertake negotiations with different people (relatives, friends, acquaintances, and ex-employers in the United States) who can help them once they are on the other side. Social networks are crucial for most women, and as others have shown, female networks are essential for Mexicana migrants.[35]

For young single women, one of the most important elements of the planning involves convincing their parents to support their decision to migrate. It is not "seeking permission" to migrate exactly, because in many cases Mexicanas have made up their mind to go regardless of their parents' perspectives. But for women with close family ties, it is important to get their family members to agree and provide emotional support. Twenty-six-year-old Maria, for example, began planning to leave for the United States after protracted conversations with a neighbor who described the income-earning potential in the United States. This meant convincing her father, a task that required a period of more than six months, and then contacting a paternal uncle who lived in Santa Barbara. Maria's father "agreed" to her trip on the condition that she travel with her brother and, once arriving in Santa Barbara, live with her uncle, for whom she would provide domestic assistance. This uncle would also provide an initial loan to pay for the costs of a coyote, or human smuggler. From the time she originally conceptualized the idea to go north to the time she began the journey, eight months had gone by.

Thirty-three-year-old Lulu also sought the blessing of her parents, but would have left even if they had not provided it in a "reasonable" amount of time. Ever since she was a little girl, Lulu had a desire to go to the United States, like her father did six months out of every year. To this end, she saved the income from a job she took for this purpose for a period of two years. Once she had enough money to pay for her transportation and a little extra for living expenses, she worked at convincing her parents. After two months, her parents grudgingly agreed, and she made plans to cross the border clandestinely with her father during the spring. They had both decided spring was safer because neither the cold nor heat would be unbearable. The plan she had worked out through phone conversations was to join a friend's family and begin work as a hotel maid. Her father would then return to Mexico by himself.

Jacklyn, on the other hand, did not have parents who initially and actively opposed her trip when she announced plans to go to Santa Barbara and join her sister. When she told her father that she had been thinking and talking about leaving for over a year, he counseled her to reflect and think about it carefully a little longer, because "the United States changes people." Because she respected her father, Jacklyn did continue to reflect, but eventually came to the conclusion that it was necessary for her to undertake the journey so that she could help provide for her family. She had never been outside of Merida, and so through phone conversations had her sister describe the bus trip to Tijuana and the types of things she might expect on the way. She also sought information about clandestine crossings so that she could arm herself psychologically. She did not want to be a burden, so she asked her sister to help her find a job as child care provider, so that she could be assured employment upon arrival.

Of course, not all women are able to exactly plan the journey north. This is particularly the case for women with weak social networks in the United States prior to their arrival. After saving or borrowing money, some women left Mexico only with the possibility that an estranged parent or sibling might help them once they got to the other side. Ernestina, for example, carefully planned for her trip north—saving money, arranging for care of her children while she was in the United States, and buying goods she thought necessary for her children. Once this was done, she planned the bus trip north to Tijuana. Not until she was safely across the border in the United States, however, did she plan to call three of her brothers whom she had not seen for longer than ten years. Waiting to call, I learned, was a common tactic. When I asked María why she had not called estranged relatives prior to leaving for the United States, she said it was too much of a risk. It was easier for these relatives to say no, if the petitioning relative was still in Mexico. But if they were already at the border, it was much more difficult to refuse. Thus, even apparently last-minute actions reveal forethought by Mexicanas crossing the border.

Margarita made the decision to leave Guadalajara with her son, even without a concrete invitation from a relative or friend. She hoped that once she arrived in Tijuana, her father, whom she had not seen in fifteen years, would help her. She had no idea whether the phone number she had been given would still be good when she arrived, whether he would be there, and even whether her father would accept her. This type of waiting strategy is a gamble that does not always work, and some women end up homeless, sleeping under freeway underpasses, and gratefully taking the first live-in domestic job that becomes available. Most often these jobs are the lowest paid and most exploitative, as it is obvious that these Mexicanas have limited options.

A central part of women's journeys north is the planning that takes place before they leave. These everyday separation practices, in turn, become part of the broader system of meaning that shapes local Mexican cultures.

CROSSING THE BORDER

For undocumented women who cross the border on foot, the trip is a test of their bodies, their character, ingenuity, and desperation. Crossing the border is no easy feat. And yet, if we look at the literature on transnationalism, this very crucial part of the trip for Mexicanas is for the most part absent. This absence serves to negate the trauma of crossing experienced by growing numbers of women who seek jobs as private household workers in the United States.

This absence, as well, gives the mistaken impression that Mexicanas who go in search of work in a transnational space are like any other job seeker, but they are not. They are criminalized by their crossing, and the southern U.S. border zone is militarized to guard against their entrance.

The historical process of border militarization began in 1848 after the U.S.-Mexican War and the American conquest of half of Mexico's former territory. In the last three decades, however, militarization has been spurred to new levels. The U.S. recession of the 1970s was the context within which Leonard Chapman, head of the Immigration and Naturalization Service (INS) and a former general, first conceptualized Mexican immigrants as a "national security threat." In subsequent decades, the United States invested unprecedented amounts of money, men, and machines to keep the United States safe, not only from Mexicans reconfigured as criminals intent on stealing U.S. jobs and social services, but also from the "communist menace" in Central America and drug runners from Latin America." [36]

By 1992, when President Clinton took office, the INS budget had swelled, and much of the infrastructure of deterrence had been laid: night scopes, ground sensors, barriers, armed tanks, and agents were in place along the border. Under the Clinton administration, Congress continued to approve ever-growing budgets for border control, totaling more than four billion dollars for the 2001 fiscal year. [37] Policy in dealing with potential "illegal" border crossers has also changed since 1993. One of the most deadly of these policies, proposed by military intelligence, is to reroute migrants from crossing in populated areas to physically difficult terrain. "Operation Gatekeeper" in California and "Operation Hold the Line" in Arizona are two examples of these policies, both involving more fencing and more agents in populated areas. [38] Since 1993, more than sixteen hundred migrant deaths have been documented, with numbers mounting in the last two years. These deaths are primarily a result of dehydration, hypothermia, and drowning in extreme terrain and weather conditions. [39]

Extreme conditions found in the deserts and mountains are by no means the only danger lurking in the night, however. Human rights organizations also regularly document "abuses" of power at the hands of the border patrol, including sexual violations, beatings, and shootings. [40] Additionally, thieves, drug smugglers, and vigilantes, as well as coyotes themselves, prey on vulnerable people who often carry the money they need to cross the border. The sums are not inconsequential because the increasing difficulty of crossing has raised the amount that migrants need for an "illegal" entry. During the 1980s and early 1990s, the cost of a guide was approximately three hundred dollars, but now it is more in the range of eight hundred to thirteen hundred dollars. [41]

The crossing is often a traumatic event, one with the very real probability of harm or death, and women who survive the experience can have psychological and physical scars. As is the case with victims of torture, Mexican women's narratives about their crossing vacillate between wanting to share the details and then wanting to guard the memories from anyone who, however well meaning, could trivialize their experiences.[42] Initially, Mexicanas I interviewed glossed over events and provided me with a broad and vague description. I respected this boundary, but in each case, the Mexicana would come back to her memories and later verbally guide me to the border, to a fateful day that had altered her in a deep and meaningful way. For example, when first recollecting her memories of crossing, Lupe said, "I have no words to describe what I felt when I saw my children scared, dirty, and tired. What I can tell you is that under no circumstances would I do it again." Her sentence was final, her eyes averted, and I did not press. Only later, Lupe's memories began to slowly unwind and details began to spot her narratives. "Do you remember," she asked me, "when I told you that I crossed?" "Yes," I answered. "You know, that I crossed without papers?" she asked me. "Yes, Lupe," I answered, "You didn't tell me, but I guessed—there's a lot of people who cross that way." "Yes," she answered, "lots of people, right?" I nodded. She went on, "I don't know—one is always left with the memory, and one thinks that one is unique." Then without prompting, and again without looking at my eyes, she said, "It's awful. One feels like a trapped animal—maybe worse because you never imagined it would happen to you." She began her crossing narrative by formally saying, "We made our way to the border, and it was very cold that night." In between long pauses, she continued:

I was really worried because Joaquin was only one, and with so much cold children can get very ill. And also, I had my other children [ages five and eight], and really all I could think about was them—they were too little. Imagine a child of five walking across the hills? No, it is not just, and I knew it was not just, but one has to eat their rage so that it does not stop you. What gave me strength was that my cousins were there with me, and they each took one of the children—and, well, I had invested so much time, and I had left my life behind, and I really had no other choice but to go forward. And so the coyote . . . there were two . . . took us across and we walked a while—I don't know how long. One becomes disoriented with so much worry, but I think very soon . . . The people started shouting, because the lights [border patrol helicopter] were coming toward us. And one of the coyotes told us to get down, but obviously everyone was scared, and I just remember that I couldn't move. Fear paralyzed me, because I was afraid that if I ran they would kill my child. And the worst part was that I couldn't immediately see the other two [cousins and children], and I just shouted out, "Francisco, don't run, they'll kill us." And thank God, he heard me. He shouted back to me, "Here I am cousin." And, I didn't hear anymore because there was a lot of shouting—I don't remember how many men [border patrol] there were, at that time it seemed a lot. I don't think I moved, but the baby's crying and everything else, I was very nervous, and I don't know, one of the agents hit me as he tried to hold someone else, and I fell, and all I could think of was to hold on to my baby. But he fell out of my hands anyway, and that's when I just could not [stand it.] I began to cry out of fear, yes, but also rage. There I was a grown woman with a child, where could I have gone? But the only thing that mattered to them was to get us. I swear to you, I am a good person, but in that moment I wanted to do something to him [border patrol agent]. There I was like an animal, worse, a nothing. I get so angry [she began to cry] . . . but I did nothing. I stayed there and waited for them to load us on the van."

Guadalupe was transported back to Tijuana, and it took her two days to build up the "courage" to try crossing again. The second time, they made it across without being chased by the border patrol. Once in the safety of her cousin's home in Los Angeles, Guadalupe realized that something in her had "changed." The crossing had marked her in a way that others could not visibly see, but which she could feel. "From that day," she said, "I became harder and more aggressive."

This realization of change was one that other women also described. However, they did not always become harder, but rather just the opposite—they became "damaged," more "nervous," and psychologically vulnerable. Elvia, for example, a small, thin woman with radiant hazel eyes and a pale complexion was thirty-two years old when I first met her. She was constantly moving, getting up from our conversations to undertake small chores, or cutting off the conversation and beginning a new topic. One afternoon as I sat on her bed, and she organized her closet while talking about her small son Horacio, she surprised me by slowing down. She sat beside me and asked if I wanted to know about how she came to the United States. I said yes, and she began to tell me her story in a detached, matter-of-fact voice, as if relating the plot of a movie. She looked at me until she got to the part relating the beatings and the rape. Then she began to cry softly, self-consciously, looking down at her hands, and only occasionally up into my eyes. She began her narrative with, "I came over the mountains with three coyotes. I didn't know there were going to be three, but they just passed us along to each other." She continued:

When we got to the last coyote, we were put in a house, and there were six of them—all wearing guns. Here we were supposed to call the people responsible for paying our way. . . . One of the women who couldn't reach her relatives was really pretty, and I could tell the coyote liked her. He told her, "If you can't find your relative, I can help you get a job and then you can pay me." She said she would like to do this, and he told her to follow him. I had my money with me, but I didn't want to tell them, because I was afraid they would take it without taking me across. [Meanwhile,] a man called his relatives, but the number was no longer in service. The coyotes told him he better find someone soon, or he was going to be sorry. I could tell he was really scared, so I went over to sit by him. He asked me if I thought they would really hurt him, and I said, "No—no one can be that bad." A few hours later, the pretty woman came back, and I could tell she was not well, but, she didn't say anything. . . . [By now a day had gone by] and other people had also not been able to contact their relatives. The coyotes yelled at them, and threatened. I got really scared then, because if I didn't tell them I had the money with me, they would do to me what they were threatening to do to the other people, and if I did tell them, I ran the risk of having the money taken from me. I took the risk and told them. The man who couldn't reach his relative came over again, and asked me for a favor: If anything should happen to him, please call his wife in Tepic, so she would know. I said, yes, and wrote her number down, as well as that of his relative in Los Angeles. . . . Then they took out some of the men who had not been able to reach their relatives. The rest of us were inside the house. Pretty soon we started to hear screams, and my son was at the window—I went to pull him away, and then I saw the blood all over the ground, and bodies being kicked. I couldn't turn away, and I saw my friend run to the bathroom, but they got him. We were all crying inside the house, and the pretty woman told us the coyote had lied to her. He had taken her in his truck and then raped her. The other woman who had not been able to reach her relatives became hysterical, and all of us were hysterical with her. Then those of us with money decided to try to help her, and we collected what we could, but it wasn't enough. We needed four hundred dollars. Then another woman who had a gold bracelet and some rings took them off and put it in with the money. Then the screaming stopped and the coyotes came back in to take our money. We gave it to them, and also the money and jewelry for the woman. But he wouldn't take it. He asked us, "What I am going to do with a bracelet?" Then he told the pretty woman to follow him again. He came back a long time afterwards, but she was not with him. He told us it was time for us to get in the truck, because it was almost dark. He told the woman who had no money to just stay in the house. We didn't know what to do, we were so scared. We walked outside and there was blood everywhere, and we had to step in the blood to get to the truck. We didn't see any bodies. Even the men—who are stronger than women—told us to not say a word, to just stay quiet. We got in the truck, and no words were said.

When she finished her story, she shook her head and closed her eyes for a long time. Finally, she looked up again and asked me, "Why is it so difficult to work?" Why, indeed. Five years after she asked me, the question is still in my mind.

In the context of structural constraints produced by globalization, increasing numbers of single Mexicanas of diverse social class, backgrounds, age, family types, and region yearn for a life that is different from that which economic crisis produced or made worse in their home country. As they dream about a new life, the United States looms large. A pattern and culture of migration in central western Mexican states, as well as evolving networks in new sending areas of Mexico, help support this yearning. Migration is conceptualized as feasible for growing numbers of people, including single women. Yearning is then followed by active planning to find the support and means necessary for making the trip and having some type of security once they reach their destination. But prior to getting to their destination, Mexicanas who must cross the border clandestinely face fear, dislocation, and sometimes injury. These experiences alter the women's sense of themselves, and not always positively, as is often suggested by the bulk of the transnational literature. It is therefore necessary to address transnational migration as a nuanced process and to document the diversity of experiences faced by both men and women.

In the excerpts of narratives I have provided, Mexicana's words shed light on experiences that generally remain "invisible, unknown, and unimagined" as U.S. employers consume the labor that is women's lives.[43] But through these narratives we are able to perceive the tensions inherent in physical movement across political borders—power-laden spaces that at once hold women's hopes for the future as well as a violence that explode their imaginings. This violence, this individual suffering—when multiplied by the many women who form part of the increasing south to north migration—becomes a story of social suffering on the borderlands. To ignore the pain that marks women's narratives of crossing is to sanitize history and not fully understand the meaning of Mexican labor migration in the New World Order.

I extend my gratitude to all the Mexicanas who, in the hope that their words might make a difference, shared pieces of their lives with me. I also thank Guadalupe Luna-Martinez, Andrew Wiese, and Ivonne Zárate for their unfailing and generous research support. Finally, I thank the Ford Foundation for a Postdoctoral Fellowship for Minorities that provided me with the time and money necessary to write.

1. Saskia Sassen, *The Mobility of Labor and Capital: A Study in International Investment and Labor Flow* (New York: Cambridge University Press, 1988), 55–84.

2. Susan González Baker, Frank D. Bean, Agustin Escobar Latapi, and Sidney Weintraub, "U.S. Immigration Policies and Trends: The Growing Importance of Migration from Mexico," in *Crossings: Mexican Immigration in Interdisciplinary Perspectives*, ed. Marcelo Suárez-Orozco (Cambridge, Mass.: Harvard University, David Rockefeller Center for Latin American Studies, 1998), 79–112.

3. Globalization refers to a new stage in the evolution of capitalism as a world system, characterized by a broad array of economic and social processes that are distinct from those found in the twenty-five-year period after World War II. The most widely recognized among these transnational processes is "the growing number and variety of corporations that organize their profit making activities across state boundaries" (Giovanni Arrighi "Globalization and Historical Macrosociology," in *Sociology for the Twenty-First Century: Continuities and Cutting Edges*, ed. Janet Abu-Lughod [Chicago: University of Chicago Press, 2000], 2). Other important transnational processes associated with globalization are transterritorial movements of workers and "culture."

4. The principal proponent of increasing westernization as a result of globalization is David Harvey, *The Condition of Postmodernity: An Enquiry into the Origins of Cultural Change* (Cambridge, Mass.: Blackwell Press, 1989). In response to this conclusion see Arjun Appadurai, *Modernity at Large: Cultural Dimensions of Globalization* (Minneapolis: University of Minnesota Press, 1996).

5. Aihwa Ong, *Flexible Citizenship: The Cultural Logics of Transnationality* (Durham, N.C.: Duke University Press, 1999), 11.

6. Leo Chavez, "Immigration Reform and Nativism," in *Immigrants Out!: The New Nativism and the Anti-Immigrant Impulse in the United States*, ed. Juan Perea (New York: New York University Press, 1997), 67.

7. Dorothy Roberts, "Who May Give Birth to Children?" in Perea, *Immigrants Out!*, 205–22.

8. Chavez, "Immigration Reform and Nativism," 68; and Pierrette Hondagneu-Sotelo, *Gendered Transitions: Mexican Experience of Migration* (Berkeley: University of California Press, 1994).

9. Ong argues that the subaltern migratory subject is reified as an unidimensional "valiant resistor." She notes that poor "immigrants are thus converted from being mi-

norities to be assimilated into the host society into being some kind of universalized lower-class subjects who attain subaltern vindication" (Ong, *Flexible Citizenship*, 9). Michael Peter Smith and Luis Guarnizo also argue that identities forged from "below" are not inherently subversive or counterhegemonic (*Transnationalism from Below* [New Brunswick, N.J.: Transaction Publishers, 1998], 23). For a broader discussion about this reification trend in anthropology, see Sherry Ortner, "Beginning," in *Life and Death on Mt. Everest: Sherpas Himalayan Mountaineering* (Princeton, N.J.: Oxford University Press, 1999, 17–25).

10. Hondagneu-Sotelo, *Gendered Transitions*, 194–98.

11. Linda Basch, Nina Glick Schiller, and Cristina Szanton Blanc, *Nations Unbound: Transnational Projects, Postcolonial Predicaments, and Deterritorialized Nation States* (Basel, Switzerland: Gordon and Breach Science Publishers, 1994), 7; and Roger Rouse, "Mexican Migration and the Social Space of Postmodernity," *Diaspora* 2:2 (1991): 8–23.

12. Smith and Guarnizo, *Transnationalism from Below*, 12.

13. Michael Kearney, "Borders and Boundaries of State and Self at the End of Empire," *Journal of Historical Sociology* 4:1 (1991): 52–74.

14. Sarah Mahler, *American Dreaming: Immigrant Life on the Margins* (Princeton, N.J.: Princeton University Press, 1995), 75.

15. Leo Chavez, *Shadowed Lives: Undocumented Immigrants In American Society* (New York: Harcourt Brace, 1998). For critique of lack of focus on women, see Juan Gomez-Quiñones, "Outside Inside—The Immigrant Workers: Creating Popular Myths, Cultural Expressions, and Personal Politics in Borderlands Southern California 1986–1996," in *Chicano Renaissance: Contemporary Cultural Trends,*, ed. David Maciel, Isidro Ortiz, and Maria Herrera-Sobek (Tucson: University of Arizona Press, 2000), 49–92.

16. Mahler, *American Dreaming*, 75.

17. Some examples include Americo Paredes, *Folktales of Mexico* (Chicago: University of Chicago Press, 1970); Enersto Galarza, *Barrio Boy* (Notre Dame, Indiana: Notre Dame University Press, 1971); Yolanda López, *Who's the Illegal Alien, Pilgrim?* (Offset lithograph, 1978); Gloria Anzaldúa, *Borderlands/La Frontera: The New Mestiza* (San Francisco: Spinsters/Aunt Lute Books, 1987); Sandra Cisneros, *Woman Hollering Creek and Other Stories* (New York: Random House, 1991); and Carlos Vélez-Ibañez, *Border Visions: Mexican Cultures of the Southwest United States* (Tucson: University of Arizona Press, 1999).

18. Various scholars have observed that there is both a new and increasing demand for Mexican immigrant women to labor as domestics. In particular, see Ruth Milkman, "The Macrosociology of Paid Domestic Work," *Work and Occupations* 25:4 (1998): 483–510; Maria Ibarra, "Mexican Immigrant Women and the New Domestic Labor," *Human Organization* 59:4 (2000): 452–67; and Pierrette Hondagneu-Sotelo, *Dómestica: Im-*

migrant Workers Cleaning and Caring in the Shadows of Affluence (Berkeley: University of California Press, 2001).

19. I undertook two phases of fieldwork among sixty-five Mexican immigrant women in Santa Barbara—the first phase between 1994 and 1996 and the second between 1998 and 2000. The term *Mexicana* is the self-referent most commonly used by the women I interviewed.

20. Wayne Cornelius, "From Sojourners to Settlers: The Changing Profile of Mexican Immigration to the United States," in *U.S.-Mexico Relations: Labor Market Interdependence*, ed. Jorge A. Bustamante, Clark W. Reynolds, and Raúl A. Hinojosa Ojeda (Stanford, Calif.: Stanford University Press, 1992), 155–93.

21. Carole Nagengast and Michael Kearney, "Mixtec Ethnicity: Social Identity, Political Consciousness, and Political Activism," *Latin American Research Review* 25:2 (1990): 61–91; Rouse, "Mexican Migration," 8–23; and Robert Smith, "Mexicans in New York: Membership and Incorporation of a New Immigrant Group," in *Latinos in New York: Communities in Transition*, ed. Gabriel Haslip Viera and Sherrie Baver (Notre Dame, Ind.: University of Notre Dame Press, 1996). For studies on Mexican families and women, see Denise Segura, "Ambivalence or Continuity? Motherhood and Employment among Chicanas and Mexican Immigrant Workers," *Aztlán* 20:1 (1993): 119–50; Patricia Zavella, "The Tables are Turned: Immigration, Poverty, and Social Conflict in California Communities," in Perea, *Immigrants Out!*, 131–61; Maria Patricia Fernandez-Kelley and Saskia Sassen, "Recasting Women in the Global Economy: Internationalization and Changing Definitions of Gender," in *Women in the Latin American Development Process*, ed. Christine Bose and Edna Acosta Belén (Philadelphia: Temple University Press, 1995), 99–124; Chavez, *Shadowed Lives*; Vicki Ruiz, "By the Day or the Week: Mexicana Domestic Workers in El Paso," in *Women on the U.S.-Mexico Border: Responses to Change*, ed. Vickie Ruiz and Susan Tiano (Boston: Allen & Unwin, 1987), 44–62; Rosalia Sólorzano-Torres, "Female Mexican Immigrants in San Diego County," in Ruiz and Tiano, *Women on the U.S.-Mexico Border*, 41–59; Julia Curry-Rodriguez, "Labor Migration and Familial Responsibilities: Experiences of Mexican Women," in *Mexicanas at Work in the United States*, ed. Margarita Melville, Mexican American Studies Monograph, No. 5 (Houston: University of Houston Press, 1988); Adela De La Torre, "Hard Choices and Changing Roles Among Mexican Migrant Campesinas," in *Building with Our Hands: New Directions in Chicana Studies*, ed. Adela de la Torre and Beatríz M. Pesquera (Berkeley: University of California Press, 1993), 168–80; Hondagneu-Sotelo, *Gendered Transitions*; Antonia Castañeda, "Language and Other Lethal Weapons: Cultural Politics and the Rites of Children as Translators of Culture," in *Mapping Multiculturalism*, ed. Avery Gordon and Christopher Newfield (Minneapolis: University of Minnesota Press, 1996), 201–14.

22. Pierrette Hondagneu-Sotelo argues that single women represent a minority of the women involved in migration. Those that do come, she says, derive from "weakly

bound families" that provide little economic or patriarchal control. She also argues that the single women in her study do not, on their own, instigate migration, but rather act opportunistically for adventure or earnings. Nonetheless, she notes that the migration process will eventually include more single women (Hondagneu-Sotelo, *Gendered Transitions*, 87).

23. E. Valentine Daniel, "Suffering Nation and Alienation," in *Social Suffering*, ed. Arthur Kleinman, Veena Das, and Margaret Lock (Berkeley: University of California Press, 1997), 309–58.

24. Douglas Massey et al., *Return to Aztlán: The Social Process of International Migration from Western Mexico* (Berkeley: University of California Press, 1987); and Wayne Cornelius, "Ejido Reform: Stimulus or Alternative to Immigration?" in *The Transformation of Rural Mexico, Reforming the Ejido Sector*, ed. Wayne Cornelius and David Myhre (La Jolla, Calif.: Center for U.S.-Mexican Studies, University of California, San Diego, 1998), 229–46.

25. Hondagneu-Sotelo, *Gendered Transitions*, 87.

26. Massey et al., *Return to Aztlán*.

27. Massey et al., *Return to Aztlán*, 144–45.

28. Douglas Massey and Jorge Durand, *Miracles on the Border: Retablos of Mexican Migrants to the United States* (Tucson: University of Arizona Press, 1995).

29. Massey et al., *Return to Aztlán*, 143–44.

30. David Fitzgerald, *Negotiating Extra-Territorial Citizenship: Mexican Migration and the Transnational Politics of Community*, Monograph 2 (La Jolla, Calif.: Center for Comparative Immigration Studies, University of California, San Diego, 2000).

31. Sassen, *The Mobility and Labor of Capitol*.

32. Alberto Ledesma, "Narratives of Mexican Immigration to the United States," in *Culture Across Borders: Mexican Immigration and Popular Culture*, ed. David R. Maciel and Maria Herrera-Sobek (Tucson: University of Arizona Press, 1998), 76.

33. Ledesma, "Narratives of Mexican Immigration," 67–98.

34. Chavez, *Shadowed Lives*, 25–43.

35. Mary O'Connor, "Women's Networks and the Social Needs of Mexican Immigrants," *Urban Anthropology and Studies of Cultural Systems and World Economic Development* 19:1 (1990): 81–98; and Hondagneu-Sotelo, *Gendered Transitions*, 72–75.

36. Timothy Dunn, *The Militarization of the U.S.-Mexico Border, 1978–1992: Low Intensity Conflict Doctrine Comes Home* (Austin: CMAS Books, University of Texas at Austin, 1996), 18.

37. Wayne Cornelius, "*Muerte en la Frontera, La Eficacia y las Consecuencias 'Involuntarias' de la Politica Estadounidense de Control de la Inmigración, 1993–2000*," *Este Pais* 119:6 (2001), 2–18.

38. Peter Andreas, *Border Games: Policing the U.S.-Mexico Divide* (Ithaca: Cornell University Press, 2000), 15–50.

39. Michael Huspek, Roberto Martinez, and Leticia Jimenez, "Violations of Human and Civil Rights on the U.S.-Mexico Border, 1995–1997: A Report," *Social Justice* 25:2 (1998): 110–30.

40. Karl Esbach et al., "Death at the Border," *International Migration Review* 33:2 (1999): 430–54.

41. Cornelius, *"Muerte en la Frontera,"* 3.

42. E. Valentine Daniel, *Charred Lullabies: Chapters in an Anthropography of Violence* (Princeton, N.J.: Princeton University Press, 1996), 139–43.

43. William Cronon, *Nature's Metropolis: Chicago and the Great West* (New York: W.W. Norton, 1991), 384.

Inmensa Fe en la Victoria

Social Justice through Education

ANITA TIJERINA REVILLA

Throughout my higher education studies, I have been involved in several student organizations that rally behind cultural enrichment, racial justice, and empowerment efforts for oppressed communities. After my undergraduate studies, I worked for a nonprofit organization that was devoted to providing equal education to poor and minority students in schools. In both of these community and professional environments, talk of equality and social justice surrounded me. Students, professors, coworkers, and activists all expressed their commitment to creating social justice and equality, and I was able to witness how those concepts filtered into their daily practices. Some of their actions contradicted their preachings, but many of their actions also confirmed them. Along the way, I decided that social justice and education would become my lifetime commitments as well.

Today, as I seek to develop my career as an activist scholar, I dedicate myself to learning how to best realize this vision of justice through education. I believe that the best way to do this is by studying the lives of people who have made this same commitment. It is especially important to consider the experiences and perceptions of students who are engaged in activism against oppressive conditions such as racism, sexism, homophobia, and classism because it is through them that we can learn how to incorporate social justice into our academic lives. For years, these students have been creating their own supplementary education as the traditional curriculum has failed to address their specific struggles and histories. Moreover, as these students formulate their identities, they develop visions for the world in which they want to live. An understanding of these experiences and visions is crucial for forwarding the goals of social justice education because without the perspective of students, educators will find themselves unable to meet their students' needs. Hence, this article will introduce a case study or *testimonio* of a young woman who is an undergraduate student involved in a struggle for justice.[1] Through her, my hope is that we can learn something about our goals as social justice educators.

METHODOLOGY

This case study stems from a larger project in which I studied for four years a student advocacy organization at the University of California, Los Angeles. The organization, Raza Womyn, is a Chicana/Latina student organization founded in 1979 and officially recognized at the University of California in 1981. I became interested in learning about the organization and the women who participate in it after attending their fourth annual Chicana/Latina conference in March 1999. The members of Raza Womyn organized a full day of workshops, dialogue, and performance for the purpose of creating consciousness and awareness about issues pertaining to Latinas and Chicanas. They stated in their conference program that the desire to "carry on the tradition of struggle of economic, political, and social justice" guided their work. They were particularly interested in advancing an ideology of change that they called "reconstructing revolution." The *mujeres*, the women, explained that they pushed themselves beyond old definitions of revolution that fight against racism but fail to struggle against other -isms and phobias, such as classism, sexism, and homophobia.[2]

While my research examines both the organization and the women who participate in it, this article focuses on the experiences of one participant in particular. She is the one member of Raza Womyn who has consistently been the center of focus of my study. Her name is delia.[3] She is twenty-two years old and in her fifth year of college. When I first met her, she was nineteen and in her second year at UCLA. The data in this article date back to my first extended encounters and discussions with her.

I have formally interviewed delia on five occasions for a total of fourteen hours, which included two focus group interviews and three individual interviews. The focus group interviews took place on March 9, 2000, and April 1, 2001, at UCLA. At each focus group interview, four members of Raza Womyn talked about their reasons for joining, their experiences with racism, classism, sexism, and homophobia, and their commitments to social justice. The individual interviews took place on November 2, 1999, November 28, 2000, and April 1, 2001. They lasted a total of nine hours and consisted of the participant's life history and academic trajectory, as well as her involvement in Raza Womyn. Transcribed interviews and audiotapes are stored in my personal files at home. Over the past four years, I collected approximately two hundred hours of naturalistic and participant observation of Raza Womyn at several different locations, including weekly meetings, annual conferences, workshops, and community and social events. delia has been present at nearly all of the Raza Womyn activities observed over this period of time.

delia was the first woman in the organization to welcome me into the Raza Womyn space. I felt that I could approach her because every time we met, she embraced me with a warm smile and a friendly word of love. This is something that has endured into the present and is extended to everyone she encounters—on the buses that she rides, in the communities she is involved in, on the university campus, and in the intimate space of Raza Womyn gatherings. Initially, I had some trouble tracking down this busy woman, but I persisted by e-mail and by phone. When I finally talked to her to explain the project and my desire to join her at work and in other spaces, I apologized for being too persistent. She responded, "Don't worry about it. We've [Raza Womyn] missed you." I explained that I also wanted to go to the Raza Womyn meetings for my observations, and she agreed eagerly. I asked her if she thought the *mujeres* would feel uncomfortable with me participating in the meetings as a researcher because I did not want them to feel that I was intruding in their space. She dismissed my fear and said, "*Mujer*, you are a Raza Woman; of course you can come." Upon joining them at their meetings and feeling their warm welcome, I soon took to heart the Raza Womyn motto: "Remember, you don't join Raza Womyn, you are Raza Womyn."

I asked delia if I could spend time with her during the day so that I could observe her in the midst of her work as a tutor and college advisor to middle and high schools students in South Central Los Angeles. At the time, delia worked for an organization called Youth Opportunities Unlimited (Y.O.U.) as a tutor at three different South Central locations, including John Hope High School (John Hope), Y.O.U. High School, and Bethune Middle School. She welcomed me to join her at work, and I observed her for ten consecutive weeks at two different schools and at a community center. Since then, over the past four years, I have spent at least three hours a week when school has been in session with her at Raza Womyn meetings and also have joined her on numerous occasions for a variety of activities on and off campus. This article will only present the results of the observations and interviews I conducted in the initial observations. I joined her on Monday mornings from 8:00 a.m. to 1:00 p.m. at John Hope and Y.O.U. I also observed her at a South Central community center called Community Coalitions, at meetings in the Raza Womyn office on campus, and during Raza Womyn activities at UCLA.

Throughout this period, delia and I engaged in dialogues about personal and academic issues. She often asked me for advice and talked to me about the dilemmas that she faced as an activist and as an educator. She encouraged me to talk to the students about my experience in college and to "listen to them be-cause they really need someone to listen to their dreams." During our encoun-ters, we spoke freely and shared information with each another, and I forged a friendship and bond with delia that made this project both enjoyable and truly meaningful. Recognizing my potential subjectivities as a researcher who also defines herself as a Chicana activist, I ground my findings and analysis in the data, which in this case directly reflect the acts and words of this particular woman. From my observations, I composed fieldnotes and memos incorpo-rating information and artifacts that I collected from John Hope, Commu-nity Coalitions, Raza Womyn, and delia. After coding the data, I found that delia's vision of social justice guides her daily actions as a student, teacher, and activist. Her multiple identities and personal struggles in life led her to be-come what she calls a *revolucionaria*, a revolutionary. The following *testimonio* weaves together the general theme of my observations, which is that her family background, personal struggles, and identity are intricately connected to her commitment to activism and justice. Moreover, her vision of social justice is achieved through education, which she believes needs to be drastically altered to meet the needs of young students of color.

RESEARCH SITES

delia tutors on Mondays, Wednesdays, and Fridays. She spends her mornings from around 8:00 a.m. to 11:00 a.m. at John Hope, noon to 2:00 p.m. at Y.O.U., and 3:00 p.m. to 5:00 p.m. at Bethune Middle School. All of the schools are in the same vicinity, near Manchester and Highway 110. John Hope is on the corner of Seventy-Ninth and Towne streets, in the center of a residential area in South Central Los Angeles. Some neglected apartments surrounded by a large black iron gate are across the street. Directly adjacent to John Hope is Fremont High School, which covers most of the block, except for the small piece at the corner where John Hope is located. A peach colored building (part of Fremont High School) and a six-foot gate separate John Hope from the other campus. John Hope consists of two bungalows housing three classrooms, an adminis-trative office, restrooms, a teachers' lounge, and a storage room. The bungalows are painted a dingy peach, and the brown paint on the doors is peeling. Eight picnic tables serve as delia's tutoring space and the students' lunch area. Three tables are old and warped, and two others are broken: one is missing the seats; the other is turned upside down. delia informed me:

> The buildings here are falling apart. The weeds are growing all over the place, and the grass hasn't been cut for weeks. The only space that the

students have is the basketball half court. Over there, past the field, there is a fenced-in storage area with old desks and empty plant pots. This is not an adequate learning environment for these youth.

Y.O.U is larger than John Hope. It is at least half a city block long, and the school is made up of four brown wooden structures. The buildings are in relatively good condition. It is visibly clean and maintained, but from the outside, it does not look like a safe and comfortable space for a learning environment. A six-foot black electronically-controlled surveillance fence surrounds the entire campus, and we are buzzed in through two different doors before we can enter the campus; the first locked door leads to the front office, and the second leads to the classrooms and open courtyard.

Twice delia and I went to the Community Coalition center located on the corner of Vermont and Eighty-First streets. From the outside, the building looks like a warehouse with a door and no windows, so I was surprised when I learned that inside there was a space open to all community members, from youths to seniors. I learned that Community Coalition organizes Latino/a and African American youth to become involved in several groups organized around the different issues that affect the local community. They also are a resource center equipped with a library, a computer lab, and personnel to serve the community.

Besides the two high schools and the Community Coalition resource center, I also observed delia as she worked to organize Raza Womyn activities. The Raza Womyn office is shared with two other student organizations—Chicanos for Community Medicine and the Iranian student group. The very small office is packed with six desks, three computers, seven file cabinets, ten chairs, and a round table. The *mujeres* primarily use the roundtable as a meeting place and work table. An altar is arranged on the heater by the window. *Veladoras* (candles), a statue of the Virgen de Guadalupe, and postcards with pictures of Latinas/Chicanas adorn the altar, along with several flowers made of crepe paper and a Native American hand-drum. A poster of Emiliano Zapata and a raised fist decorates the left wall, along with an announcement of a *testimonio* given by Maria Guardado, an activist and survivor of military persecution in El Salvador. On the right wall, a bumper sticker is posted with a statement against grapes, "Uvas No." A picture of a Chiapas revolutionary, a Zapatista, shooting the middle finger in resistance to the Mexican government, and a huge white cloth with a woman symbol painted on it is taped to the wall on the right. The office space is alive. It is warm and inviting, especially during the weekly meetings when anywhere from three to ten women come in to organize, share, laugh, and sometimes cry about the world beyond the walls of the room.

I also observed delia in action at the Mujer Expression Night—a dark, brisk, and quiet evening at UCLA. There was a desolate feeling on the campus, but as I walked into the room, active bodies of *mujeres* preparing for their special night livened up the evening. The traditional Latina/o paraphernalia and decor were absent, but the *mujeres* created an ambiance of intimacy and culture that took over the elite space called the Grand Chancellor's Salon. They set up twenty trays of tamales and several cases of red, grape, and orange colas. The smell of the tamales brought back memories of my grandmother's kitchen at Christmas time. Chicana/o and Mexican *recuerdos* were sold, including Frida Kahlo candles, Mexican jewelry, and Latina/o art. The people within the room provided a strong contrast to the polished hardwood floors, marble fireplace, and chandeliers of the room.

It is important that I provide a detailed description of delia and the five sites where I observed her because this study seeks to portray the student, the activist, the teacher, and the woman. In essence, her social and personal networks or communities of resistance reside at these sites, and they determine and foster both her identity and her commitments.

TESTIMINIO

At age twenty, delia stands five-feet, eight-inches tall, a cinnamon-skinned student who identifies herself as both a Mexicana and Chicana. She is Mexicana by birth and Chicana by political identification. She has long, brown wavy hair that reaches halfway down her back when it is loose or tied in a braid, but usually her braided hair is rolled into a bun. The bun starts tight and neat at the beginning of the day, and by midday it ends up loose with several strands of thin hair surrounding her face, which she proudly refers to as her *greñas*, messy hair. She dresses in worn jeans or pants, T-shirts with political messages printed on them, and thrift-store sweaters. She consciously purchases her clothing at thrift stores and garage sales in an effort to avoid malls and stores, which she views as capitalist traps. The thing that does not change in her wardrobe are her old, faithful, brown *huaraches*, her Mexican sandals.

Every time I see her, she has at least three bags filled with her belongings. One bag is a baby blue Mexican satchel filled with at least twenty books. The books range in subject from politics to Chicana/o studies, and from feminism to labor movements. She always has a journal, just in case she has a wonderful idea for working with her youth or for organizing with Raza Womyn. Another bag is her multicolored tapestry satchel that she uses as a purse, and the third is a forest green backpack jam-packed with more books. The backpack is adorned with at least ten buttons with different political statements on them: one has a woman symbol with a fist in the center of it, another says "No Grapes," and a third declares, "No violence against women!"

The first time I asked delia to tell me about herself and to identify who she is, she replied, "My name is delia—Chicana, revolutionary, feminist. I was born in Guadalajara, Mexico, and came to the U.S. when I was eight years old. I grew up in San Diego, by Chicano Park." That was in June 1999, and when I interviewed her again in November of the same year, she answered, "I am a Chicana feminist. I identify as a *mujer*, as a *Mexicana*, as an *hija*, or daughter, as a student, a *revolucionaria*, a *mujerista*, *activista*, *organizadora*, conscious." Her strong political stance is evident in every part of her identity, consistently identifying herself as a revolutionary dedicated to change through activism and the organizing of communities.

delia is the youngest daughter in her family, and she has two older brothers. Her family crossed the U.S.-Mexican border in Tijuana when she was eight years old. She has a vivid memory of the long, cold night they spent in the brush, ducking at the sight of every headlight that whizzed by them as they walked many miles toward San Diego. Her father warned them that they should shut their eyes whenever cars passed so that the passersby would not be able to see their eyeballs and locate them in the brush, just in case the cars carried the *migra*, the Immigration and Naturalization Service agents. She remembers the fear she felt upon awakening and learning that a snake had crawled onto her long hair while she slept, but her parents' quick thinking saved her from being harmed. After making it safely through the night, they were able to hitch a ride to San Diego. Her family thought that they were going to a better place in the United States, but the job offered to her father turned out to be a false promise. They found themselves homeless and penniless, and they were forced to move from place to place, living first in a garage, then in small apartments, in the family van, and in an orange orchard until finally they were able to secure a home in Logan Heights.

delia spent her early years in Mexico, and her experience with race there was very limited. She recalls her first memory of race in the following way, "When I was in Mexico, I was five years old. I got off the bus with my mom and I saw a black man. I had never seen a black person before. That was my first exposure to a person of a different race." But her limited exposure to the reality of race would expand once she entered the United States. It was in American schools that delia began to recognize that she, too, was a racialized being. As a Mexicana, she is neither white nor black, and while some may argue that Mexican is not a race, delia's negative experiences would prove to be the result of racism and nativism.[4]

As early as elementary school, delia experienced the viciousness of race/ethnic backlash in California against Spanish-speaking Mexican immigrants. She recalls entering grade school speaking only Spanish, and being ridiculed by her classmates, both brown and white. She sadly admits that both her teachers and her classmates made her ashamed of her voice and of the sound of a Spanish-speaker's accent—eventually resulting in her silence in school. She confided:

> When I came here to the U.S. everything was different. Since I didn't know English I was put in ESL [a English as a Second Language class]. Then I was given tests, and I was put in a GATE [Gifted and Talented] program. Even though I knew English enough to function, the way the teacher and the other students would treat me was like I was inferior. I wasn't good enough.

The harsh treatment she experienced remains fresh in her mind as she remembers that she was discriminated against, both because of her accent and because of her brown skin. Lighter-skinned Mexican American students made fun of her because of the way she looked and spoke, so she isolated herself. She said, "It came to the point where I wouldn't really talk in class because I was afraid that I would pronounce a word wrong and that they would make fun of me. So, as a Mexicana, I felt worthless." Her self-esteem plummeted and although she scored highly on tests, she did not believe she was an intelligent person because even her teachers made her feel "stupid." It got to the point where she started to believe that, she said.

delia's mother and father raised her and her brothers near Chicano Park in San Diego in a historically Chicano/a neighborhood called Logan Heights. As an adolescent, she had difficulty dealing with the fact that her parents worked as janitors. When asked if class or the level of her family's income had ever been a factor for her, she answered:

> My parents are janitors. They clean buildings. They wash toilets, vacuum, and throw away the trash in offices. I would feel ashamed because all the other kids would say my father is a teacher . . . or he's the owner of this building. I felt like, well, I felt ashamed, like what am I gonna say? It was really hard, but also I always used to see how all the other kids who weren't brown were able to do all the extra curricular activities after school. I couldn't do it because, for one, I had to go home.
>
> My mom had to work two jobs. And sometimes I had to have dinner

for her ready so she could eat really fast and go to her next job. I am the only *mujer*, the only daughter. I was expected to be there and clean dishes, the house, everything. . . . So that was an issue as I was growing older. I knew it wasn't fair. I wondered, why is it that they have access to those things and I don't?

The injustices that her parents experienced as laborers caused her to begin questioning the privilege that she witnessed in the special school she attended for academically proficient students. It was during high school that she began to question the shame that she felt because of her parents' occupations. She feels that as she matured, she learned to appreciate the love and sacrifices that her parents made for her and preferred their love to the material wealth that other children had. She said, "I realized that I shouldn't be ashamed of what my parents do because after all, it's a job. They're doing it. It's an honest job, and they do it. And then soon, in high school, when they would ask me what they do, I would tell them, proudly, 'They're janitors.'"

delia's exposure to class injustice by way of her parents led her to a fierce criticism of money and capitalism. She asserts that she purposely surrounds herself with "beautiful people, like the *mujeres* in Raza Womyn," because she wants to escape from the capitalist culture of the university. She said to me, "I see how people of color try to fit in and try to pretend like they have money. Some of them do, but some of them are just trying to fit in. It makes me sick. I'm bitter because there *is* a class difference." The discussions about the dangers of capitalism and negative consumerism led her to a passionate discussion about the youth with whom she works. She says that she is saddened by the fact that her students' goals are led by materialistic visions, and she considers it her responsibility to educate them about these issues. She declared:

Capitalism blinds people from what they really need to do and from how much they hurt if they only look at profit, at how much they can make. . . . Many times we're taught to see education for how much money we are gonna get out of it. Our youth . . . instead of having us teach or recognize the knowledge and the freedom that we can get from education, the freedom of mind, the freedom to express yourself, the freedom to know so much. . . . Instead, we are taught about how much money you can get. . . . Many times we ask people to do things, and they ask, well, how much are we gonna get paid for it? You know? We've lost the feeling, the need to do stuff because we need to do it and we must do it. We've lost that because we're so into how much are we gonna get for it. If we're not gonna get nothing, we don't want to do it. And it's just so sad.

So, I guess I feel like I need to start working on deconstructing that little by little in my students. I know that I'm not going to be always there in the lives of my students, but maybe I can create that little seed that will trigger that in the lives of my students, and maybe for them to start thinking that there's more important things than just money.

As delia solidifies her critique of classism and the woes of capitalism, she shares her feelings with her students. She regrets not being taught about the many injustices that her people have encountered in the United States, and she believes that it is up to her to provide this information to the youth with whom she works. She feels that this knowledge will help put an end to the inequalities that she and others have faced.

When delia was a second-year student at UCLA, she was a sociology major, planning to pursue master's and doctoral degrees. She hoped to pursue those higher education degrees to become and continue as an activist, teacher, school principal, and social worker. She also dreamt of creating a community center that would serve as a space for youth. When I asked what her goals were, she smiled and told me, "There's so many things that I want to do. . . . I want to do everything!" delia's short- and long-term goals included continuing to work with youth and to work with students in continuation and alternative schools because she believes that they are most in need of academic and emotional support. She laments that her students have been forgotten because of the negative conceptions that they have been tagged with in their schooling experience. She acknowledges that most of them have been placed in low-level academic tracks, and she is determined to show them that she cares about them and that she understands them. She believes in their potential to succeed and recognizes their talents and capacities in life. She lauds their abilities to write, express themselves, sing, and play sports, but she shakes her head and notes that "no one cares" about them. She explained:

> I see so much anger and frustration in my youth. I feel like I have to be there in order to listen to them, in order for them to understand that, "Look, you're not alone. Don't feel like there's no one here that doesn't understand you and don't feel that no one sees that you can make it. Because I believe in you." I've seen that it has an impact on some of my students. And just for them to be constantly seeing me . . . because it's hard, because society has fucked up on them, and they don't trust a lot of people. It's hard for them to start trusting.

I observed that delia's verbalized commitment to her youth transfers into action. She works extremely hard to juggle her life as a student, a teacher, and a mentor. At John Hope, I watched her clean dirty picnic tables in the campus courtyard because these table were the only spaces that were available. She was not given class time or classroom space, but she did not let that hinder her activities and discussions with the students. She recruited her junior and senior students as they passed by the tables, and she asked them to sit down for a few minutes to fill out applications to take the SAT exams. Some of the students turned her away saying, "Nah, I don't want to fill one out. SATs are a bunch of bull and a waste of time." delia never despaired, nor did she force the students to join her. Several of the female students and a couple male students either sat down to fill out applications or told her that they would take one and bring it back to her. She confided in me that the administration at John Hope expects her to be only a tutor for the students, but she has dreams of her students pursuing higher education—dreams that few of the teachers or administration share. She chooses to share college preparatory materials with the students and helps them collect information about college possibilities. Some teachers complained when their students stopped to talk to her about the SATs. Mr. Blackburn, a white male, yelled at a student and told her to hurry up and come to class. She replied, "I'm doing something. Can't you see I'm talking to her about this stuff?" He responded, "No, I can't." She told him, "I'll be there in a minute." She ignored him and continued to talk to delia about the SAT and college.

While she was helping students fill out SAT forms, she was also assisting other students with class assignments. Then she was called away by a teacher to help students in the classroom, and students barraged her with greetings and questions. One student even asked her to help him find work. When she told him where to go and who to talk to, he asked her to go with him. She put her hand on his shoulder and said, "I can't go for you. You have to go and show them that you want the job. I can't go for you or hold your hand." He agreed, "Yeah, I know. I'm eighteen now. I'm an adult." She said, "Yeah, you have to be responsible and show that you want to work." On at least two occasions, I heard students asking delia for assistance with finding a job, and she advised them.

delia told me that she also shares information with her students about community projects and activities that she believes are both educational and consciousness raising, such as an antipolice brutality march, Raza Womyn activities, and *Dia de los Muertos* celebrations. Sometimes she takes students with her to the university or to special events outside of school. This is something that created conflict for delia because the administration of the school felt that she was "getting too close" with the students, and they also disapproved of the off-campus activities to which she took the students because they were "too political."

When I visited Y.O.U. High School with delia, I was pleased to see the welcome that she received from the students. When she walked in the classroom, a young black female exclaimed, "delia! Thank God you're here today!" Another student, a Latino male, pleaded with delia for help because the substitute teacher, Ms. Macias, had given his mother a bad report about him, which he swore to delia was a lie. delia talked to him privately and tried to calm him down, and she recommended talking to his mother, but he rejected that advice, insisting that his mother trusted the teacher more than she trusted him. Ms. Macias had many problems with the students at Y.O.U. Every time I observed the classroom, she was busy disciplining the students or chastising them. delia later told me that Ms. Macias quit three weeks later because according to delia, "She couldn't deal with the students. She thought they acted like 'animals.'"

delia's ability to engage the students at Y.O.U. amazed me because I was able to contrast it with the teacher who was instructing the class before her. He was conducting an English lesson on how to use "I am" and "We are" in a sentence. He walked around the class chastising the students because they were talking instead of working on their assignments. He approached some students at one table and asked them if they had completed the sentences. Annoyed, they answered, "We already did it!" Distrustful, he asked, "Where is it? Let me see me it." One of the female students angrily replied, "We're already done!" Then they ignored him and talked to each other. Exasperated, the teacher walked toward another table. Once the period ended, the teacher went to another classroom, and delia began to address the students. A student named Maria stood up to move the television set out of delia's way, providing her a space to write on the dry-erase board. delia immediately wrote the directions for an assignment on the board entitled, "Self portrait through writing." She wrote:

Describe yourself:
How do you look (physical appearance)?
How do you feel and what do you think about yourself?
How do you think people see you?

The students worked quietly on the assignment for at least ten minutes. It was the longest amount of time that the students had been quiet all morning. Although there were a few new students who were not originally in the class, most of the students remained in the class from the previous period, and even they were engaged in the assignment. The assignment that they were working on before was a simple exercise of writing sentences using "am" and "are." This assignment was apparently much more challenging, but the same students worked on it without needing much assistance. Once the students completed the assignment, they volunteered to share the very personal things that they wrote about themselves. One of the students asked, "Are we gonna read our self-portraits?" delia said, "Oh yeah. You want to read yours first?" The young woman said yes and read her portrait aloud. She described herself as a happy person and happy to be in school. Two other students read their descriptions of themselves. A female student said, "People may think I am a bad ass, but I'm not." A male student stood up and read, "Some people think I ain't shit, but they don't know me." He continued, "Sometimes I see myself as a boy wonder because I constantly have to fight so much negativity all around me." He sat down after reading his self-portrait. Just then, Ms. Macias, who was still in the room but had been forgotten by the students, chimed in, "That was really good," and the female student started to laugh. Ms. Macias asked, "Why are you laughing? Don't you think it's good?" The student told her, "Nah. Yeah, I think it's good. I'm laughing cause you said it was good." After that, none of the other students volunteered to read their self-portrait. It was obvious that the students had very negative feelings of distrust and disconnection with Ms. Macias, and I wondered why their relationship with delia was so different. I guessed that delia identified with her students very differently than the other teachers did, which was evident in her oral and physical communication with them. Consequently, the students behaved differently with her.

delia continued to talk to the students about college, graduation, and the need to work together and speak freely with each other. She asked students to volunteer to tutor the middle school students at Bethune Middle School at least once a week. She encouraged them to participate by saying, "It's important to start learning to educate our young people." The level of respect that she offered her students was evidently appreciated because many of the students volunteered enthusiastically. She talked at length to them about the need to use education as a way to liberate them from conformity, and she never talked down to them. All of them signed up to tutor at least once a week, and some volunteered to go more than once a week. Something that delia tells me often is that she feels that her students are treated like small children with little or no respect for their intelligence. This is why she adamantly rejects calling her students "kids"; instead, she refers to them as "youth," "young men and women," or "*jovenes*." While she no longer works with these same youth, she continues in her efforts to gain access to higher education for youth and to demand respect for them.

As a student, delia has been fortunate to find a group of women who have offered her support and space for development. I first met delia at the 1999 Raza Womyn annual conference. The conference is a grassroots effort to educate others for social justice. More specifically, the conference is one facet of an entire movement in which the women are involved. The women in the conference program wrote:

> This year's theme . . . represents our internal passion, the ability to motivate our selves and create change. It is the fire that burns within us to destroy the many "isms," such as sexism, racism, homophobia, and classism that attempts to dismantle our communities. The theme also tries to embody the way we look into the face of ourselves to see the reflections of those that continue to carry on the revolution. Our sisters, mothers, great-grandmothers, the neighbor across the street, the women at the bus stop, and the women half way across the world, all carry on the tradition of struggle of economic, political, and social justice.[5]

In a focus group interview I conducted with four women in the organization, a member of Raza Womyn stated, "The main goals of the conference are raising consciousness, creating productive dialogue, building solidarity, and providing a safe space for all *mujeres*." The women do not view consciousness as the only outcome of their work, but they do see it as the first and most needed step toward social change. The personal growth and empowerment of *mujeres* is extremely important to these women. They view this as the central and most urgent goal of the organization; nevertheless, they do not lose sight of a social movement that will create a more just society.

The members of Raza Womyn, as women of color at a historically white university, have been forced into the margins and have also chosen the margins as a site of resistance.[6] Raza Womyn have experienced immense marginality and isolation in their own personal and educational experiences, but they have also found strength in their collective gathering and activism, which is achieved because of the strength that they receive within their marginalized space. The issue of "safe space" is key to their vision of collective action and a social movement. As one woman put it:

> There's a really safe space to go, where you can go and be who you are. What that's doing is, it's giving you the energy, and the language, and the courage, and the strength to go out and use that in other parts of your own activism, or in the collective activism of the group. So that without that, you can have some sort of goal. You can say, "Yeah, we are part of a *movimiento* and blah, blah, blah," but if you are not actually practicing it in your daily language, then you can just dump it all out—it's not really worth anything.

The organization has given the women a space to empower themselves to continue their academic and activist work. They further recognize that oppression is exerted not only from the wealthy, white-dominated institution, but also from males and heterosexuals in other organizations as well. As one woman stated:

> I think that a lot of the organizations that we've all once been a part of, and had to leave for one reason or another, who talk a lot of revolution talk, are exactly the people who are hurting us and are doing the things that are pushing us down and silencing us. They are not giving us the space to be who we are. So that I feel personally that I can't be part of a movement if I can't even be myself, and if I can't say what I need today, and if I'm constantly being silenced.

Thus, for these members of Raza Womyn, it has been necessary to challenge both institutional and individual oppressive ideologies that have pushed them into the margins, but at the same time, they rejoice in the separate space that they have created for themselves.

I initially believed that delia's consciousness and sophisticated critique of injustice was rooted in her involvement with this organization, but when I asked her how she came to her definition of social justice, she answered, "A lot has to do with my involvement with Raza Womyn, but I think that it has to do with my experience and involvement with my community, especially youth." When I asked her who taught her about the injustices that exist, she laughed and said:

> Who taught me? I guess I just started seeing it and talking to people. It would just come up. And I would be like, what does that mean? Like okay, go look for this, ask people. Some of the Raza Womyn taught me some stuff. . . .

Just my own research, my own interests about it . . . Some classes. Chicano/a studies classes usually . . . basically. Some of my feminism classes, education classes . . . I took Chicanos and Education and it opened my eyes to many things that I had questions about. So, it cleared some of those questions. And just in terms of talking to people, talking to older people in the community . . . It started making me realize that there's something more to this. Why are we living the way we are?

delia's exposure to books and discussions about justice and inequality began at the university, but the books only added to her understanding of her lived experiences. Her participation in Raza Womyn gave her a space where she could engage in dialogues about these issues, and it provided her with a group of allies, other women who had very similar experiences. It was within this group that delia was continuously discussing her obstacles as a teacher and a student, and together they came up with ideas and ways to deal with these issues in their daily lives.

In delia's work as an educator, she has met several obstacles. She says that her most immediate struggles at work are lack of resources and time, as well as lack of support from the administration, especially at John Hope High School. She explained:

> The administration . . . You know, like I have projects that I want to do or simply just talk to them about different issues. [The administration replies], "Well, you're imposing your political ideology. . . . So you can't say this or you can't do that." Also, I'm very limited with funding, so if I want to do a project here and there, or if I want to take them to places, "No you can't do that." Obstacle . . . with, like, time. If it were up to me, I would have [projects going on] day and night.

delia has been discouraged from inviting students to protests and rallies for justice. For example, she was told that an antipolice brutality march is not educational and that it would discourage the police from responding if the school ever needed their help. She once shared her frustrations about the situation at John Hope with me. The following is part of a conversation the two of us had about it:

> delia: It's crazy shit cause like any kind of little shit, their just trying to get me, you know?
> Anita: Uh huh. Why? What happened now?
> delia: Because, what was it, like two weeks ago. The students were complaining that the tables were so dirty to eat on. So I suggested to them, "Hey what's up if we stay after school and clean up, you know? Like just wash them and sweep a little . . . to make our campus more welcoming so we want be here. I mean it's ours, so we gotta take care of it." They were, like, "Yeah, yeah." At first, they were, like, "What? Us? Stay after school? Heell nah." So I was, like, "But check it out. We'll be eating. We'll be kicking it with some music or whatever." And then I suggested to them that we could clean up the garden in the back you know, like, where we were. I was, like, "How about planting some flowers or whatever?" Well, I was, "How about just hooking it up with something? Something to make it look nice?" Some of the young girls were, like, "How about planting some flowers and stuff like that, you know?" I was, like, "That's a good idea. We can do it." But then today, the project director, she came up to me, she was telling me [we can't do that]. . . . She came up to me again. It's like every time she comes up

to me, she has complaints from Dr. Darren [the principal]. First of all, why can't you just say it to my face, you know?

Anita: Yeah.

delia: She said, you know, she doesn't want me to be organizing the students to be doing anything.

Anita: Why?!

delia: I'm, like, ugghh! She tells me, "She [the principal] feels that you are a threat, and that you're [making] too much attachment to the students instead of behaving like a guest at her school. She's feeling that you're [making] her decisions.

Anita: Taking her school away?

delia: Exactly. I'm acting, like, that's my school. I'm like, nah. First of all, that school is the students' school. You know? I'm not there for her. I don't even want to see her face. That's why I don't even go in the office.

On one occasion, delia shared with me that the office aide at John Hope told her that Dr. Darren was jealous of delia's relationship with the students. It was very difficult for delia to work in this situation, where all of her actions were being scrutinized and questioned. While she found it to be a great challenge because she had no support from her coworkers, her commitment to the students did not falter.

Another significant obstacle for delia is the contradiction that she struggles with internally concerning her beliefs about higher education. She said:

They're so much shit that goes on. Hell nooo. Enough with this. And sometimes I think, Why am I going to school? It's crazy how, like, I hate going to the institution of UCLA. I hate being there. You know? I'm like, I just have to go there in order to get that diploma, but if it were for me, I know that I could do so much reading. And sometimes I just feel like I'm just wasting my time there. I have to take classes that I'm, like, this is just wasting my time. I don't have to do this. I need to be doing other stuff, working outside in my community. I could be reading my own shit, you know? Educating my own self. Reading.

But a lot of the stuff that I go through, it's not helping me. All they want to do is brainwash me, institutionalize me, and put more ideas of theirs in me. And I get so frustrated, like, do I have to go? It's crazy how, like, over there I'm hating to go to the university and over here I'm telling my students go to college, educate yourself. You know?

When I asked delia how she reconciled this contradiction for herself, she replied:

I think of it like, we have to. In order for them to do something with their lives, in order for them to start doing something, start taking . . . educating ourselves and putting ourselves in higher positions where we can do more and start taking control. I don't want to say control, but start taking charge. Start changing the way things are, because if we're always . . . well, letting others do that for us, the society, the system is always gonna stay the same. I don't want the students to conform.

I ask my students not to conform to satisfy or to think that only going into higher education is going to give you a better life. . . . I think that it's important to get into all the institutions and start changing the way things are done. . . . Economic justice, social, all of that shit, start changing it. We gotta just take the initiative and do that shit. Educate ourselves and do it. By any means necessary. If it means that we gotta get violent, you know, we gotta do that shit because if we're always gonna be positive and try to say well this and that, hoping that everything will come along, nothing's gonna happen! No! We gotta do something.

As delia shared her frustrations and goals, I thought back to the conference and considered the call for "collective revolution" that was asserted in the conference program. Many activists are familiar with a notion of revolution. It is a term and even a vision that has long been associated with social justice movements. However, it has been defined and envisioned very differently by different activists. Thus, I wondered what it was that delia envisioned as a revolution. I asked her what it means to be revolutionary, and she answered:

It means fighting for what I believe. Even if it means to die for it. Like not putting up with anything that I know is wrong, that I know is hurting me and that I see hurting human beings, not just, yeah my people of color, but in terms of everyone. A *revolucionaria* fights the injustices that exist. It means that we fight for our mental freedom. . . . To be able to do anything that we want to because we are free.

Being a *revolucionaria* means we need to express ourselves. I am a *revolucionaria* in terms of being a *mujer*, being who I am. It just means so many things. I guess ultimately it means not being afraid of doing what you believe you have to do. And for sure understanding what you need to do. . . . Yes, I will die for this, for one of my students . . . just for them to survive and be able to be free with their minds. I will die. And I am not afraid of it, well maybe I am, but I am willing. I'm not afraid of change because change has to occur. If not, things are always gonna be the same.

delia's vision of social justice and the means by which to achieve it has gone through many revolutions as well. Today, she is taking a class on nonviolent movements, but she still supports the armed struggle of the Indigenous people in Chiapas. She never ceases in her hunger for knowledge and in her immense faith in victory.

My observations offered me wonderful insights, and they helped me better understand the issues that this particular Chicana student activist faces in her work. I learned that many things informed delia's commitment to social justice, including her childhood, adolescence, personal, professional, and academic experiences. When delia was silenced as a young Mexican immigrant child in her elementary classrooms because of her language and skin color, she became determined to regain her voice and cultural pride. Because she, herself, had experienced the feeling of isolation and attack from peers and teachers, she was better able to understand and work with students in continuation and alternative schools. Growing up in a working-class Mexicana/o environment taught her to appreciate love, respect, and family, and to despise material wealth. As the only daughter of a traditional Mexican father, she was expected to act according to patriarchal female expectations. She challenged that and has pushed herself to reject all societally-imposed gender and sexuality roles.

Raza Womyn did not teach delia about social injustice—she experienced and recognized the injustices in her daily life. Raza Womyn provided the space to engage in dialogue, to develop her critique of the injustices and to organize to eliminate those injustices, and it offered her a reason to remain at the university. Consequently, she has been able to solidify her beliefs and maintain her identity as a *revolucionaria*. Her commitment and sentiments are inspirational to me and to many who know her. Education is integrally connected to her struggle. She fights oppressive education by seeking alternative sources of knowledge from her family, community members, activists, organizers, youth, elders, and Raza Womyn. She has an immense faith in victory over all injustices, and she actively participates in the struggle against oppression.

NOTES

1. *Testimonios* are testimonies. In her introduction to *Telling to Live: Latina Feminist Testimonios* (Durham, N.C.: Duke University Press, 2001), Luz del Alba Acevedo, describes *testimonios* as "stories of our lives . . . [that] reveal our own complex identities as Latinas" (1). She further asserts that "*testimonio* can be a powerful method for feminist research praxis" (3).

2. The words *mujer* and *mujeres*, meaning woman and women, are generally used by the participants of Raza Womyn to refer to women of Chicana, Mexicana, and Latina ancestry, but beyond the literal definitions these words imply a connection and

sense of identity between Chicanas/Latinas. I will use these words to refer to the women of the organization, following their common practice.

3. I purposely do not capitalize delia's name because she does not do so. She asserts that rules and regulations, especially in the act of writing, are conformist and oppressive. She feels that in order to freely express herself, she must break all the rules of writing. Therefore, in the tradition of black feminist scholar bell hooks, she chooses not to capitalize her name.

4. On the social construction of race and its effects on Chicanos/as, see Ian Haney Lopez, "The Social Construction of Race," in *Critical Race Theory: The Cutting Edge*, ed. Richard Delgado (Philadelphia: Temple University Press, 1995), 191–203; and Juan Perea, "The Black/White Binary Paradigm of Race: Exploring the 'Normal Science' of American Racial Thought," *California Law Review* 85 (1997): 1213–58.

5. Henry Giroux, "Theories of Reproduction and Resistance in the New Sociology of Education: A Critical Analysis," *Harvard Education Review* 53 (1983): 257–93. Giroux is a critical theoriest who argues that we should study resistance to develop a radical pedagogy that builds student's abilities to engage in social justice struggles. He urges educators to understand resistance in schools because he views schools as social sites that have significant impacts on the experiences of subordinated groups.

6. See Delores Delgado Bernal, "Chicana School Resistance and Grassroots Leadership: Providing an Alternative History of the 1968 East Los Angeles Blowouts" (Ph.D. diss., University of California, Los Angeles, 1997). Bernal expands on Giroux's theories of resistance and uses them in Chicana school resistance research. Also see bell hooks, *Yearning: Race, Gender, and Cultural Politics* (Boston: South End Press, 1990); and Daniel G. Solórzano Octavio Villalpando, "Critical Race Theory: Marginality and the Experience of Students of Color in Higher Education," in *Sociology of Education: Emerging Perspectives*, ed. Carlos Alberto Torres and Theodore R. Mitchell (Albany, N.Y.: State University of New York Press, 1998).

Contributors

KATHERINE BENTON-COHEN is an assistant professor of history at Louisiana State University, where she teaches U.S. women's history and the history of the American West. An Arizona native, she is a graduate of Princeton University and the University of Wisconsin–Madison. She is writing a book about the role of gender in the history of racial division in Arizona.

MARÍA ANTONIETTA BERRIOZÁBAL, the daughter of Mexican immigrants, was born in Loredo, Texas, and has lived in San Antonio most of her life. She started working as a secretary upon graduation from high school to assist her parents so that her five siblings could complete their college education. In 1979, after twenty years of college work, she earned a bachelor's degree in political science from the University of Texas, San Antonio. In May 1981, she was elected to the San Antonio City Council, becoming the first Latina to be elected in San Antonio or any other major Texas city, where she served with distinction for ten years. Berriozábal has been helping to build community in her beloved San Antonio for over forty years.

YOLANDA BROYLES-GONZÁLEZ is a professor of Chicano studies and German studies at the University of California, Santa Barbara. She is a native of the borderlands and rooted in Yaqui-Mexican-Chicana culture. Her books include *El Teatro Campesino: Theater in the Chicano Movement, Lydia Mendoza's Life in Music/La Historia de Lydia Mendoza, Norteño Tejano Legacies*, and her anthology *Re-emerging Native Women of the Americas: Native Chicana Latina Women's Studies*. Broyles-González is a recipient of the Distinguished Scholar Award from the National Association for Chicana and Chicano Studies. Her research and teaching focus on Chicana/o studies, popular culture, gender, oral tradition, and the popular performance genres of the U.S.-Mexico borderlands.

ANTONIA CASTAÑEDA, born in Texas and raised in the state of Washington, is an associate professor of history at St. Mary's University, San Antonio, Texas. She earned her Ph.D. in nineteenth-century social history from Stanford University.

GABRIEL S. ESTRADA is an adjunct faculty member in American Indian studies/ American studies at Palomar College and coordinator of the Native American Educational Network featuring California Indian curriculum and media. He earned a Ph.D. from the University of Arizona in comparative cultural and literary studies. He is Nahuatl/Spanish/Rarámuri/Basque from a mixed-class background.

PRISCILLA FALCON, a Mexicana activist, is an associate professor at the University of Northern Colorado, Greeley. Falcon earned her Ph.D. in international relations from the University of Denver in 1993. She is engaged in on-site research and documentation of the role of women within the Zapatista National Liberation Army in southern Mexico as well as the role of women within the popular peasant movements in Oaxaca, Mexico.

DEENA J. GONZÁLEZ was the first Chicana to receive a Ph.D. from the University of California, Berkeley, History Department, in 1985. She taught at Pomona College in Claremont, California, between 1983 and 2001. She now chairs the Department of Chicana/o Studies at Loyola Marymount University in Los Angeles. Author of *Refusing the Favor: The Spanish-Mexican Women of Santa Fe, 1820–1880* and coeditor, with Suzanne Oboler, of the forthcoming *Encyclopedia of Latinos and Latinas in the U.S.*, she has written over twenty articles constructing the field of Chicana history.

GABRIELA GONZÁLEZ is a Ph.D. candidate in the History Department at Stanford University and is completing a dissertation on gendered transborder politics and activism in south Texas from 1900 to 1960. González completed her undergraduate work at the University of Texas in Austin and has master's degrees from the University of Texas at San Antonio and Stanford University. She has taught courses in women's history and the politics of race and gender in the United States during World War II.

VIRGINIA GRISE, a native of San Antonio, is a Chicana cultural worker, writer, performer, and teacher. As a member of Esperanza's Teatro Callejero, Grise has performed in the streets of San Antonio's South Side and West Side and in the plazas of downtown. She graduated from the University of Texas at Austin with degrees in history and Spanish and a minor in Mexican-American studies. After graduating, she taught in a public high school for two years, where she was awarded a National Endowment for the Humanities Fellowship to study the teaching of Chicano and Latin American literature to native speakers of Spanish. She also taught writing in the juvenile correction system, created Latinos Unidos, a student organization for immigrant and Chicano high school students, and organized communities and families in East and South Austin against the segregation of schools in the Austin Independent School District. Grise has traveled to Chiapas as a Peace Observer and is working on a recovery project and theater piece about the Chinese presence in Mexico.

JUDITH L. HUACUJA is a Chicana scholar researching Chicano, Latino, and Latin American art activism in the Americas. With a Ph.D. in art history from the University of California, Santa Barbara, she is an assistant professor of contemporary and Latin American art history at the University of Dayton. Huacuja teaches and researches across the disciplines of ethnic studies, women's studies, and visual culture. Her publications include "Chicana Community and Cultural Praxis," in *Culture and Society in Dialogue: Chicana Literary and Artistic Expressions*, and "Yolanda Lopez, Print Media Artist" and "Amalia Mesa-Bains, Multi-media Installation Artist," both in *St. James Guide to Hispanic Artists: Profiles of Latino and Latin American Artists*. Recent curatorial work includes "Three Generations of Chicana Art," an exhibition of paintings, prints, video, and installation work at the University of Dayton Rike Gallery.

EVELYN HU-DEHART is a professor of history and ethnic studies and director of the Center for the Study of Race and Ethnicity in America (CSREA) at Brown University. She is the editor of *Across the Pacific: Asian Americans and Globalization*. Her ongoing research concerns the Chinese diaspora in Latin America and the Caribbean, with publications to date focusing on Mexico, Peru, and Cuba.

MARÍA DE LA LUZ IBARRA is an assistant professor in the Chicana and Chicano Studies Department at San Diego State University. As a sociocultural anthropologist, her research and writing has focused on Mexican immigrant and migrant women's work and settlement patterns in southern California. Her recent work includes *Emotional Proletarians in a Global Economy: Mexican Immigrant Women and the Ethics of Care* and *Transnational Identity Formation and Mexicanas' Ethics of Care*.

AMY KASTELY was lead attorney for the Esperanza in its successful lawsuit against the City of San Antonio. She is a long-time political activist and has worked with Esperanza and other community organizations on numerous social justice issues. Kastely teaches at St. Mary's University School of Law. Her work challenges the ways in which law and legal practice create and maintain systems of race, class, gender, and sexuality. Her published writing includes *Contracting Law*, with Deborah Post and Sharon Hom; *Out of the Whiteness: On Raced Codes in and White Race Consciousness in Some Tort, Criminal, and Contract Law*; and *Cogs or Cyborgs?: Blasphemy and Irony in Contract Theories*.

YOLANDA CHÁVEZ LEYVA is an assistant professor in the Department of History at the University of Texas, El Paso. She was born and raised on the Chihuahua-Texas border, where she learned the power of memory and keeping stories alive. Her research and teaching interests include Chicana, border, and public histories. She is working on a book manuscript that explores the intersections of memory, Indigenous pedagogy, and hidden histories. She earned her Ph.D. at the University of Arizona.

CLARA LOMAS is professor and chair of the Department of Romance Languages at Colorado College. She holds a Ph.D. from the University of California, San Diego. She is widely published in journals and other scholarly publications and is coeditor of *Chicano Politics after the 80s*. She has edited and introduced the autobiographies of Leonor Villegas de Magnón in both English and Spanish editions. Lomas was a Fulbright Scholar during the 2001–2002 academic year in Mexico City where she conducted research. She is working on a manuscript titled "The Alchemy of Erasure: On Mapping Women's Intellectual History of the Borderlands" and an anthology coedited with Clair Joysmith, "*One Wound for Another/Una herida por otra: Testimonios de Latinas in the U.S., 11 septiempre 2001—11 enero 2002.*"

EMMA PÉREZ is a historian, creative writer, and feminist critic. Her publications include *Gulf Dreams* and *The Decolonial Imaginary: Writing Chicanas into History*. She is an associate professor of history at the University of Texas, El Paso, and is writing a historical novel titled *Blood Memory, or Forgetting the Alamo*.

ANITA TIJERINA REVILLA is a Ph.D. candidate at the UCLA Graduate School of Education and Information Studies. She is studying race and ethnic studies in the division of Social Sciences and Comparative Education. Her research focuses on the intersection of race, class, gender, and sexuality in the schooling experiences of women and students of color.

GRACIELA I. SÁNCHEZ, director and cofounder of the Esperanza, is a native of the West Side of San Antonio. A dedicated activist/cultural worker, Sánchez has worked to eliminate racism, sexism, homophobia, and class elitism. She has been director of the Esperanza for fourteen years. As director of this community-based cultural arts/social justice organization, Sánchez does everything from programming cultural arts events, proofreading the monthly news magazine *La Voz*, writing grants, consulting with and giving workshops for other grassroots groups, and developing major donor and capital campaigns, to cleaning toilets and mopping floors.

CARMEN TAFOLLA is a native of the West-Side barrios of San Antoino. She has written five books of poetry, seven television screenplays, and numerous short stories and children's works. She is the former director of the Mexican-American Studies Center at Texas Lutheran College and has held numerous university positions, including associate professor of women's studies at California State, Fresno, and assistant to the president at Northern Arizona University. She holds a Ph.D. from the University of Texas and lives and writes full time in San Antonio.

DEBORAH R. VARGAS earned her Ph.D. from the Department of Sociology, University of California, Santa Cruz, with an emphasis in women's studies. One of her oral history interviews with Rosita Fernández was conducted for the Latino Music Oral History Project, Smithsonian Institution. She is revising her manuscript, "*Los Tracaleras*: Texas-Mexican Women, Music, and Place," for publication. She is a University of California President's Postdoctoral Fellow at the University of California, Davis, in Chicana/o studies.

THERESA A. YBÁÑEZ is an artist and an educator currently living, teaching, and making art in San Antonio, Texas. She has taught for fifteen years in public schools in San Antonio and Oakland, California. She also worked overseas, teaching and working for a children's museum in Kuwait. Ybáñez continues to exhibit her art and is working on several children's books.

Index

Printed in the United States
207105BV00010B/15/A